Planned Press
and
Public Relations

This book is dedicated to my wife Frances, son John and daughter Valerie

Planned Press
and
Public Relations

Third edition

FRANK JEFKINS
BSc(Econ), BA(Hons), DipPR(CAM),
FIPR, FAIE, FLCC,
MCIM, ABC

BLACKIE ACADEMIC & PROFESSIONAL
An Imprint of Chapman & Hall
London · Glasgow · New York · Tokyo · Melbourne · Madras

Published by
Blackie Academic & Professional, an imprint of Chapman & Hall,
Wester Cleddens Road, Bishopbriggs, Glasgow G64 2NZ

Chapman & Hall, 2–6 Boundary Row, London SE1 8HN, UK

Blackie Academic & Professional, Wester Cleddens Road,
Bishopbriggs, Glasgow G64 2NZ, UK

Chapman & Hall, 29 West 35th Street, New York NY10001, USA

Chapman & Hall Japan, Thomson Publishing Japan, Hirakawacho
Nemoto Building, 6F, 1–7–11 Hirakawa-cho, Chiyoda-ku, Tokyo 102,
Japan

DA Book (Aust.) Pty Ltd., 648 Whitehorse Road, Mitcham 3132,
Victoria, Australia

Chapman & Hall India, R. Seshadri, 32 Second Main Road, CIT East,
Madras 600 035, India

First edition 1977 (International Textbook Co.)

Second edition 1986 (Blackie & Son Ltd)

This edition 1993

© Frank Jefkins, 1993

Typeset in 10/12pt Palatino by Photoprint, Torquay, Devon

Printed in Great Britain at the Alden Press, Oxford

ISBN 0 7514 0016 5

A catalogue record for this book is available from the British Library

Library of Congress Cataloging-in-Publication data

Jefkins, Frank William.
    Planned press and public relations / Frank Jefkins -- 3rd. ed.
        p.   cm.
    Includes bibliographical references and index.
    ISBN 0–7514–0016–5 (alk. paper)
    1. Public relations.   2. Publicity.   I. Title.
HM263.J38   1993
    659.2--dc20   92–47028
                                                  CIP

Preface

The world of public relations has changed so much since the second edition of this book was published that much of this edition is entirely new material. There are also some innovations and new topics.

The chapter on campaign objectives has been expanded to discuss 34 typical objectives, while the chapter on evaluating results demonstrates how these 34 objectives may have been achieved.

The development of video as a public relations medium, both replacing film and expanding the uses of screened communication, is a major one. The variety of uses and kinds of video, corporate or business satellite video, videoconferencing, video news releases and satellite media tours are all fully described. So too is the international despatch of paper press releases by satellite.

The book contains new examples of opening paragraphs and complete news releases, good and bad, with practical comments on their strengths and weaknesses. The author is grateful to all those who submitted releases to quote. This remains the only book to teach how to write a news release.

A new chapter looks at some of the new situations confronting public relations practitioners such as the Grey Revolution, Networking, Effects of Bad Advertising, Environmental Issues, Lobbying in the EC, Products versus Services, and the Family Revolution.

This book is on the recommended reading list for CAM students, and this edition has been aimed at the Diploma student. Past exam papers are now included in the appendices.

A new case study concludes the book, and this is the 30 year public relations story of Rentokil, with which the author was associated for five years.

Acknowledgements are due to many people who have contributed material to this new edition. Their names, or the names of their organisations, appear in the text.

FJ

Contents

PART ONE
PLANNING PUBLIC RELATIONS CAMPAIGNS

1 Is Public Relations Tangible or Intangible?   2
Hypothetical objectives   3.

2 What Is Public Relations?   6
Abuses of public relations   6. Agency or consultancy?   6. Credibility   7. The adversarial situation   7. PR exercise   8. Purpose of public relations   8. Public relations function and its parameters   9. Definitions   9. The public relations situation   11. Attributes of a public relations practitioner   14. Ways in which public relations differ from advertising   14. What is propaganda?   15.

3 Planning a Public Relations Campaign   16
Why plan?   16. Cost effective public relations   17. The six-point public relations planning model   18. Constraints imposed by the model   18. Time — the biggest constraint   19. Analysis of the six-point model   19. Appreciation of the situation   21. Seven kinds of image   21. Methods of appreciating the situation   23. Sampling   25. Social grades   26. Predicting consequences   27. Public relations strategy   27.

4 Defining the Objectives   28
Sources of objectives   28. Thirty-four possible public relations objectives   29. Analysis of 34 typical objectives   30. Selecting priorities   43.

5 Publics   44
What are publics?   44. Eight basic publics   44. Some practical examples   44.

6 The Media of Public Relations   49
How public relations and advertising media differ   49. Nature of the media   50. Knowing the media   50. Studying the media   50. Existing commercial media   51. National newspapers   52. Breakdown of the British press   53. International press   53. Newspapers   53. Magazines   54. Directories, yearbooks, annuals   57. Television   58. Radio   59. Public and trade exhibitions   60. Educational literature and print   61. Direct mail   62. The spoken word   63. Miscellaneous public relations media   64.

7 Public Relations Costs and Budgeting   65
The financial facts of public relations life   65. The public relations budget   66. Is it cheaper to operate in-house?   67. Costs of an in-house department   67. Costs of a consultancy   70. Accounting for consultancy services   71. Methods of assessing consultancy fees   72. Job numbers and contact reports   74. Preparing estimates for consultancy proposals   74. Skeleton budgets   74. The value of budgeting   83.

8 Assessing Results   84
Proving the tangibility of public relations   84. Three ways of evaluating results   84. Evaluating media coverage   85. Measuring press coverage effectiveness   87. Achieving the 34 objectives   88.

9 Planning Public Relations Events   109
Three kinds of public relations event   109. Radio and television   111. Planning a press conference or reception   111. Planning a facility visit   118. Royal protocol   123.

10 Exhibitions and Exhibitors   125
Two public relations aspects   125. Public relations support for exhibitors   125. Public relations support for exhibitions   129. Exhibitions in developing countries   131. Private exhibitions   132.

11 Sponsorship   133
Why sponsor?   133. Advertising objectives   133. Marketing objectives   134. Defining purpose and

suitability 134. Kinds of sponsorship 136. Public relations advantages 137. Public relations spin-offs 138. Charity sponsorships 138. Hospitality and participation 139. Sponsored programmes on TV and radio 139.

PART TWO
ORGANISATION OF PUBLIC RELATIONS

12 In-house Public Relations Department or Outside Consultancy 146

Public relations versus advertising situation 146. Positioning of an in-house public relations department 147. Advantages of the in-house department 148. Disadvantages of the in-house department 148. Advantages of the consultancy 149. Disadvantages of the consultancy 149. Types of consultancy 150. Specialist consultancies 151. Services of a consultancy 151. Freelances 151.

13 The Press Officer and the Press Office 152

Role of the press officer 152. Ten responsibilities of the press officer 152. To whom is the press officer responsible? 153. How are press officers recruited? 154. Desirable qualities of a press officer 156. The press office 158. News release distribution 160. Press cutting services 161. The dos and don'ts of good press relations 161.

14 Public Relations as Part of Other Duties 164

Other people's job specifications 164. Combined jobs and job titles 164. Other executives 165. Personnel management/human resources management 168. Management 168.

PART THREE
CREATIVITY

15 How to Write a News Release 172

A special literary form 172. No puffery 172. The editor as referee 173. A bad example 173. Journalists need training 174. Writing for particular journals 174. A typical example 174. Quotations 175. Six kinds of news release 175. The Frank Jefkins seven-point formula for writing publishable news releases 175. What is the subject? 177. A practical example 178.

16 The Opening Paragraph 180

17 Presentation 184

Why presentation is important 184. Three purposes of presentation 184. Modern editorial needs 185. Essential elements of presentation 185.

18 Some News Releases Analysed 195

Why are so many releases dreadful? 195

19 Feature and Syndicated Articles 209

Non-speculative articles 209. Articles by staff writers 209. Articles by outside contributors 210. Supplied articles 210. Negotiating publication 211. Syndicated articles 212. Articles and advertisements 212. How to write feature articles 214. Plots for articles 214. Seven-point article plotting and research model 215. Presentation of articles 217. Special advantages of public relations articles 217.

20 Photography for Public Relations Purposes 220

Publishable pictures 220. Quality of pictures 221. Kinds of photographer 221. Use of public relations pictures 221. Faults to avoid 222. Some useful hints 223. Captioning 223. Copyright 224.

21 Video 225

Three essentials of documentary video making 225. Systems and formats 226. Types and uses of videos 226. Corporate video: satellite business TV 227. Videoconferencing 229. Video news releases 229.

22 House Journals 235

Internal and external house journals 235. Different kinds of house journal 235. Considerations for printed house journals 237. Planning issues, obtaining material 237. External house journals 238. Production of house journals 238.

PART FOUR
PRACTICE OF PUBLIC RELATIONS

23 **Professional Codes of Conduct**   242
     Value of professional codes   242. Complaints procedure   242. The IPR Code of Professional
     Conduct   243. The PRCA Investor Relations Code of Practice   247. Other codes   248. Code for
     Communication on Environment and Developments   248.

24 **Overseas Public Relations**   250
     Some problems discussed   250. Means of conducting overseas public relations   252.

25 **Academic and Professional Qualifications**   257
     London Chamber of Commerce and Industry   257. Communication Advertising and Marketing
     Education Foundation   258. West Herts College/PRCA Diploma in International Public Relations   258.
     Bournemouth University   259. Dublin Institute of Technology   259. Leeds Metropolitan University
     Business School   260. Napier University, Edinburgh   260. St Mark and St John College,
     Plymouth   261. University of Stirling   261. Institute of Public Relations   262. International Public
     Relations Association   262. International Association of Business Communicators   262. British
     Association of Industrial Editors   262.

26 **Special Areas of Public Relations**   264
     The grey revolution   264. Networking   265. Effects of bad advertising   265. Environmental
     issues   266. Lobbying   268. Products versus services   268. The family revolution   269.

27 **Case Study: Making Friends for Rentokil**   271
     Introduction   271. The public relations operation: information and objective   274. Planning and
     strategy   274. Public relations specification   274. Execution   275. Film and video   275. Press, radio
     and television   275. Books   276. Photographs and slides   276. Lectures   276. Wallcharts and
     leaflets   276. Rentokil Serviscene   276. Trade Association support   276. Evaluation — some
     examples   278. The local authority market   278. The hospitals market   278. The woolly bears
     picnic   278. National catch a cockroach month   278. The Manx Pied Piper   279. Conservation groups/
     animal welfare/animal rights   279. Financial records   279. Summary   280. What's in a name?   280.
     The nature of public relations   281. Necessity of a well-informed public   281. Activities generate
     news   282. Some achievements   282

Appendix 1   **CAM Diploma Syllabuses**   284
Appendix 2   **CAM Diploma Past Examination Papers and Case Studies in Public
              Relations Practice and Public Relations Management**   285
Appendix 3   **Bibliography**   297
Appendix 4   **Addresses of Societies and Education Organisations**   300
Appendix 5   **Services**   301

Index   303

A group planning a public relations presentation (reproduced by courtesy of British Gas North Thames).

PART ONE

Planning Public Relations Campaigns

CHAPTER 1

Is Public Relations Tangible or Intangible?

Critics of public relations, and even some of its practitioners and supporters such as management, regard it as being intangible. They do not believe it is possible to measure its achievements. If this is true why waste money on something which produces no results? Why should we waste our working lives on something of so little value?

Why do some people think public relations is intangible? I would suggest two reasons.

First, they think that public relations is about gaining favourable images, favourable media coverage, favourable climates of opinion, and favourable this and that. Favourable is the most stupid word ever applied to public relations. In the real world of public relations we have to deal with the good and the bad, and a lot of it is very bad these days with crises and disasters on every side. It is nonsense to try to pretend that things are better than they are, or that they can be presented as being better than they are. So let us forget the word 'favourable'; it has no place in real life public relations. It is a myth perpetuated by those who are afraid of the truth.

The second reason is that public relations is too often haphazard, unplanned and without purpose. People are expected to do this and that, run after one thing and chase after another, because management thinks that public relations is something that can take care of all the odd jobs nobody else wants to do. By

this I mean irrelevancies like buying airline tickets or meeting people at the airport which have nothing to do with public relations. This happens because public relations is not seen and used to achieve definite purposes.

We do not spend money on an advertisement just for fun or just because we like a newspaper or are friends with the advertisement manager. We do not erect a building unless we have a genuine need for it as an office, hotel or some such definite premises. In every other walk of life we do things because they will satisfy some desire or intention. Astronauts are not fired from the earth in rockets just to wander aimlessly in outer space. So why should public relations lack purpose, why should it be an aimless expenditure of time and money, why should it be intangible?

The tangibility of public relations is the theme of this book.

Public relations is about creating understanding through knowledge, and that could be about bad things such as why the plane or the train is late, or why there is a price rise, or about good things such as an improved service or a new product. Understanding is the key word, and this may be about how an organisation functions or a product works. This is factual, educational information. A product is more likely to be bought, used, enjoyed, bought again or recommended if people understand it. This is market education.

Public relations is also about effecting change. People hold irrational fears, or prejudices, or are disinterested, or are just plain ignorant. Public relations has to convert hostility, prejudice, apathy and ignorance into positive states of mind. This conversion may not be favourable but it can be sympathetic or interested or knowledgeable.

Think about the international situation and the role of public relations in creating positive attitudes about other countries and other people. Why should we be hostile towards foreigners, or to people of different languages, religion, culture or colour? Mainly, because they are different, and prejudice is often produced by resistance to differences. Apathy occurs because we are too taken up with our own interests, too isolated and insular, too uncaring about matters that do not touch on our immediate lives. We are sometimes shocked by television into discovering that there are places and people we had hitherto ignored, whether they be in Ethiopia, Bangladesh, the Sudan or the Philippines. As for ignorance, how many readers of this book know exactly where the majority of foreign countries are on a map of the world? These are some of the immensities of the public relations task, and they have nothing to do with favourable this or that, but about simple facts.

The nature of public relations is often misunderstood, which makes it difficult to talk of tangible public relations. On the one hand we have management regarding public relations as a sort of fire-fighting exercise to get them out of trouble, while on the other hand we have the media denigrating any political initiative they do not like as 'only a PR exercise'. We try to operate in a world in which neither our betters nor the media know what public relations is.

But we, its practitioners, have to be sure of what we mean by public relations, and it is our responsibility to convince management and the media of its true nature. This we can do only if we demonstrate the value of public relations to both management and the media. If we do not, we become a mere shuttlecock between opposing forces.

Every organisation needs public relations — but why? Specific questions have to be asked. Why does a bank, or an airline, or an oil company, or a hotel or any organisation, commercial or non-commercial, need public relations? Not just to gain some vague aura of favourable acclaim. No, but because it has a communication problem to solve, perhaps many such problems to solve.

If customers are unaware of your banking services, if potential passengers are unaware of the world's cities you fly to, if people believe your explorations are harming the environment, if the locations of your hotels are not fully known, you have communication problems. Many organisations have such problems.

It is the task of the public relations practitioner to identify these problems. He or she needs to discuss the communication needs of every department and function of the organisation, just as a finance minister will examine the financial needs of every ministry. In this way real public relations objectives can be defined.

HYPOTHETICAL OBJECTIVES

Let us consider some hypothetical objectives.

We will start with the community in the vicinity of the organisation. They could be customers of a store, or the people who live near our factory, the suppliers of public services or the local authority. How well do we maintain a good neighbour policy?

Do people complain about the noise, dirt, smoke or fumes you produce? Do local people know who you are and what you do? When you are recruiting local staff do applicants understand your business? If you are seeking planning permission from the local authority do officials and councillors know what you do and understand the importance of your building programme? Does the local hospital understand the nature of accidents that could occur at your premises? Just how well do the people around you know and appreciate who you are and what you do, or are you no more than a gate and a brick wall to them? Public relations begin on the doorstep and good community relations can be a very important responsibility for many organisations.

Next comes management–employee relations. Some companies such as IBM consider this to be so important that they have an internal communications manager at their plants. This is not a job for personnel managers, but it is a public relations function. It concerns downward communication from management to employees, upward communication from employees to management, and sideways communication between employees.

There are some managements who think that boardroom decisions have nothing to do with their employees. They have everything to do with their employees. Staff stability and security depend on the company's plans for its future prosperity. Members of staff should not be the last people to know what is going on. They should not learn about company decisions from the media: they should be told before announcements are made to the media. This elementary courtesy is often overlooked.

It is very easy for antagonism to exist between employees and management. They resent being regarded as drones. Nowadays many of them own shares in the business. They do not just sell their labour and obey orders. Greater intimacy between employees and management is inevitable in industries where there are small labour forces and greater use of technology such as computers and robotics. But it is even more important in international and multi-national corporations where employees are scattered world-wide and are remote from central management.

Dealer relations are another vital area of public relations. How well does a company communicate with its distributors who may be wholesalers, retailers, franchise holders, agents, factors or exporters, and may exist in many parts of the world? How well are all these distributors informed about company policies and developments, new products, advertising campaigns and so on? Are retail staff trained by the company, are there awards for sales successes, are there works visits, is there a dealer magazine? Just how does the company communicate with distributors over and above the routine calls made by sales representatives? Or does it leave everything to the sales force? There is a world of difference between public relations and salesmanship.

Financial relations cover a whole range of financial activities and concern shareholders, investing institutions such as banks and pension funds, investment analysts who write advisory reports on companies as investment prospects, and the City and Business editors and journalists who write about financial matters. Associated with this will be interim and annual reports; share, scrip and rights issues; take-over bids; and government privatisations of public enterprises. Here it is necessary not to create too favourable a situation which might provoke an unjustified rise in the share price, resulting in a costly fall later on. This type of public relations can be very sensitive.

Consumer relations — which some may think is the only form of public relations — also has an important place in this total picture of public relations activity. Here we are concerned with educating the market about a product or service, and in the case of a new one it will probably have to take place over a period of months leading up to the eventual launch. Thus interest, confidence and anticipation can be created so that when the advertising breaks, consumers will be familiar with the product. This tends to apply more to technical products such as camcorders, computers or new motor-cars rather than to FMCGs such as confectionery, drinks or foods. But even with mass selling popular lines, it is necessary to educate consumers about their use, whether it be paint, flour or knitting wool.

Finally, let us consider crisis management since this has become a universal public relations responsibility. Any organisation can suffer any sort of crisis. Many calamities occur because high technology has to compete with human error, as we have seen with oil, nuclear and airliner disasters. Other crises are unexpected and perhaps bad luck — the chairman dies, a product goes out of fashion, or a small fault makes it necessary to recall a product. Today, because of the eagerness with which the media will pounce on dramatic stories, and the instant news resulting from satellite world coverage by TV companies such as CNN, the public relations practitioner becomes a leading member of a crisis management team.

From all these observations on the complex role of public relations it should be agreed that when public relations pursues clearly defined objectives, the extent to which these objectives are achieved becomes assessable. Thus public relations becomes tangible, and its cost-effectiveness becomes apparent.

(Adapted from the author's Keynote address to the 12th International Summer School, Public Relations Management, held in London in July 1991 by the Frank Jefkins School of Public Relations.)

CHAPTER 2

What is Public Relations?

It is said that there is nothing new under the sun, and this is probably true of public relations which has a history stretching back for centuries, but in recent years there have been changes and developments, and even new abuses of public relations. Let us deal with the last of these first, although there are other misconceptions which will be challenged later in this introductory chapter.

ABUSES OF PUBLIC RELATIONS

An increasingly common abuse is the use of the meaningless expression 'a PR', by top public relations people, by journalists and in trade journals such as *PR Week*. The term is incomprehensible. It is not English. No one can be 'a public relations'.

Purists demand that we should spell out 'public relations' which is fair enough because there can be confusion with proportional representation and other subjects with the same initials. But there is no crime in referring to 'PR' where its meaning is clear, and again this applies to 'PRO' whatever preferences there may be for other designations such as public relations (PR) practitioner or public relations (PR) manager or director. The peculiar expression 'a PR' is a crime against both language and commonsense. Its origin is probably a form of journalistic slang, like the

journalistic expression 'handout' for a news release.

AGENCY OR CONSULTANCY?

The second abuse is the use of 'PR agency' for public relations consultancy. It is physically, financially and legally impossible for an external public relations service to genuinely operate as an agency. Presumably, this is why the British consultant's trade body calls itself very correctly the Public Relations Consultants Association.

Let us explain the physical, financial and legal aspects: a consultancy does entirely different advisory and creative work, it does not need 'recognition' from media bodies in order to earn income, and it is not anyone's agent and so not subject to the legal 'custom of the trade' that the agent acts as principal and is liable for debts incurred on behalf of clients. Clearly, a public relations consultancy which pretends to be an 'agency' does not know what business it is in.

An odd compromise exists in Germany where there are two divisions, the Society of Public Relations Agencies for organisations with at least five employees, whereas consultants are individual advisers rather like the American concept of public relations counsellors.

The use of the word 'agency' in this context is misleading, and could confuse clients who understand what advertising agencies are. The two operate very differently, in services provided, skills or personnel, and methods of remuneration.

An agent is remunerated by commission on the advertisement space it buys, houses it sells, goods it sells and even bets it takes. Agents used to be nicknamed 'ten percenters', hardly an apt name for a professional public relations consultant! A consultant is paid a fee by the client, and not commission by the media for whom it really acts as agent. This fee is based on working hours and expertise like that of any other professional. While it is true that there are advertising agents which rebate commission and charge fees they still need to be 'recognised' by the media owners. The expression 'PR agent', used by American consultancies and copied by some British and continental European ones, is probably derived from the American 'Press agentry' business associated with the publicising of Hollywood movie stars, which has nothing to do with public relations. It is probably used by the British advertising, marketing and public relations trade press because it cannot get away from advertising agencies and equates public relations with advertising. Moreover, only consultancies are likely to buy space in these journals, and to them the larger world of in-house public relations is either unknown or ignored, although another quaint invention of *PR Week* is the 'in-house PR'.

CREDIBILITY

Right from the start — because this will define how programmes are planned and even how a simple news release is written — we need to be clear what we mean by public relations. Essentially, any message communicated must be credible if it is to work. When we signal SOS we are seeking rescue, no less. So with any public relations message, whatever the medium used. This should be obvious commonsense but unhappily it is not because so many business people and other leaders do not want messages to be credible, and the media so often have some of our top business leaders expecting their public relations people to be trouble-shooters, with the media reacting scornfully as happened over the Lord Hanson–ICI take-over debacle. In this case, a consultancy was accused of not saving Lord Hanson's face.

THE ADVERSARIAL SITUATION

Not all, but much of public relations needs to convey its messages via the mass media of the press, radio and television. Perhaps one major difference — and there are many based on economic, geographic, demographic and political differences between the USA and Britain (and Europe as a whole) — is that in the USA the press enjoys the status of the fifth estate and is part of the democratic process, whereas in Britain the press is merely a commercial undertaking (and often a personal one) as we saw with the Maxwell scandal. Not even the American Hearst empire compared with that.

Here lies the key to the relationship between public relations and the media, which will be discussed again in the chapter on the Press Officer and the Press Office. The purposes of the two sides are different to the point of conflict.

However factual and impartial the public relations message, however sincerely it follows the Ivy Ledbetter Lee principle of aiming to be of interest and value to its audience, the public relations message represents the interests of its originator. In contrast, the media message aims to attract and please readers, listeners and viewers in such numbers that the medium will survive and generally make money. Ultimately, the jobs of journalists and editors are at stake. Consequently, the reason for using public relations material will be the extent to which it will help the media and their staff to succeed and survive. In other words, will the public relations story help sell papers? Only then will the public relations practitioner justify his or her existence and so satisfy employer or client. It is a mercenary world, and not surprisingly public relations often turns to creating its own private media over which it has complete control. It has no control over what the mass media say.

PR EXERCISE

A frequent media misconception is to call any initiative they dislike 'a PR exercise', and in this and other ways public relations is used as an expression of contempt for dubious 'smoke screen' or trouble-shooting activities. Usually it refers to political initiatives which the media, with a curious adoption of self-righteousness, consider insincere.

The media, which are constantly inaccurate — see the regular corrections published in *The Economist* and *The Independent* — or intrusive like the mass circulation tabloids, have the temerity to abuse public relations whose information is usually more meticulously checked for accuracy than the average newspaper story produced in the heat of rapid daily reporting. Some newspapers, such as the *Financial Times*, are appreciative of public relations material.

The more 'intellectual', the less its liking for public relations as frequently expressed in newspapers such as *The Guardian* and *The Independent* (which are probably best omitted from press reception guest lists!), and are evidenced by the acid comments on public relations in the Weasel feature in the *Independent Saturday Magazine* (whose letter columns consist mainly of criticism of the accuracy of the magazine's articles!).

PURPOSE OF PUBLIC RELATIONS

A simple explanation is that public relations is a reversal of the words, and is no more than

'relations with the public'. But that is inadequate. For what *purpose* is it necessary to have relations with the public or, more precisely, with various publics? The elementary purpose is to create understanding through knowledge. The object of this book is to show how the communication skills of public relations can be used for this very difficult but practical purpose which concerns any sort of organisation.

Although it may have certain associations, this purpose isolates public relations as a practice quite distinct from advertising, sales promotion, marketing, selling, personnel management, industrial relations or propaganda.

If understanding does not exist, none of those seven separate and different activities can function properly. A hospital is a combination of many people performing different jobs, but it will not function without a doctor. Yet a doctor is not also an administrator, nurse, orderly, cook, receptionist or ambulance driver. The public relations practitioner, like the doctor, is a specialist professional, vital to the successful operation of the whole organisation. He also has to integrate the communication functions of many others in the organisation. There can be a public relations element in other people's work.

The misunderstandings come from various quarters, but are sometimes provoked by unskilled, untrained practitioners themselves. Let us look at the three chief sources of misunderstanding. Public relations itself needs public relations!

Management of all kinds, and especially marketing management, frequently expect it to be something quite different from creating understanding. This ranges from seeking free advertising to pretending bad things have not happened. It tends to think solely in terms of favourable images. The word 'favourable' has become the curse of public relations. We may have to help members of our publics to understand why something unfavourable has happened, as with the recall of a faulty product, a fall in share price or a factory closure or relocation.

PUBLIC RELATIONS FUNCTION AND ITS PARAMETERS

A very good analysis of public relations appears under this heading in Gold Paper No.7, *Public Relations Education — Recommendations and Standards*, published by the International Public Relations Association in 1990, and the following is quoted:

Professional public relations operates in every sphere of life:

1. Government — national, regional, local and international.
2. Business and industry — small, medium and transnational.
3. Community and social affairs.
4. Educational institutions, universities, colleges, etc.
5. Hospitals and health care.
6. Charities and good causes.
7. International affairs.

Public relations practice is:

1. Counselling based on an understanding of human behaviour.
2. Analysing future trends and predicting their consequences.
3. Research into public opinion, attitudes and expectations and advising on necessary action.
4. Establishing and maintaining two-way communication based on truth and full information.
5. Preventing conflict and misunderstandings.
6. Promoting mutual respect and social responsibility.
7. Harmonising the private and the public interest.
8. Promoting an understanding of democracy.

A typical public relations activity will have four parts:

1. Analysis, research and defining goals and objectives.
2. Drawing up a programme of action.
3. Communicating and implementing the programme.
4. Monitoring the results, evaluation and possible modification.

These 19 functions and parameters may seem formidable, idealistic and optimistic, and far removed from the typical management and certainly marketing acceptance of public relations, but they are those of an international body with senior members in 70 countries, and its own code of practice with Universal Declaration of Human Rights overtones known as the *Code of Athens* which was adopted in 1965. In the Gold Paper it lays a foundation for tertiary training in public relations (see Chapter 25).

The four parts of the public relations activity are, in effect, identical to the Six-Point Public Relations Planning Model in which the planning aspects of this book are based. Our six parts are Appreciation of the Situation, Defining Objectives, Defining Publics, Defining Media and Techniques, and Budgeting and Evaluating Results.

These 19 items also demonstrate how completely different public relations is from advertising. It calls for personnel with broader backgrounds, different qualifications, more perceptive and wide-ranging mental abilities, and less specialisation than advertising personnel. This will be brought out more extensively when we consider the attributes of the public relations practitioner at the end of this chapter.

DEFINITIONS

There are many definitions of public relations, some of which suffer from semantics as when we contrast American and British ones. That grand old man of public relations, Ed Bernays, who wrote some of the first books on public relations over 60 years ago, and was greatly honoured on his 100th birthday in November 1991, once called public relations 'engineering consent' which certainly has a very different and unfortunate meaning in British English.

We have to be very careful about the difference between American English and British English as in the case of the notorious Philip Kotler definition which referred to 'planting commercially significant news' since 'planting' (like 'engineering') suggests something highly disreputable, and the very thing which public relations is accused of doing by the media. And since Philip Kotler is the most widely read marketing writer it has led to the marketing world's general misunderstanding of public relations as free advertising and its general contempt of it, especially when Kotler also equates public relations with 'publicity'.

Not surprisingly, there is not much sympathy between the Chartered Institute of Marketing and the Institute of Public Relations, and public relations is so absent from the CIM Diploma that CAM will award exemption from the CAM Certificate to CIM Diploma holders with the exception of the public relations paper which must be studied and passed by those wishing to take the CAM Diploma in Public Relations.

Probably the two most explicit definitions are that of the IPR, and the one known as the Mexican Statement which resulted from the World Assembly of Public Relations Associations held in Mexico City in August 1978. Each definition is now given and analysed.

> Public relations practice is the planned and sustained effort to establish and maintain goodwill and mutual understanding between an organisation and its publics. (IPR)

This is a revised version of the IPR definition which appeared in the previous edition, the word 'deliberate' being omitted, 'goodwill' being added and, in recognition of common usage, 'publics' has replaced 'public'.

Two things are significant in this broad definition. It emphasises that public relations should be *planned* — a main theme of this book — just like planning any other operation. It should not be haphazard or 'played by ear',

subject to the whims of some superior. Of course, it can be planned only if it has a purpose and seeks to satisfy specific needs, that is to achieve tangible *objectives*. The tangibility of public relations is discussed in the next chapter and becomes an integral part of the Six-Point Public Relations Planning Model.

The second important point is 'mutual understanding', meaning that public relations is a two-way process. We not only seek the understanding of our numerous publics but aim to understand them too. The definition also stresses the continuous nature of public relations. There are no short, sharp bursts (as often occurs in advertising) for to be successful public relations, in one form or another, must be an endless flow of educational and informative communication. It goes on and on relentlessly.

> Public Relations Practice is the art and social science of analysing trends, predicting their consequences, counselling organisation leaders, and implementing planned programmes of action which will serve both the organisation's and the public interest. (The Mexican Statement)

This comprehensive definition goes much further than the first one, and virtually supersedes the IPR definition however amended. It follows the principles of the Six-Point Public Relations Planning Model which, as the reader will have by now discovered, is a universal concept.

The Mexican Statement begins by stressing that *research* is necessary in the first instance, and its findings must be *studied* before a programme can be planned. How else can we properly appreciate the situation? The IPRA Gold Paper No.7, to which reference has already been made, complains about the lack of research in public relations and lists forms of applied research which mostly require expensive field surveys. But that is not always the case: scientific research is not always necessary and inexpensive research by means of observation and experience is equally valid.

Next, this definition brings out the advisory function of public relations, which is perhaps the most professional aspect of both in-house and consultancy practice. This is why public relations calls for well-trained, well-qualified mature people, is not the place for school-leavers, and why many practitioners are graduates or second or third career people. The average age of CAM candidates is between 25 and 35 years. Unlike advertising, which can recruit young people such as art students, this is not so in public relations although younger people can be recruited as trainees and junior assistants in large in-house departments or consultancies. But they are unlikely to advise employers or clients, or be taken seriously by them. It takes a mature mind to advise organisation leaders on how to solve their communications problems.

The Mexican Statement continues with the carrying out of programmes and closes with the responsibility of serving not only the organisation's interest but the public interest. Thus, public relations should behave responsibly, and that may be news to those critics who regard public relations as a dubious practice.

The social responsibility is, of course, implied in the IPR and PRCA Codes to which all members are expected to subscribe. Unfortunately, in Britain public relations is not a registered profession and anyone may call themselves a public relations practitioner. There are many cowboys and cowgirls who pretend to be practitioners but who would not qualify for membership of the IPR, and especially with the new requirement of the CAM Diploma or its equivalent. These people worsen the adversarial situation with the media.

THE PUBLIC RELATIONS SITUATION

The foregoing definitions make it clear that public relations is very different from advertising which aims to *make known in order to sell*, and while advertising educates the market to a

certain extent it does so in a biased and persuasive way. This is justified if it is to be competitive and to achieve action, whether it be enquiries or sales. Similarly, propaganda is biased and persuasive in its appeal to supporters, adherents and donors. A major difference between public relations and advertising or propaganda is that if public relations is to succeed it must be free of bias. It has to be impartial and provide hard facts. If it fails in this respect, credibility is lost. Credibility is vital, as pointed out earlier in this chapter.

This is sometimes a hard lesson to learn. The PRO may be enthusiastic about the product, service or organisation, and loyal to the organisation or client, but once partiality creeps into his or her work it invites disbelief, scepticism, and the work is doomed. Management, especially marketing management, will not always understand this, as is so often seen when their amendments and 'more exciting headlines' destroy news releases, making them unpublishable.

A lot of rubbish (at least 70 percent of all news releases) received by editors is not always the fault of the named authors. But these PROs and press officers have to earn the status necessary to tell employers and clients what is publishable. After all, management does not tell the architect to put the basement on the roof.

It is, therefore, necessary to determine the limits of public relations in order to clarify its purpose and, again, distinguish it from advertising and other practices. We come back to *understanding*, which is its primary purpose. This can be demonstrated by the Public Relations Transfer Process. This model epitomises the crucial situation in which public relations has to operate, first having established the extent and nature of the negative situations. The purpose is usually to convert one or more of these bad situations into better ones. Clearly, this is a lot more complex than the banal attempt to create favourable images, favourable situations, or favourable mentions in the media. The gross oversimplication and

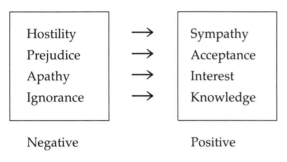

Hostility	→ Sympathy
Prejudice	→ Acceptance
Apathy	→ Interest
Ignorance	→ Knowledge

Negative   Positive

Figure 2.1   Public Relations Transfer Process

unreality of the 'favourable' idea of public relations has long been one of its handicaps. The achievement of understanding, no more, is a very different, difficult, plausible and realistic concept. It is a tremendous task.

Let us look at the Transfer Process more closely, for it really is the essence of our subject and a major theme of this book. It is the anatomy of public relations. Much of the problem-solving in public relations is to do with converting those four negative states into more positive ones. Success will never be one hundred percent because new situations are always occurring, and new people have to be converted. They have to be converted by facts, not persuaded by sales talk.

1. *Hostility.* Almost any organisation will have to contend with some degree of hostility. Most of the public services which serve almost everyone — the police, Post Office, the gas and electricity undertakings, British Rail and so on — cannot possibly please all of the people all of the time. In the commercial world there are people who at different times and for various reasons may be hostile to their products or services. There are countries which provoke hostility which could harm their trade and tourist interests. Even charities and other voluntary bodies arouse criticism from time to time.

The communication task will be to present the facts, not lurk behind a protective wall of silence or subterfuge, in order to be under-

stood. People may not love you, but with understanding they can sympathise and be tolerant. But if the hostility is unjustified a good informative programme can reverse the situation. Research may be necessary to find out what are the grounds of hostility; they may be misinformation, lack of information, or some other mischief such as false information from a rival source. Respected opinion leaders, being misinformed or uninformed themselves, can do great harm to an organisation.

2. *Prejudice.* Overcoming prejudice may be difficult, as happens with racial or religious differences. Prejudices are often deep-rooted and bound up in environment, family upbringing, educational, political or religious background, nationality or ethnic group. There can also be prejudice about names, colours or shapes which affect products. There are people who will never board an aeroplane or ship or go abroad. Some prejudices may seem petty or immature. Yet, often they can be overcome through better understanding.

In Asia today almost every motor-car is Japanese, yet, as a result of wartime occupational experience, there was both hostility and prejudice towards Japanese motor-cars at one time. In January 1992 American–Japanese prejudices surfaced following President Bush's abortive trade trip to Japan, which resulted in misunderstandings about Japanese intentions regarding imports of American goods. The Japanese are very sensitive about their 'uniqueness' which can read like hostility and prejudice towards foreigners. In that same week there were eruptions of prejudice. Los Angeles transport officials infuriated the Japanese by cancelling a £68m contract to buy commuter rail cars from Sumitomo Corporation for a new 300 mile mass transit system. Meanwhile, Yoshio Sakurauchi, speaker of the Lower House of Parliament, said 'American workers want to get high salaries without working. They cannot take orders because 30 percent of them are illiterate'.

Who would have taken a holiday in Russia

before Thomson Holidays promoted cheap weekends in Moscow with wide coverage by travel writers? Who would have bought English wine, until comparatively recently, but now there are many English vineyards. Some people are still prejudiced about travelling to France by the Channel Tunnel.

3. *Apathy.* Here we have a dreadful negative state. The police have done a tremendous public relations job with their Neighbourhood Watch programme to encourage householders to protect their property from burglars, and with the *Crime Watch* programme on BBC1 TV. Apathy is understandable: people are wrapped up in their own affairs and resist new ideas. Apathy is a kind of protective conservatism, but it may be very much in people's interests to be aware of beneficial products and services. Local authorities and Government departments have to fight apathy to get people to enjoy rights, services and facilities to which they are entitled. It was apathy which made it necessary for the use of motor-car seat belts to be made legally compulsory. In our changing world, apathy is often to do with life-styles and older age groups, and people do not want to change. This is particularly true in developing countries where Ministries have to use public relations tactics in order to effect social changes which call for revolutionary changes in life-styles. No wonder some of them call their information services departments of public enlightenment!

4. *Ignorance.* The world has become so complex that all of us are inevitably ignorant about a great many things. When new products and services are introduced, advertising alone will not break the barrier of ignorance, and informative, educational public relations is essential. It is surprising how those responsible for marketing will go straight into expensive advertising for an unknown product or service, and then be disappointed by the take-up. When Findus launched their Lean Cuisine range, they began with an extensive pro-

gramme months before they launched their advertising campaign. On the other hand the Sinclair C5 electric tricycle arrived unknown with a burst of advertising, and was savagely criticised and mocked on *Spitting Image*, the satirical TV puppet show. The new concept of a CDi for the popular market occupied Philips with an educational programme lasting more than a year before the launch.

The market has to be prepared for new things, but the marketing world is not in love with market education, which includes the trade as well as the consumers. When public relations is accepted as an integral part of the marketing mix, and not as mere publicity and an optional extra (*vide* Kotler), it can be a great asset in demolishing ignorance and paving the way for successful advertising. We have seen major examples in the privatisation of state enterprises supported it is true by lead-up advertising. Sony used public relations a year before their compact video camera appeared on the market. Advance knowledge can build up interest, curiosity, expectation and awareness which can be an excellent prelude to a product launch.

From the above it will be seen that public relations opens up an immense array of possibilities for use of its techniques. But as will be seen in the next chapter, the user must be clear about its purpose. When there are well-defined objectives, it can be a very economical means of achieving specific results.

But the philosophy must be clear too. There must be no confusion with other practices, and public relations is not a substitute for advertising. It relies on facts and frankness. Once suspect, it loses credibility. Unless the message is believed, the effects will be disastrous. This calls for impartiality and accuracy.

If the mass media are being used, it calls for understanding of how they operate and when and in what form they require information. The public relations practitioner has to do the favours, not expect them, and this can involve appreciating that the objectives of the media are very different from those of his client or organisation, as was explained earlier. To sell newspapers and magazines, and to win radio and TV audiences, it is necessary to satisfy readers and audiences. Sometimes the mass media will not be appropriate, and special private media may have to be created. Part of the philosophy of public relations is therefore knowing *how* to communicate, not just how to write a news release. What then are the attributes of a good public relations practitioner? They also express the philosophy of public relations.

ATTRIBUTES OF A PUBLIC RELATIONS PRACTITIONER

Here are the six essential attributes of a public relations practitioner.

1. Ability to communicate, whether the message be written, spoken, printed, photographed, broadcast, filmed or videotaped.
2. Ability to organise, which means worrying about every detail including costs.
3. Ability to get on with all kinds of people, which means understanding and liking people, not flattering them.
4. Integrity so that one is trusted inside and outside the organisation and especially by the media.
5. Imagination, which is necessary in every aspect of public relations, whether it be planning a campaign or a simple event, briefing photographers, buying print, editing house journals or handling anything else creative.
6. Perhaps most important of all, willingness to learn and find out, and to realise that in this profession one never knows it all.

A person with these all-round qualities should succeed in public relations which calls for get-up-and-go people who realise that it is mostly hard work.

Added to that, it will help the practitioner if he or she has taken the trouble to learn their craft and holds the CAM Diploma or one of the degrees now available from British colleges and universities. Membership of the IPR will signify his or her experience and recognition as a professional.

WAYS IN WHICH PUBLIC RELATIONS DIFFER FROM ADVERTISING

A number of comparisons have been made already, but the following are worth highlighting.

1. *Language*. The type of language differs between the two, advertising relying on persuasive and sometimes emotional wording whereas public relations depends on factual wording free of emphasis, self-praise and superlatives.
2. *Editorial versus sales*. Public relations deals with those who produce the editorial content of the press or the programme material of radio and television. Advertising deals with the advertisement space or air-time selling side of the media.
3. *The purpose*. This is fundamentally different. Advertising aims to persuade and sell, public relations aims to educate and inform. The latter can of course make the former more effective. We are more likely to buy what we understand.
4. *Costs*. The largest costs in advertising are media and production, but in public relations they are time and materials.
5. *Media*. When the mass media are used, different ones may be used for advertising and public relations, but public relations also has its own private media which is often aimed at small audiences.
6. *Breadth of public relations*. Whereas advertising is mostly limited to the marketing function, public relations applies to all functions of an organisation, and to organisations which do not advertise.

WHAT IS PROPAGANDA?

We prefer to regard propaganda as biased information and as the means of making known in gaining support for an opinion, creed or belief. It requires the sacrifice of time, money, heart and mind for a cause which might be charitable, political, religious, national or ethnic.

However, it is only fair to admit that there are other views which were discussed by Tim Traverse-Healy when he researched and compiled his IPRA Gold Paper No.6, 1988, *Public Relations and Propaganda — Values Compared*. Tim Traverse-Healy surprised himself in his generous study of the beliefs of eminent academics, practitioners and writers. Some of them saw public relations and propaganda as being identical, although others offered reservations about their different purposes. Propaganda is not necessarily a bad thing in the Goebbels tradition and may be used legitimately to promote good causes such as Save the Children. Propagandists may also use public relations to explain themselves. It can be a good thing to understand what Christians, Buddhists, Jews and Muslims believe in without sharing their beliefs.

Bernays, that lucid writer, has a definition more nearly ours when (as quoted in the Gold Paper) he describes public relations as 'Ideally it is a constructive force bringing to the public facts and figures resulting often in accelerated interest in matters of value and importance, to the social, economic and political life of the community'.

And who would disagree with the late Sir Tom Fife-Clark, first president of IPRA in 1955–1957, who believed that it was 'the duty of practitioners to provide people with the unvarnished facts about policies as quickly and as fully as possible so that in the light of them the public could make up its own mind about public issues, develop its own assessment and arrive at its own decision'.

The root of confusion seems to be in the role of public relations as a means of effecting change. If this is a matter of overcoming unvarnished hostility, prejudice, apathy or ignorance, this is surely praiseworthy, and is not to be condemned as disinformation or propaganda. The author is quoted in the Gold Paper as saying 'The popular belief that public relations is a form of propaganda nullifies its purpose and destroys its credibility'. Credibility again! Yet Dr Jon White (formerly of Cranfield) makes the alarming assertion that 'propaganda and public relations both have the same overall aim'. How is that possible?

We prefer Professor Van der Meiden's distinctions: 'The objective of public relations is the achievement of consent; of propaganda to build a movement. The intention of public relations is to achieve true dialogue; not so with propaganda. The methods of public relations involve complete openness; propaganda if needs be obscures the facts. Public relations strives for understanding; propaganda for a following.'

Tim Traverse-Healy is certainly to be congratulated for bringing together for the first time such a diversity of views on propaganda.

CHAPTER 3

Planning a Public Relations Campaign

WHY PLAN?

For the purpose of this chapter the author offers his own definition: *Public relations consists of all forms of planned communications, outwards and inwards, between an organisation and its publics for the purpose of achieving specific objectives concerning mutual understanding.* The key words are 'specific objectives'.

There could be no more damning a condemnation of public relations than that it is intangible, but *effective* public relations is not. Why should anyone spend money on something incapable of showing that the money was well spent? There was a time when some people thought that a collection of press cuttings was sufficient reward. Perhaps press cuttings represented that vague idea of 'favourable media coverage' or, worse still, 'free advertising' with a fallacious calculation of column inches or column centimetres on an advertisement rate card basis.

That is no way to evaluate even press relations because it is highly unlikely that the same space on the same date in the same publication would ever be bought. It is a mythical yardstick. A truer measure of media coverage would be the number of people who had the opportunity to read, watch or hear the message, based on readership or audience figures. Better still would be a measurement of the *effect* of media coverage, based on the number of enquiries received or as a result of a survey into recall or shift of attitude or opinion. Today we measure the *quality*, not the quantity, of media coverage.

However, if one plunges into public relations in a haphazard fashion, failing to determine objectives, failing to define publics, failing to plan campaigns, techniques and media, failing to budget labour, materials and expenses and control budgets, failing to allocate resources including labour, and failing to evaluate results against precise objectives, that can scarcely be described as responsible professional public relations. Unless there are *targets* or *objectives* there is nothing against which to evaluate results.

It happens, but why does it happen? There are two reasons. First, because management does not know what it wants from public relations, or because management wants it for spurious reasons. Second, because practitioners do not present planned programmes to management, but allow themselves to be dogsbodies who are expected to do this and that as and when commanded. Unfortunately, a lot of public relations — and a lot of which provokes criticism — is of the latter kind. It is an abuse of public relations, a waste of opportunities to make it work, and it undermines the authority of the practitioner.

COST EFFECTIVE PUBLIC RELATIONS

If public relations is to be cost-effective, it should be a planned operation, planned like a marketing strategy, a sales or advertising campaign or a factory production schedule, that is, with a definite end in view. It can come about in one of two ways: either management will present its communication aims to the in-house PRO or the public relations consultant, and a budgeted programme will be drawn up and presented for approval; or the PRO or consultant will present management with its recommended and costed plan of action. This does, of course, presuppose that the situation has been researched and appreciated and that there are reasons and purposes on which to base a plan of positive action.

In the case of the consultant, this is likely to be true in any event because it will be the method of either winning the account or securing a renewal of the business.

The situation may be different with the in-house PRO. Much depends on his position in the organisation. To whom does he or she report, the chief executive or someone down the line such as the marketing manager or director? Perhaps (as we shall see in chapter 14) he or she doubles as advertising manager or marketing services manager, and the public relations role is more obscure. Again, what status is enjoyed as an adviser to management? Ideally, the PRO should operate independently, and be answerable only to the chief executive, but this is not always the case. We have to accept that the positioning of the in-house practitioner is not always perfect.

Nevertheless, and whatever his or her position, public relations is labour-intensive and it will be productive and successful only if time or labour are deployed over planned assignments to achieve definite purposes. Otherwise time will be frittered away here and there and nothing in particular will be achieved. This can happen when there is no management by objectives system.

Does this make sense? It does in almost any other walk of life. Newspapers are not published every morning by accident, nor do buses, trains, ships or aeroplanes arrive at their destinations unless that was the planned intention of the operators. A doctor runs a surgery, visits patients, attends a clinic, all according to plan. Schools have curricula of studies, timetables of classes. The rest of the world works to planned objectives, so why should it be unusual in public relations? Why should public relations be the sort of hit-or-miss, do this, do that, plaything of management that it so often is?

When lecturing on the topic, the author is often confronted by amazed PROs who pretend that planned public relations cannot happen. They are in the wrong business. Planned public relations is the only thing that can happen if it is going to work. It does happen, of course, in all successful growth companies as demonstrated in the case study at the end of this book, in those that have survived the recession, and in the public relations consultancies that have survived recent cut-backs.

There are two ways in which objective planning can be accepted as the norm: when management knows how to use and buy public relations services, and when in-house PROs assert and earn their status by presenting management with their planned and costed programme for the coming financial year. It is not a case of preparing an isolated campaign or press reception, but of organising a year's work on the basis of the available time, money and other resources such as equipment. No one can be in two places or doing two jobs at the same time, and that also goes for vehicles, cameras, word processors, VCRs, and other equipment.

This is where one begins to realise the importance of the six attributes and the need for training and qualifications with which the last chapter closed. This happens less today, but some years ago it was thought that if one wanted a PRO all one had to do was hire a journalist. What would the average journalist, fresh out of a newsroom, know about planning intricate campaigns based on labour, materials and expenses? About as much as the journalists interviewed by the author, when he was a consultant, who said they knew all about running press receptions because they had attended so many! The gin-and-tonic PRO is a ghost of the past. Today's PRO is a businessman, a budget-minded miser accountable for every hour and penny that is spent, and proud of the documented and recorded achievements gained by varied skills and knowledge.

Yes, public relations is an exciting and satisfying occupation because its results are assessable, visible and there to be proud of. The IPR, for instance, makes its annual Sword of Excellence awards for successful PR campaigns. The top people in PR are all telling of their *tangible* achievements. And they are earning top salaries and fees. The justification for tangible, objective PR has become big business. We are not therefore being idealistic in presenting the following Six-Point Planning Model which has been a main feature of the author's books since first published in *Marketing and PR Media Planning* in 1974.

THE SIX-POINT PUBLIC RELATIONS PLANNING MODEL

This model follows a blend of the definition at the beginning of this chapter and of the Mexican Statement given in the previous chapter.

1. Appreciation of the situation or the communication audit.
2. Definition of objectives.
3. Definition of publics.
4. Choice of media and techniques.
5. Budget of the cost of labour, materials and expenses.
6. Evaluation of results.

Separate chapters are given to the last five points, and after a brief look at the general principles of the model we shall first consider

the constraints which it imposes, and then examine how the situation may be appreciated.

The model sets out a logical sequence of decisions and actions, and places public relations in its problem-solving role in the effort to achieve mutual understanding. It asserts the management function of the practitioner who directs and takes responsibility for a plan of action. He or she is the spokesperson for the organisation or client, operating an intelligence system and acting as the eyes, ears and voice of the organisation represented. The public relations practitioner is not a puppet on the master's string.

CONSTRAINTS IMPOSED BY THE MODEL

While the six points of the model are far-reaching, they also impose restraints. The nature of the programme will depend on the results of auditing the situation. It is no use planning a grandiose programme if it is irrelevant to, say, the extent of hostility, prejudice, apathy and ignorance revealed by the initial study. There may be more publics than can be reached within the limits of available resources, and some may have to be disregarded. Or media capable of reaching them do not exist: can we afford to create our own media? The budget will affect everything. How will results be assessed? That also may cost money. There could be a constraint on what is carried out because of research costs. The budget has to be sufficient to cover initial and post-research, and to conduct a campaign sufficiently substantial to achieve the desired results.

The above is very different from some of the haphazard public relations undertakings of the past when initial and post-research was never considered. But that was rather like spending money on medicine or medical treatment without first diagnosing the ailment and then making sure that the treatment had succeeded. Although public relations is often remarkably inexpensive and economic it cannot be done on the cheap, and one of the reasons management has become disenchanted with it has been that too little was spent to produce any worthwhile results. These failures have been rather like a 10p each way bet on an odds-on favourite and failing to win a fortune.

TIME — THE BIGGEST CONSTRAINT

However, the biggest constraint is *time*. Enough time must be allocated for each job in the programme, remembering that a total year's programme may entail a variety of separate assignments such as a new share issue, a new product, a house journal, the setting up of an overseas subsidiary and maybe a merger with another company. There is a limit on what existing staff can do, or extra staff must be employed to do extra work, or a consultancy must be appointed to augment the existing staff. The only way in which more can be done in the same time is when the practitioner is sufficiently skilled to use his time economically.

In the case of a consultancy, it can undertake a workload only according to the fee, and additional work must be paid for. In the past, foolish consultants have attempted to be generous to clients by accepting more and more work for the same fee. This is possible only if the consultant is prepared either to subsidise the client by virtually receiving a lower hourly rate, or to steal time from other clients. Unbusinesslike consultants do not survive, and those who stay in business and thrive work on a time-sheet basis and have no qualms about resigning unprofitable clients. As a consultant, the author had no hesitation in firing greedy clients who would have ruined him.

There was a time when consultants charged round-sum fees or retainers for unspecified services: today contracts of service are based on carefully budgeted proposals outlining the whole programme of work so that the client knows exactly what the fee represents, and the consultant knows that this has to be done to earn his fee. The businesslike consultant is like a quantity surveyor.

It is significant that the *Hollis Press and Public Relations Annual* lists some 1200 UK consultants, but each year's listing is different. One reason is that consultancies have disappeared because they got their sums wrong, offered services too cheaply and suffered cash flow crises.

ANALYSIS OF THE SIX-POINT MODEL

1. *Appreciation of the situation*. Sometimes called the communications audit, the object of this study is to establish the current image and to discover what is the state of hostility, prejudice, apathy or ignorance. It is no use planning a campaign unless we know where we are now. It would be foolish to accept management's mirror image, which could be wrong. The various types of image will be discussed later in this chapter. The cost of this study could be a valuable investment, and it can also provide a basis for eventual evaluation of results when a similar study can be repeated to measure how the situation has changed, if it has, as a result of the campaign. This is a logical procedure which makes all the difference between money-wasting intangible public relations and cost-effective tangible public relations.

This research does not have to be expensive, and it may not require the employment of a marketing research service if information is available elsewhere. For instance, bad media coverage and published misunderstandings could be evidence enough on which to base a PR programme to correct these misunderstandings. The result should be proper understanding by the media, which would be simple to evaluate for the cost of a press cutting service.

2. *Definition of objectives.* This is not unlike a central or local department setting out its proposals when the annual budget for the government or local authority is being drawn up. The PRO or consultant needs to examine all the proposals of the different departments in an organisation to determine what communication problems have to be handled. These may embrace a new product launch, a rights offer of shares, the opening of a new factory, participation in an exhibition, a recruitment campaign and so on. As will be seen in Chapter 4, the list of possible objectives could be very long, and it will be different for different organisations. It may be prohibitively long, and the constraints of the budget — the available labour and other resources — may mean the selection of priorities. On the other hand, the defining of objectives may encourage management to see the necessity of public relations, and so agree to a bigger budget!

Without these objectives, a practical plan of campaign cannot be devised, nor can its results be assessed. It is like setting out on a journey: it has to be planned and one either arrives or one does not. Unplanned public relations never expects to arrive anywhere.

3. *Definition of publics.* Unlike the meaningless Oxford English Dictionary definition of public relations, we do not deal with 'the general public' but with many specified groups of very different people. An advertising campaign may be addressed to the mass market, or even to a large number of housewives, motorists or DIY enthusiasts, whereas a public relations campaign is addressed to particular sections of the public. Examples of publics for different organisations are set out in Chapter 5. In order to achieve our objectives, we need to define the special publics to whom our messages are to be addressed. They may be as varied as employers, politicians, distributors, schoolchildren and opinion leaders as well as customers past, present and future, actual or potential of one or both sexes and of different ages and social grades. We shall discuss social grades later in this chapter.

4. *Choice of media and techniques.* Having put our objectives and publics together we now have to decide how, or whether it is possible, to communicate in order to achieve our defined objectives through our defined publics. Suitable commercial media may or may not exist, and one of the strengths of a public relations practitioner will be knowledge of the printed and broadcast media. Media can be divided into the *existing commercial* (e.g. newspapers, magazines, radio and television and public or trade exhibitions) and *private created* (e.g. house journals, audio-visuals and visual aids, educational print, private exhibitions, sponsorships, seminars and conferences).

The public relations practitioner can never know enough about media, and it should be a perceptual study. There are numerous excellent sources of reference such as *Benn's Media Directory, Willings Press Guide, Editors,* and the *PR Planner.*

Techniques are also involved such as press events, feature articles, radio and TV interviews, corporate identity schemes, talks and video/slide shows, or sponsorships.

The choice is far wider than in advertising, but rather like direct mail advertising, it can be very selective. Each public may consist of millions or only a few people. There could be eyeball-to-eyeball communication between two people.

5. *The budget.* The three main costs are time, materials and expenses. Unless there are heavy material costs for the printing of house journals or the production of videos, the major cost will be time. Expenses — catering, hospitality, travel — should be a small part of the budget. Time, or labour, will be represented by the PRO's salary (and that of his staff) or the consultancy fee. The fee will represent the

workload estimated for the proposed campaign. In a similar way, the staff PRO's working year can be calculated in hours, and the take-up of these working hours allocated to the tasks of the programme.

This is important. You cannot build a house if you do not have enough bricks, and you cannot carry out a public relations campaign if you do not have enough time. Conversely, given a certain volume of time you can plot what it is possible to do with it. This is one of the constraints, and it is no use listing a great many objectives, identifying the right publics, and deciding on the best media and techniques if the time is not there to perform the work. If the budget and the time are inadequate, it is necessary to trim the demands.

Budgetary controls are also necessary, the most obvious kind being a simple daily time-sheet on which is recorded what is done. Time-sheets are critical in a consultancy so that time is rationed carefully between clients according to their fees. Each client should have a time-bank of hours per fee. Such time-sheets are also valuable in order to weed out uneconomic clients, charge supplementary fees for extra work, prepare monthly and annual reports and, in the event of a dispute, show a client exactly how much time was spent servicing the account. The in-house PRO can also benefit from having a record of activities.

Other forms of paperwork, including the use of job numbers, which contribute to control of expenditure, will also be discussed in Chapter 7.

6. *Assessment of results.* There are three ways of measuring results: by observation and experience; by evaluating media coverage; and by the use of scientific marketing research techniques. It all depends on the objectives. If staff of the right calibre are recruited; if complaints are replaced by compliments; if dealers are able to explain products better; if proposed hostile legislation is defeated or amended; or a take-over bid is aborted, the results will be self-evident and can be observed and experienced.

If the tone of media coverage is improved, this can be seen from press cuttings and monitored scripts of broadcasts. But if it is a case of measuring a shift in attitude or opinion, or awareness or correctness of a corporate image, a research survey such as an opinion poll or image study will be necessary. It should be a repeat of the original study made to appreciate the situation.

Methods of making assessments will be discussed in Chapter 8.

APPRECIATION OF THE SITUATION

First, let us consider the question of the *image* since this is the word which rightly or wrongly is so often associated with public relations. We are lumbered with some unfortunate jargon, including the expression public relations itself. The word 'image' has caused a great deal of argument and misunderstanding, mostly because of the anti-public relations concept that an image is something false which can be contrived, or perhaps 'polished' as journalists and advertising people sometimes claim. We even have a consultancy called Imagemaker, which is a nonsensical contradiction in terms since an image cannot be made. An image is whatever is in people's minds, according to their information, awareness or experience. It can depend on the extent of their hostility, prejudice, apathy, ignorance or otherwise. The image can therefore be a very fickle thing, different people having different images of the same thing.

This leads to consideration of the fact that while a correct image is desirable (and a 'good' one has to be earned for it is a matter of reputation), there are some variations and seven kinds can be described.

SEVEN KINDS OF IMAGE

These different types of image are given precise meanings as they apply to our subject, but they are sometimes given different lay meanings, especially mirror image which is often used loosely by journalists.

1. *Mirror image*. This is the somewhat imperfect and often quite false image held by business leaders who *think* they know how others view the organisation. It could be wishful thinking based on blindness, optimism and lack of information. An advertising agent or public relations consultant has to beware of clients telling them how the world regards their organisation. It is usually a self-imposed fantasy. That is why research is necessary to audit reality.

2. *Current image*. This is the consensus of what other people (whether staff or outsiders) really know about the organisation. It can be a shock to those at the top who had fondly held a mirror image.

3. *Multiple image*. The image of an organisation is often created by its representatives. These representatives are staff such as field sales representatives, shop assistants, telephone receptionists, waitresses, and air hostesses with whom customers and other members of the public have direct contact. Achievement of a uniform standard of service, behaviour and appearance is very much a public relations exercise, requiring careful staff selection and training, and it may include dress. If individual impressions, good and bad, are given by individual members of staff, there will be as many images as there are representatives of the organisation. This is allied to the corporate identity, that is, how the organisation is viewed physically.

4. *Wish image*. When a new organisation is created, no image exists and the wish image is the one initially promoted to create understanding of the nature and purpose of the organisation.

5. *Corporate image*. Here we have the most commonly known image, this being of the organisation itself, what it is and what it stands for, and as we have seen above there can be a mirror and a current version of it. Whether it is a good or a bad image depends on how the organisation is seen to behave and the extent of people's knowledge and experience of it. The corporate image may be helped by the corporate identity, but should not be confused with it. The corporate image or *perceived* image exists in people's minds, while the corporate identity exists in people's eyes since it consists of the logo, typography and house colour and is physically represented in forms of dress, the livery of transportation, and in print and advertising.

6. *The product image*. This can be created by advertising which develops the character of a product by emphasising its individual qualities or selling points. One pen may have a status or gift image, another will have a cheap throwaway image, although both of them may write perfectly well.

7. *The optimum image*. No one is likely to have perfect or complete knowledge of an organisation, and in public relations we have to settle for a reasonable average understanding which is correct as far as it goes.

Coming back to the use of the word 'image' in public relations, we have to be careful about talk of 'good images', 'improving the image', creating a 'favourable image' and so on as if it is in our power to pretend that a corporate image can be falsified as one which is better than it really is. An image can be only what it is, although it may happen that people do not know how good it deserves to be. Thus, the establishment of an image can be the public relations task of presenting the facts and accomplishing knowledge and understanding. Before planning a campaign, it is therefore necessary to understand what the current image is. Sometimes the image may be virtually non-existent. Before Cornhill Insurance started sponsoring test cricket it had an excellent image with insurance brokers but practically none with potential policy holders in the household insurance market. The Cornhill tests have changed all that.

METHODS OF APPRECIATING THE SITUATION

We do not necessarily have to spend money on a marketing research survey, unless we need to measure attitudes, opinion, awareness or to discover the current image, when it is necessary to question a representative sample of our public or publics. Before considering marketing research methods, let us first see what can be done within our own resources.

1. *Complaints.* The number and kind of complaint could indicate something of the hostility towards the organisation. It could also show the extent of ignorance through misinformation, misunderstanding, or lack of information. Remedies could range from writing better instructions (e.g. on labels, stuffers or in service manuals) to a market education programme.

2. *Media attitudes and tone.* Study of press cuttings and monitored broadcast scripts could reveal the hostility, prejudice and ignorance of journalists and broadcasters. This is a very real 'situation', and many organisations have suffered from misinformed and uninformed media. The remedy lies with public relations. The media may dislike public relations, and persist in maligning it, but that may well be the fault of bad public relations. But when the media persist in saying that Lagos is the capital of Nigeria, most journalists will prefer to be corrected. A lot of public relations is like that: the media get it wrong until told otherwise.

Perhaps there are no press cuttings. Why? When a consultant, the author found that his new client was not reported because when

editors had written to the company advertising manager for information he had filed the letters in his waste-paper bin. Here was a situation which literally had to be repaired.

3. *Meetings with managers, sales representatives, distributors.* How the organisation is viewed by key personnel, and by the trade, can be a valuable part of the communication audit. Interviews, similar to those conducted by management consultants, can produce an enlightening and critical insight into the current image. Moreover, such people can be encouraged to talk freely and, being interested in the organisation, they will reveal intimate details which are impossible with an outside survey conducted among strangers.

4. *Sales reports.* The regular reports by field sales representatives can also be useful in producing information about dealer attitudes and the state of the market, including competition and competitors. Study of sales figures, and annual reports and accounts, can also contribute to a picture of the organisation's fortunes.

5. *Published reports.* Secondary or 'desk' research can consist of studying reports on the trade or industry, or on consumer behaviour, as published by government agencies (e.g. Central Statistical Office), and trade bodies such as the Confederation of British Industry (CBI) together with those representing the particular trade or industry. The organisation may also subscribe to consumer panel and dealer audit reports, and these will also be useful to the public relations practitioner. It may be that this desk research will make the commissioning of original or primary research unnecessary.

6. *Image studies.* Now we begin to look at the ways of assessing the situation by means of independent scientific research conducted by a professional marketing research unit. There are many kinds of marketing research using

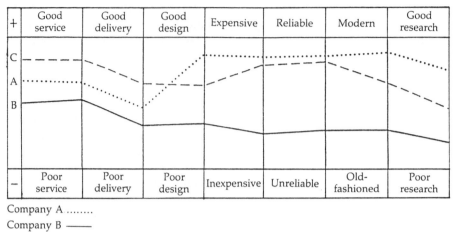

+	Good service	Good delivery	Good design	Expensive	Reliable	Modern	Good research
C							
A							
B							
−	Poor service	Poor delivery	Poor design	Inexpensive	Unreliable	Old-fashioned	Poor research

Company A ....
Company B ———
Company C – – –

Figure 3.1   Image study

special techniques and usually seeking particular kinds of information. The user of research needs to understand what needs to be known and what sort of techniques should be applied. Before commissioning research, the PRO may need to consult the marketing department, advertising agency, consultancy or the Market Research Society. Again, it is an instance of the jack-of-all-trades PRO needing to know about yet another ancillary service. The expression 'image study' is often loosely used, and confused with opinion polls which are quite different.

An image study compares the sponsor's organisation with its rivals. Those interviewed are asked how they rate each organisation, and the questions asked may be about price, delivery, research, or service or whatever makes up the image. The answers can then be represented graphically showing how each organisation is rated on a scale from good to bad. The sponsor can then make comparisons with rivals and a comparative image is revealed.

In Figure 3.1 we have a hypothetical graph, although in reality it could extend over more topics, and there could be more rival organisations. The curve for each one can be identified

by a different colour, one of them representing the sponsor, although those being questioned will be unaware of the sponsor's identity.

If the aim is to correct weak points and so earn a truer image, the image study can be repeated at the close of the public relations programme so that changes can be recorded and an assessment made of the effects of the programme. It may be, for instance, that although the first image study showed that the organisation was thought to have poor research, this was a misunderstanding which better information could correct.

7. Opinion, attitude, awareness or shift studies. These polls are often of a regular or continuous nature, as is seen with the political polls conducted by NOP, MORI, Harris and other pollsters. For PR purposes, a poll could be conducted before planning the campaign, then at mid-term and finally when the campaign has been completed. Thus, change over time can be recorded. The questions are usually of the 'Yes', 'No', 'Don't know' type, but other types of question, such as the multi-choice, can be used when, for example, respondents are asked to state which make of listed motorcars they drive.

Reference was made earlier to Cornhill's sponsorship of test cricket. The initial poll showed that only two percent of adult males were aware of the company, but following the first season of sponsorship, a subsequent poll showed that this awareness figure had risen to 18 percent.

8. *Telephone and postal surveys.* Personal interviews cost money, but there is the guarantee that every member of the sample does provide answers and, according to the methods of sampling, the results will be representative. With postal questionnaires the accuracy of the survey depends on the number of questionnaires returned. The telephone survey, best arranged by appointment, is particularly useful when the sample is small and respondents are scattered so that personal interviews would be prohibitively expensive if not difficult to achieve. However, telephone interviewing has become very popular for urgent studies such as those conducted by newspapers on issues of wide interest. Phone-in polls are conducted on the radio. The telephone survey is therefore a versatile method which can be inexpensive.

9. *Discussion groups.* Here, a group of people assemble under a chairperson who asks questions, and answers are given spontaneously like a 'brainstorming' session, the chairperson summing up with a consensus answer. The group may meet regularly and deal with various topics, or it may be recruited 'off the street' on each occasion. The weakness of the method is that the group is small and may not be truly representative.

SAMPLING

Some jargon has appeared above, and we need to be clear what we mean by 'sample' and 'sampling'. A research sample means a number of people who represent the whole 'population' or 'universe' of people we are interested in, e.g. motorists, parents, doctors, teachers and so on. We are not usually interested in the general population in 'population census' terms. The sample is like the sample taken by the wine-taster who does not have to drink the whole barrel or bottle to test its quality. Thus 100 interviews could be a satisfactory sample of 1000 motorists, provided the 100 represented all the different kinds of motorist. It is necessary for the sample to represent all the 'characteristics' of the total 'population'.

However, there are two main kinds of sample, the *quota* and the *random*.

The *quota* sample is usually smaller than the *random* sample, and consists of quotas or percentages of different kinds of people in proportion to their existence in the national census population. The simplest example would be quotas of men and women on this population basis, but it could be quotas of different kinds of doctors, teachers, motorists or farmers, or again, age groups or social grades. The quota sample lends itself to surveys of particular kinds of people. However, it has the weakness of bias because these quotas have to be found or recognised by the interviewer who could make mistakes, although interviewers are usually well trained and experienced.

In marketing research the *random* sample is not taken at random, nor are 'random numbers' used as in some sociological surveys. Instead, names and addresses are selected at regular intervals from an appropriate list (e.g. electoral register or a membership register). Thus, every *n*th name is chosen according to the size of the sample required. Interviewers are given lists of actual names and addresses, and normally they are expected to make at least three attempts to locate each given respondent before replacing with an alternative. The method is more costly in interviewing time than a quota sample, and the number of people interviewed is usually larger in order to get a proper cross-section of the population, capable of covering every characteristic. There

Grade	Class	Occupation	% Population
A	Upper middle	Chief executive	2.7
B	Middle	Executives, managers	15.2
C1	Lower middle	White-collar, white-blouse office staff	24.1
C2	Skilled working	Blue-collar factory workers	27.1
D	Working	Semi- and unskilled workers	17.8
E	Very poor	Poor pensioners, disabled, casual workers	13.1

Figure 3.2   Social grades in Britain

is no interviewer bias and so the random sample is, by the law of averages, the more accurate. It is sometimes called a 'probability sample' because the probability is that everyone in the population has an equal chance of being selected. It may also be called an 'interval' sample.

Random samples do require lists of names, and such statistical information may be lacking in Third World countries. An alternative is the 'random walk' or 'random location' method which may be used when the researcher will call at houses at regular intervals.

Criticism is sometimes made of political polls, but this is obviously unfair because voting intentions are never finalised until election day. But the results of political polls do vary, and it all depends on (a) the questions asked, (b) the date of the survey and influences that could affect answers, (c) the size and nature of the sample, and (d) whether it was a quota or a random sample. If the various rival political polls are studied closely, it will be seen that these four conditions are rarely if ever the same for each research company, resulting in different answers. Moreover, the quota sample may be 450 compared with, say 1200–1500 for a random

sample. When opinion polls are being conducted for public relations purposes, the conditions peculiar to political polls, especially during the run-up to an election, are unlikely to exist.

SOCIAL GRADES

Marketing research samples often take into consideration *social grades*, which were originally created for the National Readership Survey (NRS). Social grades differ from socio-economic groups which have not been used in the UK for the past 20 years although they are still used in countries where it is easier to classify people according to their wealth. Social grades are based on occupation, not income. This is important because two people could earn the same income but have entirely different life-styles.

In the UK, the social grades are as shown in Figure 3.2.

It will be seen that the mass market (69%) consists of social grades C1, C2 and D. They make up the millions who read the popular press and the bulk of the popular television audience. In a developing country, socio-economic groupings may be 20 percent representing the educated elitist upper and middle-class, mainly urban population, and 80 percent the illiterate, poor, rural population. The mass media of the West are mainly confined to the 20 percent minority in developing countries.

PREDICTING CONSEQUENCES

The above methods of evaluating the situation are not conclusive, but they indicate the range of methods which exists for finding out where we are now, the nature of the current image, and the extent or otherwise of hostility, prejudice, apathy and ignorance. We now have a foundation on which to base the Public Relations Plan. There are reasons for making certain recommendations. More than that, it is possible to predict that unless certain things are done, the situation is likely to get worse. In recommending a plan of action it can be justified by predicting what will happen if nothing is done. To take another analogy, after the doctor has made his diagnosis he will recommend treatment. If his advice is ignored, the patient's health will deteriorate, perhaps fatally.

This objective planning approach is obviously very different from the PRO or consultant being told what to do to please the whims of management (including marketing management) which thinks public relations is like turning on and off a hot tap. In public relations, the hot tap stays on 24 hours a day, 7 days a week, 12 months a year as proposed by the practitioner and approved by management.

PUBLIC RELATIONS STRATEGY

In this chapter we have outlined the parameters of planning public relations programmes, but this is only the beginning. Next, it becomes necessary to choose the strategy. It may be desirable to improve dealer relations, or keep the City better informed but what tactics do we adopt? Do we organise visits for dealers, as tourist centres do by inviting journalists to visit them? Do we have occasional lunches with investment analysts to tell them about the company's plans? The range of available media and techniques is immense, calling for the practitioner's planning ability and ingenuity. A single news release may never be written, nor a press reception held, and no use may be made of mass media. After the Six-Point Planning Model comes the individual strategy to achieve the set objectives. In the case study at the end of the book, one of the strategies was to educate the market by opening information centres in Natural History Museum style in the major cities of Britain where parties of potential clients were invited for receptions, talks and film shows.

However, we must first examine the remaining five elements of the Model.

CHAPTER 4

Defining the Objectives

Without defining and setting objectives a public relations programme cannot be planned, nor can its accomplishments or failures be assessed when the programme has been completed. Objectives and results are the essentials of tangible, cost-effective, accountable public relations. As already mentioned in the previous chapter, it is possible to define more objectives than can be entertained by the budget which represents labour and resources.

How does the public relations practitioner arrive at a preliminary list of possible objectives? They are not just pulled out of the air. Some may be derived from the initial appraisal of the situation. Assuming that the total organisation is being serviced and not only marketing activities are being supported, important though this may well be, it will be necessary to discuss the communications needs of various directors, managers and executives as suggested below.

SOURCES OF OBJECTIVES

1. *The Chief Executive.* The public relations practitioner (whether consultant or in-house PRO) will need to have confidential advice on company policy. What are the organisation's future plans? This information may indicate who are involved in these plans.

2. *Marketing Director.* What marketing strategies are being planned, how may public relations be involved? New products, packages, prices? Is market education required to prepare an acceptable market situation before the launch? What about dealer relations?

3. *Company Secretary.* What corporate and financial public relations is needed? If a private company, is it 'going public' and putting shares on the market? Is a debenture or rights issue being planned? Does the City need to be better informed in order to stabilise or strengthen the share price? Is there threat of a take-over bid which has to be resisted by making the City better informed? By City, we refer to the London financial market.

4. *Personnel Manager.* Do management–employee relations need to be improved? Are job applicants of the right calibre being attracted? Is there a recruitment programme, or problems of redundancies? Are staff to be invited to buy shares or enjoy profit sharing? Is induction material required?

5. *Advertising or Product/Brand Manager.* What products or services will be advertised during the next financial year? The public relations practitioner will need copies of advertising plans and

schedules, and proofs of advertisements in order to give media support including trade press advance notices. What exhibitions will space be taken in?

6. *Sales Manager*. Will there be sales conferences for which help will be required? What about sales force communications?

7. *Export Manager*. Is support required to augment the export programme? With an international company public relations may be required on behalf of overseas agents, subsidiaries or licensees.

8. *Subsidiaries*. If the organisation is a conglomerate, consortium, or multinational, the same people as listed above may have to be considered in each subsidiary organisation.

9. *Works, Branch Managers*. Perhaps for local public relations purposes, contact should be made with those who are responsible for production or selling centres.

10. *Committee Chairmen, Department Officers*. In many non-commercial bodies such as voluntary organisations, trade and professional associations or local government, it will be necessary to have discussions with committee chairmen or department officers. They may be responsible for membership, appeals, publications or exhibitions or, in the case of a local authority, a variety of public services.

From the above list it will be obvious that no one person can supply such advice. Lines of communication are necessary, and the public relations practitioner has to know who is who and have direct access to responsible people and sources of information. He or she does not just sit in their office and wait for things to happen. The initiative has to be taken. The successful PRO knows more about the organisation than anybody else in it, and this can be the advantage of the in-house PRO over the outside consultant. That is why the majority of public relations practitioners are engaged in-house, although, as we shall see, the consultant does offer other advantages.

To present some idea of the objectives which may be defined and acted upon, here is a list of 34 possible objectives. Not all of them can be undertaken in a single year's programme and some of them refer to particular kinds of organisation.

THIRTY-FOUR POSSIBLE PUBLIC RELATIONS OBJECTIVES

1. Change the image of an organisation.
2. Explain a change of policy.
3. Keep the public informed about a project.
4. Educate the market prior to a promotion.
5. Informing the trade.
6. Overcome a public misunderstanding.
7. Organising a product recall.
8. Preparing the stock market for a new share issue.
9. Keep confidence high in the stock market, share prices up, and so avoid a take-over bid.
10. Encourage staff recruitment by showing why organisation is a good employer.
11. Similarly, maintain staff stability.
12. Improve management–employee relations.
13. Recruit right calibre of staff, with reduction in irrelevant applications.
14. Achieve move of a given percentage of staff during re-location exercise.
15. Maintain consumer interest after purchase.
16. Educate the distributors.
17. Explain the organisation's diversity of interests.
18. Maintain confidence by explaining what an organisation such as a local authority or a charity does with its taxes or funds.
19. Explain that an organisation is a voluntary body and not a state body or a quasi

autonomous non-governmental organisation (Quango) which receives official monies.

20. Gain credit for achievements which might otherwise pass unapplauded.
21. Maintain good community relations.
22. Maintain good political relations.
23. Achieve media coverage for sponsorship.
24. Familiarise a potential overseas market with the company, its policies, products or services.
25. Educate hostile opinion leaders.
26. Organise reviews of videos.
27. Liaise with exhibition press officers to get maximum media coverage.
28. Hold open days, works visits for local residents, customers, or distributors to spread knowledge of organisation's activities.
29. Keep pensioners informed.
30. Inform staff of financial results.
31. Advise staff of benefits.
32. Establish the corporate image.
33. Promotion of corporate identity.
34. Create good media relations.

The length of this list may surprise those who thought public relations was only to do with creating a good image and favourable media coverage. Yet some programmes will have objectives which are inevitably missing from our 34 suggestions.

ANALYSIS OF 34 TYPICAL OBJECTIVES

1. *Changing the image.* This has become a very important aspect of public relations in recent times as sweeping changes have occurred for economic, social and political reasons, often as a result of the impact of market forces. Long-established organisations may be embarrassed by images which have become out-of-date, or they have changed their mode of business and a new image is necessary. We have seen this with Sainsbury and Tesco which have moved up-market,

and building societies which vie with the banks. There are shipping lines which were once famous for carrying passengers and mail on regular routes which have been replaced by the airlines. Today, these shipping lines (e.g. P & O) run car ferries, cruise ships and container ships. Generally, their image has changed from selling berths to selling holidays or freight. Or a ladies' perfume firm may enter the men's toiletry market, while a resort once famous for donkeys and candy floss may re-emerge as a hoverport or sophisticated conference centre. Changing an image can be a very positive objective calling for the highest skills, and for public relations at many levels of the organisation in addition to the efforts of the in-house public relations manager or the outside consultant.

A case in point is Rentokil which has been involved in an ever-changing image for the past 30 years, its succession of images representing rodent control, woodworm and dry rot control, weed control, hygiene services and the supply of office plants.

2. *Change of policy.* It may be a pricing policy, as when the maker of a luxury line enters a more popular market; or a rationalisation policy when it is decided to sell through a different system of outlets; or a packaging policy as occurs when a liquid medicine is re-issued in tablet form in handy blister packs. Some recent policy changes have been for banks to issue interest-bearing accounts, door-to-door milk retailers to offer franchises to milkmen, and hypermarkets and supermarkets to bake bread on the premises instead of buying from plant bakeries.

Policy changes may, of course, be announced by advertising, or as part of a normal advertising campaign, but it may be foolish to rely on advertising alone. If the change of policy helps to promote sales, then advertising may well be the ideal means of communicating the message, but if the policy change merely suits the convenience, economy or some other aspect of the company's administration, offers no apparent benefit to the customer and possibly (as with rationalisation) is against some customers' interests, advertising could be ineffectual and wasteful. Too much should not be expected of advertising. Public relations techniques, however, could be more effective since they are concerned with information and goodwill and not with persuasion and selling. It is in such situations that we see the great distinction between the two forms of communication. Properly used, each can serve different purposes and produce different results. A positive public relations objective can exist here.

3. *Informing about a new project.* A new project such as a tunnel, bridge, new city, special ship or aircraft, motorway, airport or shopping precinct may be a long-term job about which many people from financiers and politicians to the owners and eventual users need to be continuously informed for a variety of reasons. There may be contentious issues regarding safety, over-running costs and disputed dates of completion. The Channel Tunnel provoked numerous communication problems. With many such projects many publics have a right to know, or believe they have a right to know, what is going on. Meanwhile the media will seek opportunities to dramatise any negative aspects, and will seldom praise the project. In the case of the Channel Tunnel there was some crass comment from the media about rabies and terrorist hazards, but some excellent coverage by television since the topic was visually exciting. A deliberate attempt by the owners, Eurotunnel, to keep people informed took the form of a purpose-built exhibition centre near Folkestone which carried a large working model railway layout. Thus, in such circumstances an on-going objective is to maintain a progress report as the work proceeds.

4. *Market education.* This is one of the most important and valuable ways in which public relations can help marketing, acting as it were as marketing's third arm. It is certainly adopted by makers of complicated equipment, such as computers, who understand that the market will not buy or lease items unless their uses and benefits are fully appreciated. There is an old saying that people like the things they know best, or, to paraphrase another saying, familiarity breeds content.

Too many products have been launched on an ignorant market and have proved to be costly disasters, simply because marketing managers put all their faith in block-buster advertising and failed to see public relations as any more than Kotler's concept of product publicity or free advertising. Market education, adopted over a period of from six months to two years before the launch, can be more decisive than test marketing which is often too late to have a significant effect, as seen by Nielsen's admission that fifty percent of new products fail even when test marketing results looked promising. (Incidentally, test marketing is not to be confused with product pre-testing. It tests the total marketing strategy and seeks to gain a given percentage of sales in a miniature of the broadscale market.)

Market education applies particularly to new products or services which require explanation rather than to fast moving consumer goods (FMCGs) where advertising has to be dramatic and score from impact and surprise. Even so, it helps if the market has faith in the *manufacturer*, and it is surprising how many products are launched with no identification in the advertising of the maker's name, a curious abuse of commercial pride. This is poor public relations, and it fails to exploit the halo-effect of goodwill stemming from the company's past reputation.

Market education can include both the trade and the consumer because it is essential that the retailer has confidence in the product and can explain it to the customer. It is no use — as happens sometimes — if the retailer can only say 'full instructions' are given with the product. If customers have to find out for themselves, they are likely to walk out of the shop. The training of shop sales people is part of market education.

5. *Informing the trade.* The support of the trade depends on its being knowledgeable about the company's efforts to promote its brands, or about changes which concern the trade. Much of this can be done through the trade press, but also directly by means of a dealer magazine, by material supplied by visiting sales representatives, and sometimes through trade exhibitions and dealer conferences.

This information will include schedules and samples of forthcoming advertising, details of sales promotion schemes, new packages or containers, price changes, and also the appointment of new sales staff, opening of new depots, appointment of new wholesalers and so on.

It is therefore a good public relations objective never to overlook distributors and to devise means of keeping them informed.

6. *Overcoming misunderstanding.* It may or may not be the fault of the organisation that the misunderstanding has occurred, but such a barrier to goodwill can only be removed by convincing people that the problem no longer exists. People may have thought that a product was dangerous when it has since been proved quite safe. The media are apt to raise unfounded scares which can be very damaging to a company. By demonstration and example, the situation may be reversed, although this may take time, patience and persistence.

For example, on one occasion a government research station published a report, which was on sale at HM Stationery Office shops, condemning a certain product in the building industry. There was nothing wrong with the product, only that it had been mis-used by a particular firm. It took nearly a year's public relations work (involving free use of the product on major works) to prove that the product could be used efficiently by a reputable company.

At one time there were 'old wives' tales about the nature of woodworm which were not helped by advice given in women's magazines. The impression was created that woodworm resulted from dirtiness, and that furniture infested by the insects should be burned. It was even recommended that paraffin should be poked down the holes with a knitting needle, although the holes were the exit holes of the insects! All this nonsense had to be contradicted by facts such as that wood boring insects could fly in the open window on a warm day, and that timber of a certain age (as used in roofing timbers) was attractive to the insect. The fortunes of companies like Rentokil, Cuprinol and others in the timber preservation business depended on overcoming popular misunderstandings fostered by women's magazine journalists.

But some subjects invite misunderstanding. Either because they are outside the limits of experience of those who misunderstand, or because their very name invites misunderstanding. It took a long time for people to understand what was 'open' about the Open University. Girobank suffered from a similar misunderstanding. There are still people who think that a transistor is a radio set, and not everyone understands what a mouse is in relation to a computer. Misunderstandings also occur in the use of words, as with the differences between American and British English. We talk about road shows (as occurred with various privatisation schemes) which meant a travelling presentation by road, but putting a show on the road in America means putting it on the railroad or a train.

7. *Organise a product recall.* Occasionally it may be found that a product has a fault which needs to be rectified. There is no shame in this, and many famous companies have won the respect of customers because of their frankness and anxiety to replace a product or correct a

fault. This usually requires a press advertisement explaining the problem, supported by media stories.

In recent years another kind of product recall has been hard on reputation and costly to undertake, and this has been when products have been deliberately contaminated (or there has been a hoax to that effect). This sort of crisis situation is doubly difficult because both the retailer and the manufacturer are under criticism, and the retailer takes defensive action by removing the supposedly dangerous product and demanding its collection by the manufacturer. Here we have short-term public relations objectives to protect both the customer's interests and the company's reputation (whether this be the retailer's or the manufacturer). Fortunately, these attempts by terrorists and extortionists have generally been short-lived, as in the cases of Mars and Heinz.

8. *Preparing the Stock Market.* A new share issue will succeed on the Stock Exchange only provided that large blocks of shares are taken up by institutions such as pension funds, insurance companies, unit trusts and other large buyers of shares. In recent years we have seen this extended to privatisation share offers involving the general public. When a company goes public and seeks a market quotation, or when a quoted company seeks to raise funds by a new share issue, rights issue or a debenture, the money world has to be informed about the company's trading prospects. But in the case of a privatisation it may be necessary to convince the City first of the likely success of the flotation, and then members of the public who do not normally buy shares have to be educated about the procedures.

Many people comprise the money market and they are not all investors themselves. There are those who are capable of giving advice for or against investments. They include City Editors (who edit financial pages, sections or magazines in newspapers), investment analysts (who write reports about the financial strengths and weaknesses of companies), market makers, brokers and banks, all of whom need to be kept fully informed if they are to give reliable advice. This does not mean providing fake information to inflate the value of shares, and financial information needs to be handled discreetly for it can be very sensitive. The Stock Exchange itself is so anxious to avoid 'insider trading' (in which shares are bought advantageously on the basis of secret knowledge) that it applies special procedures to avoid sensitive information being available to prying eyes.

9. *Stock Market confidence.* A company's quoted share price may rise or fall according to confidence or loss of confidence in the company's performance. Sometimes share prices can also be affected by external market forces over which a company has no control.

However, a falling share price can be dangerous and could incite a take-over by a predator company which is looking for a bargain. We saw this with Dalgety and Spillers, Dixons and Currys, Guinness and Distillers, British Airways and British Caledonian.

The public relations objective may be to avoid risk of a take-over bid by making sure that the money market is kept aware of a company's strengths. Consistent confidence can keep share prices high or at least steady. Some take-over bids have resulted from laxity in keeping the market informed.

While it is true that shares are bought and sold as the opportunity for taking a profit occurs, or because the market has fallen and there are some bargains to be had, a number of shares are retained and voting rights are exercised. There are those who remain loyal to a company and are its strength if there is a take-over bid. Will they support the board of management and not sell their shares? This depends very much on whether their knowledge of the company's affairs is such that they have faith in its greater ability to succeed than the predator.

10. *Staff recruitment.* Two objectives may be involved here: to educate the employment market and attract recruits to apply for jobs, or to attract the right sort of applicants when jobs are advertised. Even in a period of recession and unemployment these objectives can be important because certain vacancies still have to be filled.

Jobs are advertised in the local and national press, and in specialised trade, technical and professional journals. What image do applicants have of the prospective employer, the job or the industry? What reputation does the organisation have as an employer? The firm seeking staff may be a complete mystery to those reading its recruitment advertising. Job applicants form a public which needs to be well-informed if response and the right response is to be achieved by recruitment advertising. But so often we hear employers complaining about either the dearth of applicants or their irrelevance to the job advertised.

Some employers make excellent use of public relations techniques such as videos for school-leavers, attendance at career evenings at schools, and the running of weekend courses at residential training centres. More simple public relations activities can include press relations aimed at the publications read by possible recruits, and some newspapers run features on career prospects. Another method is to offer an audio-cassette tape in a recruitment advertisement which can be played back on a cassette-player to discover more about the company and what it has to offer.

11. *Staff stability.* A company invests money in recruiting and training staff, so a sensible objective is to maintain staff stability. This is not always a matter of satisfactory salaries or wages and working conditions. Job satisfaction can take many forms. In the past, a good deal of industrial friction resulted from poor management–employee relations and a lack of information about what was going on. A vicious grape-vine created misunderstandings. Today, with streamlined work forces, as seen

in what used to be our major heavy and manufacturing industries such as coal, steel and motor-cars, and with more high-tech staff in more modern industries, internal communication has improved. It becomes even more imperative in these more tightly knit work forces for management to be candid about its policies, wishes, successes, prospects and problems, and to be willing to invite a dialogue with employees.

A number of innovations ranging from various electronic forms of communication to share owning and profit sharing have created better internal relations. A public relations objective may therefore be to ensure that techniques such as house journals, videos, speak-up schemes, organised notice boards, staff meetings, quality circles and where necessary eyeball-to-eyeball relationships are fully used.

12. *Improve employee–management relations.* This requires the development of upward communications between employees and management, downward communications between management and employees, and sideways communications between members of the staff. These are forms of communication which transcend old-fashioned class and trade union differences and conflicts. An independently edited house journal or a video house magazine can be one method of achieving good all-round relations, and so can other methods such as Works Councils which have proved so successful in some continental European countries. A deliberate public relations objective of this kind is far more practical than the idea of management seeking staff loyalty, whatever that means.

13. *Right calibre applicants.* Inevitably we have touched on this in 10 above, but getting the right calibre applicants could be an objective in itself. Some jobs may attract scores of applications, which can be time wasting and disappointing for both sides. A filter system is

desirable. This may be comparatively easy if certain academic qualifications or years of experience are demanded, but some recruitment advertisements can encourage the most hopeless candidates to apply. It may not be entirely satisfactory to depend on 'head hunting' employment agencies.

Public relations can be employed to create an understanding of the type of people who are employed by the company — whether they are technically proficient, give good service or provide reliable advice — according to the nature of the business. No others need apply for vacancies!

14. *Re-location.* When an office or factory moves to another location, it can present opportunities for some employees, but it can be a traumatic situation where families are concerned. Other people's jobs, families, friends and children's education can all be upset by a move. It may be a realistic public relations objective to get 25 percent of the staff to accept the move. To do even this, the attractions and amenities of the new location have to be explained to whole families. A special kind of video has been created to overcome what is called 'the trailing spouse syndrome'.

Once again there is an investment problem regarding the recruitment and training of staff, especially key employees with special skills whose work contributes a great deal to the success of the company.

15. *Maintaining consumer interest.* This can be a constant public relations objective in the sense of 'once a customer, always a customer'. This is where customer relations embraces all features of the after-market, that is what happens once the customer has made a purchase. After all, if they are never likely to make a repeat purchase they can always recommend. One company, which is expert at all forms of public relations, claims that 60 percent of its business comes from recommendation. No doubt that is why it rarely spends

money on advertising and pays handsome dividends to its shareholders.

By educating existing customers about new or additional uses so that (a) more of the product is bought, such as cooking ingredients, or (b) the product is enjoyed so that a repeat purchase of the same product, or of another variety of it, is achieved, sales can be increased.

This can be explained more thoroughly if we take some typical examples. A simple food product like flour can be used for many cooking purposes if the domestic cook is given useful recipes, and one of the oldest and most famous cookery books is McDougall's which is offered from time to time on flour bags. A sewing machine may be used more productively if users are given ideas on what to make. A motor-car owner can be made more interested in touring, car maintenance, economical driving or be given satisfactory service, so that he remains loyal to that make. A photographer can be encouraged to buy accessories and use a camera more creatively. The same applies to many other products such as lawn treatments, garden insecticides, DIY materials, and various hobbies such as philately and numismatics.

Looking after the customer, inviting queries and even complaints, offering advisory and maintenance services, keeping the customer interested in his or her purchase, all help to establish confidence and ensure further or future business.

One of the biggest problems that some manufacturers suffer is underuse of their product. A camera, sewing machine or cake mixer gets put away in a cupboard and virtually forgotten. It is a form of apathy, one of the evils with which public relations has to contend. Oddly enough, it is often a problem when there is a product recall because a fault has been discovered — but where are the products? For example, it was remarkable how few coffee pots were returned when it was discovered that their handles were liable to fall off! So, a public relations objective may be to encourage people to use products they have bought or been given.

16. *Educating distributors.* With most retail products, even the most popular FMCGs, it is wise to make sure that stockists not only know what they are selling, but how the product will satisfy customer needs. They also have to understand the company, its policies, its advertising and its standing in the industry. Mistakenly, some companies in their eagerness to maximise profits rely too heavily on 'selling in' techniques of trade terms or 'selling out' tactics of sales promotion, and are careless about dealer opinion and education. The retailer is not just a shelf-filler and order taker, not even a giant supermarket chain with a central buyer who seeks advantageous deals. This is very important today when there is serious risk of a national brand being delisted in favour of an own label.

Market education is an aspect which marketers ignore at their peril, as they inevitably do if they have no appreciation of the range and value of public relations.

For instance, it has occurred that new products have been advertised and customers have been drawn to the point of sale only to be rebuffed by shop assistants who (a) do not understand the product and can neither explain nor demonstrate it; or (b) are sceptical about the ability of the product to perform as claimed in the advertisement.

When prospective buyers, made enthusiastic by advertisements, are met by retorts across the counter such as *'You can't always believe what you read in advertisements'* or *'Well, that's what they say'*, or *'I haven't tried it myself'* and so on, there is a lack of distributor education and the advertising is nullified. The customer either buys nothing or accepts a substitute. This is the story of marketing which places unjustified faith in advertising but ignores public relations. One has only to look at the CIM syllabus and the average marketing course to see why. A lot of marketing lecturers think sales promotion is public relations!

Sales conferences, dealer external house journals, videos, slide presentations, works visits, demonstrations and trade press news coverage can all contribute to the familiarisation of stockists with a product, how it is made, what it is made of, what it does, its place of origin and the benefits it offers customers.

Not all products are sold in supermarkets, and it is noticeable that supermarkets concentrate on FMCGs such as foods, drinks and toiletries whose packages make their contents self-explanatory. Almost everything else needs distributor education, and even new FMCGs need a certain amount of initial explanation before supermarkets and chain stores will have confidence in stocking them. For example, instant tea is far from new, but it has been a very slow starter.

Sometimes evidence of distributor education is necessary to convince customers, and following attendance at a training course, the distributor (e.g. of motor-cars and sewing machines) will display a framed proficiency certificate.

Certain trades lend themselves to distributor education, to mention only the wine and travel trades where the merchant or agent often has first-hand knowledge of what he or she is selling. This is appreciated by the customer who is seeking advice.

From these remarks, it will be seen that distributor education may well be a primary objective of public relations, and ideally it could result from feedback from sales management.

Following on from the above, another important public relations objective can be to familiarise distributors about the company so that when sales representatives call, whether during the regular journey cycle or on a 'cold' call, they are not strangers from an unknown company.

This 'ice-breaker' type of public relations may concentrate on trade press stories, or a dealer magazine if the number of distributors is not prohibitive, or on news about a company's financial and trading progress. Regarding the latter, retailers are quite likely to read the business and financial pages in their daily or Sunday newspaper.

17. *Explaining diversity.* There may be considerable merit in making people aware that a company engages in a variety of enterprises. Some companies may be disliked because they are thought to be monopolies, when in fact their best known activity is only one of many. Others may be thought to be limited to the business with which most people associate them. Policies vary: some conglomerates do not wish to reveal the breadth of their business and prefer member companies to enjoy autonomous status (e.g. Toyota and Daihatsu) free from the influence of the parent company. Others prefer the parental image to have an umbrella effect (as with Lucas, ICI and Sterling Pharmaceuticals).

It is particularly interesting in the case of the multi-nationals or trans-continentals that no two are alike and one cannot generalise about how they should communicate. So we are faced with certain dilemmas: for instance, does an airline or airport authority wish to publicise its ownership of hotels? Is it better that airline and hotel groups should operate independently or as admitted associates? Or should it sell off its hotels as British Airports Authority has done? Does a steel corporation wish to admit that it makes plastic pipes, or a cigarette company that it makes potato crisps? CPC (Corn Products) does not broadcast its interests in well-known brands of cooking oils, soups, mayonnaise, cornflour, industrial adhesives and cattle foods, which was probably just as well when one of its cattle food ingredients was found to be contaminated with mercury!

Nevertheless, in spite of all these reservations, it may be a public relations objective to reveal the diversity of a company's operations.

18. *Maintaining confidence.* Lack of information can cause doubts, worries or unwillingness to continue giving support. Voluntary organisations receive subscriptions, but what do they do with the money? Local authorities levy community charges or some form of tax but how and how wisely do they spend our money? Keeping the providers of funds aware of where the money goes can only help to maintain the flow, minimise criticisms and create satisfaction, again on the principle that we like the things we know best.

A delicate situation here. If the organisation is too lavish in producing literature to explain its work, there can be criticism that this is a waste of donations or other payments. Yet a clear public relations objective can be the need to provide information on expenditure.

To take another case, privatisation has resulted in millions of shareholders, all of whom are entitled by law to receive the annual report and accounts of the companies whose shares they own. These reports are expensive pieces of print, and the result has been twofold. The companies' print bills have risen alarmingly, while large numbers of small shareholders resent being bombarded with these lavish documents. A solution — which serves the purposes of providing essential information and maintaining confidence — has been to invite shareholders to accept an abbreviated version.

Another question of confidence has resulted from these millions of new small shareholders being inundated with direct mail shots simply because share-lists are available to those who wish to use them. Out of self-protection, a number of reports and accounts now include warnings about this irritating practice, advising shareholders to ask the Direct Mail Preference Service to have their names and addresses deleted from mailing lists. At least these companies are trying to deflect the blame.

Confidence may also have to be maintained because of changes in a product (or its packaging) which may suggest that the new version is inferior to the original one. 'Nothing is as good as it was' is a customer lament which may or may not be true. But customers do have to be assured of the durability of the product — the plastic may be lighter but just as strong as the metal — and this may have to be explained in the instructions or on the packaging. It can also be part of distributor education.

19. *Explaining needs of charities.* Here is an objective for a non-commercial voluntary body. It needs money, support and voluntary help. It has nothing to sell in the normal sense of the word, except maybe gifts and Christmas cards which help to raise funds. Secondhand goods may be needed for charity shops, or supplies such as food for the homeless at Christmas.

But more than that, in many cases it is necessary to explain that it is an independent voluntary body, even though it may be thought that a modern caring state should pay for the upkeep of orphans, research into diseases, the lifeboat service, the preservation of stately homes, gardens and historic places, and even the complete financing of disaster funds throughout the world. To do so would increase taxation enormously, deprive voluntary bodies of the generosity of thousands of well-wishers, take away the independence of excellent organisations and burden the Government with increased administration.

The National Trust, the Royal National Lifeboat Institution, Barnardos, and the World Wildlife Fund operate perfectly well as private bodies rather than as Government agencies or even as Quangos. Yet it is wrongly assumed that many charities and voluntary bodies are state organisations which do not need public support, and so a public relations objective for them is to establish a correct image of their independence.

20. *Credit for achievement.* Praiseworthy and newsworthy activities sometimes go unreported when awareness of them could greatly increase knowledge, understanding, goodwill and respect. These achievements may go unreported merely by default, but too often they are neglected because they are taken for granted, and people inside the organisation do not appreciate that they would be novel and laudable in the minds of outsiders, *if only they knew about them*.

This author once toured a company in search of material for feature articles. He was met by a stonewall attitude of staff who met his enquiries with statements such as 'We always do this. So what?' They possessed a gold mine of anecdotal work experience stories which made a series of published articles. In fact, almost any company has a fund of such publishable material and it is a worthwhile public relations objective to exploit it.

21. *Community relations.* Most organisations have neighbours. They may annoy them through noise, effusions, unsightliness or other inconveniences. Or they may simply ignore them. But it is a very true saying that public relations starts on the doorstep.

The reasons for maintaining good community relations can be many when the trouble is taken to think about them. At all times, responsible behaviour can only enhance the company's reputation and ensure a permanent store of good feeling that can help the company when it needs it most. This may involve acting as a local benefactor, caring about the environment and avoiding pollution, being known locally as a good employer, supplying equipment to local technical colleges, participating in local events, awarding prizes at shows and sports meetings, sponsoring local bodies, holding 'open days' and above all keeping the local media aware of company personalities and happenings. The need for a 'good neighbour' policy should make this objective a priority.

Good behaviour is not all. How, precisely, does an organisation want or need to be regarded by members of the local community? As a contributor to the export drive and participation in Europe, a good employer, a conserver of local resources and amenities, a local benefactor, an inventive or innovative producer of new products, a member of a national or multi-national group, a bringer of work and prosperity to the area — what *exactly* is the objective of the public relations programme?

It is no use being generous, informative and socially responsible — although the latter has become increasingly essential with today's concern about green issues — unless it has a *purpose*. This should not be confused with an ulterior purpose like trying to camouflage a problem. But if there is an 'open day' or factory visit, it can be arranged in one way if it is explained what the factory does, and in another way to demonstrate the working conditions and recreational facilities. The purpose of one might be to enlighten townspeople, while that of the other would be to provide an insight for prospective employees.

Public knowledge about an organisation can have its benefits. People are more likely to tolerate rather than complain about any problems it causes. The local authority is more likely to understand the reasons behind requests for planning permission. The local press and radio may take an interest in its activities. Opportunities to work for the company will be taken up readily. Generally, it will be accepted as an important feature of the community, and people may be proud to be associated with it.

22. *Political relations.* Very important today are a company's relations with politicians such as local government councillors and officers, local MPs, Members of both Houses of Parliament and of the European Parliament in Strasbourg, Government Ministry and Department officials and Lobby correspondents. A formidable list of people can have some sort of legislative influence upon the affairs of the company, and today this also includes EC directives from Brussels.

In this complicated political web, a company needs to be kept informed, and it also needs to keep the various politicians and legislators informed about the company. Lobbying, that is presenting a company's case to ministers and MPs, or the giving of evidence to select committees, and knowing when Bills are having their readings in the House, can fully occupy the wits of a public relations practitioner.

In fact, it may well be necessary to hire a firm which specialises in political liaison work, while some large companies pay MPs fees to keep them informed. This is not a matter of bribery and corruption: the MP has to declare his or her interests and must not serve a client in a clandestine way. This is a subject which has exercised considerable Parliamentary debate regarding the efficient registration of Members' interests. The IPR maintains a register of its own members who are MPs and represent public relations interests.

So here is another objective which may have to be fitted into the overall public relations programme. For some companies, political liaison may be a constant concern, whereas for other companies, this aspect of public relations may be rare.

23. *Sponsorship.* Whether sponsorship be for advertising, marketing or public relations purposes, there is bound to be a public relations input since a principal objective is likely to be media coverage, especially on TV. Sponsorship has become a more versatile activity since the new rules introduced by the Independent Television Commission and the Radio Authority in 1991, while for some years there has been considerable relaxation of the ability to sponsor whole programmes on BBC TV and local radio.

It may be an objective to engage in sponsorship as a public relations medium or to support sponsorship which has taken over where media advertising, such as TV, has ceased to be cost-effective. Sponsorship is discussed in more detail in a special chapter.

24. *Familiarising overseas markets.* As a preliminary to marketing (or manufacturing) in another country or region of the world, it can be essential to familiarise potential buyers with the company, its products and brands. A

company or product may be a household name in its home market, but unknown abroad. For younger readers it may seem strange that twenty-five years ago names like Sony, Toyota and Toshiba were unknown in Britain. Honda motorcycles became popular about then, but Mazda was better known as a brand of electric light bulb than a motor-car. The first Datsun (Nissan) car appeared in Britain in 1969, and people wondered what it was. It looked like a copy of the Ford Cortina.

Global markets rarely exist because of ethnic, religious and other inhibitions. In Arab countries, the first product to arrive generally becomes a generic so that all lorries are called Mercedes, sewing machines Singers and toothpastes Pepsodent.

It becomes a public relations objective, therefore, to familiarise overseas markets by means of public relations tactics, remembering that media may be few or different, and there could be numerous languages. House journals, videos, exhibitions and trade fairs may be necessary in the absence of media facilities. The assistance of the Department of Trade and Industry, Overseas Services of the BBC, British Overseas Trade Board, British commercial attachés to Consulates and High Commissions, and commercial services such as those of EIBIS and Two-Ten Communications may be sought.

Overseas markets are not necessarily far away, for close at hand is the Single European Market and the greater Europe which has emerged in Eastern Europe and beyond the EC and EFTA countries.

25. *Educating hostile opinion leaders.*

Opinion leaders (or formers as they are sometimes called) can be anyone who expresses an opinion about an organisation or its people, products or services. They can be parents, priests and schoolteachers as well as celebrities who express their opinions through the media. If they are misinformed or wilfully hostile or prejudiced, they can cause great harm. Often, it is a matter of ignorance. One way or another we are confronted by at least three of the negative elements of the public relations transfer process. Sometimes, mis-information is given out in innocence and with sincerity.

A public relations objective may be to identify misleading opinion leaders and to correct them. This can be a delicate operation because it would be folly to alienate people whose influence is powerful. Repeating the transfer process, it is a matter of converting negative into positive attitudes by providing convincing information. Face-to-face talks, educational literature, videos, works visits and so on may be used in this process.

There are times, however, when it is impossible to reverse the influence of a powerful opinion leader. Hardly any man has worn a hat since the Prince of Wales, in the 30s, stopped wearing one. Even the Anthony Eden homburg and the Harold Macmillan Russian hat failed to catch on.

26. *Organise reviews of videos.*

This follows on from the reviewing of industrial films which have now been replaced by videos. If it is desired to gain audiences for videos, either by direct requests or by borrowing from a library in which they have been placed, it can be helpful if they are reviewed in appropriate journals. They may also be entered in contests which will result in reviews.

When producing a video, its distribution should be determined in advance; it will simply lie on the shelf if its existence is unknown, or be used only occasionally by its maker. A video should be made to work, hence the objective of seeking reviews.

27. *Liaison with exhibition press officers.*

This is a subject which will be fully discussed in the chapter on Exhibitions and Exhibitors. Here we list an important objective if the company engages in trade, public or overseas exhibitions. Part of the overall public relations strategy should be to be familiar with the company's exhibition plans, and to work closely with exhibition press officers from the moment a contract has been signed to take stand space. It is no use leaving it until the day the show opens and arriving at the press office with a pile of press kits. Advance discussion with the press officer of the exhibition will probably reveal that a given number of news releases and captioned photographs are required, not elaborate press kits which journalists do not want, and which have to be dumped after the show.

28. *Open days and works visits.* Apart from press facility visits, the company may have open days for the public, or regular works visits for parties. The latter can be a major activity, organised through motor coach companies, or it may depend on clubs and associations making applications. If it is policy to welcome such visits — as happens with breweries, newspapers, potteries, motor-car manufacturers and other firms — a public relations objective may be the organising and handling of such visits. The training of guides may be a public relations responsibility, and public visits may be a public relations initiative.

29. *Informing pensioners.* The company's pensioners represent a large body of people who, for various reasons, remain concerned about the activities of their former employers. There can be house journals addressed to pensioners, and special days, events and clubs in which they may participate. Nowadays, many employees retire at a comparatively early age, and belong to the grey market which may well be interested in buying the company's products at a discount. Pensioners are therefore an important public whose interests are worthy of being a public relations objective.

30. *Staff and company results.* A special public relations objective should be to make the staff aware of interim and final company results, whether or not staff own shares. A number of companies do this either by special editions of house journals, or by videos in which the accounts are explained in easily understood terms, and all members of the staff are shown these videos as soon as possible. International companies fly such videos all over the world so that all their staff are made aware of the company results, whether they be good or bad. This can be extremely important because employees rarely understand how the company obtains its money and what it does with it. Profits are often a tiny fragment of the millions involved, wages and salaries, taxation and bank charges, costs of raw material and production, and research and re-investment absorbing large sums. Thus it becomes a major public relations objective to explain all this to staff.

31. *Advise staff of benefits.* In co-operation with the personnel department, it may be the role of the public relations department to keep staff advised about benefits such as pension schemes, discounts on purchases, and profit-sharing schemes. This may require news items in the house journal, notices for display on notice boards, and the production of explanatory literature, while induction material — perhaps in video form — will be required for new recruits. This becomes another objective to include in the public relations plan.

32. *Corporate image.* This has been included rather late in the list, although it may be implicit in some of the objectives already discussed, because there is sometimes a false notion that establishing the corporate image is the sole purpose of public relations. But as has been shown in the previous 31 instances there can be a lot of other public relations considerations.

Public relations is not just about 'creating a favourable image' which is too often the sort of misconception found in marketing books. Nevertheless, *establishing* the corporate image is important in the sense that a correct image depends on the perceiver having a sound knowledge and extensive experience of the organisation. It is not a question of whether the corporate image is a good one but whether it is a true and justified one. The image is in the eye of the beholder, and depends entirely on the perceiver's knowledge and experience.

This knowledge and experience will vary according to a person's relationship with an organisation. A customer, employee, shareholder or dealer may have a quite different corporate image. It is therefore nonsense to talk about 'creating a favourable image'. What matters is whether it is correct or not. A public relations objective can be to ensure that particular publics have a true image of a company — as a manufacturer, as an employer, as an investor or as a supplier as the case may be.

33. *Promoting use of corporate identity.* It is a costly process to create a corporate identity scheme which may comprise a logo, colour scheme, typography, livery of transportation, dress of staff and many other items. The idea is to create unity and uniformity which distinguishes the organisation as we see with airlines, banks and stores.

There should therefore be a public relations objective to see that everyone responsible for buying or supplying print, advertising, decor, uniforms and so on comply with the strict instructions contained in the manual. This is imperative because it does sometimes happen that although a corporate identity scheme has been designed there are people who ignore the instructions when buying, say, stationery.

34. *Media relations.* Finally, a sensible objective is to try to create good relations with the media so that reports are accurate and their tone is at least sympathetic. One does not expect favourable coverage, but one does expect journalists to get it right. Much depends on how willing you are to be frank, and how well you understand the editorial and production needs of the media.

So this objective requires a deliberate policy of trying to understand the media, giving them what they want how and when they want it while still recognising the adversarial situation that the purpose of the public relations practitioner and the journalist are contradictory.

The length of this list may surprise those who thought public relations was only to do with creating a good image and gaining favourable media coverage. Not all these 34 objectives apply to the same organisations, and for budgetary reasons not all of them can be entertained as will be discussed below. Meanwhile, with these 34 examples of possible objectives we have:

1. Shown the variety of objectives which may have to be built into a programme of work covering, say, 12 months.
2. Shown yet another reason why programmes must be planned in advance, and not handled haphazardly as and when something comes up.
3. Shown that the desired objectives may justify a larger expenditure than might otherwise be contemplated by employer or client.
4. Shown that it is highly likely that there are more desirable objectives than can possibly be handled by the proposed budget (meaning resources of labour, equipment, materials and expenses), and that priorities (*see below*) will have to be determined.
5. Shown that time will have to be rationed so that the selected objectives can be met by doing certain things at certain times. This will be helpful if some objectives are short-term or seasonal.
6. Shown that given set objectives and reasonable resources to handle them it will be possible to assess results. In other words, if we know where we are going, we plan to arrive.
7. Shown that ideally the in-house PRO or the consultant should be responsible to the chief executive since all sections of the organisation have to be serviced. We are concerned with the communications of the total organisation, not merely one

department such as personnel or marketing. Corporate and financial, Parliamentary liaison and crisis management are matters for the board of management as advised by the PRO or consultant.

We shall return to these 34 objectives in the chapter on Assessing Results.

SELECTING PRIORITIES

A long list may be produced, but it is likely that a short list will have to be made of those items which are feasible within the budget. It is silly to attempt too much and so whittle down the possibilities of success. Of course, some objectives will be short-term and a number of these can be fitted into the whole programme. The following are six ways of deciding on priorities.

1. What is the *importance* of the objective? Each objective could be given a rating to discover its relative importance.
2. How much *time* will each objective require?
3. How *feasible* is it — is there a reasonable chance of success?
4. Are *media* available, or do they have to be created?
5. Is there enough *money* to cover the cost of attempting each objective? This means cost of labour, materials and expenses.
6. Who are the publics with whom we need to communicate in order to achieve the objectives? That is the subject of the next chapter.

CHAPTER 5

Publics

WHAT ARE PUBLICS?

In advertising, we speak of target audiences and to be economic, advertising is aimed at the largest number of potential buyers, even though this may be a special segment of the total market. In public relations, we do not concentrate on virtually one large audience, but on many special groups of people, some large, some small. These groups are called *publics*, as stated in the IPR definition.

This distinction highlights another of the numerous differences between advertising and public relations. It shows the breadth of public relations activity compared with advertising, simply because it is concerned with the total communications of all sections of an organisation with all the people with whom it has or should have communications. This is demonstrated by the following list of eight basic publics.

EIGHT BASIC PUBLICS

They are described as 'basic' because, as will be demonstrated, different organisations will have variations of this list.

1. The community — those who live adjacent to the site or premises.
2. Potential employees — who may live

locally or elsewhere, work for other organisations, or be attending school, college or university.
3. Employees — broken down into the various categories in the organisation.
4. Suppliers of services and materials.
5. The money market — shareholders, banks, insurance companies, brokers, investment analysts and so on.
6. Distributors — wholesalers, agents, retailers and so on.
7. Consumers and users, past, present and future.
8. Opinion leaders or formers — all those whose opinions may help or harm an organisation.

It will be noticed that the media have *not* been included as a public, although some authors do include media. Strictly speaking, we reach publics through the media. However, individual writers and broadcasters such as columnists and presenters may be regarded as opinion leaders.

SOME PRACTICAL EXAMPLES

The following six examples show the special publics which apply to certain kinds of organisation; obviously those for a commercial company will differ from those for a charity or local authority. Just as one of the planning tasks is to list the possible objectives (and to eliminate those which are not feasible), so is it necessary to list all the publics with whom we should, or would like to, communicate. Again, constraints will have to be applied, because of either the limitations of time, money and resources, or lack of media (or prohibitive cost of creating media) to reach them.

Figure 5.1 shows a basic list of publics for local government. This list can be revised according to the kind of authority and its special responsibilities or interests. Some local authorities, for example, have special interests or attractions so that special publics are involved. The town or city may be an exhibition centre, have an airport or industrial area or be popular for retirement.

The 'visitor' category could embrace shoppers, commuting workers, tourists, cultural patrons, sports fans and so on.

Figure 5.2 shows a typical set of publics for a toy manufacturer, and here we begin to see the pattern of publics for manufacturers in

Staff
Trade unions and professional bodies
Wage tribunals
Local government associations
Government departments
Local MPs
Other local authorities
Local associations
Local industry and trade
Taxpayers
Users of public services
School children
The investment market
Suppliers of goods and materials
Potential residents
Potential industry and commerce
Visitors

Figure 5.1   The publics for local government public relations

Staff
Trade unions, professional bodies, trade associations
Distributors: wholesalers, retailers, direct response marketers, credit traders, coupon/stamp
   gift distributors, exporters
Parents
Teachers
Children
Suppliers of raw materials, services
Potential staff, e.g. unskilled operatives
Members of community adjacent to factory
Local authority officials and staff
Local MPs
Shareholders and investors
Opinion leaders who may either object to, or praise certain toys
Government officials, e.g. Department of Trade — competitive imports

Figure 5.2   Typical publics for a toy manufacturer

Staff
Trade unions, professional bodies, trade associations
Distributors, agents and overseas distributors
Motoring associations
Road safety organisations
Motor sports enthusiasts
Buyers and those who influence car buying — drivers, fleet owners, spouses, driving schools, travelling salesmen
Suppliers of components and accessories
Suppliers of raw materials, e.g. steel, body finishes, glass
Suppliers of fuel to operate plants
Potential staff (from apprentices to graduates)
Members of community adjacent to factory
Motor insurance companies
Government departments
The police
Motoring correspondents
Dissatisfied owners
Secondhand market
Opinion leaders *re* design, road safety, environment, etc.
Holiday and travel trade
Rail, sea and air ferry operators

Figure 5.3   Typical publics of a motor-car manufacturer

general. Figure 5.3 shows how the pattern can be varied as the market differs or is extended.

A basic list of publics for a voluntary organisation is given in Figure 5.4. This list can be varied, but it applies in general terms to various organisations which depend on voluntary workers and donated funds and either conduct charitable work or seek support for their cause.

Voluntary bodies are not confined to charities but could include professional and special interest associations, institutes and societies.

From the examples given already, it will be seen that public relations always has to operate at two levels — internally and externally. The internal operation may be as elaborate as the external, when it has to be directed at members who may lose interest and resign

Members
Subscribers, benefactors
Users of services provided
Potential supporters — either workers or donors
Opponents and critics
MPs
Government departments
Local authorities
Other associated organisations
Opinion leaders

Figure 5.4   Typical publics for a voluntary organisation

Staff
Potential staff
Credit customers
Regular and casual customers
Customers in outlying areas
Community adjacent to store: involvement in e.g. award of trophies, participation in carnivals
Suppliers of services
Suppliers of own-name goods
Suppliers of branded goods
Local authority
Motorists and motoring organisations for organising car-parking facilities
Builders for furnishing show houses
Social interest groups, e.g. travel clubs, youth clubs, sports clubs

Figure 5.5   Typical publics for a department store

unless there is sufficient communication to convince them that the organisation is active and worth supporting. This activity may well involve participation, which is one of the surest ways of combating the cry, 'What do I get for my subscription?' Apathy may have to be overcome.

Let us examine the possible publics for a few more examples.

A department store (Figure 5.5), because of the variety of its goods and services, can make very effective use of public relations if trouble is taken to analyse buyers and potential buyers into separate publics. Some can be addressed by, say, a simple newsletter mailed to members of clubs and societies, especially if special discounts can be offered.

In Figure 5.6 we list the publics for a company whose products may be unknown to the man in the street, a company which manufactures building, engineering, electrical or electronic components — anything from expanded polystyrene to transistors.

These breakdowns of the publics of different organisations are by no means exhaustive, but they indicate the market analysis which is necessary in the preparatory stages of planning a programme.

Staff — office, factory, sales, delivery
Potential staff — apprentices, engineers
Specifiers, e.g. design engineers, architects
Contractors
Technical teachers at universities, technical
   colleges
Trade unions, trade associations
Community in vicinity of factory
Technical information centres, e.g. building
   centres
Technical writers
Government research establishments
Overseas agents

*Figure 5.6   Typical publics for a technical
component manufacturer*

Unless the publics are defined, the media cannot be selected and public relations material cannot be prepared to satisfy interests and needs. Nor can the extent of activity be measured in labour and other costs. In defining publics it is possible to recognise the size of the communication problem, and such may be the constraints of time, money and resources that some publics may have to be neglected, others concentrated upon. The temptation to fly in all directions — the cause of so much public relations failure — is resisted when the total communication span is seen in all its impossible immensity and variation. No practical programme can be planned until the publics have been identified and priorities have been declared.

When publics are defined, we are obliged to consider how to reach them. A standard mailing list and mass distribution of a news release is useless. Suppose the analysis shows that in a relocation situation the wives, husbands and children are vital publics. How do we communicate with them? Or suppose we are about to market a new domestic rodenticide. How do we communicate with Public Health officials?

In the next chapter we shall consider the media of communication or the means whereby our message can be transmitted to our chosen publics.

CHAPTER 6

The Media of Public Relations

HOW PUBLIC RELATIONS AND ADVERTISING MEDIA DIFFER

Here we strike another difference between public relations and advertising. In advertising we speak of above-the-line and below-the-line media, the first group consisting of press, television, radio, cinema and outdoor, and the second group including a great range of media such as direct mail, exhibitions, sales literature, point-of-sale material and all kinds of novelty and give-away material. But in public relations we are concerned with the mass communication media plus private, created media such as house journals, videos, audio visuals, educational print, private exhibitions, seminars and conferences. Much public relations media is not to do with mass communications but is aimed at small groups or even individuals. Where the mass media are concerned, the public relations practitioner deals with editorial and production staff and not with those selling advertisement space or airtime.

The media of public relations communication may coincide with those used for advertising, but generally a public relations programme uses far more media, and can also introduce its own specially created media. Whereas an effective advertising campaign will exploit the fewest number of publications or commercials to reach the largest number of potential buyers at the lowest possible cost, a press relations programme is likely to use a wider spread of publishing and broadcast media. This is not to say that a news release should be distributed on a blanket mailing irrespective of its suitability for certain publications.

Again, public relations and advertising may use entirely different media. Public relations material for a FMCG might be used by the women's press, but television might be used for advertising purposes.

Media vary considerably from country to country, and according to the size of the country. Britain is fortunate in having a national press, but the press is more regionalised in large countries such as Australia, Canada and Germany, and especially in the USA. The number of languages, ethnic groups and religions will have their effects too. While English predominates in Britain, countries in Asia may have publications and broadcast programmes in English, Chinese, Indian, Malay and other languages. In developing countries, where only a minority are literate, people are poor and there is lack of electricity for TV, the mass media are elitist, and other media such as mobile film or video units may be essential forms of communication.

NATURE OF THE MEDIA

As we have already said in Chapter 2, there is an adversarial situation in which the interests of public relations and the media differ, calling for understanding and compromises. The so-called 'freedom of the press' is a myth, and when the late Lord Thomson came to Britain and bought Scottish Television he was honest enough to say it was a licence to print money. The late Peter Jenkins, writing in *The Independent* on February 6 1992, said 'the commercial interest in selling newspapers is promoted into a spurious doctrine of the public right to know'. That applies to most British media, not merely the big circulation tabloids, and the *Sunday Times* has been a major culprit, to quote only the attempt to denigrate Neil Kinnock prior to the 1992 General Election.

KNOWING THE MEDIA

The study of media is therefore a universally important aspect of public relations, and the skilled practitioner will be a master of media, knowing what is available, how they differ and how to use them to the best advantage. In Britain, where *Benn's Media Directory* records no less than 12 000 titles, keeping up with the media is no mean task. How does one do it? How does one reach the stage when one can literally dictate a selective mailing list for each individual news release?

It is a poor PRO who keeps a standard mailing list, and mails stories to news media irrespective of whether they are evening, morning, Sunday, weekly, monthly or quarterly, and without checking (or knowing) whether they are relevant or not to the particular story. It is seldom likely that a particular story is suitable for the 'national press', the 'women's press', the 'trade press' or the 'regional press', which are meaningless generalities. Much of the hostile attitude expressed towards public relations by media

critics is because they are sent irrelevant stories by PROs who do not know their media or cannot be bothered to be selective. You can only be selective when you know what you are selecting.

STUDYING THE MEDIA

Media should be studied constantly. Information abounds in directories such as *Benn's Media Directory*, *PR Planner*, and the excellent series of *Editors* volumes, while *Advance* gives monthly advice on editorial features. There are other useful directories such as *Willing's Press Guide* and *Advertisers Annual*, while the user of mailing services such as PIMS and Two-Ten will have updated monthly media lists. The addresses are given in the bibliography (Appendix 3).

Information about media changes can be gleaned from the trade press, and every public relations office should subscribe to or receive *UK Press Gazette* and *Campaign* at least, and there are several more specialist journals. From these weekly journals, the PRO will learn of those which have folded, changed their titles or format, been launched, or changed their printing process. A large number of titles vanished with the recession, but doubtless remained on standard mailing lists! Twice a year, ABC circulation figures and NRS readership figures are published. Every week BARB issues audience figures for television programmes.

First-hand knowledge of the media and their versatility is even more valuable. Every opportunity should be taken to look at publications — in reception rooms, other people's homes, in newsagents and on railway bookstalls. Media come and go and change and should never be taken for granted. Many former broadsheets are tabloids, colour newspapers are common, and free newspapers are not only plentiful but improving in editorial quality.

Similarly, it is necessary to study the broadcast media, watching and listening to programmes, studying the listings magazines such as *Radio Times*, *TV Times*, and others which have emerged since the deregulation of listings, and becoming familiar with programmes, producers and presenters in order to recognise the opportunities (and the problems!) of getting coverage. We do not just send news releases or invitations to TV or radio stations, but work with the right individuals who are numerous and have specialised interests. There is also the new technique of *video news releases* which are discussed in Chapter 21.

This is only a useful beginning, because we have to create our own media, and that may require a good knowledge of printing, photography, and video production, and the preparation and use of all kinds of audio-visual and visual aids. We often say in this profession that every day is a new day, and that we never stop learning. But that is the fascination of public relations. There is never a dull moment provided we are prepared to admit that we never know it all, and accept that we never will! Unfortunately, too many public relations people know too little about media, which is like a surgeon being ignorant of anatomy.

EXISTING COMMERCIAL MEDIA

The press, television, radio and public or trade exhibitions are the mass media, the macro-media compared with micro-media created privately by the public relations world.

In Britain, BBC radio and TV is currently non-commercial, although there is pressure for the BBC to augment its finances by accepting advertisements. For the purpose of this section, however, we shall include the BBC. Nor must we overlook satellite television such as British Sky Broadcasting. In most other countries all broadcasting is commercial, that is it relies on selling air-time to advertisers for its income. In some other countries broadcasting is wholly state-owned, perhaps coming under the control of the Ministry of Infor-

mation. Who controls broadcasting, and how independent it is, may have considerable bearing on whether or not public relations material is accepted. On the other hand, scarcity of broadcasting material may make public relations material such as videos or taped interviews very welcome. Video material can also be distributed overseas by satellite news services such as Visnews.

Both press and broadcast media are going through changes which need to be observed and understood by the practitioner. They could offer increased and different opportunities for media coverage. For example, under the special Codes on sponsorship introduced by the Independent Television Commission and the Radio Authority in 1991, new opportunities are now available for the sponsorship of broadcast programmes (see Chapter 11), while the BBC has permitted various forms of sponsorship in recent years.

Following the initial challenge by Eddie Shah, and the Battle of Wapping at the *Daily Mirror* East End plant, trade union resistance has been overcome and we have seen the demise of Fleet Street and its old letterpress plants and restrictive practices. Now, London's national newspapers either have new web-offset-litho plants on the outskirts of London, or use strategically located contract printers. This has made viable small circulation newspapers such as *The Independent*, vastly improved photographic reproduction, and made possible some colour printing in newspapers. The *Daily Mail* has adopted flexography, a letterpress process in advance of offset-litho. At the same time, the paperless newsroom now uses single stroke keying which dispenses with the old hot metal composing room and plate-making foundry. Journalists work on computers to write and sub stories, compose and design, and it is possible for a story to be written and on the printing press in minutes.

Meanwhile the world becomes more literate, and throughout the developing countries, more and more newspapers and magazines appear and circulations grow. One of the biggest growth areas has been the Middle East. Only a few years ago, companies interested in public relations coverage in the Gulf states sent their news releases to potential buyers; now they can send them to editors in the normal way.

Let us analyse the types of publications which exist in Britain.

NATIONAL NEWSPAPERS

In many countries there are, for historic and geographical reasons, many newspaper centres, and consequently no national newspapers although there may be chains of newspapers or regional editions like the German *Bild*. London has always been the capital of England and it is the national press centre. Other parts of the United Kingdom — Scotland, Wales and Northern Ireland — also have their national presses although the London papers circulate there too. However, in Scotland the *Daily Record* is virtually the Scottish *Daily Mirror*. Thus, as is often said, by means of the national press it is possible for a story to reach the nation's breakfast table.

The British press differs from many others for another reason. In some countries there may be newspapers appealing to readers of different Christian denominations, religions, political parties or ethnic groups, but in Britain the national daily and Sunday newspapers are classified by class or social grades. The social grades of A, B, C1, C2, D, E as set out in Figure 3.2, Chapter 3, can be related to the nationals as shown in Figure 6.1.

It is important to understand this class breakdown, which is peculiar to the British press, because it determines which newspapers go on the press lists for particular stories. It is rare that one story will qualify for the whole of the national press.

Circulations increase as one goes from social grade A to social grades C2, D and E. Roughly, *The Times* sells 400 000 copies compared with *The Sun*'s 3½ million. The day when *The Times* printed a nude is still a talked-about occasion; there are nudes in *The Sun* every day. Only *The Times* and *The Financial Times* report business appointments regularly, giving each a line or two; the others do so only occasionally. Yet PROs send pin-up pictures to *The Financial Times*, and three-page biographies of business people to the national press in general. Not surprisingly, we have the adversarial situation described in Chapter 2.

Although most papers print editorial pictures in colour, and carry colour advertise-

A	Upper middle class	*The Times, The Financial Times, The Sunday Times*
B	Liberal-intellectual-teacher	*The Guardian, The Independent, The Independent on Sunday, The Observer*
	Managerial middle class	*The Daily Telegraph, The Sunday Telegraph, The Observer, The Sunday Times*
C1	Lower middle class	*The Daily Express, The Daily Mail, Today,*
	White-collar, white-blouse	*The Sunday Express, The Mail on Sunday*
C2,D E	Skilled and semi-skilled working class, others	*The Daily Mirror, The Sun, The Daily Star, The Sport, The Sunday Sport, The Sunday People, The News of the World, The Sunday Mirror*

Figure 6.1   Social grades and UK national newspapers

ments, it is still necessary to supply black and white photographs to newspapers, unless there has been a special agreement with the editor.

Modern offset-litho and flexography printing methods, and particularly contract printing, call for earlier copy deadlines and fewer editions. It is noticeable that in *The Independent*, for instance, no news appears later than *News at Ten* on ITV. Newspapers printed in London such as *The Sun* do carry later news.

BREAKDOWN OF THE BRITISH PRESS

While there are more than 8000 national newspapers and magazines, the regional press should not be overlooked, and most cities throughout the UK have a daily newspaper — usually an evening — but there are still a few morning and even Sunday newspapers published outside London. There are, in fact, more than 100 regional dailies. In addition there are some 800 regional weeklies and more than 800 free newspapers which are given saturation distribution by door-to-door delivery. There are also some specialised local magazines dealing with industry, farming, Chambers of Commerce membership, and local interests.

To these regular daily, weekly, monthly or quarterly publications may be added a large number of directories and yearbooks which are authoritative works of reference. It can be in the interests of many organisations that these volumes contain entries and correct information about themselves.

Thus the British press represents a huge and varied outlet for public relations information provided it is targeted and timed correctly. A more precise breakdown of the British press is as follows:

National mornings
London evening — only one remains
National Sundays
National consumer and special interest magazines, including the weekend magazines which accompany many newspapers, and the many TV/radio listings magazines
National trade, technical and professional magazines — these separate groups not to be lumped together as the 'trade press'
Directories, yearbooks, annuals and diaries
Regional mornings
Regional evenings
Regional Sundays
Town, suburban and regional weeklies
Regional magazines such as county, local interest, Chamber of Commerce, National Farmers Union and business journals
Civic newspapers issued by local authorities
Local directories, guide-books, maps
Free weekly newspapers
Free magazines
Local magazines such as Tenants' Association or parish magazines

INTERNATIONAL PRESS

International newspapers and international editions are a growing feature of the world's press. *The International Herald Tribune* uses a satellite to produce in South-east Asia and the Far East, *The Wall Street Journal* has its European editions. *The Financial Times* has extended beyond its Frankfurt edition with a North American edition, and *USA Today*, the first US national, has its international edition.

NEWSPAPERS

Outside London there are more than 100 daily newspapers, most of which have special correspondents and special-interest features which will welcome material of interest and value to their readers. They are well worth cultivating and to some degree they correspond to the daily newspapers found in large cities abroad where only these and no nationals exist. Britain is unique in having both types of daily, although the further one gets away from London, the more influential becomes the local daily, and vice versa.

Most of these regional dailies adopted web-offset-litho printing many years before the exodus from letterpress-dominated Fleet Street. Consequently, they are well printed, often in colour.

Some of them have London offices, and they receive national news from the Press Association. Two-Ten Communications, which has access to PA computers, can supply public relations news releases, feature articles and photographs to regional newspapers.

A comparison of the number of stages involved in letterpress printing compared with web-offset-litho is made in Figure 6.2.

The *free newspaper* has existed for as long as it has been possible to finance a newspaper solely from advertising revenue. Free newspapers are usually locally distributed and hand-delivered to every house in the distribution area. They attract advertising because of their saturation coverage of the domestic market. Advertisers consist mainly of stores, house agents, motor-car agents, restaurants and entertainments. Although editorial space is limited and there are many classified advertisements, some free newspapers run domestic advice features, and welcome public relations material.

Another form of free publication is the civic newspaper. This came about largely because the local press was failing to adequately report local government affairs.

The *alternative* or *community* newspaper has become an interesting development dating from the 1970s with some one hundred of these radical papers being either sold or distributed door-to-door. Income is seldom derived from advertising and comes from sales, donations or in some cases from local authority grants. The alternative newspaper is a kind of ground-roots consumerist paper, sometimes the class counterpart of the rate-payers' association magazine, with a circulation area no larger than a housing estate. It should not be ignored in community relations campaigns.

MAGAZINES

It is in this publishing sphere that Britain has a diversity of titles second only to the USA, and they range from popular weeklies to technical journals which are read all over the world. In many overseas countries, the British and American press are the only journals available on particular subjects since it would not be an economic proposition to publish such specialist journals in that country. Conversely, some subjects are so specialised that they are an economic proposition in Britain only provided there is a substantial overseas circulation. There is, therefore, an English-language magazine covering almost every subject one can think of.

Magazines can be divided into certain broad categories and a useful indication of them can be found in directories such as *Advertisers Annual*, *British Rate and Data*, *Benn's Media Directory* and the *Editors* series. The following sections contain only a selection of the main categories. We will start with two groups which have made a dramatic appearance at a time when recession and cut-backs in advertising expenditure have seen scores of titles fold.

Weekend magazines. For many years there were only what used to be called the 'colour supplements' of the *Observer*, *Sunday Times* and *Daily Telegraph*. Then they became common throughout the Sunday press, while *The Independent* has its *Magazine* published on Saturday. From an advertising point-of-view, these weekend magazines have captured a large volume of magazine advertising revenue.

Listings magazines. At one time the *Radio Times* and *TV Times* monopolised the publishing of advance details of BBC and ITV programmes, respectively. But with deregulation in 1990, any publisher could buy the listings from the BBC and ITV. At first a number of new titles appeared, with the *Radio Times* and *TV Times* losing half their circulations while having to print all plus British Sky Broadcast-

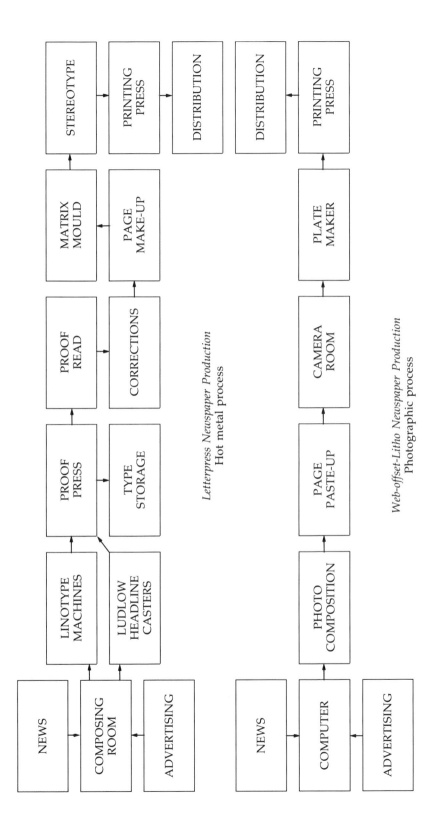

Letterpress Newspaper Production
Hot metal process

Web-offset-Litho Newspaper Production
Photographic process

Figure 6.2 Letterpress compared with web-offset printing process

ing programmes. A latecomer was *TV Quick* from the German publishers H. Bauer and printed in Germany, which spent millions on a sledge hammer advertising and price-cut launch campaign. Subsequently, *The Sun*, *Daily Mirror* and *Sunday Express* found a subtle way to publish a listings magazine. Their value as public relations media is problematic, but some contain editorial features.

Women's magazines. These extend from multi-million circulation weeklies such as *Woman* and *Woman's Own* to more specialised women's journals dealing with childcare, dressmaking, home interests or certain age groups. There are women's magazines catering for readers as different as factory girls and the wives of tycoons, and their contents will range from romantic strip cartoons to room-by-room descriptions of stately homes. In the middle are the cheaply produced colour gravure or offset-litho weeklies with their regular output of knitting patterns, recipes, romantic serials, make-up advice, and coloured advertisements appealing to the mass women's market. They may, however, suffer from the competition of colour TV advertisements just as popular daily newspapers suffered from black-and-white commercial TV. In recent years a number of English language versions of French and German magazines have appeared in Britain. These form part of the trend to publish European magazines in different languages.

Children's magazines. In this group we find few titles of long standing, and this ever-changing readership obviously demands new fashions in reading matter.

Specialised magazines. It would be invidious to analyse all the specialised interest groups, but most interests and hobbies have their own journals, to mention only gardening, motoring, philately, politics, religion and sports. Sometimes these publications are described as

'class' magazines. They can generally be bought from retail newsagents.

From a public relations point of view the existence of so many titles makes it possible for almost any public to be reached, and it is therefore one of the characteristics of British public relations that this remarkable accessibility is available. It can only be exploited if the public relations practitioner has a rich knowledge of press media.

Trade, technical and professional. These three are often lumped together perhaps because they are not usually sold over the counter — unless specially ordered — and may be distributed on a postal subscription, or mailed free of charge to 'request' readers under what is known as 'controlled circulation'. These 'cc' magazines may have bigger circulations than purchased ones because they do not rely on sales and can be mailed to as many people as the publisher chooses, thus achieving high penetration of the market. Since they are thus able to attract more advertising they can afford to be bigger magazines. Their format is often different from traditional journals with advertisements and editorial side by side, often accommodated on broad pages, and resembling catalogues of new products, materials and services to prospective buyers.

They may not carry feature articles, but this varies. For instance *PR Week* carries news and articles and is an attractive proposition to advertisers because, with the promise of 15 000 copies a week, it has great penetration of its market.

There are some magazines which cover all three fields, but generally speaking a trade magazine covers the distribution of goods, the technical magazine appeals to technicians, while the professional journal is typified by the legal and medical press. Subtle distinctions should be noted carefully. In compiling mailing lists it is easy to be misled by the similarity and important to select those which are relevant to the story. A good PRO should know, for instance, who reads the 200 or so titles which may be contained in lists of, say, computer, engineering or farming magazines.

One of the great problems about media selection in the sphere of trade, technical and professional journals is how to select the right ones for the mailing list for a particular story. It is rare indeed that stories can be mailed to standard lists: most stories require a tailor-made list to suit the content of the story. This cannot be emphasised enough.

Local magazines. These can be general-interest magazines dealing with local history, glossy journals covering local social life, industrial journals, agricultural or Chamber of Trade and Commerce journals.

In addition to the publications themselves, there are groups of journalists who specialise in certain subjects. There are also home page editors, and the specialist correspondents. These journalists are sometimes editors of specialist magazines as well as being columnists in newspapers. Sometimes they write in a great many different newspapers and magazines, also broadcasting and appearing on TV. Allied to these are freelance writers who again generally keep to particular subjects.

House journals. In this category we have internal and external private magazines. They sometimes accept outside contributions, the larger ones sell advertising space, and while the majority are issued free of charge, some are sold. Most house journal editors are members of the British Association of Industrial Editors which holds an annual contest and presents awards to encourage high standards of editing and production. Some 900 house journals are currently published in Britain.

House journals or private magazines are another public relations medium and are dealt with separately later on in this chapter.

There is also an untidy group of general-interest magazines.

An important point to remember about magazines compared with newspapers is that they are usually planned, edited and printed over a period of days, weeks or even months, and not hours as in the case of a newspaper. So, if sending news releases to magazines they may have to be sent earlier than to newspapers if simultaneous publication is desired, and similarly it will be necessary to negotiate publication of feature articles a long way ahead. For example, it may be ideal to have a holiday article published in January or February, but it will probably have to be negotiated, written and submitted in the previous summer and autumn. A press reception for magazines could be organised three months before one for newspapers in the case of a Christmas gift product. If consumer and trade/technical press journalists were to be invited to a press reception or works visit, it would be better to have separate ones as the interests of each group would be different. Once again, it is essential to know your media, and its special needs regarding planning, editing and printing needs.

DIRECTORIES, YEARBOOKS, ANNUALS

These reference books divide into two kinds, those which merely list members or provide a directory of names and addresses, and those which contain informative articles and technical recommendations such as standard specifications.

These annual publications must not be overlooked, and it is the responsibility of the PRO or public relations consultant to see that the organisations he represents are correctly listed in every appropriate work of reference, whether or not there is a charge for entries. Publications include telephone directories, Yellow Pages, Thomson's local telephone directories, professional membership registers, trade directories, yearbooks and diaries. Many diaries give 'useful tips', but is the information correct?

There are yearbooks which contain authoritative articles, and incorrect or out-of-date information could be detrimental to the organisation's interests. The author had experience of a directory which was referred to when clients were considering tenders for contracts. Unfortunately, the information was out-of-date which meant that companies using different and more modern techniques had their tenders rejected because they did not use the methods and materials recommended! When the author had the feature corrected his company was able to compete successfully for contracts.

Some directories (e.g. *Advertisers Annual, Hollis Press and Public Relations Annual*, and *Benn's Media Directory*) may be in daily use, but if they lack required information, this is unhelpful to the organisations which are not represented. Such directories are the 'Bibles' of their industries, and their compilers will welcome entries. The public relations practitioner will find the names and addresses of nearly 2000 annual publications in a special section in *Benn's Media Directory*.

TELEVISION

This is the greatest snare and delusion among public relations media. The temptation to use TV as a public relations medium must often be resisted because it has to be recognised that TV is primarily an entertainment medium and personalities and subjects likely to please audiences will be presented, not people who would like to express their point of view to a large audience. Material can easily suffer from the effects of editing and the juxtaposing of material which was not expected during individual sessions. A poor performer in an interview can be crucified.

TV is unlike any other medium. It has many of the attributes and characteristics of the film yet it is viewed on a small screen and in domestic circumstances, so that the captivity of the cinema is missing. In some countries of the Third World, TV is state-controlled for the purposes of propaganda or education, but

although Britain has a public service TV it is really the modern escapist medium of the masses. However, people will watch things they would not read about, and there is the magic difference that TV commands over every other medium. People watch it: it has the original appeal of the silent cinema. To the PRO, TV means that if your managing director looks like an unpopular politician you keep him off the box, although he might be excellent in a radio interview.

The chart in Figure 6.3 indicates the sort of television programme which attracts the largest audiences, and they are mostly soaps or comedy series. *Coronation Street*, Britain's longest running soap which has been broadcast for more then 30 years, regularly tops the

1. Coronation Street (Mon)	20.45	25 Nov
2. Coronation Street (Wed)	19.84	20 Nov
3. Coronation Street (Fri)	19.23	8 Nov
4. Only Fools and Horses	18.93	3 Feb
5. London's Burning	18.86	1 Dec
6. The Darling Buds of May	18.35	21 Apr
7. Auntie's Bloomers	18.24	29 Dec
8. You've Been Framed	17.81	10 Feb
9. Denis Norden's Laughter File	17.39	22 Sep
10. Blind Date Wedding of the Year	16.89	20 Oct
11. The Grand National	16.80	6 Apr
12. EastEnders (Thurs)	16.77	21 Nov
13. EastEnders (Tues)	16.72	12 Nov
14. Big	16.46	4 Dec
15. Watching	16.43	8 Feb
16. Best of Blind Date	16.42	9 Feb
17. Ruth Rendell Mystery	16.34	1 Dec
18. Casualty	16.06	29 Nov
19. News (ITN)	16.00	7 Apr
20. The Bill (Tues)	15.90	12 Nov

Figure 6.3   Top 20 TV ratings of 1991 (millions of viewers). (Source: William Phillips)

audience ratings. Game shows, current affairs and even natural history programmes do not score big audiences. Esther Rantzen's *That's Life* struggles to get eight million viewers.

There are ways in which TV can be used successfully in public relations programmes but it is a medium to consider with caution. It is a visual medium with many pitfalls for the individual who may be interviewed and it is also a tedious medium which can consume a large amount of budgeted labour. Is the large expenditure of time and money justified by the small amount of eventual screen time, the way in which the subject will be treated, and the kind of audience who will watch it? The biggest danger of TV is its appeal to client's or employer's vanity although the net public relations value may be nil.

Even if an organisation lends its premises free for filming, often when the scenes appear on the screen there is nothing that could possibly be of public relations value to the provider of the facilities. Television is notorious for taking all and giving nothing.

However, there are certain ways in which the practitioner can achieve good media relations with this medium and they fall under the following headings.

1. *News* for regional and national bulletins. This usually requires advance notice and provision of independent facilities quite different from those of a press reception or press facility visit. If pictures are supplied they must be in colour.
2. *Discussion programmes* and chat shows if the organisation can produce a personality who televises well.
3. *Series* in which the organisation can feature on its own merits, as when it provides a topic for the series (e.g. *Coronation Street*, gardening, motoring and sports programmes).
4. *Give-away programmes* which are prepared to purchase one's products for use as prizes, provided the product can be identified by viewers, because it is unlikely to be named.
5. *Documentary videos* which may be used in whole or part as programme material.
6. *Properties* for use in sets or products which actors may use, such as cars in crime series.
7. *Library shots* (e.g. pictures of aircraft specifically taken by airlines for use in films and TV series). Visnews is a particularly useful supplier of all kinds of news and location material to the TV companies. They provide archival and news services, and also video news releases as described in Chapter 21.

Just as there are PIMS services in press relations, and the Two-Ten Communications press and radio services, so there is the Visnews sponsored filmclip service for TV.

However, TV programmes are planned and sometimes 'canned' a long time in advance, and it may be useless to propose an idea for next week's show when the series is half-way through. It is best to keep in touch with producers and their staff and try to anticipate future possibilities, as when a series comes off and it is announced that it will be returning in a few months' time.

Another possibility is coverage on BBC TV News or Independent Television News. The best advice here is to tell TV news editors well in advance about your event so that a camera can be booked. Studio interviews are also possible if the subject is of sufficiently wide interest. This topic is also discussed in Chapter 9 which deals with organising public relations events. Alternative television is discussed in Chapter 21.

RADIO

The transistorised portable or car radio has created not only a huge increase in numbers of listeners but also in kinds of listener and in listening hours.

Some of the advantages of radio are:

1. Radio is listened to at all times of the day, but especially outside peak TV viewing hours such as in the morning.
2. It has the power of immediacy.
3. It is simple to deal with — by post, telephone or personal visit to the studio.
4. It can reach illiterates, either by transistor or rediffusion, as in Third World countries.
5. Professional services are available, and these will be detailed below.
6. It is easily monitored by tape-recorder.
7. With such a large network of stations which are more localised than TV, it is possible to use radio locally, nationally and (through the BBC External Services) internationally. Overseas listeners (including British people living abroad) also listen to broadcasts from British stations. In 1991, national independent (that is commercial) radio was inaugurated by the Radio Authority.
8. Receivers are compact and can be carried about or fitted into motor-cars.

In addition to instantaneous broadcasts there are talks, magazines, series and serials which can incorporate public relations material if it suits the programme. Many programmes offer scope for public relations stories, background information, themes and interviews. Nowadays, phone-in programmes are popular. Anyone who listens to LBC broadcasts in the London area will realise that there are many opportunities for public relations coverage such as studio interviews and supplied taped interviews, provided the information is of interest and value to a large radio audience, which will vary according to the time of day.

Two-Ten Communications offers radio services. A taped interview begins with the discussing and planning of the feature with the client, followed by the briefing of the radio reporter and the interviewee. A three-minute recording is made, either in the studio or outside with portable equipment. Then the

recorded tape is edited and copies are made for each local station. A cue sheet is prepared for each station. Tapes and cue sheets are then despatched to the selected producers in every local radio area.

Another Two-Ten radio service is to arrange live interviews with local radio presenters, the interviewee being in Two-Ten's London studio.

PUBLIC AND TRADE EXHIBITIONS

There is a tendency nowadays, especially in advertising agencies to regard all forms of exhibition as public relations. Public and trade exhibitions consist of stands which are just as much a form of advertising as a TV commercial. One reason for this confusion is that the exhibition is classed as a below-the-line advertising medium, and since public relations sometimes wrongly suffers the below-the-line classification, the two are associated.

Public relations does concern the exhibition in two interesting but separate ways. There can be public relations activities *in addition* to the exhibit itself such as advance media relations, invitations to visit the stand, press receptions and associated video shows or seminars. There is also the purely public relations exhibit when the exhibition medium is used as part of a public relations programme. The police make good use of this technique to create a public understanding of their services with exhibits mounted at large gatherings where there is a ready-made audience.

Having made these distinctions about the public relations aspects of exhibitions there are, of course, occasions when a stand at a public or trade exhibition might be taken for public relations purposes but this really applies to organisations such as voluntary bodies which choose to use advertising media as part of their overall communications programme. A large public exhibition may be just the place to promote the work of a charitable institution and to seek support by explaining its work.

The exhibition has the virtue of reality. Things can be actually seen, handled, sampled, compared, and questioned. These are irrevocable tests, inviting criticism, and consequently having great power to create and establish knowledge, understanding, and goodwill. The best way to overcome doubts is to invite people to convince themselves, and an exhibition provides exactly this opportunity. But again, the difference between an exhibition stand for advertising purposes and one for public relations has to be stressed. The demonstrators and salesmen on the former may use slick, high-pressure salesmanship methods, whereas those staffing a public relations stand will be more restrained and informative. Sometimes this is mistaken to be the contrast between 'hard sell' and 'soft sell', but it is wrong to describe the first as advertising and the second as public relations when they are both advertising.

The merit of the exhibition for public relations purposes is that there can be personal confrontation — one of the finest forms of communication — and the willingness to invite comment. They are ideal for testing reactions to prototypes of new products.

The use of public relations techniques on behalf of exhibitors or exhibition promoters will be discussed in Chapter 10. Here, the point is worth making that this is a very neglected area, often being no more than a last-minute supply of unwanted press kits to the exhibition press room. Public relations in support of exhibitors begins months before that. Private exhibitions, whether permanent, mobile or portable, will be discussed in the next section on private, created media.

EDUCATIONAL LITERATURE AND PRINT

Public relations literature is explanatory and educational reading matter which tells a story, rather than sales literature which seeks to persuade and sell. Typical examples are factual accounts of the history and activities of an organisation, cookery recipe leaflets, or handyman's guides to decorating and household tasks. The public relations effect of this literature can be to inspire confidence in an organisation, to encourage a housewife to extend her range of cookery skills by showing her what can be produced, or to make the houseowner wish to improve their home by teaching them how to do it.

Public relations may consist of leaflets, folders, booklets, books, and other pieces of print including wall charts, diaries, postcards, and pictures for exhibiting and framing. A leaflet is a single sheet printed one or both sides; a folder is a larger piece of print which folds down to a convenient size; a booklet consists of more than four pages, the binding being perhaps wire-stitched or saddle-stitched. Larger booklets may require side-stitched, sewn, and/or glued bindings with drawn-on covers, until we come to the book which consists of 8- or 16-page sections or signatures bound together.

Posters make good public relations aids. There are people who collect posters such as those of Guinness or airlines, while double-crown advertising posters are often used for decorative purposes in clubs and canteens and their supply can be a public relations service. Educational posters for display in schools are another use of posters, typical ones describing manufacturing processes or the produce of foreign countries, e.g. tea, coffee or cotton.

Calendars serve both advertising and public relations purposes, enjoying permanent display for a year, and if well-produced they not only create goodwill but give pleasure. Calendars can be produced in one of two ways: the stock calendars offered by firms such as Eversheds Ltd of St Albans and Impact Calendars of London can be overprinted with the sponsor's name and address, or pictures can be produced specially for an original calendar.

Annual Reports and Accounts are often produced by the public relations department as part of financial public relations, or shareholder relations, and they provide an opportunity to explain the activities of a company. They are usually well designed, illustrated and printed.

DIRECT MAIL

Here we come to a medium which some marketing people tend to regard lock-stock-and-barrel as a form of public relations. It is a term which is apt to cause considerable misunderstanding, and some explanations are offered here.

Direct mail is usually taken to mean the advertising medium whereby goods or services are made known by post, whether or not an immediate sale is urged. A book publisher may use this medium, including an order form for a direct response sale, but a department store may distribute a sales catalogue by post and seek to encourage personal shoppers. Moreover, there is no such thing as mail-order advertising in the sense of a medium. Mail-order trading, or direct response marketing as it is called today, may be achieved by the use of the media of press or direct mail.

Direct mail advertising, or postal publicity, is a medium which enjoys the advantages of privacy and selectivity and the ability to send a comprehensive message in the form of supporting literature.

It is particularly interesting, then, that while the advertising tactics of direct mail may not be applicable to public relations (other than as an advertising medium as in the case of a charity appeal), the mechanics of direct mail are frequently used by the practitioner. The simplest example is the news release which is clearly best distributed by direct mail techniques. For instance, some measure of personalisation can be most desirable so that stories are not sent to 'The Editor' but to the 'Home Page Editor' or the 'Science Correspondent' although it helps if the mailing list can be so up-to-date that the envelope can be personally addressed by actual name.

Similarly direct mail is implied when despatching house magazines to the home addresses of employees, or direct to distributors, customers or other external readers. But here we are only using the technique of *direct* distribution, and the need for maintaining a reliable list. A folded and wrapped journal can be less attractive to receive and read than one which arrives flat and in a natural condition as when an envelope is used.

Again, a brochure describing an organisation, its history and facilities, range of services, equipment, techniques, and qualified or skilled staff, might well be direct-mailed to clients and potential clients.

In the same way, invitations to an exhibition stand, video show, seminar, demonstration, dealer conference, works visit, press conference or press reception require the direct mail techniques of accurate mailing list, planned contents, correct timing, and reply facilities.

There are certain occasions when direct mail can be selected as the best means of conveying a public relations message, as when the PRO wishes to distribute a message to opinion leaders such as Members of Parliament, teachers and others who can be personally addressed by letter. The information can be presented in a personal style and bear the signature of someone influential such as the president of the organisation. The letter's value will depend on its ability to improve the recipient's knowledge of the subject, and it should therefore avoid pressing a case too vehemently. The same tactics can be approached by a voluntary organisation seeking new members, donors or other supporters.

Direct mail is therefore a very versatile medium suitable for either advertising or public relations.

THE SPOKEN WORD

Mention has already been made of the importance of personal confrontation. The spoken word is a public relations technique which can be applied to an individual conversation just as much as to the addressing of an audience which may or may not be visible. The skills of public speaking cannot be enumerated here, but ability to express oneself clearly, intelligently, and interestingly is fundamental to a well-trained practitioner. Whether it is necessary to converse on the telephone, address a press reception, face a TV interview or speak at a public meeting, the spokesperson should be an expert in the use of this medium which is particularly suitable for public relations purposes. Few media can be more convincing, because we are right down to basic human contact and communication, and it can be very difficult to project a message through a human personality which is not readily acceptable to the majority in the audience. This is the great test of TV, which can be disastrous to those who, however sincere, are unable to project themselves sympathetically.

By introducing TV we have perhaps complicated the spoken word by associating it with the visual impression created by sight of the speaker. Nevertheless, it is only on the telephone or radio that the speaker cannot be observed, and so when talking, the speaker does have to be well presented and with the fewest possible distractions. When considering the spoken word as part of a public relations programme, it is therefore essential to decide whether the organisation has people of the right ability, whether they should be trained in public speaking or TV/radio interview techniques, or whether they may have to be specially engaged for the occasion.

Exactitude is of paramount importance in public relations planning, and where the element to be planned and managed is as unreliable as the human personality in circumstances where rigid discipline is probably impossible, the PRO or consultant has to direct operations in an inoffensive yet persuasive manner. The chairman or managing director who will not prepare advance notes, attend a rehearsal, take well-meant advice or use a microphone is a menace to a public relations operation, and may well turn the occasion into a disaster. The VIP who sensibly places himself or herself in the hands of the PRO, and co-operates in every way, is an asset of tremendous value to the organisation.

It is not that the PRO will present a favourable but false image, but that from often very rough material a personality will be extracted which does not irritate listeners or viewers by its faults. There are several habits that the practitioner must seek to eradicate from speakers such as hands in pockets jingling money, rocking on one's heels, taking off and putting on spectacles repeatedly, gesticulating with the hands, walking up and down, running hands through hair, scratching one's nose, loosening one's collar, pulling one's ear and hitching up one's trousers. These mannerisms are, of course, indications of nervousness and all the PRO really does in preparing a speaker is to help this person to relax and help him or her to do nothing else except speak clearly and pleasantly so that the message is conveyed convincingly. The spontaneous quips from newsreaders indicate the relaxed speaker. By way of contradiction, it must be acknowledged that there are speakers whose mannerisms are characteristic, as are those of certain conductors of symphony orchestras.

In addition to avoiding the bad habits mentioned above, the following tips are worth noting on behaviour while addressing an audience.

1. Smile from time to time. Look relaxed and appear to be enjoying the occasion.
2. Make useful movements and gestures. Do not stand rigidly with your hands behind your back as if not knowing what to with them. Use body movements which are expressive.

3. Do not irritate audiences by moving about too much. Do not pace up and down, waving your arms.
4. Do not stand with hands in pockets.
5. Never smoke while speaking.
6. Do not hold your hand over your mouth.
7. Try to produce response from your audience — smiles, laughter, nods of agreement.

MISCELLANEOUS PUBLIC RELATIONS MEDIA

There are certain other techniques which may be used independently or impinge on what has been said already.

House style or *corporate identity* means the adoption of a uniform appearance, colour scheme, typography, symbol or some other means of identifying the character of the organisation. This applies particularly to all forms of print from stationery to advertisements and can also extend to signs and notices, staff uniforms, badge ties, ashtrays and cuff-links. This is dealt with more thoroughly in Chapter 26.

Another form of corporate identity is the *livery* that distinguishes vehicles, ships and aircraft which is well represented by road tankers, ships' funnels and the decoration of aircraft. Identity is an important part of communication and an excellent example is the house styling and livery of the world's airlines.

Corporate identity is very much a public relations responsibility because it is the means by which an organisation communicates physically. The scheme has to be adopted throughout the organisation and it will be fully exploited in marketing and advertising. Organisations are identified and distinguished by their logos, colour schemes, livery and dress.

Flags are another form of identification and a company flag can do much to assist in good neighbour relations, helping to break down the anonymity that can create an unnecessary barrier.

Airships became impressive with the large Goodyear airships, capable of carrying six passengers in the gondola, but in recent years smaller two-man airships have become popular for both advertising and public relations purposes.

Hot-air balloons, painted in the colours of their sponsors, have become a colourful form of sponsorship, with balloon races and long distance flight feats. Again, they have lent themselves to a blend of advertising and public relations activities.

CHAPTER 7

Public Relations Costs and Budgeting

THE FINANCIAL FACTS OF PUBLIC RELATIONS LIFE

Probably because in some ill-informed quarters a strange idea exists that public relations is free advertising, the reckoning of public relations costs is sometimes misunderstood. The costing of public relations work is no different from the costing of anything else comprising labour and materials which are combined with the intention of carrying out a task effectively and economically and, in the case of a consultant, profitably.

Some employers of internal public relations staff and a good many consultants have very little idea of the real costs of their work. It is truly amazing how many employers will turn a conveniently blind eye to overhead expenses; how users of outside services will accept a service with an arbitrarily conceived and seldom ever justified overall fee; and worse still, how many consultants abhor time-sheets and operate unprofitable consultancy services which are more like charities for selfish clients. Far too many clients literally believe that public relations is free publicity, and pay extraordinarily tiny fees presumably because they cannot conceive of the work costing much to perform. Yet it is extremely labour intensive, unlike advertising where the costs are largely on media purchases.

This remarkably unrealistic state of affairs can only be ended when users of public relations services understand what they are buying, what it costs, and what constitutes value for money.

There is, nevertheless, a very genuine reason why some users of public relations are confused about costs. They are or were in receipt of very extensive free services from their advertising agents because of the curious commission system. However, this is rapidly giving way to various kinds of fee systems, especially with the newer creative à la carte agencies which do not engage in media buying and so receive no commission income. The commission system, which is convenient to the media owners, really means that the media owners subsidise the service — that is, the advisory and administrative work undertaken by account executives, space buyers, production, print buying, progress chasing and other staff. The commission system not only prevents the advertising agency from making a proper professional charge for work done, but the cost of the work is hidden from the client. Costs cannot be hidden in public relations because only the client can provide the consultancy with income.

Consequently, it comes very hard to have to pay for somewhat similar services when carried out by a consultancy, and the different method of charging is even more perplexing when it comes from the public relations department or subsidiary of the advertising agency whose services are apparently free. In fact, advertising agency owners or consultancies do not themselves always appreciate what they should properly charge, and there was a time when some advertising agencies tried — most unprofitably — to throw in public relations services as freely as others, overlooking the fact that this required a heavy subsidy from agency resources.

So, we must start with the assumption that everything must be paid for, and that as personnel become better selected, trained, qualified and experienced they will be able to command salaries equivalent to those earned by advertising personnel. Inevitably, the service will cost and be worth more when performed by more competent practitioners. As with advertising, vast progress is likely to occur in a short space of time once public relations recruits understand how much they need to learn.

One curiosity of public relations costing needs to be disposed of right away, and that is the practice of tacking a little something on to the end of an advertising budget (or deducting it from this budget) for public relations. The public relations executive is then told he has a certain sum to spend before he has had any opportunity to make a study and present proposals. This practice often occurs in advertising agencies where the account executive has no understanding of public relations. This is yet another reason why there should be a separate budget and separate negotiations for public relations services even when they are to be carried out by a department or subsidiary of the advertising agency.

THE PUBLIC RELATIONS BUDGET

From the above introductory remarks, it will be seen that a public relations budget is completely different from an advertising appropriation. The emphasis will be on what can be done with a certain amount of time (which has a money value) or how much time is required.

Let us now examine the items which constitute a public relations budget, looking at this from the points of view of both the staff PRO and the outside consultant. The five basic elements are: labour, office overheads, materials, equipment and expenses.

1. *Labour*. Salaries of management and specialist staff. Salaries of secretarial, clerical and accountancy staff (including National Insurance and pension fund contributions). Fees to freelance, consultancy, and other outside staff. This is likely to be the major cost.
2. *Office overheads*. All rent, rates, insurance, heat, light, telephone (including switchboard), office services, client liaison.
3. *Materials*. All stationery, photography, postage, print, visual aids, exhibition stands, video, slides and other items.
4. *Equipment*. Office equipment including copying machine and possibly word processors; TV set and VCR; cameras, camcorders; and vehicles such as staff cars for mobile activities. Some organisations have their own video studios.
5. *Expenses*. All out-of-pocket expenses incurred by staff such as fares, hotel bills and entertainment of guests, plus catering costs for functions and events.

The consultant will expect to make a gross profit of at least 15 percent and this means charging a service fee capable of recovering salaries and overheads, although some income may be derived from commissions or quantity concessions on certain materials such as print and photography. Expenses are charged at cost, and where these are heavy, as with catering for a press reception, they are best charged direct to the client by the contractors, otherwise they may represent interest-free loans.

There is a somewhat old-fashioned argument that it is unprofessional for a consultant to accept commissions from suppliers, but the consultant who handles videos, house journals, exhibitions and sponsorships may depend on these commissions for a part of his income. The amount of consulting or counselling done by such a consultant may occupy only a minor part of the time or workload with most of it occurring in the original planning stages and then at subsequent progress meetings. The bulk of the fee will be taken up by the time expended on carrying out the programme. Few consultancy fees can be regarded as retainers for advice, although such an item can, and should, be specifically written into a consultant's budget proposals. However, in most cases the consultant is literally selling time and expertise and this is the chief form of remuneration.

IS IT CHEAPER TO OPERATE IN-HOUSE?

No, it is bound to be more expensive.

The client may say an in-house department can be operated more cheaply than a consultancy fee, thus saving the consultancy profit. This is possible only if the consultancy is employed full-time and more than full-time, and if the consultant is conveniently located.

It has to be recognised that although the consultant may have to bear and charge the overhead expenses of an office in the centre of a city, compared with the lower costs of an office in a provincial factory, the cost of sharing those city facilities is a very modest investment in more efficient services. However, the pros and cons of internal and external services will be debated in Chapter 12.

The sort of false argument occurs when the client resents paying consultancy fees and thinks that for a smaller and even the same outlay, an in-house department can be run. An effective department cannot be run on this sort of outlay for two reasons. (i) If a small fee is being paid only a proportion of an executive's time is being used, and consequently if a PRO was employed full-time he or she would have to indulge in extra activity which might well incur numerous other costs such as house journals, videos, seminars, works visits and so on. This in turn would probably involve further expenditure on additional salaries. (ii) While a staff PRO and secretary may be engaged for the cost of their salaries they still have to be housed, equipped, serviced and supplied at a minimum cost of at least their salary bill again. And since the additional volume of work is bound to require additional staff such as an assistant and an office junior with their own overheads, it is unlikely that an internal department comparable with a consultancy service can be undertaken more economically. It may be undertaken differently or more efficiently but that is another matter associated with the intimacy of in-house public relations. It can therefore be misleading to compare consultancy costs with department costs.

Generally speaking a consultancy is engaged when (a) an internal department is not justified by the volume of work; (b) specialist and perhaps *ad hoc* services are required; or (c) the internal department is so busy it needs outside help.

COSTS OF AN IN-HOUSE DEPARTMENT

Let us now look more closely at the costs which may concern the internal public relations unit, assuming that the internal unit is at least an embryo department consisting of a public relations officer or manager, and his secretary. Anything less than this is not a serious attempt to undertake public relations, but mixed operations will be discussed in Chapter 14.

Labour

The staff of a large public relations department may consist of some or all of the following personnel.

Public relations manager

Assistant public relations manager
Press officer(s)
House journal editor
Photography and audio visuals officer
Print designer and buyer
Sponsorship manager
Exhibitions manager
Events organiser
Works visit organiser
Librarian
Secretarial staff
General office staff

The budget must therefore include their salaries, pension funds, insurance, and taxes as may be appropriate under current policy or legislation, and successive budgets must allow for bonuses and salary increases.

Each organisation's public relations department will vary according to its particular needs, and two seemingly identical companies serving much the same market could undertake the work in very different ways. This is the great advantage of public relations over advertising as a means of communication, since more than one method can be adopted with equal effectiveness. However, in a sizeable campaign, the house journal and the documentary video will both occupy important places in the programme, but a smaller campaign could use either one or the other. Today, a number of organisations produce corporate video programmes with satellite transmission. (It will be seen from these remarks that already we are relegating press relations to but a place in a programme, and not the whole programme as it is sometimes regarded.)

A modest in-house department will therefore consist of at least a PRO, a press officer, two secretaries, and a clerical assistant or copy typist.

Costs could be lessened if more specialist duties were supplied by outside consultants, photographers, video producers, exhibition stand designers, house journal producers and others. It is by no means a case of making a distinct choice between either an internal department and a consultancy; many sensible and valuable combinations are possible, and these combinations are an important aspect of costing. For example, it is pointless maintaining even a two-man video unit unless at least three productions a year are to be made or, again, unless the unit can double on other duties, photographic or otherwise. There is no investment in idleness. For instance, a video studio can also produce training and servicing videos.

Other costs

There is, however, one contributory aspect of public relations which can seldom be budgeted accurately, although some allowance should be made when the cost would otherwise have to be met out of department salaries. Here we mean all the innumerable activities which the PRO may inspire but which may well be instigated by a public relations-oriented management which recognises that public relations is something implicit in the proper management and conduct of the organisation.

With this in mind, it is difficult to understand the thinking of those who regard public relations as a luxury. It is like sex, existing whether we like it or not. All that is new is the integration, planning and control of the relations which an organisation inevitably has with its numerous publics.

The public relations-conscious organisation will therefore operate through public relations-minded executives or officials, and their staff, in every department. Good relations is often no more than good manners. In an industrial organisation, the works manager, personnel manager, purchasing officer, sales manager, production manager, maintenance engineer, warehouseman, transport manager, and other departmental heads can all contribute by creating and maintaining good relations with their respective publics. To these may be added branch, area and field managers who may be in charge of retail outlets, depots, or sales offices. Their public relations costs are difficult to place in the budget, and the recognised cost of an organisation's public relations may be related only to the central, inspirational department whose duties must include direction and instruction through the staff house journal, internal memos, staff meetings and conferences, and possibly by means of videotape or slide presentations. The internal role of the staff PRO must never be overlooked, and the topic is mentioned here because time has to be allowed for it when allocating staff and salaries.

In local government, this sort of thing is even more apparent because much of the success of a local authority PRO's work will depend on the co-operation he obtains from committees and committee chairmen, but especially from his fellow local government officers. A major cost of local government public relations is the time spent on integrating the communication requirements of a very complex organisation which has a crying need for contact with its public. Nowhere is public relations more seriously needed than in establishing communication between the local government service and the taxpayers. Since the majority of taxpayers never enter its doors, it is not enough to look upon the public library as an official information service.

Office overheads

An internal department requires more than just offices for executives and secretaries; it is very much a workshop needing working areas for assembling, packing, designing and making up. This is expensive.

Once again, it may be cheaper to use a consultant who has all these facilities or to use one of the mailing services such as PIMS or Two-Ten. An organisation cannot expect to undertake its own public relations work unless it is prepared to devote a sufficient slice of office accommodation to its staff and their equipment.

The location of the office is also important, and ideally it should be in a principal city, in close proximity to communication media, and other facilities, and preferably centralised. This can mean a high office rent, but this should not be shirked if there is a serious intention to set up a fully operative public relations department. However, the office should not be isolated from the main centre of production and employment as frequent visits may be necessary. Public relations staff should maintain good communication with the entire organisation, even if this has scattered locations, and this could incur installing direct lines, telex, fax, or having a press officer in each location. If an organisation is based out of London, a London PRO is an asset, although this is sometimes overcome by having a location-based PRO supplemented by a press information service through a London consultancy. This also applies in other regions or countries where there are city-based media centres. However, some of these locational problems can be overcome by the use of fax and PC facilities, but not always.

From the above argument it will be seen that office overheads should include the cost of maintaining contact with the local branches, offices, factories, mines or mills wherever they may be in the UK or overseas. The public relations department cannot be fully operative unless it is a central hive of information, the eyes and ears of the organisation.

Normal office overheads will also include rent, rates, light, telephone, cleaning and other service charges. It is essential that these be included, and the PRO should not be housed in a couple of spare offices free of charge so that no real cost is budgeted.

Materials

Public relations work has its own creative and production costs. A story may be published free of charge in a magazine — as it deserves to be if it is genuine news — *but it is not produced free of cost*. As we have already said, salaries and office overheads have to be allocated. Now we must consider the materials used by the labour in the office. The following is a list of some of the items which come under this heading:

   (i) Envelopes: for news releases
                 for photographs (card backed)
                 for MSS, brochures, etc.
                 for correspondence.
  (ii) Letterheadings.
 (iii) Printed news release headings.
 (iv) Photographic caption blanks, preferably printed with identification details including the logo.
  (v) Invitation cards for press receptions.
 (vi) Plastic press packs.
(vii) Copier materials.
(viii) Suitable binders, files, etc. for press cuttings, photographic records plus normal office supplies. Use may also be made of the organisation's computer, e.g. for addressing purposes when mailing house journals or news releases.

The above list can be adapted or extended according to the special needs of the organisation which may require other materials such as all kinds of printed material, blow-ups of pictures, video-tapes, slides, charts, and other visual aids, and the various materials required by specialist staff such as house journal editors, photographers, video producers, exhibition designers, and events and sponsorship organisers.

Expenses

This is an item which has to be realistically anticipated and rigorously controlled. Lavish expenditure is stupid, but if staff are expected to give up their spare time and be separated from their homes and families they deserve the compensation of first-class travel, decent meals, and first-class hotel accommodation. Hospitality for guests may be an expense associated with sponsorship, which will be discussed separately in Chapter 11. Expenses are likely to include the following items:

Car expenses, either supplying vehicles or paying a mileage rate
Fares
Telephone calls
Overnight hotel expenses
Meals while travelling
Entertainment of visitors, contacts
Catering expenses for press receptions, seminars, other public relations events
Hire charges for halls and equipment such as microphones, screens, OHPs, VCRs.
Hire of transport — cars, vans, caravans, coaches, trains, aircraft
Supply of newspapers, trade magazines, yearbooks, directories

The expense will obviously vary according to whether one is perhaps mainly researching technical articles about installation or doing something more elaborate such as touring an exhibition or road show.

COSTS OF A CONSULTANCY

Having established an appreciation of the more likely costs of an internal department, it now becomes a straightforward matter to understand the costs of an outside consultancy, whether one is a consultant or a client.

The costs are basically the same in items and calculations except for two considerations. First, the consultant has to make both a living and a profit, and earns this by offering factors of convenience, knowledge, skill and facility; second the consultant can offer a share of his or her organisation which, while very economical to the client who has no need to run a fully fledged department, is naturally limited to the size of the fee. The price of outside services has therefore to be measured within these parameters.

This has to be understood. Some people wrongly suppose that consultancies are expensive, but as with most things in life you get what you pay for. In this case one is buying time and expertise.

Now it is easy to reconcile the contrasts and contradictions between the cost of placing advertising through an advertising agency and public relations through a consultancy. If advertising were handled internally, the advertiser would not enjoy the commissions granted to advertising agencies, granted because it is more convenient to account collection to deal with a minimum number of agencies instead of a maximum number of advertisers. Moreover, agencies are permitted only limited credit whereas most clients somewhat selfishly take long credit if they can get it. Even where the commission system has been replaced by fees, advertising tends to be less continuous than public relations so that again it can be very economical to share agency facilities.

But both in-house and consultancy are equally free of the commission system to a major extent. This is because the greatest advertising expense is usually space in the press, time on TV or radio, sites for posters and signs, or printed material, all of which produce commissions to pay the agency for giving the client free administration and other services carried out by some of the most expensive advertising agency staff such as account executives and copywriters. The greatest public relations cost, especially as far as the consultant is concerned, is *time* and the value of that time according to the practitioner's experience.

The client buys time, not so many inches or centimetres of press cuttings, minutes of interviews on TV or mentions in news bulletins. These are the consequences of using time effectively. The client does not pay by results in the physical sense. Payment is for effort expended, although clearly if the results of the effort were disappointing the client might well decide to change the consultant or stop using public relations.

The trouble is that some clients tend to expect a certain monetary value of press cuttings (calculated on an advertising space rate basis) for a fee of a similar amount. They fail to understand that at an hourly rate (by the simplest computation of executive hours) a day's work costs so much, and if the consultant spends only a day a month with his client, for progress meeting and gathering material, at least a proportion of the fee is spent talking to the client. And this does not take into account the time spent on day-to-day liaison. But while this can be easily explained it is sometimes more difficult to convince clients that apart from outgoing initiated effort there is constant incoming enquiring activity which also occupies time and eats into fees. Generally speaking, the consultant's main source of income is the sale of his or her time and expertise.

ACCOUNTING FOR CONSULTANCY SERVICES

The consultant is wise to *invoice* his client under three headings:

1. *Fee*, based on an hourly or daily rate which covers labour, overheads and profit. This is usually charged one to three months in advance.
2. *Materials*, such as press relations materials, photography, and other goods.
3. *Expenses*, being reimbursable items for fares, hotels and catering, large sums being best invoiced direct to the client since the consultant cannot afford to give extended credit on, say, a hotel account for a press reception. (Some consultants pay such bills themselves but may add a percentage when charging their clients.)

It now becomes necessary to determine how the hourly rate shall be calculated. It would be simple if consultants could together agree on a minimum fee structure so that clients could know the approved scale, although there would be nothing to prevent the better qualified or more successful consultant charging a higher rate if this was merited. A minimum rate would avoid price cutting and give consultants a basis for organising their own office economy. However, a standard rate is difficult because overheads vary as does individual expertise.

A well-known way of arriving at an hourly rate is to take the joint salaries of an executive and his or her secretary and multiply them by three. In other words the executive is capable of handling accounts to this value per year. The 'three times' method, despite its seeming an over-simplification, is extraordinarily accurate. However, this does tend to imply that this executive has to be a jack-of-all-trades with little if any division of labour among specialist 'backroom' staff.

At the other extreme there is the system which can be applied to a consultancy with specialist departments which enable the account executive to be confined to advising, planning, and directing. Under this method all members of the staff are given values based on their salaries plus overheads and proportionate profit on-cost. Each employee from managing director to messenger boy has to complete a job sheet, and the client is charged the monthly sum total of all the rated time expended by various personnel. The account executive would be responsible for controlling time expenditure within the agreed fee.

A bad practice is the provision of costly competitive speculative schemes, for which no payment is made by the prospective client. The client calling for such presentations could appoint no one and pirate the ideas. The best professional practice is for the client to invite a chosen consultant to carry out a pilot study and make recommendations.

The following is a summary of the methods of assessing consultancy fees. The variety is surprising and it represents the failure of either the IPR or the PRCA — although there are more than a thousand consultants in the UK — to establish a method of charging that is generally intelligible to clients. The recom- mendations that have been suggested are very ill-defined.

METHODS OF ASSESSING CONSULTANCY FEES

1. *Arbitrary all-in annual fee.* This is the consultant's calculated guess, usually unrelated to any objective planning as set out in Chapter 4 and permitting the consultant very little opportunity to justify what is being done for the fee. It is a most unsatisfactory method of charging fees, although at one time it was almost the only one known to consultants. This method was just as unsatisfactory to the consultant as it was to the client. If the consultant really did a good job, the chances were that there would be over- spending and money would be lost on the account. Either way there was no means of forecasting, controlling or charging out at a profit the three types of cost that had been incurred. This 'method' still persists in many parts of the world. Sometimes it occurs in countries where public relations is comparatively new and consultants tend to charge what they think the client will be willing to pay. It can mean a very poorly paid consultant! Fees must cover costs and show a profit. Clients cannot be sub- sidised.

2. *Retainer plus* charges for time, materials and expenses. The term *retainer* is often confused with *fee*, but the two have no connection. A retainer means that a payment has been paid to ensure that no rival client is serviced. No work can be expected for a retainer. It merely grants the client *exclusivity*. With this method (which should be unnecessary with proper costings) the client makes a token payment, and is then invoiced for the actual work done on a proper basis of

hourly fees plus the cost of materials and expenses. It is a method favoured by some of the larger American-owned consultancies. But there are well-known consultancies which charge retainers when they mean fees.

3. *Hourly rate to cover all staff* (but based on account executive's time) plus overheads and profit, plus materials and expenses. This is a reasonable and commonly used method. The rate can be varied according to the seniority and experience of the account executive.

4. *Hourly rate per member of consultancy staff* (salary plus percentage) plus materials and expenses. This is an excellent method which has the advantage that it calls for the estimate of labour resources when planning the budget and by means of time-sheets enables budgetary control to be conducted during the progress of the campaign. It is especially applicable when the consultancy is large enough to have a division of labour between people with different skills or expertise.

5. *Annual fee charged and consumed monthly.* The fee may be calculated by one of the methods described in 4 and 5, but control is now exacted on the month-by-month expenditure. If no work is done in a particular month, the fee is still charged because (and this is perfectly fair) the consultancy had staff and other resources available to service the account and these had to be paid for whether or not the client made use of them. But if the client consumes more than the agreed month's ration of the annual fee, a suitable charge is made according to the excess hours recorded on the time sheets. This can apply to very busy accounts with unpredictable demands on time.

6. *Annual fee and supplementary fees.* Similar to 5, this method assumes that the time is fully taken up each month, but if the time sheets show a danger of the allotted time being exceeded the client is asked whether more than the monthly instalment of the annual fee is to be incurred. It is one way of controlling the ever-demanding client who does not understand the limitations of a fee. If such control is not exercised, the consultancy could go out of business.

7. *Time bank system.* Not very popular, this method follows the calculations outlined in the hourly rate methods, but spreads the time over longer periods, usually three months, so that the client is permitted to have peaks and troughs in the consumption of time, even though the fee is charged on a monthly instalment basis.

8. *Ad hoc.* Payment by the job, based on time, materials and expenses, is a convenient way of charging for short-term assignments.

9. *Based on advertisement rate.* There are some journalists who have either set themselves up as consultants, or who are still working on publications and offer their services in a freelance fashion, and have no idea how consultancy work is paid for. They are capable of measuring the inches or centimetres gained in editorial columns, multiplying the total by the advertisement rate per single column centimetre and billing the client accordingly. They are oblivious to labour and hourly rates that cover overheads and show a profit. The only reason why they get business is that their clients equate public relations with journalism. It is not a method to be taken seriously.

With this curious mixture of fee systems two things are essential: consultants must explain to their clients exactly what they can expect for their money and how they will be charged, and clients must take the trouble to find out how and for what they will be charged.

So not only must fees be capable of being proved against strict records, but materials must be specified, and likewise the nature of expenses must be clearly stated. There should thus be no reason for a client to dispute an invoice, because every item should be in accordance with agreed policy and programme. Moreover, if the invoice specifies how many news releases were despatched the client knows that a job has been done, and a client has every right to be pleased to receive a busy, detailed invoice because it indicates the effort made by the consultant. In case of dispute, the consultant should be able to produce time-sheets to prove expenditure of time.

JOB NUMBERS AND CONTACT REPORTS

All this needs to be supported by a simple *job number* system which can be applied to orders for goods and supplier's invoices, and to invoices charged out to clients. If a job number is raised every time some complete job, such as a photographic session or a press reception is set up, this number can be used as the code on every document, for every agenda item at meetings, and in contact reports (minutes with a right-hand column for allocated personal responsibilities) submitted by the consultancy after meetings.

Clients should never prepare minutes of such meetings, and if the responsibility is accepted by the consultant, the contact report can become part of the control system of the account. Thus, long-winded verbatim reports by a client's secretary with little understanding of what is going on can be avoided, and precise reports can be produced referring only to decisions and responsibilities. The contact report can be produced quickly and circulated to the client so that any misunderstandings can be eliminated in a matter of hours. It should state the occasion and give the distribution list which may include people on both sides who did not attend the meeting.

These contact (or progress) reports are usually kept in a *facts book*, and are very useful if there are any misunderstandings, and they

can form the basis of a progress report on the year's work.

PREPARING ESTIMATES FOR CONSULTANCY PROPOSALS

Costing thus begins for the consultant at the time of preparing proposals. From experience, the time required to perform certain tasks will be known. Figure 7.1 shows a dummy estimate which might fit a proposal for a medium-size account.

Clearly, the items mentioned can be changed to suit each potential client. No mention is made of support for exhibitions, or of general news stories about the company and its personnel while financial public relations is not listed in this example. It does, however, indicate the 'shopping list' method of showing the client what may be expected for a given fee. The calculations mean the number of items times the estimated number of hours times the hourly rate.

When producing a speculative scheme, probably in competition with rival consultants, a problem can be estimating an acceptable total fee. It is easy to say that the client *should* spend so much, and that it is the professional task of the consultant to advise on the *right* expenditure, but in most cases the client has already worked out a total marketing budget and has *allocated a certain sum* for public relations. The consultant can supply only as much or as little service as the client is prepared to pay for, and if the client will admit the desired ceiling, the consultant can work to that figure. Of course, the consultant can always say whether this budget is sufficient to achieve the client's objectives. But it would be nonsense if the figure was some set percentage of the total advertising appropriation!

SKELETON BUDGETS

An indication has been given of costings in outline. It is pointless to quote actual figures

12 Progress meetings	12 × 0 × £0.00	000.00
3 Press receptions	3 × 0 × £0.00	000.00
Editing 4 issues house journal	4 × 0 × £0.00	0 000.00
12 New product stories	12 × 0 × £0.00	000.00
Information bureau service	0 × £0.00	000.00
4 Feature articles	4 × 0 × £0.00	000.00
Organising works visit	0 × £0.00	00.00
Script for video	0 × £0.00	000.00
		£0 000.00
Estimated material cost		000.00
Estimated expenses		000.00
		£00 000.00

Figure 7.1   Consultancy budget

since these will vary according to time, place, quantity, and other controlling factors. But we can itemise expenses and the following section gives skeleton budgets for some specific exercises. If these skeletons are remembered as patterns of predictable expenditure, it is possible to produce rough estimates based on known costs by a process of quick calculation. This can be valuable when dealing with superiors, colleagues, or clients. One must adopt the habit of budgeting all costs. When doing this it is wise to err on the higher side and seek to present final accounts which are slightly under estimate. This always inspires greater confidence than when estimates are exceeded, which is what most people pessimistically expect!

1. A press reception

Figure 7.2 shows a typical estimate for a press reception in which it is assumed that the maximum necessary expenses are incurred such as a hired venue and outside catering. Demonstrators can be engaged for the occasion, or staff at their normal rates of pay.

Some costs, such as rent or hire of microphones, are fixed unless a larger hall has to be taken. Some hotels do not charge a room rent if there is a bar and catering. Rents can depend on whether the premises are required for a couple of hours, half a day, or a day, and this cost could be doubled if the room had to be prepared the day before. These costs must be discussed with the hoteliers, and comparisons made before giving a firm booking.

The same applies to menus, catering charges, and what in fact a catering quotation means. There can be an immense difference between finger buffets; a small extra payment per head could be money wisely spent, since the initial preparations by caterers are costly. Drinks are much the same wherever one goes, but with catering one has to be sure what one is buying, and casual ordering can be disappointing. It is a simple matter to ask the hotelier what each item on the menu means, and the same description can mean very different things from one hotel to another! If, as is often appropriate, the buffet is served about noon, a finger buffet as served at cocktail parties is useless and it is necessary to provide

	£
Printed invitation cards, reply cards, white envelopes	00.00
Postage on invitations	00.00
Telephone: checking names on invitation list, following up non-replies, refusals, etc.	00.00
Hire of room	00.00
Hire of VCR, TV set	00.00
Hire of microphones	00.00
Average 3 drinks at £0.00 per head	000.00
00 buffets at £00.00 per head	000.00
00 coffees at £0.00 per head	00.00
Gratuities	00.00
Press kit wallets	00.00
News releases, copies of speech	00.00
Display panels for photographs	00.00
Photography and prints	000.00
Captions	00.00
Order forms for photographs	00.00
Visitors' book	0.00
Samples/souvenirs for guests	000.00
Lapel badges	00.00
Artwork for tent cards, displays, notices	00.00
Taxi fares transporting materials, staff	0.00
Special effects: costume hire, decorations, musicians, lighting, etc.	000.00
Incidentals	00.00
Contingency fund	000.00
Total	£0000.00

Figure 7.2   Budget for a press reception

either substantial well-filled sandwiches augmented by hot items, or better still, a fork buffet.

There is no need for the bar charges to be exorbitant. If there is an initial reception, then the programme of talks and demonstrations followed by a bar and buffet, the average consumption will be three drinks per head. Excessive drink costs occur only when there is a stand-up cocktail party with waiters or waitresses carrying round trays of drinks, that is a press reception with no programme, or when there is a surfeit of hosts who carry on drinking after the guests have gone.

2. A press facility visit

An extra budget is given in Figure 7.3 for the costs of a facility visit. It is similar to a press reception except that it involves a more detailed tour programme at the location, travelling arrangements, and full host responsibilities for catering throughout the trip with the possibility of overnight accommodation.

The economics of transport and catering have to be carefully weighed. It may be cheaper to charter an aircraft than to use a train because fewer meals and less entertaining would have to be provided. The flight might

	£
Transport for main party:	
(a) to and from location 00 at £0.00 per head	00.00
(b) to and from airport, seaport, rail terminal 00 at £0.00 per head	00.00
Transport for local or short distance parties:	
(a) helicopter	
(b) private car	00.00
(c) minibus	
(d) coach	
Catering:	
(a) Breakfast 00 at £0.00 per head	00.00
(b) Lunch 00 at £00.00 per head	000.00
(c) Tea 00 at £0.00 per head	00.00
(d) Dinner 00 at £00.00 per head	000.00
(e) Coffee 00 at £0.00 per head	00.00
(f) Bar 00 at £0.00 per head	000.00
Overnight accommodation 00 at £00.00 per head	000.00
Hire of:	
(a) Marquee, hall	00.00
(b) Chairs	00.00
(c) Tables	00.00
(d) Umbrellas	00.00
(e) Protective clothing	00.00
Extra staff costs for escorts, guides including rehearsals	00.00
Provision for route signs, cordons, etc.	00.00

Figure 7.3   Extra budget for facility visit

also add to the pleasure of the journey. For this budget most or all of the items listed for a press reception may be required, with the possible additions or variations shown in Figure 7.3. These are adjustable items and are given here as a guide to what may be required since so much depends on the geographical position of the venue, its accessibility, and the nature of the visit.

For example, if the location is inaccessible by rail, road transport is essential and a greater proportion of time will be occupied in travelling. It may not be feasible to make road-stops for refreshments because of the time loss, but it is possible to hire a modern coach with refreshment facilities.

Again, the full party may not always come from one central starting point, and various forms of short-run transport may be required to bring in, say, regional press, radio and TV representatives.

It may not be practical to cater for a large party of visitors at the factory or installation, and there may not be a large enough catering establishment within handy distance. In these circumstances, it is more convenient to bring the caterers to the guests, and premises such as a marquee may have to be hired and furnished or adapted.

Visitors are not allowed in some food factories, on construction sites or down mines without protective clothing such as caps, helmets, goggles, coats, boots or wellingtons, and quantities in a range of sizes must be hired or purchased for the occasion.

If the party is to make a tour, it could be a wise precaution to place directional signs or arrows along the route, and also to cordon off areas not to be visited. Items on the route may require explanatory placards. All these signs must be allowed for in the budget. We have already mentioned escorts and guides, but uniformed commissionaires may be required to man entrances and direct visitors. Scale plans may be required so that all concerned may have identical visual instructions.

A number of people in a strange place have to be managed in a discreetly disciplined manner, and the costs of achieving this have to be borne in mind. In such circumstances even the most intelligent guests behave irrationally, get worried, and can panic because what is thoroughly familiar to the host is totally strange to the visitor. The imaginative PRO will anticipate what is required. Money spent on directional signs, hand-drawn instructions, and large legends explaining what is being shown, could impress by their helpfulness and be a major public relations aspect of the entire operation. So allow for such costs.

From these remarks, the reader will see that planning and costing are logical mental disciplines which are complementary to each other. The good PRO is a worrier about details, and the budget preparation is the time for establishing details. The budget provides a checklist for action.

3. An industrial or documentary video

Now let us think about the costing of a documentary video. A typical outline form is shown in Figure 7.4 and again, it must be but an outline.

A big influence upon the cost of video

	£
Script writing fees (treatment, shooting script)	00.00
Shooting, sound recording and editing	0000.00
Post production effects	00.00
Location expenses	000.00
Actors', commentators' fees	000.00
Musical score, composition of, hire of	000.00
Titling	00.00
Copyright fees (e.g. library shots)	00.00
Translations, dubbing language sound track	00.00
Cost of copies in cassettes	000.00
Distribution costs: e.g. postage, packing, air freight, library and bookings administration	000.00
Synopsis leaflets for audiences	000.00
Distribution services, showing to selected audiences	000.00
Preview for industrial video critics	000.00
Advertising to attract borrowings	000.00

Figure 7.4   Budget for a video

making may be whether it is made by a staff or an outside production unit. When shooting is necessary over a protracted period the staff unit could be more economical. Since no two videos are alike, the skeleton costing scheme is probably more incomplete in this instance. There are, however, certain basic decisions to be made which have a direct bearing on cost. These are: (a) length; (b) recorded sound or dubbed commentary; (c) colour or black and white; (d) extent of location shooting; (e) employment of actors, commentators. Then there is the cost of showing and distribution.

The budget is made out to allow for inside or outside production. The original may be made on the industrial Sony/Umatic system, but copies may be required on the domestic VHS formats, and sometimes other formats for overseas use, e.g. North America.

Among the points to be specially remembered here are whether sound is to be recorded during shooting, or whether the video can be silent with music, commentary, and sound effects dubbed in afterwards; whether own staff or professional actors are to be used; whether locations will be distant, time-consuming, and dependent upon weather or seasons.

Nowadays, creative post-production effects can be introduced using computer graphics and systems such as Quantel Paintbox.

4. A house journal or company newspaper

Next let us look at the costs of producing and distributing a printed house journal. Here again there are so many variables that the skeleton is a check list for adaptation to actual needs. Determinants are as follows: (a) frequency of issue; (b) format; (c) number of pages; (d) colour or black and white; (e) method of distribution; (f) editorial costs; (g) art/photography; (h) paid contributions; (i) income.

Income. To dispose of the last item first, it is possible for house journals to have income which can partially offset costs, make them self-liquidating or actually make the publication a profitable venture. There are two ways of doing this. One is the traditional method of the publishing business, that being sale of advertisement space, but as always this is possible only when the readership has value to advertisers because of quantity or speciality. The other, which is becoming more widely accepted, is the sale of copies. The willingness of staff to pay for their house journal is a measure of its excellence and success.

These remarks chiefly apply to *staff magazines*, for it is less easy to charge for copies of dealer magazines and ones for external distribution to customers and others. Some externals are actually sold on bookstalls, especially in developing countries where journals are few in number. The status of the house magazine is greatly increased when readers are prepared to buy it. Putting a cover charge on a house magazine is also a means of controlling distribution in organisations with very large staffs where the enormous print order for a totally free distribution would be prohibitive and wasteful.

So we can seriously regard some house journals as having a balance sheet. The editor may be responsible for working within a cost budget, a break-even budget or a profitable budget. The majority of house journals will be regarded as part of the public relations programme, with an allocation from the main appropriation for the medium.

The first eight determinants can now be commented upon in some detail.

Frequency. How often will the periodical be published? Weekly, fortnightly, monthly, quarterly? Most other costs will be multiplied by the frequency figure, and the number of issues therefore has a big bearing on total costs, while conversely the total budget can determine the number of issues.

Format. Size of page — whether newspaper or magazine — and the volume of material to be carried as determined by the number of columns and column width (if any) will also have a bearing on paper, typesetting, design, proofing, and machining costs. Size will also concern envelope costs and maybe postage.

Number of pages. Printing costs (including paper) can be quoted in multiples of four pages, but the pages have also to be filled and editorial, photographic, art, and reproduction costs must be worked out according to the number of pages. The number of pages (and the quantity and weight of paper) also concerns postage rates.

Colour or black and white? Each colour beyond the first means an extra printing plate and an extra working. Full colour requires four colours, yellow, magenta, cyan and black. Very good effects can be achieved by using black and a second colour, and very economical use of two colours can be obtained if the second colour is used on the outside front cover, outside back cover and on the two inside pages which are printed together in the four-page plate, all other pages being printed one colour, usually black. Some fairly inexpensive colour work is available with web-offset printing.

Method of distribution. Handing out copies is by far the cheapest method of distributing staff journals but seldom a very satisfactory one. It depends on how and where distribution is made. If copies are taken round from office to office or bench to bench, this method may be all right. An often better but costlier method is to post copies direct to employees' homes where other members of the family have an opportunity of reading about the organisation. Dealer and other external magazines generally require posting. If posted, an accurate mailing list must be maintained.

If the journal can be mailed flat it is more attractive to receive and more inviting to read. A rolled and wrapped magazine can look a mess when unwrapped, and a paper or plastic film envelope is usually preferable. This is an important point. Do not put readers off before they have even opened the journal. The question of folding should be faced when planning page size and choosing paper. Some house journals are printed on too heavy paper, a false attempt to achieve prestige which only succeeds in making the journal look unrealistic. Many a house journal budget is swollen by excessive paper costs.

Editorial costs. Allowance has to be made for the time and professional expertise which will be devoted to the work of producing the journal. This can range from a few spare hours put in by an executive to the employment of a full-time editorial staff or outside consultancy services. It can also include the services of local correspondents, and the costs of layout and design. It is advisable to keep an editorial time-sheet. The editor will have to plan issues, seek material, write some of the contents, rewrite many contributions, prepare issues for the printer, and read proofs.

If desk top publishing is adopted, the demands on the editor's time can be enormous. Now he or she has to be able to write, edit, design, apply typography, and supply the printer with the complete job ready for printing. This can be so time consuming that it may pay to put the job out to a specialist firm such as Dewe Rogerson who have all the necessary equipment and trained staff.

Art and photography. Costs can be minimised if a typographical style is decided for text and titles. The purely photographic 'cold setting' associated with offset-lithography can be both economic and efficient since each character is perfect, whereas hot metal characters can be damaged. One problem with house journals is that photographs are often obtained from amateur sources, and the prints are of varying quality and of different standards so that reproduction up to a good overall standard can demand retouching. The costs involved need to be severely controlled. If feasible, it is better to have all photographs taken professionally.

			£
Editorial costs:	(a)	Editor	0 000.00
	(b)	Contributions	000.00
Art costs:	(a)	Layout and design	000.00
	(b)	Art work	000.00
	(c)	Photography	000.00
	(d)	Retouching	000.00
	(e)	Reproduction fees	00.00
Printing, including typesetting			00 000.00
Envelopes			000.00
Postage			000.00
Other items (e.g. prizes in contests)			000.00
			£00 000.00

Figure 7.5 Budget for a house journal

If the magazine is produced by a consultancy, art costs are the ones which can be high, especially if the outside service tends to be more concerned with *designing* journals than *editing* them.

Paid contributions. Last on the list is the question of buying contributions. Cartoons usually have to be bought, or reproduction fees have to be paid. Some external journals are produced like regular magazines and big-name contributors are sought. Authors may be approached through literary agents and fees agreed. If the editor of a staff journal wishes to reproduce a cartoon from, say, a national newspaper or magazine, he may be able to do so at a nominal fee agreed with the art editor or syndication department if it is a big publishing house. It is not usual to pay members of one's own organisation for contributions, except as a special inducement to attract material.

From the above analysis it is clear that there is an assortment of variables, making it less easy to suggest a reasonably well-defined list of items for even a skeleton annual budget, so the basic form shown in Figure 7.5 must be adapted as required. It is more applicable to journals produced by traditional methods rather than by a DTP system.

Since printing is a major item for consideration in more respects than cost, preliminary discussions with more than one printer will be necessary before any progress can be made with the budget, even before decisions can be made on format, number of pages, and frequency.

House journal costings, in the hands of the amateur, sometimes suffer from either one of two erroneous extremes. First, there is the situation where editing a house journal is regarded as a spare-time task, almost a hobby, and second there are the lush, heavy art-paper, multi-coloured art studio dreams which are excessively expensive and deserve the scorn of professional editors.

5. Support for an exhibitor

Exhibitions are not included in these examples because so much depends on the venue, size of stand, and what is being exhibited. But it is worthwhile glancing at the budget for public relations support for a participant in an exhibition shown in Figure 7.6. Here it should be

	£
Feature articles to coincide with exhibit	000.00
Writing news releases for (a) local press; (b) trade press; (c) city editors; (d) DTI; (e) sales staff, overseas agents, etc; (f) press room; (g) stand; (h) press reception on stand	000.00
Organisation of VIP visit to stand	000.00
Attendance by interesting personalities, e.g. girls in national costume	000.00
Translation of news releases for overseas press, both for home and overseas exhibitions	000.00
Reproduction of releases	00.00
Postage on distribution of releases, including air mail direct to overseas press	00.00
Envelopes for releases, card for photos	00.00
Invitation cards to (a) press preview, or (b) reception on stand; or (c) reception in private room or at nearby hotel; or (d) open invitation to press to visit stand	00.00
Entertainment of guests invited above	000.00
Press packs for guests (NOT for Press Room!)	00.00
Photography for (a) feature articles; (b) press previews; (c) press room; (d) press visitors as invited; (e) press material on stand. Half-plate black-and-white prints fully captioned	000.00
Supply of special information, facilities, photos, articles, requested by press visitors to stand, press room	00.00

Figure 7.6   Budget for exhibitor support

remembered that this support can begin between three and six *months* before the exhibition opens. For example, monthly magazines previewing the exhibition will often want copy six to eight weeks in advance. Too many PROs accept the lack of 'secret new product' news as an excuse for doing nothing, but usually some information about the company and what it does or makes can be supplied.

In all this, there will be liaison with the exhibition press officer from the moment that stand space has been booked.

It is necessary to bear in mind the different publics who can be interested in one's participation, at home and abroad, and to think in terms of before, during, and after the show. This can be a very exacting exercise, valuable because it enhances the influences of the exhibit quite in addition to helping to attract visitors to the stand. It can be important to the the suppliers, shareholders, distributors, and potential overseas buyers that you *are* exhibiting, and your presence has public relations value over and above the exhibited products or services themselves. These points seldom seem to be fully appreciated. In this section we must not forget overseas trade fairs, joint ventures, and store promotions in overseas cities, the participants in these seldom bothering to exploit public relations possibilities to the full.

From these outlines of possible budgets, it will be seen how ideas, techniques, media, timing, and costs go hand-in-hand. For convenience the process is broken down into chapters, but in practice one plans with all the means in mind. Selection of the means is guided by knowledge and experience of their comparative merits in relation to costs. A good practitioner can estimate costs from experience and be able to do so mentally so that in the middle of, say, a board meeting, questions can be answered and proposals made with a fair idea of financial feasibility. For the consultant, working within an agreed fee and expenses which could mean financial disaster if exceeded, the ability to make rapid costings is essential to profitability.

THE VALUE OF BUDGETING

There are two other sides to costing which must be emphasised. First, it is worth reiterating that when a consultant is making proposals to a client, the fees quoted should be based on sound costings which should be set out price-list fashion so that the client knows what is being bought. Nice round-figure arbitrary fee quotations are worthless, ambiguous and unfair to both consultant and client. They do not reflect the hard work that costs the money in professional public relations. A properly calculated proposition will reveal the volume of work that will be put into the account, not how many lunches or gins will be bought. Needless hospitality (which should not be confused with courtesy) is the fetish which has cursed public relations.

Second, when budgets and estimates are presented frankly at all stages, no one is able to criticise the accounts afterwards, provided costings have not been exceeded through carelessness. With an agreed budget, the staff PRO or consultant is always in the position to resist extra demands from management or client unless there is a subsidiary fund to cover the new expenditure. A budget is both a discipline and a refuge.

In budgeting, it pays to be conservative and it is worth reminding ourselves that it is always psychologically sound if final costs are a little less than the original estimates. Good costings are always capable of being trimmed slightly, but this can be done only if every expense is anticipated, and even then allowance should be made for contingencies. But these do not have to be spent, and there must be strict control of all spending, suppliers being told that there is a strict budget.

While it is true that in the past a great deal of money has been frittered away on needless wining and dining, it has nevertheless tended to come from small budgets and has been at the expense of genuine public relations activity. The majority of editors regard their entertainers as being quite mad, for in the end they will publish only what is of interest and value to their readers and so keeps them in their jobs. Such antics only help to convince editors of the superficiality of the public relations world. In a sense, the need to take an editor out to lunch in order to get a story published points to (a) the poverty of the story and (b) the ignorance of the practitioner. Consequently, entertainment should be a diminutive item in the budget.

One of the revelations of budgeting is that so much can be done for so little, compared with the high cost of advertising.

For the in-house practitioner, budgeting possesses a special benefit. If a scheme is presented to management, the inevitable businessman's retort is 'What will it cost?' The PRO should be ready with his budget. That is one way in which the in-house practitioner can earn respect and gain status. Management may not understand public relations, but it does understand figures.

CHAPTER 8

Assessing Results

PROVING THE TANGIBILITY OF PUBLIC RELATIONS

In this chapter, we shall substantiate the claims made in Chapter 1. Evaluation is the practical conclusion of objective planning. Either the objectives have been achieved or they have not, but there may be degrees of success or failure. An inquest may point to good or bad use of techniques, sufficient or insufficient expenditure of labour or money. It is idle to expect results unless there were precise targets in the first place. It is impossible for public relations to work wonders if it is not decided at the outset what wonders it should perform. If those results are to be tangible and worthwhile they need to be more than a collection of press cuttings, or something vague like a 'favourable climate of opinion'. Businessmen need to know what they are getting for their money, and public relations professionals need to be proud of the service they have manifestly provided.

In Chapter 4, we listed a great variety of possible objectives. Now, the question is, did the *planned and sustained public relations effort* (to quote from the IPR definition) succeed in achieving these desired results? Many evaluations will be qualitative rather than quantitative, and sometimes negative rather than positive. At the end of this chapter, we shall attempt to match results to the 34 possible

public relations objectives discussed in Chapter 4.

The mistake is often made of trying to relate public relations to sales and profits, although it may very likely relate to annual trading results and the total picture of the organisation. That total picture includes industrial relations, stock market quotation, growth and future prospects, corporate image and reputation. It may be that as a result of public relations, there is a greater employee stability, better understanding in the financial world, improved international prospects, better trade and customer relations, less risk — if any — of a take-over, and encouragement to enter into new developments. The public relations contributions to an organisation's success and prosperity are varied and numerous, and quite different from those of marketing, advertising and selling, although public relations may well enhance the ability to market, advertise and sell effectively.

THREE WAYS OF EVALUATING RESULTS

Results can be measured in three ways: (i) by *observing* change; (ii) by *experiencing* change; and (iii) by using market research methods to *measure* change. As was shown by the Public Relations Transfer Process in Chapter 2, public relations is mostly about effecting change. Conditions are rarely so perfect that a static position is required, and usually the original study of the situation will have revealed the necessity for change from an inferior to a superior situation.

We can observe changes in industrial relations, management–employee relations, the stability of staff and success in recruiting the right people. Similarly, we can experience changes in dealer relations, or in what is said by opinion leaders, and in the level of complaints.

We can observe, experience and measure change in media relations.

But if we wish to measure the change in opinions, attitudes or awareness, or in the nature and accuracy of the image, we need to repeat the form of research applied originally to appreciate the situation. The reader may refer back to the end of Chapter 3 to reconsider the possible research methods. Here we shall consider some other techniques, starting with the evaluation of media coverage.

EVALUATING MEDIA COVERAGE

Since the industrialised or Western-style countries are rich in mass media, it is inevitable that public relations will exploit media opportunities to the full. It is far easier to communicate with large numbers of people, very quickly and inexpensively, when there are thousands of newspapers and magazines, and numerous TV and radio stations. Media relations may occupy a large part of the programme simply because it is sensible to make use of communication vehicles which already exist.

However, this has provoked misunderstandings about how to evaluate media coverage, mostly because the mass media are also used for advertising purposes. Some businessmen and marketing people can see media only in advertising terms. They also confuse publicity with advertising, although the former may be invited or uninvited.

It is a simple matter to quantify media coverage by adding up the column inches or centimetres of press coverage, the area occupied by pictures, and the minutes of TV and radio coverage. We can arrive at a *volume* of media coverage. It is a bit vague because page sizes, column widths and type sizes will vary, and it might be more realistic to count the number of words printed.

A volume count becomes unrealistic if we now try to calculate what all this would have cost on an advertisement rate-card basis. There are still people who evaluate media coverage on an *advertisement value* basis. No doubt it looks good. It flatters PROs and consultants and pleases employers and clients. Look what we got for nothing, they gloat! Nothing? What about all the labour, materials and expenses? Nothing costs nothing.

The fallacy lies not in the free advertising myth, but in that the editorial programme space and time is priceless and — more important still — the same space and time would not have been bought in that media, in those positions, in that quantity or on those dates. For instance, a sponsored golf tournament might occupy hours of broadcast time, and the cost would have been prohibitive in advertising terms.

Moreover, a good news release contains no puffery and does not seek a free advertisement. The IPR Code of Professional Conduct expects members to respect the integrity of the press. Visnews, in supplying video news releases, avoids any taint of advertising because of its international reputation as a news provider to broadcasters.

There are, however, some practical ways of evaluating media coverage by *value* instead of *volume*.

1. *Readership and audience figures.* It is possible to take circulation figures (ABC), readership figures (NRS), TV audience figures (BARB), or radio audience figures (RJAR) for each cutting or monitored broadcast, and so calculate the estimated

Publication	Ratings	Release 1	Release 2	Release 3
The Times	4	X	X	
The Financial Times	4		X	X
The Daily Telegraph	4	X	X	
The Guardian	4		X	
The Independent	4		X	
The Daily Express	3			
The Daily Mail	3	X		X
The Sun	2			
The Mirror	2	X		
The Daily Star	1			X
Total score		13	20	8

Figure 8.1   Press coverage rating chart

number of people who had the opportunity to read, or view or listen to, the public relations material. These may be called OTS figures — opportunities to see.

2. *Ratings chart.* Values can be given to different publications (or broadcast programmes) according to their value to the sponsor of the story. Rating values differ from one organisation to another, but such a chart might look like Figure 8.1 for an organisation primarily interested in publishing financial and corporate news.

If the organisation was interested in the popular press, the quality ratings would be different. For instance, if the story was about a new Rolls-Royce model, the first two newspapers would be given the highest rating, but if it was about a motor-cycle the popular newspapers would be rated high.

3. *Ratio of publication.* This is an interesting way of measuring the right publications to send stories to, or perhaps to reveal which apparently suitable publications were not accepting stories from the organisation. How many journals printed the story? *What was the hit rate?* The result of this study might also suggest that there was something wrong with the *quality* of the release mailed! That could call for a self-critical analysis. Why were your stories rejected when, perhaps, those of rivals were used? The subject of writing releases will be dealt with in chapters 15–18, but here we can hint at the possibility that the first paragraph was not written in the style used by newspapers the world over; the release was too long; it was badly timed; or it was sent to the wrong journal. Perhaps it was sent to too many journals as happens when standard mailing lists are used instead of compiling a new list to suit each story.

This method of evaluation could be an eye-opener. Send out a hundred bad releases on a poorly compiled mailing list and get one press cutting, and the hit rate is one percent, but send out an excellent publishable story to one journal and get it published and the hit rate is 100 percent!

4. *Tone of coverage.* Now we are progressing.

What is the tone of the coverage? Is it critical, appreciative, or has it improved? This result is self-evident, but before-and-after comparison can be made when the objective was to improve the tone of coverage. Value judgement ratings could be presented with a bar chart or graph in order to provide a physical representation of a change of tone, and this could be really significant. Different colours could be used to distinguish the curves for different publications.

5. *Picture record*. It can be very expensive to send out photographs with every release. A check on which publications actually print your pictures could save money. In future, pictures could be sent to those editors who have printed pictures in the past, for others who do not seem to use pictures, availability of pictures could be stated at the foot of the release. It will also be found that some journals never use supplied pictures, but prefer to take their own.

From the above five methods it will be seen that media coverage can be measured in ways which provide valuable information about the success or otherwise of the press relations campaign. Here there is information of value to employer or client, justifying the campaign, and other information which will enable the practitioner to modify and improve the media relations output. The practitioner can thus *maximise* press coverage once it is known what happens to releases and pictures. Without such research and statistical feedback it will never be known what has been actually achieved, where perhaps things went wrong, and how better results can be gained. Without this information there will merely be a collection of press-cuttings. They are history. This leads us to yet another form of media evaluation.

6. *Effect of media coverage*. What did the media coverage actually *do*? We have already noted change of tone, but were there any physical results? For instance, did people write or phone in for more information? Sometimes an address or telephone number may legitimately appear in a news story, feature article or broadcast item. Did people make enquiries at your stockists? The number of enquiries received by the organisation or by suppliers can be totalled.

Similar information can also be deduced from questionnaires which ask why people bought a product — were they recommended, did they see an advertisement, did they read about it in the press? — and so on. Such questions could be incorporated in a general marketing research survey conducted for marketing purposes — this is where public relations and marketing can work together — or it can be included on a card supplied with purchase of the product, e.g. a guarantee card which has to be returned.

MEASURING PRESS COVERAGE EFFECTIVENESS

A scientific approach to the measurement of press coverage effectiveness probably dates back to 'content analysis', an American method of analysing what was going on in Germany during the Second World War by analysing coverage in the press. Some thirty years later, the idea was taken up by American firms anxious to monitor the value they were getting from press coverage. A number of services emerged such as that of the News Analysis Institute of Pittsburgh who used a computer to evaluate all the variables such as circulation, reader exposure, space secured, markets penetrated, pictures used, newspaper front pages and magazine covers, name or product name in headline, page-or-longer articles, type of presentation, story distribution and advertising values. The Americans like this final evaluation which is really irrelevant. The two basic American approaches have been *image tracking* as developed by A.J. Bar of Washington, and *content comparison* which Dr Walter Lindenmann of New York developed.

A number of systems have also been created in Britain, one being that of Media Measurement of Milton Keynes whose managing director David Phillips has written a book on the subject, *Evaluating Media Coverage* (Kogan Page, 1992). Media Measurement provides press coverage measurement and evaluation services, using a continuous content analysis research programme. It looks at the 'editorial space universe' which fluctuates from month to month, but does so within definite bounds, the public interest fluctuating also. Computer modelling software has been created to compare different campaigns with the editorial effectiveness of in-house press officers and public relations consultancies. This makes possible the prediction of cost and effect for press relations activity and the auditing of the effectiveness of past activity compared with cost.

ACHIEVING THE 34 OBJECTIVES

In Chapter 4 an analysis was made of 34 possible public relations objectives. Now let us take the logical step and consider what sort of results each of these objectives might have achieved. No actual programmes have been discussed in the preceding chapters so these are hypothetical results. Nevertheless, they do help to demonstrate the tangibility of public relations when a management by objectives approach is applied. Possible results in each case are listed briefly, followed by more detailed discussion.

1. Make known a change of image

(i) The new or current activities are now known and understood by relevant publics.

(ii) The organisation is now correctly classified in works of reference such as directories.

(iii) The media identify the organisation by its new image.

The problem here is that the old image will tend to linger on. It took Rentokil a long time to get rid of the *woodworm only* image, and to win recognition as experts in all kinds of *pest control*, *property preservation*, *hygiene* and *supply of office plants*.

It took Burroughs at least three years to change over from an *adding machine* to a *computer image*.

Woolworth have gone through a process of intensive sales promoting TV and press advertising, new store lay-out, and up-market merchandising to kill the image of the *bargain bazaar* of affectionate memory.

We have seen many changes in company names and images in the motor-car industry such as Datsun changing to Nissan, while the chief British motor-car manufacturer has had many changes leading up to the current Rover. Famous names like Hillman, Talbot and Triumph have merged into Peugeot.

British Rail has changed from dirty, old-fashioned trains to ultra-modern high-speed inter-city electric trains, and established an image of *more efficient transportation*.

In days gone by — forty years ago — Calor Gas was associated with old-fashioned-looking appliances and fuel for those who had no supplies of town gas or electricity. Today Calor Gas is a *modern fuel*, there are modern appliances, and the fuel is used by industry, in caravans and on yachts.

The banks have changed their images of secrecy behind frosted glass windows and heavy oak doors to one of shop-like premises where customers can be seen at the counters. The Co-op has lost much of its left-wing political image. The big local co-operative societies with their department stores, numerous bakery, milk, laundry, coal, funeral and other services, and their member-shareholders and dividend on purchases, have mostly disappeared. In many parts of the country, the 'co-op' is a CWS supermarket or late-opening store. The Co-operative Permanent Building Society has buried its former Co-op image by taking the new name Nationwide.

Hard to believe though this may be, Save the Children has changed its image from *saving starving British children* after the First World War to that of an *international relief organisation*.

Special problems occur when former colonies become independent and adopt new names such as Ghana, Zambia or Malawi — usually of important local significance — but which are confusing to strangers abroad whose geography has to be relearned. Siam became accepted fairly quickly as Thailand, but it may take time for Myanmar to replace Burma, while new names have appeared with the dissolution of the USSR. Not every country enjoys the world-wide publicity of Zimbabwe which is not an easy name for Westerners to conjure with.

2. Change of policy

(i) The supply of goods through wholesalers, instead of direct to retailers, or the other way round is known and understood by the trade.

(ii) New methods of payment or credit facilities are known and understood.

(iii) The product range has been expanded or reduced and this is understood.

(iv) The organisation has diversified into other areas of business, as banks and building societies have done, and this is known and understood.

(v) An industrial product is now available to the consumer market, and this is understood by the new market.

The above examples indicate a few of the results which may be achieved. Again, the measure is of knowledge and awareness of the new policy, and the *opinion survey* is the surest way of testing this. An opinion survey could include questions to discover *attitudes* to the change of policy as well as *awareness* of it. This could be important, and a public relations operation in itself.

But much depends on the change of policy. For instance, if the change is likely to be disliked or resented, it will be necessary to monitor criticism or complaints. The success of the public relations could be measured against the extent of articulate opposition. In the case of a retail product, a postal questionnaire could be sent to retailers to detect the extent and nature of customer reactions. Rationalisation of product lines, packing in plastic rather than glass, or making products obsolescent and unrepairable after a certain time, can arouse resentment.

Another method might be to assess comment by the media including readers' letters. Consumer features and phone-ins could be monitored to see whether they were dealing with complaints about our product or service.

Looking at sales figures, a check could be made on whether sister products have suffered any fall in sales. The danger of a change of policy is that it can have many implications. While the rationalisation of a product range may cause temporary annoyance, a new more convenient pack could provide 'added value' and increase sales.

In the transport business, a change of timetable or the introduction of new equipment may have a good or bad effect on goodwill, and the success of the public relations programme will lie in the extent to which goodwill has been maintained or improved. Side effects may have to be considered: larger aircraft may carry more people more comfortably and more cheaply, yet passengers may be frustrated because it takes longer to handle check-ins, baggage reclaim and customer processing. The assessment must therefore consider all aspects. The same problem could apply to the introduction of new car-ferries, hovercraft, jetfoils, trains or buses.

3. Informing about a new project

(i) The nature and purpose of the project is understood.
(ii) Prejudice or hostility towards it have been overcome or minimised (e.g. the Channel Tunnel or changes in the National Health Service).
(iii) The duration of the work and the anticipated completion date is understood.
(iv) The benefits to various publics are understood by the money market (e.g. the City of London).

The extent of knowledge and understanding of a long-term project could affect the attitudes of influential people — MPs, local authority representatives, journalists, broadcasters, investment analysts, shareholders, potential customers, employees, all kinds of people — and so public relations activity in the form of progress reports and news stories could be valuable. Their effectiveness can be monitored by checking the knowledge and understanding of the publics concerned.

The research techniques may range from questionnaires and various kinds of independent surveys to assessing what is being said by the media. The *fairness* and *accuracy* of media reports will be a measure of the success of public relations endeavours. This will be more significant than the *volume* of coverage gained. The tally of column inches or centimetres will be less significant than what is actually *said* in *those* columns. A whole page article in *The Sun* might be valueless, whereas a couple of paragraphs in the *Financial Times* might be very important, while the opposite might be true for another subject. Thus a qualitative assessment will be necessary here.

Some projects can have traumatic effects on all kinds of people affected by them, as has been seen with not only the Channel Tunnel itself but the rail link. Proposals to build new superstores by supermarket chains provoke all kinds of resentments, as do those for new nuclear installations, motorways and extensions to airports.

4. Market education

(i) Retailers are familiar with the product and are able to explain it to customers.
(ii) Consumers or users understand the product.
(iii) If it is a new product not yet launched there is favourable anticipation of its availability.
(iv) If it is an existing product there is good understanding of its various benefits and uses.

The results of public relations activity could influence the advertising campaign in two ways:

(i) When it was decided that the selling situation was sufficiently favourable because prospective buyers were sufficiently well informed, advertising *could commence* and
(ii) the *weight* of advertising could be determined by the extent to which the market had been familiarised. Some launches require excessive sledge-hammer advertising campaigns simply because there has been a lack of market education. Some marketers — and advertising agencies — are reluctant to use the public relations techniques of market education.

The state of the selling situation could be learned by the use of research appropriate to the subject. An *opinion survey* could test knowledge and awareness; a more *structured questionnaire* applied to a *field survey* could study customer preferences and willingness to purchase. *Product pre-tests* and *hall-tests* could define specific likes, dislikes and preferences. The marketing strategy as a whole could be *test-marketed*. The extent of *dealer-response* would indicate not only the ability of the sales force but the lack of sales resistance due to market education. *Here we see public relations in the role of ice-breaker.*

5. Informing the trade

(i) Distributors, especially retailers, understand the company's range of products, and how to obtain them.

(ii) Because they appreciate the saleability of the products, and consequently their profitability, retailers never permit themselves to be out-of-stock.

(iii) Similarly, because of their belief in the products, retailers make sure they are displayed prominently, and make the best use of point-of-sale display material.

(iv) Being aware of forthcoming advertising, retailers ensure that they have stocks to meet anticipated demand, thus effecting adequate distribution. (This does not always happen. In 1992 a new pharmaceutical product was advertised on television, but shops sold out and wholesalers were unable to replace stocks. Obviously, the distribution system had been poorly informed about the advertising campaign and orders had been too timid.)

Results can be assessed in much the same way as discussed in Chapter 14, although perhaps less positively. Dealer education is more on-going so that better customer relations are established for the company through the medium of the distributor. It is a form of double rewards since customer relations are improved for the retailer too. But with a familiarisation programme as discussed under this heading, we are concerned mainly with improving the *supplier–dealer* relationship. Thus, the more the dealer understands the supplier, the more readily is he likely to receive and welcome the supplier's representative. The measure of this kind of public relations is likely to be found in salesmen's

reports — even if salesmen credit themselves with improved relations and sales!

One test could be a mailed questionnaire to distributors to record and measure their knowledge and understanding of the company. If this could be done *before* and *after* the public relations effort with an interval of at least six months, it would be possible to chart the effect of the campaign. This could be done *image-study* style by an independent research unit. The questions could be asked about a number of companies who also supplied the sample of distributors, the sponsor's identity not being revealed by the organisers of the poll who would identify themselves as independent researchers.

6. Overcoming misunderstanding

(i) Essential publics are now satisfied that the problem no longer exists.

(ii) These publics understand the efforts that have been made to rectify the unfortunate situation.

(iii) These publics are complimentary about the organisation's efforts.

(iv) The media now report the organisation in the normal way and do not refer to the problem.

(v) Adverse effects such as fall in consumer sales, retail orders or share prices have been reversed.

If sales had dropped as a result of ill-will, and misconceptions had been erased by public relations efforts, there would be a marked return to healthy sales which would need no testing.

But it might be a more complicated situation as in the case of ITT when research had revealed a list of misconceptions held by top businessmen, academics, civil servants and the business press. The famous ITT corporate image campaign using dramatic corporate advertisements (e.g. *Who The Devil Does ITT Think It Is?*), and publication of the international external house journal *Profile*, among other things, led the public relations team in Brussels to be well satisfied with the response and change of attitude among these influential publics. The results revealed themselves mostly in direct response ranging from a better informed business press (e.g. the *Financial Times*), and the willingness of the *Guardian* to publish a feature article (written by an ITT PRO) dismissing its previous criticism, to the hundreds of complimentary letters which ITT received.

Perhaps another measure of success in overcoming a misunderstanding will be the extent to which the problem is forgotten. By gaining credit for a company's genuine achievements it is possible to make excellence bury a past misadventure. This is a positive way of dealing with a negative situation, a swings and roundabouts approach. In public relations it is seldom wise to be apologetic. Some crises are self-inflicted.

How many people now remember whose meat pies contained foreign bodies, which manufacturer of chemicals was blamed for the death of farm livestock, which travel company's brochures offended against the Trade Descriptions Act, or whose canned fish poisoned a number of people? Bad memories do not linger on. It is a psychological trick that people tend to remember the good and forget the bad, as instanced by the common expression 'the good old days' as if they had not also been bad! This is one reason why one should not be too sensitive about criticism or errors: it is better to get on with projecting positive stories than trying to correct some of the errors that inevitably occur in the media.

7. Organise a product recall

(i) A satisfactory proportion of faulty products has been recalled.
(ii) The organisation is praised for its action, (as Marks and Spencer were when they recalled soft toys which were found to be dangerous for children).
(iii) There is a favourable response from the trade in handling returned products,

and in appreciating the company's action.
(iv) A calamity has been converted into a praiseworthy effort.
(v) The company's image has been enhanced by the way the recall was handled (e.g. Figure 8.2).

Many companies have experienced product failures which have required replacement, modification or refund, and reputations have been rescued by prompt action, using both advertising and public relations to make known the need for recall. At first sight this may seem disastrous. To admit there are bits of broken glass in a baby food, for instance, could imply negligence and destroy confidence in the product, and it may seem very undesirable to make any such admission.

In fact, the company's insurers may insist that no admission be made, and very diplomatic procedures may be necessary. This did happen when mercury was accidentally introduced into a cattle food, and the PRO had to work with food ministries to temporarily stop the movement of cattle across European frontiers until it was discovered whether tainted meat had had any effect on humans. Although this was an industrial product, the company also made leading brands of foodstuff and unfortunate publicity could have devastated sales. In this case the result was a very satisfactory one, but it took a month of cautious behind-the-scenes public relations work to avoid a worse situation.

Marks and Spencer were in the news again in February 1992 when they announced the withdrawal of two kinds of Italian wine which had been found to be contaminated, although not dangerously, with slight traces of fungicide, offering refunds on returned bottles. The speed of the recall, and the widespread national publicity given to it, did no harm to Marks and Spencer's reputation.

To deny any fault in the product can cause immense mischief, as did occur with a certain

Figure 8.2   A recall advertisement which appeared in the British press in March 1992

make of motor-car which was involved in a serious accident, and with a pharmaceutical product which caused crippled children. Generally, it is foolish to attempt to cover up a product fault, and a generous response is more likely to be provoked if a fault is admitted and dealt with quickly.

8. Preparing the stock market

(i) A new share, rights or scrip issue has been taken up successfully.
(ii) A flotation has been over-subscribed.
(iii) A privatisation scheme has been successful.

(iv) Those who advise shareholders — investment analysts, financial journalists, bankers and brokers — were well-informed about a new issue.

As will be seen from the case study in Chapter 27, when a company which has no counterpart among quoted companies goes public and offers shares for the first time this can be a risky business, unless the market is sufficiently well informed about the company's history and prospects. In this case the company's regular attention to public relations paid off.

The stock market is very susceptible to success and very cautious about the unknown. If a private company is 'going public', or a quoted company is launching a new share issue or raising a debenture, the success of such a venture will depend on the *confidence* of the market.

The most important part of this market consists of the investment analysts and city editors on the one hand, and the big institutional buyers such as pension funds, insurance companies and unit trusts on the other. Confidence depends on knowledge. The company *record* is all-important.

There was the remarkable case of the Rolls-Royce privatisation, when there were fears that the public would not take up the shares because of the company's earlier bankruptcy, but so great was the British public's affection for Rolls-Royce that the flotation was a success.

A painstaking public relations programme over preceding weeks, months, maybe years, can make sure that a deservedly good record is thoroughly known and understood. The results lie in the take-up, and better still the over-subscription of the shares, as with the privatisation of British Gas.

Even shares with a poor market can gain from better knowledge. The shares of a building products firm fell from 120p to 30p, but when it became known that they were entering the solar energy field the shares rose to 38p in two days.

9. Stock market confidence

(i) The share price has been kept steady because the money market has been made aware of the company's stability, success and good prospects.
(ii) As a consequence, a take-over bid has been averted.
(iii) A fall in share price has been averted because misleading information or false rumours have been successfully countered.
(iv) Shareholder loyalty has been maintained.

The stock market can be volatile and is easily influenced by market forces over which the company has no control, and yet its fate may depend on what happens not only on the London Stock Exchange, but on stock exchanges and bourses throughout the world which are subject to 24-hour satellite communication and computerised speculations.

Moreover, financial information is very sensitive and cannot be issued as randomly or freely as product information. Share prices must not be boosted artificially, and yet those dealing with shares need to be correctly informed.

10. Staff recruitment

(i) Job applicants understand what the employer does and what the advertised job entails.
(ii) Objections to the industry or kind of job have been overcome or minimised.
(iii) Sources and advisers of recruits, such as schools, colleges, universities, careers advisers and head hunters understand the career opportunities offered by the organisation.

Success or failure will be self-evident by the number or calibre of applicants and the level of actual recruitment but it will still be sensible to record the extent of the success or failure. The personnel department will have the figures of applications, offers, acceptances and refusals.

A further test may be to include in application forms (if they are used), or to ask at interview, questions which probe the applicant's understanding of the organisation. What proportion of applicants or interviewees appear to have been reached by the public relations effort? Does the image of the organisation coincide with that projected by the public relations activities, including the explanatory panel in the recruitment advertisement?

If the public relations effort has been aimed at certain areas of the country, or at certain places of education, do the new recruits originate from these sources? *In other words, results should be married to objectives.* If the aim was to recruit more university graduates, what proportion of applicants *are* graduates, and what is the percentage increase in the number of graduate applicants?

Another method of testing the results of recruitment public relations is to draw a graph of advertising and monthly recruitment figures with an additional curve for the impact of public relations. If an increase in the number of recruits follows this effort it will prove the effectiveness of the programme, assuming that recruitment advertising has been of a similar weight throughout the year.

To explain this more clearly, Figure 8.3 is a chart with curves for a constant monthly expenditure on advertising and varying numbers of applications, plus one for a special public relations effort, say, in the summer vacation when graduates might be seeking jobs, although a recruitment information campaign could be applied at any time of the year. This is merely a demonstration.

11. Staff stability and 12. Improve employee–management relations

(i) There is a reduction in staff losses.
(ii) There is a reduction in absenteeism.
(iii) There has been an increased take-up of equity schemes.
(iv) There is better understanding of the organisation's policies.
(v) There is better understanding of the organisation's managerial structure, and who is responsible for each function.
(vi) There is evidence of greater job satisfaction.

Again the results will be self-evident: either staff stay, or stay longer, or they leave. But more precise information may be necessary. How much *longer* do they stay? How many *more* people stay longer or permanently? For some staff, such as secretaries, married women, trainees or people dependent upon

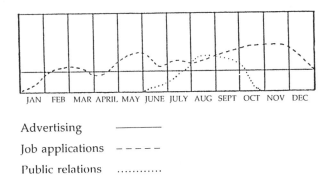

| | JAN | FEB | MAR | APRIL | MAY | JUNE | JULY | AUG | SEPT | OCT | NOV | DEC |

Advertising ————
Job applications – – – – –
Public relations ············

Figure 8.3 Public relations effort compared

promotion prospects, we may have an average figure of staff turnover and replacement. Has there been an *improvement* in these figures? Or how *long* do people remain with the organisation *after* their period of training? Such figures could be a measure of job satisfaction, not merely loyalty or even inertia.

A questionnaire could be distributed among employees, and this could reveal the extent to which employee relations were dependent upon communication. Such a questionnaire using the *semantic differential* method of rating, could be worded as shown in Figure 8.4.

QUESTIONNAIRE
TO BE COMPLETED BY EMPLOYEES

Please place tick (√) in boxes as appropriate

	Very good	Good	Fair	Fairly poor	Poor	Bad
Working conditions	☐	☐	☐	☐	☐	☐
Salary/wages	☐	☐	☐	☐	☐	☐
Bonus/profit sharing schemes	☐	☐	☐	☐	☐	☐
Promotion prospects	☐	☐	☐	☐	☐	☐
Staff training programme	☐	☐	☐	☐	☐	☐
Social facilities	☐	☐	☐	☐	☐	☐
Canteen facilities	☐	☐	☐	☐	☐	☐
Communication with management	☐	☐	☐	☐	☐	☐
Company's trading performance	☐	☐	☐	☐	☐	☐
Company's trading prospects	☐	☐	☐	☐	☐	☐
Company's environmental behaviour	☐	☐	☐	☐	☐	☐
Company's public image	☐	☐	☐	☐	☐	☐

Figure 8.4   Employee questionnaire

This is just a simple example, and more or different questions could be asked according to the nature of different organisations, and also according to the public relations efforts which have been made to create job satisfaction through better knowledge and understanding of the company. The final report would show the percentage of employees expressing various degrees of satisfaction or dissatisfaction. This could also be broken down into types of employees — e.g. office staff, factory staff — expressing various views. Confidentiality is important, and the identities of employees should not be requested.

However, the 'face-sheet data' could identify useful information such as sex, age, marital status, department or branch, length of service and so on so that the findings could report the percentages of different categories of employee who gave certain answers. This could reveal weaknesses in communication which could be rectified through the internal media.

But according to *The Economist* on February 5 1992, such figures can be misleading. Japanese-owned factories are not always models of industrial efficiency. There may have been no lay-offs in Californian factories for five years, but 'their unusually high employee turnover meant that, to reduce staff, they never had to sack anyone'.

13. Right calibre applicants

(i) Applicants of the right calibre, e.g. educational background, training, qualifications, experience and so on are being attracted to apply for job vacancies.

(ii) The number of irrelevant applications has been reduced.

(iii) Consequently time has been saved in interviewing prospective candidates.

Once more, the success or failure of the public relations effort will depend on the experience of the personnel department. Has the number of irrelevant applicants been reduced, and are applications now being received from people better qualified to fill the jobs advertised? This should mean that time has been saved in examining applications and that better appointments have been made.

This screening process can be a great service to the busy personnel manager. It is not only a matter of saving the personnel manager's time: it is poor public relations for a company if it has to disappoint large numbers of applicants who could have been deterred from applying in the first place. Far better, for example, if a vacancy advertisement for a public relations person stated 'must be able to speak German', or 'must have five years experience in High-Tech public relations' or 'holds the CAM Diploma'. Thus, public relations enters into the wording of the advertisement.

14. Re-location to new venue

(i) The desired percentage of staff have agreed to move to the new location.
(ii) The need for the move has been understood by employees and their families.
(iii) The trade union(s) is reconciled to the move, and there has been no industrial dispute.
(iv) Social and other arrangements on behalf of the staff have been successfully negotiated with organisations at the new location.

This is a sensitive issue which has to be resolved to the satisfaction of everyone involved, and it usually calls for a programme of internal public relations activity which may take weeks or even months. Initially, such a move is bound to be unpopular with a lot of people for whom it is a very disturbing prospect.

Has the company succeeded in transferring the desired number of staff to the new location? Since willingness to move depends so much on information, the public relations effort is considerable and its success or failure will be reflected in achievement or otherwise of the target figure. The desired percentage will depend on (a) the number of trained or experienced personnel the company wishes to retain; and (b) the number of staff who can be replaced by available labour at the new location. The cost of training new staff may affect the viability of the move. For example, one company set a target of encouraging 25 percent of its present staff to move from the old location in London to a new one in Brighton some 50 miles away. With the help of a model public relations programme, this was achieved.

15. Maintaining customer interest

(i) The desired percentage of customers is making repeat or replacement purchases.
(ii) There is good take up of 'piggy backed' accessories for products such as motorcars, cameras and computers, customers understanding their value and how they can extend the benefits of the basic product.
(iii) There is evidence that customers are buying sister products with which they are now familiar.
(iv) Customers are communicating with the organisation about their satisfactory experiences of the product, or are making useful suggestions.

Customer interest will depend on the nature of the product, but here we have an after-market situation which public relations activities can stimulate. It may be to do with food ingredients and cookery books, recipes or demonstrations, how to get the most out of a piece of equipment, or how to profit from financial services.

The positive result will lie in sales — have they been increased, maintained, revived or repeated as the case may be? Are products and services being used in new ways, used regularly, is new interest aroused, or do customers make repeat purchases or renewals?

Sales figures alone may not reveal the whole

truth, and more specific information can be gained from *consumer panels* or *omnibus surveys*. Such research can reveal who buys what, where, when and in what quantities, and questions can be asked about usage.

Media monitoring — e.g. press cuttings — will also show the extent to which the product or service continues to be discussed or recommended, whether new uses are proposed, or whether it has been superseded by rival products or services. Consumer interest may depend on the product's regular acceptance by the media, so the negative effect of disfavour could be important. A problem may be that a product is ignored or regarded wrongly by the media, and this would be reflected in either the absence or the content of media coverage. Vital results could be the extent to which a public relations programme has overcome disinterest or misrepresentation.

16. Educating distributors

(i) There has been a reduction in customer complaints.

(ii) Dealers are re-stocking more quickly. Advertising is more effective. Do sales respond to current advertising? Do customers mention advertising? Are there more requests for the product by name?

(iii) Dealer audit research shows a better market share for the product.

(iv) Dealer relations have improved — salesmen more welcome, orders more forthcoming. Dealers more familiar with the product.

(v) Dealers have become more willing to use point-of-sale material, permit in-store displays/demonstrations, and generally co-operate with sales promotion exercises.

(vi) More dealerships have been opened. Requests have been received from prospective stockists.

(vii) Accounts have been paid more punctually, improving cash flow.

(viii) More dealers have attended stand at trade exhibitions.

(ix) Entries have increased in dealer competitions, e.g. window display contests.

(x) More dealers have attended dealer conferences, and similar trade functions.

A longer list of results has been given here because this is sometimes a neglected area of public relations. The manufacturer is remote from the final customer, but distributors — especially retailers — have a face-to-face relationship with customers. Good dealer relations must never be overlooked.

17. Explaining diversity

(i) Consumers/users are now aware of the diversity of the organisation's activities.

(ii) The money market, from investment analysts to shareholders, are now aware of the diversity of the organisation's activities.

(iii) The media are similarly aware so that they understand the size and importance of the organisation.

(iv) Where necessary, distributors are well-informed about this diversity.

Awareness of the diversity of an organisation's activities can be measured by an awareness or opinion survey. What percentage of what kind of people are now aware of the organisation's diversity compared with the base period before commencement of the public relations programme? Before the campaign mentioned earlier, the diversity of ITT's business activities were not widely known. It was thought to be a 'telephone' or 'cable' firm, yet it also engaged in hotels, insurance and cosmetics.

But there can be other means of checking according to the nature of the organisation. If it is possible to invite customers to fill in questionnaires — as hoteliers, airline and package-tour operators do — questions can also be included to discover what respondents know about associated companies. The semantic differential method can be used as described in section 11 *Staff stability*.

Practically, the 'halo effect' or 'reflected glory effect' of using a common logo, or a phrase such as 'a member of the so-and-so group of companies' or 'an XYZ company' could result in greater confidence on the part of distributors and consumers, which in turn should be reflected in more business. The umbrella effect of the parental image of a conglomerate can be one of strength and improved reputation.

The revelation that a company is engaged in numerous enterprises quite different from the one normally or originally associated with it may create a better overall reputation. Tate and Lyle have often been regarded as a sugar monopolist whereas they are engaged in many other industries. Similarly, ITT were not only involved in electronics and telecommunications, and Ocean Transport have many land-based operations. Some tobacco companies have diversified into other products such as potato crisps, drinks, sauces and even fashion goods. Guinness, with its acquisition of Distillers, now markets spirits as well as beers. These revelations are sometimes made in corporate advertisement and announcements of the annual reports and accounts, and a measure of success may be the number of applications for publications which are offered in these advertisements. (N.B. ITT is mentioned because it was a classic example of public relations, but it has now been taken over by the French company Alcatel.)

Creating the larger picture of an organisation — *filling out the corporate image* — will be one of the objectives of many public relations activities to mention only press receptions, feature articles, videos, external house journals and exhibitions.

18. Maintaining confidence

(i) Public confidence has been maintained in an organisation or its products or services in spite of adverse publicity (e.g. sales have not been affected in spite of protests by pressure groups or by a scandal concerning a company personality).

(ii) Trade confidence has remained high in spite of the above situation.

(iii) Employee confidence has been maintained in spite of rumours of take-over bids or other destabilising influences.

As we have pointed out already, confidence is a mercurial quality, and it is necessary to keep the temperature up!

Confidence is expressed in the following ways: automatic renewal of orders, recommendations, a good share price, ready stocking of the product, or strong market share. In other words, there is a general air of buoyancy. Gaining credit for achievements, sponsorships, always being in the news, regular reports of progress — all such efforts aim to maintain confidence, always assuming that this confidence is justified by the satisfaction of buyers, users and other publics ranging from employees to the stock market.

While once again the results of the public relations endeavours may be self-evident, it is unwise to be complacent, and an image, opinion or consumer panel survey may detect changes in the *degree* of confidence enjoyed by the organisation and its products or services. If such a survey makes comparisons with other firms, it may be found that there is greater confidence in a rival, meaning reduced confidence in the sponsor of the survey.

Consequently, it may not be enough to say 'there is still confidence' in an organisation if it is endangered by new confidence enjoyed elsewhere. People may prefer to fly by those airlines which fly newer aircraft, such as versions of the Airbus; buy where their credit or charge card is accepted; or fill up at garages with self-service. The extent to which people are more willing to travel to France by Channel Tunnel, rather than by air or sea can be a matter of confidence.

Willingness to change and offer new and better services may be a means of maintaining confidence, and public relations methods may have to be used to keep customers informed.

Conversely, there could be merit in a conservative policy that things are as they were, say, unspoilt. The National Trust and English Heritage are anxious to maintain confidence that natural or historic values will be maintained. There could be industrial conservation in the sense that special efforts are taken to control pollution and protect the environment.

19. Explaining needs of charities

   (i) That the independent voluntary role of the charity is properly understood.

   (ii) That it depends wholly on voluntary contributions is understood.

   (iii) That its affairs are administered efficiently is accepted.

   (iv) That its patronage by an eminent person is appreciated.

   (v) That the success of its work is well known.

   (vi) That the nature of its work is understood (e.g. different cancer charities are responsible for different work ranging from running homes for terminal patients to research).

   (vii) That its expenditure on direct mail appeals and house journals is accepted as justifiable expense.

Greater response to appeals will be the principal means of measuring public relations success, and it may not be necessary to indulge in research. Increased donations and other gifts, and more voluntary assistance, are not unlike increased sales for a commercial company, and a charity may also enjoy increased sales of goods such as Christmas cards, calendars, ties, publications and gifts.

An organisation like the National Trust can measure public relations success by an increased number of visitors to its properties.

These are direct and practical results for organisations which spend little on advertising, and rely heavily on the knowledge, understanding, sympathy and support produced by public relations activities such as house journals, year books and other print. The comparison will be between a previous situation when there had not been a certain programme, and the situation following an objective one.

For example, one Christmas a certain children's charity complained through a television programme that it was receiving an uncommonly disappointing inflow of toys, which was probably due to gifts being donated to another charity which had appealed on behalf of refugee children. The result was that the disappointed charity now received its usual inflow of toys, and the effort was quickly measurable.

Sometimes, the result of activity can be *instantly* recognised. This happened with another charity which feared a shortage of flag sellers because of a threatened rail strike, but when the charity was featured in a popular TV chat show a few days before the flag day, there was a record turn-out of volunteer streetsellers of the charity's 'flags'.

Appreciation that charities are independent voluntary bodies, and not extensions of state-funded services, can help to increase public support. Nevertheless 'independence' is a separate issue since state organisations such as hospitals also invite and receive outside aid. Consequently, this is a tougher assignment, and it could be advantageous to research the effect of public relations. Here are some ways in which this could be done:

   (i) One method will be to monitor media reports to see whether a true picture is being presented to the public. A press cutting agency could be used for this purpose, and broadcasts could also be monitored by one of the specialist agencies listed in the *Hollis Press and Public Relations Annual*.

(ii) A street survey could be conducted to poll attitudes and awareness, and if the services of a marketing research agency could not be afforded it might be possible to obtain the voluntary services of sociology students at a university, or better still have a university with marketing or sociology students adopt the survey as an operational exercise.

(iii) A newspaper, or magazine could be asked to run an independent poll among its readers, using a printed questionnaire. This does have the weakness that only interested readers may bother to mail in the completed questionnaire. Again, a publication might be willing to donate advertisement space for the insertion of a questionnaire on behalf of the charity, and a Freepost or Business Reply system could at least make return of the questionnaire postage free.

(iv) A simple poll could be organised through schools in a sample of large towns, heads of schools being asked to supply questionnaires to senior pupils who could seek answers from their parents. The school would be responsible for returning the completed questionnaires to the charity. This might be seen as an interesting and educational way of helping the charity. It would be courteous to first of all seek the agreement of the Education Officer for each educational authority.

You may consider that some of the above research methods are subject to excessive bias, and are less reliable than surveys conducted by professional research units using more statistically reliable samples and more efficient collection and tabulation of data. This is true on the basis that one gets what one pays for, but where funds do not permit independent professional research alternative 'amateur' methods can produce useful information of a limited kind inexpensively. Much depends on interpretation of the data, and due allowance being made for error. For instance, *an item of information which is repeated by many respondents could be significant*. If, for example, the same misconception occurred, it would be clear that action needed to be taken to correct this false idea.

20. Credit for achievement

(i) Stories about the organisation's achievements have appeared in the press and in TV programmes.

(ii) Relevant publics now have a better understanding of the organisation's achievements.

(iii) The corporate image has been clarified and enhanced by better knowledge and understanding of the organisation's achievements.

(iv) This knowledge has encouraged employees to be proud of working for the organisation.

(v) This knowledge has strengthened the regard of the money market, including that of shareholders.

This objective may be combined with several of the 34 objectives under discussion, and the extent of success or failure may be reckoned in other results. But assuming that this is a principal or only objective because, in the past, an organisation has been lax about telling its very worthwhile story, we can consider some methods of assessing public relations efforts to put the record straight.

We may well start from either a zero or a negative situation when there is either no knowledge or understanding to one where prejudice and hostility exist.

Let us take the last situation first. Knowledge and understanding may be warped simply by default. *Directory entries* may not be submitted because they are considered unimportant, somebody has been 'too busy' to fill in a publisher's request for information, entrants have been put off by directory rackets, or there has been ignorance of the existence of a directory. *Directories and year books are extremely valuable public relations media*, and most programmes should include attention to the possibility, and the accuracy, of entries. Some of these annuals have editorials which contain recommendations. As a simple example of the failure to use directories, that excellent publication *Hollis Press and Public Relations Annual* could contain the names of many more PROs if they would only take the trouble to submit entries.

Here is a true *example* of the result of being *absent* from important directories. A financial organisation was worried about its image in the City. An investigation was carried out and repeatedly informants gave unfavourable answers. It was discovered that informants, not knowing of the organisation, were referring to a well-known international year book, and since it contained no reference to the organisation they concluded that it was of no consequence, probably of ill-repute! Thus, statements such as *'wouldn't touch it with a barge pole'* really meant *'it's not in the book'*. Directories and year books can be Bibles of industries and professions. Sometimes, entries cost nothing.

Credit for achievement may just mean *proof of existence*, but it can also mean *appreciation of excellence*. This may influence stocking by dealers, sales, applications for jobs, success of share issues, sympathetic consideration by Government departments and local authority committees, and better understanding by opinion leaders. From this we can see how 'objectives' and 'publics' go together so that results will be related to the attitudes of these publics. Results can therefore be checked according to the effect the public relations effort has had on these publics. These results may be obvious — a new share issue has been taken up, even over-subscribed — but when less obvious, we may have to combine interpretations of press cuttings with, say, an image or attitude study.

But an important point is made in this section: public relations can be very practical — *thoroughly tangible* — when the objective is also a practical one. Intangible public relations occurs only when there is no public relations clear-cut objective, as when an organisation merely seeks media coverage for its own sake.

Another result may be that once an organisation's achievements are known, it will become a sought after subject for reports, features, radio and TV interviews and programme material. An 'interesting' organisation can produce a snowball demand for information and facilities, and such recognition and acclaim is a positive measure of public relations success. We can all think of organisations whose spokesmen are sought, quoted or interviewed when topics touching them are in the news. We may well wonder why *other* organisations are not approached. The answer is that the achievements of these sought after organisations are *recognised* and their spokespeople are *approachable*.

Seeking credit for achievement is a straightforward objective, and there is every reason for assessing results scientifically if they are not satisfactorily self-evident.

21. Community relations

(i) Local people understand what the organisation does.

(ii) Relevant local government officials, committees and representatives understand what the organisation does.

(iii) Schools, parents and so on understand job opportunities in the organisation.

(iv) Local organisations such as police, fire and health services understand the nature of the work undertaken by the organisation, including its hazards.

(v) The media are familiar with the organisation's activities and know who to contact for information.

(vi) Where applicable there is a good dialogue with trade union officials.

A good neighbour policy has to be worked

out, and there can be many rewards when the organisation needs the assistance of local people.

What results do you want from community relations? A 'do-good' programme is pointless, and may be regarded as the capitalist conscience seeking redemption, as gifts from Caesar. You really cannot buy goodwill, although the attempt is made. Rather, the organisation has to earn its rightful place in the community. The organisation should not see itself as an interloper, a foreigner, a hostile force which has to bring gifts and beg for acceptance. It has to be a joiner, a member, a contributor, a part of the lifeblood of the community. Results will not be the extent to which the organisation is liked or even admired, for *itself*, but the extent to which it has become integrated in the community.

This process of assimilation can be measured against purposes such as those outlined in Chapter 4 on Objectives. Do people understand what goes on beyond the factory gates, is the progress of the company a matter of local pride, is there a waiting list of applicants for jobs, do the public services co-operate with the company (and the company with them), are personnel invited to serve on local committees, and so on? These achievements will be the results of the public relations programme which will, of course, be inherent in the total behaviour and communications of the organisation and its people.

Some of these results may not be easily achieved in a period of recession, lay off, unemployment and closures, and yet good community relations may be all the more necessary. Recession is not the local company's fault, its good name needs to be preserved, and faith in the future must not be abandoned.

22. Political relations

(i) Local councillors, MPs and MEPs know and understand the organisation.

(ii) The needs or problems of the organisa-

tion are understood when decisions or new legislation are being made.

(iii) The same applies to local authority officials, and civil servants in ministries, departments and quangos.

(iv) There have been actions by Ministers and others with power to act which are in the interests of the organisation (e.g. a reduction in VAT or the setting of import quotas).

(v) A Bill supporting the organisation's interests is successful.

(vi) An offensive Bill has been amended or defeated.

(vii) There has been a change of public opinion, as produced by lobbying or as revealed by an opinion poll.

Since we can discuss only circumspect relations with elected representatives, or with members of the Civil Service and local government officers (not forgetting the officials of quangos), it may now be asked what results may be forthcoming and how can they be recorded? We are bound to consider the original objectives. If a Bill was to be presented to Parliament, and if enacted it would have been detrimental to our organisation, the results would lie in either the failure of the Bill to reach the Royal Assent, or of an Act which contained such amendments to the original Bill that it was not detrimental or at least less severely so.

We have to assume here that the organisation's case was not against the national interest. This is, of course, difficult and dangerous ground. Insurance companies, banks and building societies will be anxious to avoid nationalisation, but proponents of nationalisation will believe that they are acting in the national interest. Nevertheless, in a democratic country, every special interest group is entitled to lobby in its own interests.

So it may be said that a political programme can be measured by positive or negative results. Whether it be lead-free petrol, divorce laws, the slaughter of seals, or child porno-graphy, or whether it be privatisation of a state enterprise, consumer protection, safety regula-tions or import quotas — these are all topics involving political public relations which is capable of assessment. At the very least, the public relations effort — the lobbying of MPs, the informing of political correspondents, public discussion in the media, facility visits for politicians — will have contributed to the decision even if party policies and individual consciences also played their parts.

A detrimental decision made by Parliament, Council, committee or official may have been made *in the absence of better information* which a programme could have provided. Moreover, when major decisions are being made — e.g. reviews of farm prices — the Ministry or Department is helped towards making wise decisions when it has the benefit of the views of special interest groups. It is sometimes said that the National Health Act which set up the National Health Service was based on the advice of everyone except the patients. Now-adays, even the patients would be repre-sented.

23. Sponsorship

(i) That the media have given the required volume of coverage before, during and after the sponsorship, coverage having been monitored.

(ii) That the sponsor was identified in media reports (e.g. the *Ever Ready* Derby and the *Cornhill* test).

(iii) That it provided the desired oppor-tunity for hospitality for the sponsor's guests, such as customers.

(iv) That it has succeeded in positioning the sponsored product in its market seg-ment or niche.

(v) That it has familiarised the market with the sponsor's name or brand name, and what it stood for.

(vi) That goodwill has been created with desired publics such as consumers/

users, distributors, shareholders, mem-bers and so on.

Sponsorships may have a variety of object-ives, and perhaps more than one so the above are merely a few possibilities of what may be achieved. Although sponsorship is often adopted as an alternative to advertising it is not a direct alternative to media advertising. There may also be personal motives. The *Ever Ready* Derby is a major sponsorship and its principal objective was to establish the name after a series of name changes, but no doubt the particular sponsorship was chosen because Lord Hanson's partner Lord White was a horse racing enthusiast.

24. Familiarising overseas markets

(i) Chosen overseas markets are familiar with the organisation and what it makes, does or supplies.

(ii) The method of distribution is under-stood (e.g. local importers, agents, com-pany sales offices, local manufacture or licensing arrangements with an indi-genous manufacturer).

(iii) Material has been distributed overseas by the DTI.

(iv) Material has been distributed overseas by the BBC World Service.

Here is perhaps a more difficult objective, and one requiring long-term effort, but it depends on how closely the public relations effort is married to the marketing objective. There is seldom a 'world market' for a product or service, each country or perhaps region being a market with its own peculiar character-istics. The Canadian and US, the Chinese and Japanese, the Ghanaian and Nigerian markets are distinctly different. The Middle East is not just an Arab market. Within the USA, the Atlantic and Pacific Coasts, the mid-West and the South have their special characteristics. Malaysia and Singapore are not alike. Geo-graphical proximity may mean little. This overseas public relations can be of two kinds, *world-wide* irrespective of individual countries or concentrated on *certain countries*. Which is the marketing strategy?

There is the danger that if the public relations effort is to be global, the massive diffusion of the message will result in it being 'very thin on the ground'. But that may be inevitable or acceptable. For instance, a direct response trader may not mind where his orders come from so long as there is no difficulty over payment. A small number of orders may be attracted from a large number of countries, perhaps by advertising in an international magazine. Or the public relations may provoke interest from quarters which cannot be forecast, and which may lead to direct export sales, the appointment of agencies, investment in subsidiaries, or arrangement of production under a royalty agreement.

Such unpremeditated response may result from the publication of stories in journals with international circulations, whether technical magazines or newspapers such as the *Economist* and the *Financial Times*, distribution of news by the Department of Trade and Industry, or broadcasts on the BBC World Service, not forgetting the distribution by satellite of video news releases by Visnews (see Chapter 21). Before engaging in such a programme, it is essential to be prepared to handle the response that may result — and the External Services of the BBC emphasise this before handling stories. Results can be surprising and simple to check.

However, the company may have a franchise to sell only in specified countries, or the intention may be to develop selected foreign markets. In this case, global publicity may be embarrassing if enquiries and orders from outside the chosen territories have to be rejected. Results can be assessed in a more penetrating way because now the PRO will be interested in the ripples that result from the initial effort. To what extent is interest aroused in the country so that the subject is taken up, discussed, written about, commented on in radio and TV programmes and so on?

It may pay to use either a local sales agent or an indigenous public relations consultancy to monitor results. Although firms such as Romeike and Curtice can provide an international press cutting service covering major cities, it may be necessary to have observers on the spot who will collect press cuttings. Even so, they may be in a foreign language and preferably they should be translated on the spot. The PRO may, of course do his or her own mailing, taking addresses from the Europe and World volumes of *Benn's Media Directory*.

Success in achieving coverage by foreign media will depend on its relevance to the readers of that media. How does the new product apply to the foreign market? This will make all the difference to the story's acceptability.

Here, results will depend not only on defining objectives and publics but on the possibilities of gaining coverage, skill in using not simply the right media, but also the many export public relations facilities available in the UK (or in any other country), and especially skill in producing efficiently translated material. Organisations such as EIBIS take extraordinary care over their translations, and this is a factor which can make or mar an overseas communication campaign.

Although overseas public relations may sometimes seem like working in the dark and rather haphazard because the PRO is not there to see what happens, results do depend on the trouble that is taken to perfect techniques. Then the results can be measured against particular targets. The subject is dealt with in greater detail in Chapter 24.

25. Educating hostile opinion leaders

(i) The particular opinion leaders/formers are now correctly informed.
(ii) Subsequent statements by these opinion leaders/formers show proper understanding of the subject.

A one-to-one operation is usually necessary here, as hostile opinions are mostly made by individuals, but there could be a body of hostile opinion leaders. Members of a political party could be antagonists, or groups of pensioners, parents or teachers could be wrongly informed and therefore hostile. Large numbers of people are, rightly or wrongly, opposed to the European Parliament, although they may know very little about it, and unless educated they will continue to express misinformed opinions. British politicians with anti-European views do so constantly.

26. Organising reviews of videos

(i) Reviews of corporate videos have appeared in the media, resulting in requests to see or show these videos.
(ii) Media which review videos have asked to see the organisation's latest videos.

The objective here is to get the organisation's videos known and reviewed as an aid to efficient distribution, often to users whose identities may be unknown to the organisation but whose interest could be valuable.

27. Liaison with exhibition press officers

(i) Advance information about the participant's exhibit has been issued by the exhibition press officer.
(ii) The exhibitor has been informed regarding the VIP who will open the show, enabling the PRO to invite the VIP to include the stand in the itinerary of his or her tour.
(iii) As a result of this liaison, the required number of releases and captioned photographs can be supplied to the press room on the date required.
(iv) The exhibitor will be informed about press day or press review arrangements.
(v) There has been excellent media coverage locally, nationally and internationally before, during and after the exhibition.

The results from liaison from an early stage with exhibition officers can be extremely rewarding, although it is one of the most neglected areas of public relations. Last minute deliveries to the press room of elaborate press kits stuffed with irrelevant material are unlikely to produce a result apart from a heavy bill. This topic is discussed more fully in Chapter 10.

28. Open days and works visits

(i) The opportunity to visit the works has been taken up by various clubs and associations, and may have become a feature of motor-coach outings (e.g. visits to the *Coronation Street* studios of Granada TV at Manchester).
(ii) Feedback, including questionnaires, shows the extent to which such visits have improved knowledge and understanding of the organisation, strengthened community relations, and contributed to the corporate image.

Much depends on the purpose of the visit. The writer once overheard a woman declare 'I always buy Heinz. I've been round their factory and seen their foods made'. Works visits may be a kind of entertainment, but good impressions can be indelible. From a community relations point of view, 'open house' invitations can help to break down local misunderstandings.

29. Informing pensioners

(i) Interest in and knowledge about their former employers has been maintained.
(ii) There has been a good level of participation in activities or benefits organised for pensioners.

(iii) There has been a good take up by pensioners of discounted purchases.

(iv) Pensioners have supplied contributions to the house journal.

Many companies have thousands of pensioners and this is a public not to be overlooked when setting public relations objectives. The results of these endeavours should be measured since considerable expense is involved and it needs to be justified like any other. This is not an attempt to be parsimonious but to see that money is not being wasted on good intentions which are not appreciated. Pensioners welcome the opportunity of keeping in touch with former workmates and colleagues.

30. Staff and company results

(i) Employees are familiar with the annual report and accounts.

(ii) Employees understand where the money comes from and what happens to it.

(iii) Employees understand the company's trading policy and prospects.

(iv) Employees understand the consequences of resolutions passed at the annual general meeting.

Industrial democracy has progressed a little in Britain (although not as much as in continental Europe) and by various communication aids such as house journals and videos, together with greater equity ownership by employees, the financial affairs of public companies are now the business of employees. However, the extent to which they are understood will be a measure of the success of public relations in this direction.

31. Advise staff on benefits

(i) Employees are fully aware of all the benefits offered by the employers.

(ii) There is a satisfactory take-up of these benefits, indicating staff stability.

Many benefits are a means of augmenting wages and salaries, but they also provide a means of keeping a permanent staff because staff are unlikely to become involved in a long-term benefit unless they intend to stay with the company. From a company point of view, staff stability is a return on investment in recruitment and training, while contributing to quality control and productivity.

32. Corporate image

(i) Relevant publics have a current and well-informed image of the organisation.

(ii) Misunderstandings about the corporate image have been resolved.

(iii) If there has been a bad image because of some unfortunate experience, this has now been corrected and good reputation has been regained.

The test here will be to measure the extent to which our publics perceive a more accurate impression of the organisation, what it is and what it does. The opinion, awareness and image studies can be applied, and if there was an initial survey at the appreciation of the situation stage, it should now be possible to measure the shift from that situation. The extent of the shift will show whether our target has been achieved or to what extent we have succeeded or failed in our objective. This could also help us to determine whether sufficient, too little or too much money was spent on the programme, and also whether the right tactics were used.

For instance, one organisation which adopted sponsorship in order to improve awareness gained a shift from near zero (by comparison with its rivals) to 20 percent awareness at the close of the sports season during which the sponsorship took place. This was a very positive result which justified the particular tactic. The company has found it economic to extend its sponsorship over a number of years.

33. Promoting use of corporate identity

(i) Relevant publics recognise the organisation by its logo, colour scheme, typography, transportation livery, badges, uniforms and so on.
(ii) Departments or branches of the organisation are using the corporate identity scheme correctly in their print, decor, dress, livery, advertising and so on.
(iii) Suppliers of services such as advertising agencies, public relations consultancies, printers, decorators and so on are using the corporate identity scheme correctly.

These results are essential if the corporate identity scheme is to be a success. After all, its creation cost a large fee, and a style book has been issued as a guide. Nevertheless, in large organisations, people responsible for buying items which should adopt the scheme may be indifferent or careless. The wrong shades of colour may be used. Printers may not have the specified type faces. The results of usage of the scheme need to be monitored.

34. Media relations

(i) That the organisation is being reported regularly.
(ii) That reports are appearing in the most valuable media.
(iii) That reports contain correct information.
(iv) That the organisation is approached for information or a viewpoint when its subject is in the news.
(v) That the media respond well to invitations to media events.

Good media relations are a practical relationship, one of working amicably with the media, understanding their needs and not expecting favours. One of the simplest ways of establishing good relations is the supply of news releases which are publishable. As will be seen in Chapters 15–18 very few are, and bad media relations occur simply because news releases fail to resemble reports as printed in newspapers the world over. This final objective will not have the desired results until practitioners, especially consultants, learn how to write publishable news releases. The majority of releases remind one of a nurse who is unable to apply a bandage.

CHAPTER 9

Planning Public Relations Events

The planning of public relations events calls for methodical and meticulous organisation. Success often depends on experience and the press officer who has organised other kinds of events will find this experience useful. There is a lot of hard work in planning public relations events. It calls for the second attribute of a good practitioner described in Chapter 2.

THREE KINDS OF PUBLIC RELATIONS EVENT

Let us first be sure of what is meant by the three main types of media event. The loose expression 'press party' is often used in a vague sense to mean any sort of media gathering whether assembled or conveyed, but by *press conference, press reception* and *facility visit*, we refer to gatherings of accelerating complexity. In this order the first is a fairly simple affair, the second occupies a bigger place, more time and is consequently more elaborate, while the third usually involves travel to a distant location, more hospitality and possibly overnight accommodation.

1. Press conference

A press conference is organised like a meeting, the guests being seated to receive an announcement and to ask questions. It may be held in an office, a boardroom, a hotel assembly room or possibly at an airport. Hospitality is usually modest such as coffee, tea or sherry, served with biscuits, according to the time of day. A bar is not always necessary. Copies of the announcement will be available in news release form. A press conference is a fairly unpretentious occasion, capable of being called at short notice if the urgency of the news demands it.

2. The press reception

The success of this type of media event will largely depend on its being much more than a mere drinking occasion. Public relations has, in the past, gained a regrettable reputation for over-generous hospitality. Contrary to the impression held by some people, most journalists who attend press receptions come in search of a story, not a free drink. However, in overseas countries where media representatives are fewer, and are probably well known to the host, and party-going is very much a way of life, the hospitality may be more generous and prolonged.

A press reception depends for success on a programme and the promise of a story sufficient to attract a good response to the invitation. For this reason it pays to include a timed programme on or with the invitation although strangely enough this is rarely done. Some invitations do not even state the purpose of the press reception and it is a wonder anyone bothers to accept. A programmed invitation is more likely to attract the journalists who are seriously interested in the subject and best able to give it media coverage. However, the invitation will be dealt with in greater detail later on in this chapter.

A typical timetable would include: the initial reception (without formal announcement); initial refreshments according to the time of day; the business of the occasion; and a final period of hospitality of the bar and buffet kind. The business may require guests to be seated, and this session can be in a separate room away from the catering. It may include speeches, demonstrations, a slide or video presentation and an opportunity for questions to be asked and answered. Those responsible for answering questions should have anticipated the most likely questions and have their facts by them. A good question and answer period can do much to create goodwill if speakers are prepared to reply frankly and fully.

A short documentary video — not more than 20 minutes — can be a very useful part of the proceedings, and should be included if possible, but it must be relevant and recent if not actually new. It may be someone else's video, showing either production of the raw materials or use of the finished article, if the host company does not have a suitable one of its own. For example, a video showing the manufacture of laminates might be shown at a press reception for a furniture maker. The documentary or industrial video, free of advertising is undoubtedly one of the best public relations media we have, and guests at press receptions provide most receptive audiences. It gives information entertainingly and provides enjoyable watching.

If the video is the first item on the programme after the reception it will create a very pleasant atmosphere for the remainder of the party. Platform activities should be rehearsed and timed. A good 20-minute video is infinitely better than a dull 10-minute speech.

Slide presentations may also be made, and with twin projectors and cross-fade effect, perhaps augmented by synchronised sound on a tape-recorder, they can be as effective as video. They are easier and cheaper to produce, and can easily be up-dated with new slides. They may also illustrate a talk with the speaker controlling the appearance of each slide.

It can be a wise plan to divorce the business section from the refreshments. The catering bill is doubled when there is no separate business section, and the worst offenders can be the representatives of the host organisation (who mistake the event for an opportunity to indulge in some free drinking). The organiser should restrict company representatives to essential hosts such as technical experts needed to talk authoritatively to guests.

The press officer should drink sparingly if at all at press receptions, and if the event is organised by a consultant for a client it is a very bad thing for the client to see consultancy staff consuming drinks which will be included in the bill. When the catering bill for a press reception is high, it is usually because there has been a lot of drinking by people other than the press. Press drinking can be restricted to the short periods before and after the business session, which means that few guests will consume more than two or three drinks. These are points of great significance when budgets are being considered. A press reception does not have to cost a ridiculous amount of money, and it is totally wrong for press receptions to be regarded as extravagances.

Two provisos may be added. A press reception should be confined to journalists and essential hosts. Friends of the host, or customers, should not be invited, just because the host thinks it is a party. Moreover, these are rarely the people who should be interviewed by journalists. The second proviso is that with some products, such as technical ones, the consumer and trade media are best invited to separate receptions since each will require different information and will ask different questions.

3. Facility visits

Facility visits provide the press with the opportunity, and often the privilege, of attending an official opening, visiting a factory or other premises, visiting an installation, going on board a new ship, flying in a new aircraft, or being taken abroad to an overseas exhibition in which the host is participating. For the trip, anything from a private car to a chartered aircraft may be used. These events can be costly because the party has to be conveyed from point to point, fed and entertained, and on a long trip overnight accommodation, hospitality and perhaps entertainment are necessary.

There are two basic kinds of facility visit and the organiser should be clear about the kind that is being held. First, there is the visit which is purely to provide background information; second, there is the kind with a definite news story, and this will require facilities for some guests to get the story back by telephone, Telex, fax, computer or fast transport in the case of TV news. The press will expect the visit to be of one kind or the other. It is foolish to take a plane-load of journalists from one end of the country to the other to see a jam or paint factory no different from one they could see on their doorstep. Unfortunately, this happens all too often, and public relations gets a bad name for extravagant thoughtlessness.

RADIO AND TELEVISION

These three events — conferences, receptions and visits — are labelled 'Press', but radio and TV should be considered separately and differently from the printed media. A common mistake is to include representatives of BBC radio and TV news, BBC programmes, ITN, TV company programmes, IRN, BBC Local Radio and Independent Local Radio in the general invitation list. An even greater error is to simply invite BBC and ITV without realising the numerous sections which now exist in radio and TV, nationally, regionally and locally, commercially or otherwise.

Unless reporters from radio and TV are content to 'sit in' in search of material for future programmes, they should not be sent a general invitation to attend a press event. Instead, after careful selection of the appropriate programmes and stations, the respective producers, presenters or reporters should be written to or telephoned individually. This should be done in advance of the general press invitations. Broadcasters should be told of the event but asked to state their special needs in order to cover the story. They may wish to make a preliminary visit, shoot on a different day or at a different time, or tape interviews prior to the press reception. Television teams may take hours to produce a few minutes' screen time. Moreover, equipment and technicians have to be booked in good time. Much radio reporting and interviewing is conducted by freelance reporters who have to be booked to cover the story. Or the PRO himself may provide radio stations with taped interviews, using the services of Two-Ten Communications or other news agencies. Video news releases may be offered to TV stations.

The main speaker may be able to give a live or taped interview in a local radio station before or after the press reception. Again, this can be arranged in advance by the organiser. TV newscasters may read news items derived from the reception, and a still photograph may be screened while the item is being read, or parts of a video news release may be incorporated. A colour picture must be supplied, and it should be remembered that production of major evening TV news programmes, such as *News At Ten*, begins early in the morning. Material should therefore be supplied overnight if possible.

PLANNING A PRESS CONFERENCE OR RECEPTION

The following considerations must be borne in

mind when organising these two kinds of press event.

1. The purpose

There must be a good reason for the conference or reception. Would a news release suffice? Is there a big enough story to warrant taking up the time of the media let alone the expense? Are we absolutely clear what we want to tell and show the media?

2. The date

What is the best date? Many factors will control this choice: the purpose of the event, the availability of the venue. Right choice of date is vital. For example, if a new central heating system is to be introduced, the press reception should be held early in the year in order to achieve coverage in the autumn-published heating features and supplements in the women's and home interest monthlies. January would be preferable, February would be getting rather late. (If the product were a Christmas gift, the event should be in July.)

To make sure that the right speaker is free it may be necessary to work a long way ahead and there is not much sense in holding the event on a day when journalists you want are attending something else. It is by no means easy to avoid a clash of dates sometimes, but it does pay to check as far as possible. It may also pay to check dates with good media contacts who are willing to tell you what other invitations they have had.

Linked with the right date is also the right day of the week, and the right time of day. The time of day for a press gathering is much more important than is sometimes supposed. Businessmen are inclined to think first of their own convenience and availability, and to regard these events as cocktail parties which must commence at 6pm and be held out of office hours so as not to interfere with the day's work. But the guests have homes to go to. They do not all work on national newspapers whose offices are open day and night. They, too, like to keep office hours. It is no pleasure to them, and not really a duty, to have to forsake dinner at home with their families to attend a commercial cocktail party.

If the organiser does insist on an evening affair, he must expect to attract office juniors and freelance contributors to whom the invitations have been passed by more senior people who prefer to attend the other press functions which are held at more convenient times of the day.

So, generally speaking, the best time for a press conference or reception is between 11am and 1pm on a Monday or Tuesday (Wednesday is bad for journalists working on weeklies) during the first or last ten days of the month (mid-month is bad for journalists working on monthlies). Newspapermen should be given their stories before lunchtime, and an evening paper reporter will want his story as early in the day as possible. If the guests are likely to be inundated with invitations, a convenient venue allows them to attend more than one event during the same morning or afternoon. This is often true of women's magazine and women's page journalists who flit from one reception to another. *Early in the day, early in the month* is therefore a good general rule.

3. The venue

A venue should be chosen because it suits the occasion, provides the correct facilities, is conveniently situated, has the right appeal, and makes reasonable charges for exemplary catering. This is a short list of requirements, no more.

Choosing the venues for media events calls for knowledge of the advantages and disadvantages of a large variety of premises, and for this purpose it pays to continuously put on file information about all likely hotels, halls and other accommodation. If possible they should be visited and reliance should not be placed on supplied information. Careful selection is necessary and usually one finds that only a limited number of establishments are worth retaining on the recommended list.

In London there is a modern skyscraper building which possesses a magnificently appointed lecture theatre which is admirable for conferences. But there is no public transport and empty taxis hardly ever pass the door. It has earned the reputation of being a place from which it is difficult to return. Quite another problem prevents one from using certain otherwise attractive venues in some provincial cities: lack of car-parking facilities. In selecting a venue outside London, the organiser has to cater for guests travelling in from other towns, usually by car.

Let us summarise the eight main considerations to be borne in mind when booking venues for press gatherings.

1. Availability of a room or rooms of the required size, and whether this accommodation is available earlier in the day or on the previous day for preparation or rehearsal purposes.
2. Does the accommodation meet the special demands of the occasion: e.g. does it black out for video or slides; is it soundproof; is the floor strong enough for weighty exhibits (ballroom floors seldom are); are there convenient cloakroom facilities, especially for coats, hats and umbrellas during winter months?
3. Is the catering good? Are there any specialities? Guests remember the food.
4. Is the venue or its location of special interest?
5. What are the costs per head for finger buffets, fork buffets, lunches and dinners? Is there a hire charge for rooms? What is the method and rate for gratuities? (Comparative costs are more important than one might think.)
6. Has the venue special facilities such as lighting effects, staging, microphones, projectors, VCRs, TV sets or tape-recorders? Some are extremely well equipped for events. Others make heavy hire charges.
7. Is there a car-park or are the premises adjacent to one? Apart from guests' cars, space may be required for a demonstration vehicle.
8. Are transport facilities good, e.g. taxis, public transport, and is the venue easily accessible at busy times of the day? Accessibility can have a critical effect on attendance figures if a number of public relations events happen to be claiming the same people on the same day. The accessibility factor has become even more important as magazines have moved out of London altogether, and national newspapers have deserted Fleet Street.

Other considerations may occur according to the needs of the occasion. A hotel may be required to provide lunch for a press party visiting a factory or an installation. What is the capacity of the dining room? Or it might be an attraction to invite the press to a brand new hotel which has novelty appeal. It may be that outside caterers can be brought in to provide for a party in an historic venue, for example a City livery hall or the Royal Pavilion at Brighton. Perhaps catering can be arranged in a marquee in the factory grounds.

Few venues are suitable for every event, and if press parties are being held in various parts of the country, satisfactory answers will be required to many questions. The important thing is knowing what questions to ask! It is not sufficient merely to write or telephone: venues should be inspected before making firm bookings.

So we have three major problems to resolve before anything else is decided: is there a big enough story to warrant holding the event at all; and when and where do we hold the function?

4. The invitation list

This should not be a big problem for the

experienced press officer, and certainly not if he or she is dealing most of the time with a limited, specialised press. It can be more difficult for the consultancy dealing with a much bigger assortment of journals and journalists. The list should have not just the addresses of the journals but the names of the individuals who are to be invited. People do like to be known and to be addressed by name.

To produce a reliable invitation list, it is necessary to do a lot of telephoning because journalists do change their jobs with remarkable frequency. In fact, it is true to say that if the same organisation held a reception only twice a year there would be considerable changes in each succeeding invitation list. Lists can also be compiled from those published by PIMS, Two-Ten and *Editors*.

Invitations, whether cards or letters, do have to be made out to individuals as they are personal communications. They cannot be sent vaguely to unidentified persons. This may come as a shock to those who run off grubby-looking invitation letters on a copier and send them in unsealed envelopes to unnamed editors. Not surprisingly, such invitations produce little or no response and the organiser fills the reception with his own staff to make it look as if there is a good attendance. Good attendances are won by taking infinite pains.

When compiling an invitation list, it must be large enough to produce a satisfactory turn out. If the aim is to have an attendance of 40 it may be necessary to invite 60, perhaps more. Clearly, the attendance will depend upon the various factors of newsworthiness, attractiveness of venue, and convenience of place, date and time, but in addition there are always other considerations such as staff shortages in the office, personal illness, and holidays which are beyond the control of the organisers and so deplete numbers even after acceptances have been received. On these occasions, the press officer must never be over-optimistic and it is foolish to boast to employer or client that this and that paper will be represented. National

newspapers tend to accept everything and then make the choice on the day!

5. The invitations

The news may be so 'hot' that a telephone invitation will be justified, and this is possible when the invitation list is a small one. Or the list may be extremely specialised, and all the journalists will be personally known to the press officer who can ring round in the friendliest way and invite them all at short notice. But these are exceptions to the usual run of events, possible with press conferences but unnecessary with press receptions which have to be planned over a matter of weeks so that there is ample time in which to give journalists seven to ten days notice, sometimes longer.

The timing of the despatch of invitations is of importance to the overall organisation of the event. There must be a day prior to the event when a reasonable knowledge of likely numbers is required so that catering, transport, seating and other arrangements can be confirmed with banqueting managers and contractors. This day may be three to seven days in advance of the actual date. And if, for some reason, numbers are limited, it may be necessary to stagger the despatch of invitations in order to control the total number of acceptances, further invitations being sent out to make up for refusals.

Out of courtesy to guests, the invitation must either be a well-produced letter or, better still, a printed invitation card. A card is always preferable, and letters should be resorted to only when there is not time to print a card or when numbers do not justify the design and print cost. A card has many advantages over a letter. It is a special piece of correspondence, arriving in an important-looking white envelope. Out of politeness, it cannot be ignored. It does its job well. Invitation cards are often put on mantelpieces and window sills where other people see them. And if the design and printing is neat and distinctive, it will help to make the event seem worth attending. If the host is prepared to go to some trouble to invite his guests properly, he will surely go to the same trouble to make sure that the event is worth attending.

There was a time when it was thought that invitation cards had to be given the copper-plate look, but the vogue for script typefaces has now been superseded by the use of neat modern typefaces.

When designing cards, thought should be given to the way in which replies will be returned. The organiser needs to know the refusals as well as the acceptances, and the best way to obtain definite answers one way or the other is to provide an easy means of reply. When a means of reply is used, a fairly accurate idea of acceptances will be known within 48 hours, while knowledge of refusals provides opportunity for follow-ups or despatch of fresh invitations.

There are several ways of doing this: reply slips, reply cards, or addressed envelopes, but by far the best method is to incorporate an addressed reply card with the invitation card. The two cards offer four sides of printing. On the face of one card we have the invitation. On the back of the invitation, a timetable programme of the event should be set out. The reply card should repeat the basic details of the event and have space for the guest to indicate acceptance or refusal, 'I can/I cannot', and give his or her name and publication. On the reverse side the reply part must bear the organiser's full postal address and in the top right-hand corner a frame to indicate that a postage stamp is required, otherwise people will post it back in an envelope. When so many offices use franking machines a stamped addressed card is irrelevant, although advisable when writing to freelance writers and correspondents at home addresses.

The following is an example of simple, informative and effective wording:

The Directors of XYZ Ltd
have pleasure in inviting

....

to attend a PRESS RECEPTION
in the Buckingham Room
Hotel Western, Park Lane, London W1
at 11.30 am on Tuesday November 5
to view the XYZ models for 19XX

Cocktails   RSVP John Smith XYZ Ltd
Refreshments 88, Hall Street, London W1X 222

This card does require the organiser to write in the names of each guest, and names must be neatly written in by hand and *not* typewritten. If there is a very large invitation list, this handwriting may be too big a task and the alternative is to have a card which reads:

The Directors of XYZ Ltd
have pleasure in inviting you
to attend a PRESS RECEPTION

The wording of the invitation should clearly set out all the facts which will encourage the recipient to decide to attend if he or she possibly can. This wording should be cordial but not extravagant. A press reception has to be marketed like anything else, hence the attention to detail which is emphasised throughout this chapter. This marketing attitude is vital because invitations must compete with many other claims upon a journalist's time, including rival invitations.

The invitation card should also indicate the kind of refreshments that will be provided, and the address for reply should be printed at the foot of the ticket even though a reply card is attached or enclosed.

The appearance of the card will be enhanced if it carries the organisation's coat of arms, or the company logo, and it should comply with the accepted house style regarding typeface and colour.

Gimmicks are not usually advisable. On the other hand an invitation sent in July for a press reception about a Christmas gift might be printed on a Christmas card.

Should there be any sort of enclosure with an invitation card? The answer is yes if it will do anything to encourage the journalist to come. It could be a personal note, or if it is a complicated or controversial subject, it may be a good idea to include some preliminary information which will stimulate curiosity and questions. But it can be fatal to send out the news release in advance!

A telephone follow-up may be worthwhile. When telephoned, some of the people will say they have never seen the invitation, and this may be perfectly true. There may be other reasons why the prospective guest has not replied, and a few friendly words on the telephone may very likely encourage an acceptance. One has to sell a press reception.

For the day, a complete list of acceptances should be made up, and this can be checked against signatures in the visitors' book so that absentees may be sent the news releases and pictures they would have received had they attended.

6. Identifying guests

It has become accepted at receptions, meetings and conferences that everyone should wear some form of identification. This practice has the distinct advantage that it makes contact and conversation so much easier. By means of badges, preferably adhesive, which name both guest and publication, the press officer can move among the guests, quickly scanning badges and welcoming people by name. Guests will be present for only a short time, they may be unknown to the PRO or members of the host party, and there could be substitutes.

Badges of a different colour, or bearing the organisation's house symbol, should be worn by members of the host party.

The badges should be prepared from the acceptance list, and set out in alphabetical order on the reception table at the entrance to the room where the reception is being held.

7. Press kits or packs

It is not advisable to hand out press packs as guests arrive because it is difficult to eat, drink, talk and read at the same time. (Plates with holes to accept the stems of wine glasses are useful.) Packs can be available on the reception table for those who ask for information in advance. (Over-elaborate so-called press kits are an abomination at all kinds of media event and are unnecessarily costly.) Often a simple news release is all that is needed, with pictures and photographs numbered on a board and available for order. If press packs are absolutely necessary, the best are undoubtedly the pliable plastic ones which can even be rolled and put in a jacket pocket if need be. The simplest is the transparent kind, but there are more sophisticated ones with button-down flaps which are useful and more secure when material is being collected during a prolonged visit or tour. The use of clumsy cardboard wallets is incomprehensible, and no journalist appreciates the kind with glued or even stapled flaps which always seem to burst open.

These remarks therefore refute what is so often common practice, but surely the guiding rule must be: use a wallet if it provides a service to your guests, but do not use a wallet merely to try to impress them with the importance of your organisation. Journalists will not be impressed by sheer swank. They will be impressed by thoughtfulness.

8. Catering

When giving numbers to the caterers it is safe to work on a number slightly below that of the acceptance list, since not all the guests remain for the buffet. While it is extremely bad to have insufficient food, it is equally bad management and economics to have a lot of food over. The bar can be controlled by one of two methods:

the bartender can be given a maximum figure, at which point he asks the organiser whether the bar should remain open; or the bar can be closed at a certain time and coffee can be served.

The serving of coffee is an excellent device for bringing the proceedings to a close, and, since by coffee-time, numbers are sure to be depleted it is almost certain to be sufficient to order only half as many coffees as the total number of people present. These remarks are not intended to be pinch-penny but to indicate that by proper management, press events can be budgeted and controlled in a sensible and responsible manner.

Food is more important than the bar. If a host really wants to impress the press, good food is by far the best method. The food should include some substantial items and not miniature sandwiches lost under a maze of mustard and cress. The organiser should insist on not only seeing a variety of menus and prices but should clearly understand from the banqueting manager what is meant by each item. It is no good hopefully accepting a banqueting manager's vague assurance that he can 'do something for so much a head, sir'. It is sometimes surprising how much better one can do for less when one demands that each item be detailed.

9. Gifts and mementoes

Should the press be given presents at press receptions? It depends on the suitability of the gift or memento to the subject of the reception. A gift is not vital, but if it is a sample or is related in some way to the organisation running the reception, then it can be appropriate and desirable. There are some organisations from whom such a gift might well be expected, but otherwise gifts are more appropriate to facility visits, where they are an accepted courtesy. A gift should not seem to be a bribe, merely a nice gesture, and if it is a matter of proving one's case by providing a sample it will, of course, be a very good tactic.

The motor-car industry has suffered a very bad image by being too generous to journalists.

There was the famous or infamous TV programme when a motoring correspondent displayed an array of gifts he had received from manufacturers. One mini-car manufacturer gave motoring correspondents a free car. On the other hand, a nice gesture was made by the sewing machine company which presented 120 guests at a press reception with a child's toy sewing machine. But a clock manufacturer, launching a new type of clock at a press reception, gave everyone a clock and was chagrined afterwards to receive complaints that it did not work. If a new food or drink product is the subject of the reception, it will be an excellent gesture to supply samples which guests may eat or drink at home. In the case of drinks, miniatures may be sent with invitations. When St. Ivel Gold was launched, and a press dinner and dance was held at the Grosvenor House Hotel, free samples were available on leaving.

10. Managing the event

It has been stressed at the beginning of this chapter that a public relations event must be planned right down to the last detail, and that there must be a properly planned programme. The practitioner has to be both producer and stage manager. People have to do certain things correctly at stipulated times, and a press reception is not just 'played by ear'. Only the organiser can co-ordinate and manage the various elements, and everyone from managing director to distinguished guest must comply with this person's control. A good organiser will operate almost invisibly, and the event will seem to run itself, but all the same he or she must be here, there and everywhere making sure that everything proceeds as it should.

By setting out a timed programme on the invitation ticket, the organiser commits everyone concerned to a timetable. Speeches must be prepared so that copies may be available to the press; there must be a rehearsal, with or without the VIP speaker; and the organiser may take the chair and so make sure that the programme runs to time.

One of the controlling factors will be the accessibility of the venue. If more than one hotel exists of the same name, the location of the chosen one must be clearly stated. If the hotel has more than one entrance, the right one should be clearly stated also. If there is an indicator board in the foyer of the hotel, the organiser must check that the event is correctly described. If there is any risk of guests losing their way along corridors, there should be directional signs. If the event occurs in the winter or on a wet day, cloakroom facilities should be clearly indicated. We have already referred to the reception table at the door, adequately staffed to receive guests. The organiser should be present to welcome guests and do anything necessary to expedite their entry.

If the organisation or the client has been made responsible for the supply of products or materials, the organiser must make sure that they have in fact arrived and are ready for use. The same applies to the arrival of equipment.

The reception period will usually run for 20 or 30 minutes, the shorter the better. During this period drinks will be served according to the time of day, and guests will be introduced to members of the host party. In cold weather, a hot drink on arrival may be appreciated more than a bar. The reception period must not drag and will continue only so long as a reasonable number of guests have yet to arrive. If it goes on too long, journalists will become restless and want to know when the programme is to begin. The organiser must therefore take the feeling of the assembly and watch how satisfactorily the attendance is building up. The right moment must be judged to go on to the next item on the programme, making sure that the stated time is not over-run.

Throughout the course of the event the organiser must make sure that the timetable is obeyed, the showing of the video or slides, the giving of speeches, the demonstrating and finally the invitation to enjoy the refreshments and ask questions of members of the host party all taking no more than their allotted time. During this latter period, the organiser will endeavour to meet as many guests as possible and see that they are satisfied with answers to their questions and are supplied with information. The organiser should also endeavour to say goodbye to each guest on leaving and thank them for coming.

Finally the account for the hotel's service will have to be agreed. Appreciation of the way in which the hotel contributed to the success of the event will establish good relations of value to the next occasion.

The old-fashioned stand-around cocktail party press reception has long been superseded by the programmed press party from which the guests take away a good story, not a fat head and a free gift. For instance, when Necchi launched an automatic sewing machine a dress was actually made during the two hours of the reception. Women journalists went away and wrote stories that began with words such as 'The other day I saw a dress made in two hours . . .'.

Gimmicks are apt to have boomerang effects, and journalists are quick to deride attempts to invent stories. On the other hand if the product is somewhat mundane, a little originality can succeed.

PLANNING A FACILITY VISIT

While most of the items already discussed under press conferences and receptions will also apply to the preparation of a facility visit, there are several additional items to consider.

In this category of facility visit can be included all those visits by parties of journalists to factories, installations, sites and so on requiring conveyance of guests, or at least the management of guests at some distant or outside location as distinct from receiving them in the head-office boardroom or in a hotel in the vicinity of the publishing offices. It also includes trips on new trains, ships or in aircraft, provided by the owners as a facility to the press to gain first-hand knowledge and experience. It can involve no more than a single journalist who is being given facilities to write an article, or a party of almost any size. Included in this category are trips abroad to see a holiday venue, visit a vineyard, or try out a new motor-car prior to its launch.

Such visits can be very complicated planning feats calling for patient preparation over a long period. Journalists are unwilling or unable to give up a day, perhaps two days, on a facility visit unless there is justification. Complaints are made from time to time about wonderfully arranged charter-plane trips with generous hospitality and souvenir gifts, but no story!

As we said when considering the press reception, there must be a clear and valid purpose for any such event, but particularly so for one which will occupy so much of a journalist's time. It must add to his or her knowledge and experience, supply background material, show promise of future news development, or provide an immediate story. *It must be of value to a journalist in his daily work.* The journalist must go home feeling glad that the invitation was worth accepting, and not feeling that it was all very nice but rather a waste of time. Some well-known organisations do spend thousands of pounds to achieve no more than that. These ill-conceived jaunts do the public relations business no good at all. Journalists have a particularly derisive term for these non-events: *junkets.*

Let us now analyse the practical requirements of worthwhile facility visits.

1. Party numbers

The primary consideration when planning a press visit is the number of people in the proposed party.

Capacity of the premises. Visitors to a factory can be a nuisance to those working there, but this must never be apparent! A certain number of people can be handled comfortably, whether it be in a laboratory or factory or on an outdoor site. No more than 15 people might be acceptable in a research establishment, whereas six parties of 15 might be all right in a large factory.

On most factory visits, small groups need to be arranged because production operations would be lost on a crowd, and so the usual practice is to organise parties of from 6 to 12 people, each with a guide. This may therefore decide how many groups can be taken round in the available time between arrival and lunchtime, or in the afternoon before the party must leave. One method of overcoming the time problem is to let these groups follow different routes, rather than have them following one behind the other. In this way all groups can complete their tour at very nearly the same time, and visitors are not left hanging about waiting for the others to catch up with them.

This clearly calls for some good planning, and rehearsal. Guides must know what they are talking about, be capable of answering questions, yet all take about the same time in dealing with each section of the tour. There should be a manual for guides to study, and rehearsals should include practice tours which are carefully timed and observed by the organiser. It is no use detailing members of the staff for guide duties and then hoping for the best on the day.

Catering and accommodation facilities. Party numbers may be controlled by the seating capacity of the dining room at the factory, or at a local hotel or restaurant. If there is suitable outdoor space a marquee may be the answer. Again, if a large party is desirable, seating limitations can be overcome by having a cold buffet with a minimum of tables, although a party which has been tramping round a factory will prefer an opportunity to sit down and relax at lunchtime. But these are the sorts of alternatives which need to be thought about carefully, remembering that factory canteen facilities will not be available, and there are few parts of the country where large gatherings such as weddings, 21st birthday parties, annual dinners and the like are not being organised and catered for by a local hotel, baker and confectioner or brewery.

Naturally, it is more pleasant to keep a party together if an overnight stay is necessary, and a member of the host party should stay at the hotel with the guests. Local conditions may demand scattering the party among different hotels, but this should be avoided if possible. Many members of the press party will know one another and will enjoy the opportunity of staying in the same hotel. If a party does have to be split up it is a good idea to find out if any of the guests do wish to keep together, and accommodation can be organised to meet individual wishes. It may be possible to organise entertainment after dinner.

On arrival there should be an appropriate welcoming drink, even if it is only coffee. It may be possible to induce guests to travel by an early train if breakfast can be served en route and dining car seats can be booked.

Attention to small personal details can be most important to the success of an event, and if block bookings have been made the actual allocation of rooms at different hotels can be made during the coach, train or plane journey. To do this well, a team of organisers is required with hosts, couriers or guides attached to each grouping of guests. The guests must never be left unattended, never expected to move from A to B unescorted once they have joined the party at the assembly point. Sometimes it is even wise to have someone detailed with a car to pick up latecomers or stragglers so that there is no danger of anyone failing to join the party.

A point worth remembering in this respect is that if guests have to travel a long way to join the transport (as when airports are some distance from city centres), it is safer to collect people in the central place and provide transport to the airport. It is comparatively simple

for guests to assemble at a suitable well-known spot which is accessible by most forms of transport. Motor coach companies can usually advise on the best meeting places because they have picking-up points agreed between them and the police. Some airports are conveniently served by rail services so that transportation is easily arranged and controlled.

Capacity of transport. Numbers may be determined by the peculiarities of the seating capacity, or the party booking arrangements, or the mode of transport. If a coach has 42 seats it is obviously impossible to accept 43 guests. The same rule applies to aircraft. It is not always possible to provide a larger coach or aircraft. Trains are more flexible up to a point, but the organiser must discuss with the railway booking staff the make-up of the train and the kind of stock being used, since this differs considerably according to the region. It is essential to know how the seating will be dispersed, and it may be desirable to restrict the party to a single coach. Alternatively, the *minimum* size of the party could be the total seating of an entire coach.

When chartering aircraft there may be a choice of aircraft, and this choice will again depend on numbers. Similarly, if seats are being booked on a scheduled passenger service there may be an advantage in a number which secures a price reduction. These points should be discussed at the earliest possible moment with the airline.

The commercial staff of transportation operators can be exceedingly helpful, but it is wise to check everything and not rely too heavily on other people to take over one's responsibilities. On one occasion, it was discovered at very short notice that railway tickets had been wrongly dated, which would have invalidated them when presented to the ticket collector at the barrier. Fortunately the wrong date was discovered in good time, otherwise that press visit might have been calamitous. Tickets should not be posted to guests: it is safer to ask guests to exchange a voucher for a ticket supplied by the organiser at the place of departure. Guests are liable to leave tickets in the wrong suits or handbags.

From the last remark an important lesson can be learned: an organiser must be a born pessimist. He must literally make himself miserable trying to think of everything that could possibly go wrong so that he can find a satisfactory solution to it. For example, in a certain town, the police insisted that coaches must unload their passengers the other side of a busy cross-roads from their venue. This could have meant some of the party losing their way. So the organiser argued, and the police relented and permitted the coaches to unload outside the venue itself, returning at an agreed time which meant that the activities within the venue had to run strictly to time. But this sort of thing can be done only if the organiser has a sufficiently nimble mind to foresee trouble. This usually means going over the ground at the venue to see what snags can be found.

Limited invitation list. When the topic is so specialised that there is a limited invitation list, the problem is to find a date when the majority can attend. This difficulty is best overcome by offering alternative dates by telephone, and negotiating in this way until a sufficiently large party has been assembled. In this case the visit will hinge on the date acceptable by the guests.

The budget. It may be physically possible to accommodate and to transport a hundred people but the cost may be prohibitive. Whatever facilities or limitations may exist, it is essential to have the event strictly costed, and to work within an agreed figure. Every cost can be known in advance and nothing should be agreed upon without a prior quotation. 'Shopping list' budgets for press events are outlined in Chapter 7.

2. Invitations

For this type of operation the invitation must give specific details about the object of the visit and the facilities for transport and accommodation which will be provided, accompanied by a timetable from start to finish including the picking up and returning of guests. Depending upon how complicated the arrangements may be, an invitation ticket as already described for press receptions may be adequate, or it may be safer to include a covering letter setting out the itinerary.

Because so many bookings have to be finalised when numbers are known, it will be necessary to despatch invitations much earlier than in the case of a press reception. Transport contractors and caterers will want a week's notice of the final arrangements, so if time is required for sending out a second round of invitations should acceptances be unsatisfactory, the original invitation will need to go out a month before the date of the event. This means that copy must go to the printer at least a fortnight before delivery is required, and time must also be allowed either side of the printing dates for first of all the finalising of details and the design of the card and then, when delivered, the making out and posting of the cards.

Thus, at least two months in advance of the event, we must know exactly what is going to happen. Working backwards yet again, it is not going to be too soon to begin making plans three months in advance, and no doubt some thought will have been given to the idea of a press visit much earlier than that.

It is important to see that the right people join the party. Such an expensive event merits the attendance of senior editorial personnel: it is not just a day out for juniors, free-loaders and hangers-on. This can be emphasised by pointing out that numbers are restricted and that it will be a privilege to attend. It does happen sometimes that when a very attractive press visit is learned about a number of journalists will ring up and ask to be invited. And some who were not invited will ring up and complain about this afterwards. This only goes to show yet another of the pitfalls of media relations: you can be too successful.

3. Party briefing

No matter what details may have been sent at the time of invitation, each person who has accepted must be sent detailed instructions three to seven days prior to the event. The instructions should not be sent too soon, otherwise they may be mislaid, not too late otherwise they may be delayed in the post or in the publishing house's internal postal system. If necessary a map should be included showing the pick-up point, or the location of the venue. Before leaving home every guest should know exactly the programme of the visit.

It is unwise to issue only assembly instructions in advance, and then to issue the rest of the instructions during the journey or upon arrival, although it is sensible to re-issue instructions in case anyone has left them behind. Knowledge of the scheme of things will enable people to bring with them suitable clothing, accessories and equipment which might include such things as raincoats, sunglasses, cameras or field glasses. Thoughtful organisers make successful events.

Some organisers make the mistake of handing out elaborate press kits as soon as they meet guests, and when these kits are clumsy cardboard wallets it really is a problem to know what to do with them. They are likely to be discarded before the arrival at the venue! A sheet of paper that will go into a pocket or handbag is much better appreciated. Press kits can be a fetish which irritates guests. They are often a waste of money.

4. News story facilities

If journalists are likely to need working facilities so that they get stories, pictures or tapes back to their offices in time for use that day, these facilities must not only be laid on but made known in advance. Telex, telephones, typewriters, word processors, lighting facilities, computer terminals, dark-rooms, and cars to station or airport may be necessary. It is useless inviting people to cover a story which they cannot communicate to their editors in good time.

5. Timing

Following on from this is the need to time events such as VIP visits and official openings so that they occur before lunch and there is time to communicate the story to evening papers and radio and TV news services which are broadcast by 6pm onwards. This timing of press visits will be controlled by the location of the venue, and also by whether the party is staying overnight or travelling to and from the venue during the day. Day return visits present problems requiring very tight and foolproof schedules, and much will depend upon the speed of the transport. We must accept that the earliest a party may be able to leave a city centre — to which members have already travelled from their homes — is 9am, and it should be back by 5.30pm since some members of the party may well have to undertake a considerable additional journey to reach their homes. Add to this the fact that most factories close down for lunch at 12.30pm, and close for the day at 4.30pm, there are very strict time limitations within which a visit has to be planned.

Every item in the programme must therefore be timed, and this does mean going over the ground and timing every movement of the party, making special allowances for the time it takes for a given number of people to leave or enter a vehicle or building, cross roads, ascend stairs or attend demonstrations. An experienced organiser can estimate these times without having to resort to a mock rehearsal, but it does pay to go over the sequence of movements where they will actually happen. Even then it is wise to insert in the timetable some extra minutes so that the programme is flexible enough to allow for losses of time through lateness of transport, unexpected weather conditions or some other minor disaster on the day. The opposite can also happen, and there may be time in hand which has to be filled.

This programming should be so expertly done that the party proceeds comfortably throughout the sequence of events without anyone being conscious of being 'organised', only that everything runs smoothly. Although a programme may be carefully planned and scrupulously rehearsed it seldom actually goes like clockwork because trains can run late, aircraft are notorious for being late, traffic does get held up, people get lost, and something always takes longer than expected. But this does not matter if the organiser has taken the unexpected into account.

As an example, the timetable for a women's press party to a south coast town permitted various delays in transport. In the event there was time to spare and the coach took a detour along the coast. It was a day of constant adaptation as there were several substitutes in the party which meant a change in the table plan, one member missed the train but joined the party later. However, a story was written afterwards congratulating the organiser on a visit 'that ran like clockwork'.

But it may be necessary, possible or advisable to take a press party to a distant location with all its costs and troubles of transporting, feeding and accommodating perhaps a hundred people over a period of, say, 36 hours. The event could be televised, conveyed by telephone landline and shown on a giant Eidophor screen to a press audience in a London hotel. Hiring the landline is expensive, but the total operation is simpler and can be economical if it is a big story capable of earning substantial coverage.

ROYAL PROTOCOL

To minimise the presence of the media so that members of the Royal Family are not harassed by a swarm of journalists and cameramen, a rota system is operated by the press and information office at Buckingham Palace, Clarence House or Kensington Palace according to the member of the Royal Family. The arrangements vary according to the occasion, but the basic make-up of a royal rota press party is shown in Figure 9.2.

Where a single journalist or photographer is nominated, he or she does not work merely for his own newspaper but makes the story or pictures generally available.

Not all the options listed in Figure 9.2 are taken up, and over and above these options it is sometimes possible, depending on the nature of the engagement, to have additional places for non-rota or static photographers or to make minor modifications. Circular badges are issued bearing this information:

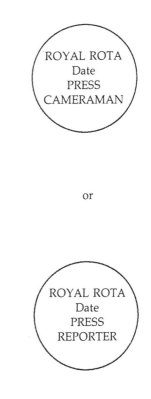

Figure 9.1   Badges for royal rota journalists and photographers

Reporting

Press Association: Court Correspondent   Carries permanent Buckingham Palace pass
   or reporter   (reporting for National newspapers)
BBC: Court Correspondent   Occasionally
IRN: Court Correspondent   Occasionally

Filming

BBC Television news cameraman   With sound recordist, lighting engineer,
                                        reporter, as required

ITN (or regional ITV Company) cameraman   "
(These all use hand-held cameras)

Photography

2 colour negative still photographers   Allocated by Newspaper Publishers'
   (1 national newspaper, 1 photographic news   Association
   agency)
1 colour transparency photographer   "

Frequent additions

Press Association photographer
In places with *provincial Press interest*:
1–3 reporters and 1–3 photographers from   Allocated by the Newspaper Society
   local newspapers
BBC local radio reporter   (In place of Court Correspondent)
Commercial local radio reporter   "

Figure 9.2   Royal protocol press, radio, TV rota system

CHAPTER 10

Exhibitions and Exhibitors

TWO PUBLIC RELATIONS ASPECTS

There are two clear-cut sections in this chapter: media relations in support of an individual participant in an exhibition; and media relations for an exhibition as a whole, that is on behalf of the organisers but also beneficial to the individual exhibitors. The chapter does not deal with public and trade exhibitions or trade fairs as such since they are advertising media, but only with the public relations aspects of these shows.

PUBLIC RELATIONS SUPPORT FOR EXHIBITORS

It is an expensive business to take stands in private or public, national or local, permanent or travelling exhibitions, to say nothing of overseas trade fairs, and DTI Joint Venture schemes which will be discussed in Chapter 24. Space has to be rented, the stand has to be designed and built, equipment has to be made ready and transported to the hall, give-away literature has to be designed and printed, certain advertising may be advisable, and much time will be occupied in staffing the stand. It is so costly that some companies will not exhibit at all, while others exhibit only irregularly or in inexpensive joint venture schemes abroad.

Nevertheless, on the whole, exhibitions such as those held at Olympia and Earls Court, London, and at the National Exhibition Centre, Birmingham, are well supported and attended. Throughout the year exhibitions are taking place every week, and the magazine *Exhibitions Bulletin* is packed with dates, venues and details. Exhibitions are, in spite of the misgivings of some firms, a major advertising medium, which suggest that the costs must be relative to results.

According to the Exhibition Industry Report 1991, published by the Exhibition Industry Federation, 779 exhibitions were held in Britain in 1990 (there were 651 in 1988 and 708 in 1989), £1403 million was spent by visitors and exhibitors, and 9.16 million people attended. Public relations support before, during and after the show can do much to increase the value of an exhibit to people who cannot or will not attend so that the impact and cost of the exhibit is spread over an infinitely larger number of potential buyers. In addition, public relations support can increase the number of visitors to the stand. These are bonuses not to be ignored.

The cost of providing this support is, relatively, very small. When preparing an estimate of time to be expended in order to arrive at an annual fee, the consultant needs to allocate no more than three to five days' time, spread over a period, to each client exhibitor. Materials and expenses will not add too much to the bill if news releases are kept to a reasonable length, press packs are avoided, and the press room is not flooded with too many photographs.

Thus we arrive at a time, materials and expenses cost which can be divided into three categories: (1) advance press relations; (2) supplying the press room; (3) attending the press previews and official opening. In the case of overseas exhibitions a further cost will be the translation of releases.

One of the largest single material costs, which does need to be rigorously controlled, is that of photographs, very few of which may be used because of the competition from so many exhibitors and the fact that most journals can print but two or three pictures at the most. Unless a picture has news value, it has no place in the press room, and many of the pictures to be found in exhibition press rooms have no place anywhere. Colour photographs should not be put in press rooms, although it may be possible to negotiate the use of colour prints by some newspapers, and colour transparencies by some magazines.

For the PRO or consultant intent on doing all possible to enhance the value of a stand at an exhibition the following plan is recommended.

1. Advance planning

When the annual budget is being prepared, it is important to know the details of the exhibition programme. This applies whether media relations are handled by a staff member or by a consultant. Time can then be allocated, and preparatory work can begin at once because it is often necessary to work from one annual exhibition to the next if the organisation is a regular participant. The practitioner will need to know names of exhibitions with venues, dates and stand numbers. A plan of each exhibition will be required so that the location is known of the stands which have been booked. Even if there is but a tentative proposal to go in an exhibition, the PRO or consultant should know about it. This means

that those responsible for exhibitions must work in close collaboration with the public relations practitioner, and vice versa. Moreover, they should understand why this information is necessary and how it can contribute to the success of participation in the show.

2. Contacting the exhibition promoter

The practitioner should contact the promoters of the exhibition and obtain any available literature and instructions to participants. For example, who is editing the exhibition catalogue? The PRO or consultant should supply the entry. What special facilities are likely to exist, such as a cinema in which the exhibitor's video can be shown, or a seminar in which company personnel might be able to take part either on the platform or in the audience?

3. Contacting the exhibition press officer

As a result of contacting the promoters, the practitioner will have learned the name of the exhibition press officer, who may be on the promoter's permanent staff or be a consultant appointed for the occasion. The PRO or consultant can then discuss with the exhibition press officer *months in advance* what will be exhibited (or at least the business of the exhibitor) and supply information which can be used to publicise the show. The identity of the official opener can be learned, and what VIPs are expected to visit the show and on which days. Generally, over a period preceding and during the event, the two can work together for their mutual advantage, making the most of opportunities for media coverage for both the exhibition itself and the individual exhibitor.

It is, of course, essential to work closely with the exhibition press officer so that one may know exactly what arrangements are being made for a press preview or press day. Some promoters are very lax about press facilities, and others do not appoint their own press officer until two or three months before the event. But we will deal with these problems in the next section on Public Relations for Exhibitions. The point is made here to emphasise the need for liaison between the public relations personnel on both sides.

4. Obtaining advance information about the exhibit

This is by far the most difficult part of the exercise, and it may be this which deters some consultants from doing more for their clients who exhibit. Exhibitors are notoriously indecisive about what they are going to exhibit, and although they may be genuinely anxious not to reveal trade secrets about a new product to be launched at the show, quite often there are no secrets and it is just inefficiency which makes information unavailable. Yet the PRO or consultant must have some knowledge of his company's or client's intentions if useful coverage is to be gained in the journals which are previewing the exhibition or publishing special numbers to coincide with the event.

5. Press previews

Monthly magazines previewing exhibitions usually require copy six weeks before publication, and some like to work even further ahead to avoid special issues being something of a tax on their staffing resources. The exhibitor who does not know what he is exhibiting is likely to be left out, or given a bare mention which is of no consequence. But the practitioner can overcome problems like this by making sure that editors are given at least a general description of what the company makes or supplies which is certainly better than a mere statement of name, address and stand number.

Another problem arises in that editors often obtain lists of exhibitors from the promoters and then write to each participant asking for information. They seldom write to the correct person, however, and very often letters never reach the PRO or consultant, so that press coverage is lost.

Nevertheless, the astute practitioner can circumvent the trouble caused by such careless mailings and clumsy handling of correspondence and produce an advance story six to eight weeks before the exhibition date; in time, that is, to distribute it to all the magazines and newspapers likely to be interested. In doing this, care must be taken to head the story with the name of the exhibition, the date, the venue and the stand number because not every editor will know these details. They should not clog up the body of the release.

At this early stage, the practitioner may suffer from the disadvantage of having no pictures of the main exhibit, but a picture can be supplied of a product which will be on the stand even if it is not the highlight or the secret new product.

From these remarks it must be apparent that the practitioner has to show considerable initiative to overcome the many obstacles to enhancing the value of an exhibit, but it can be done.

Some time prior to the opening of the exhibition, the practitioner should receive from the promoter's press officer details of press room arrangements such as the location of the press room, the number of releases and pictures recommended and the date and time of the press preview and official opening. The exhibitor's PRO or consultant should take the precaution of telephoning the exhibition press officer a fortnight before the opening date to make sure that he receives final information and tickets to the press preview if these are necessary.

Two different kinds of preview have been mentioned and in case this is confusing, it should be explained that magazines will sometimes preview an exhibition in the sense that they will publish a guide to the exhibition (as distinct from reviewing the event afterwards), while some promoters invite the press to attend a preview of the exhibition, either on the day previous to the opening or an hour or so before the official opening on the morning of the first day.

6. The press room

Owing to the physical peculiarities of exhibition halls, the offices are mostly placed close to the outer walls so that the middle area is left free for exhibition purposes, and this results in cell-like press rooms often situated in obscure places.

It pays to deliver press room material personally and, if possible, to have some say in how and where it is to be displayed. In well-arranged press rooms, the material is laid out on tables in alphabetical order (racks are a nuisance because the releases will droop forward, losing their identity), while a sample picture is given a number and displayed so that copies may be requested from the stock held by the press room staff. It is essential to visit the press room from time to time to see whether stocks of releases or pictures require replenishing.

To avoid repetition, it is sufficient to say here that the news release supplied should be brief and provide news, not a company history or something equally irrelevant, that pictures must be captioned, and that nothing else is required. Journalists do not arrive with suitcases so press kits are unnecessary. Moreover, most journalists want a few releases they can put in their pocket, or in their briefcase if they happen to be carrying one.

7. Staffing the stand

It is rarely necessary for public relations personnel to be present on the stand after the first day unless the exhibit is very much a public relations effort and they have work to do. The major part of support for an exhibit should have been completed before the exhibition opened, but a supply of news releases and pictures should be kept in the stand office, in addition to those in the press room, and the stand manager should take charge of them. In practice, a staff PRO is likely to attend the stand more frequently than a consultant, unless the fee is large enough to cover the time expenditure.

8. Press visitors to the stand

There are several ways in which the press can be invited as guests of the exhibitor. These will be in addition to the efforts made by the promoters to attract journalists and may be on a different day to the press preview or press day. It depends on the resources of the exhibitor, the size of the stand, and what kind of show it is, indoors or outdoors. The latter category includes agricultural shows from the Royal to local county ones, and big events like Farnborough Air Show.

A big exhibitor may hold a press reception on the stand, but only a limited number of these can be attended in any one day and it may be unwise to compete. In most exhibition halls, private rooms can be hired for press parties, so size of stand is not necessarily a limiting factor. The more modest exhibitor can still invite the press by sending journalists an open invitation to call at any time, when hospitality will be available. Sometimes, in spite of a press day, it is a good idea to invite the press to come back on another day for a reception and demonstration on the stand.

9. After the exhibition

As a result of the event, many new press contacts will have been made, and they can be mailed future stories or invited to public relations events. Some of these interested journalists will have asked for more information, additional pictures, opportunities to visit the factory or write feature articles, and all these things must be attended to before the interest is allowed to flag.

10. Clearing the press room

On the final afternoon, a last visit should be made to the press room to collect surplus pictures and news releases. Pictures cost money and there is no point in leaving them to the exhibition press officer to throw away. If the exhibition press officer has been helpful and the press room has been well run, it is only courteous to express one's appreciation. Public relations is a friendly world, and it is likely that there will be future opportunities for further co-operation. One thing that is guaranteed to annoy an exhibition press officer is having to dispose of unwanted press kits — unless he has been wise enough to prohibit them in the first place!

PUBLIC RELATIONS SUPPORT FOR EXHIBITIONS

Now let us consider public relations for the exhibition itself.

An exhibition press officer should be appointed to an exhibition as soon as the event has been agreed upon and with shows which are held at regular yearly or two-yearly intervals, media relations activity will be constant. Large exhibition promoters have a staff of press officers and this continuous effort is automatic, but the complaint can be made about smaller sponsors that they appoint press officers far too close to the event with the result that exhibitors do not get the support they deserve.

During the months leading up to the event, the press officer can stimulate knowledge of the exhibition and interest in it by issuing news stories and supplying articles. This is, of course, done extremely well by the press officer to the Ideal Home Exhibition through the associated *Daily Mail*, and the same steady build-up of new stories heralds other famous events.

But the press officer can do very little if he or she does not know who is going to take part and what they will be showing. Since we have already said that finding out what is to be exhibited is no mean task for the exhibitor's PRO or consultant it is doubly difficult for someone even further removed from those responsible for exhibits. Yet the exhibition press officer needs to be constantly filling in the picture of the eventual event in order to be able to talk and write about it. His job does not start and finish with the press room during the run of the show.

So, collating information about exhibitors is an important part of the advance publicity job, but first the person who can supply the information has to be discovered. Usually the person who signs the contract for the stand space, the only name that the promoters have, is useless to the press officer. The name and address of the advertising manager, publicity manager, PRO, press officer or consultant is needed. This means writing to each exhibitor as stand booking comes in, asking for the name and address of the person who will be dealing with the public relations on behalf of the exhibitor.

This request often comes as a surprise to those exhibitors who do not use public relations and do not realise that it has anything to do with exhibitions. Others respond very willingly, and are only too glad to put their PRO or consultant in touch with the exhibition press officer. A mailing list can now be assembled so that all communications from the press officer to exhibitors go direct to the person responsible for supplying information. If it is not done, much of the correspondence from the exhibition press officer to the exhibitors is liable to go astray, be mislaid, misunderstood or just not answered. And this is a pity because such a breakdown in communication may deprive both sides of valuable communication opportunities.

Ideally, the exhibition press officer should issue numbered bulletins, reporting progress to exhibitors and telling them what else may be required of them and to a greater or lesser extent this is done by the promoters of the larger exhibitions. An advantage of such a bulletin is that it does indicate that there is an active press officer, and even if one issue goes astray because the exhibitor has no public relations organisation, or fails to act upon a request, succeeding communications must surely evoke a response.

When the press officer knows what the exhibition is going to look like, having been sent artists' impressions of stands and told about special working models and demonstrations, worthwhile advance stories can be issued to arouse the curiosity of potential visitors and encourage them to book the forthcoming event in their diaries. This is clearly of benefit to exhibitors and depends entirely upon their co-operation.

The following questions must be decided: Should there be a press reception, a press lunch, a preview on a previous day, or a preview prior to the official opening at, say, 11am on the first day? How are the press to be invited and received and what facilities will be provided? Should the official opening be made at a seated assembly, or in the hall by the main entrance? All the various factors mentioned above have to be taken into consideration and no hard and fast rule can be laid down, as many matters will be governed by the subject, location, size and news value of the event.

Another controlling factor is the day of the week on which an exhibition opens. When an exhibition opens mid-week or at the end of the week, an afternoon given over to a press preview is a very good thing, giving the press ample time to gain interesting material which they can use next day or even at the weekend. But when an exhibition opens on a Monday morning a Sunday press preview will not be popular, and the possibilities of press coverage are more limited.

On these specially organised press previews, hospitality is necessary, but a 'dry' press room is preferable, especially since there is seldom a lot of space and it can be a very busy place. Most journalists are busy people and the ones who hang about drinking in the press room are mainly correspondents and freelances who have time to spare. In any case,

there are plenty of bars and the exhibitor's club to which the press officer can take a journalist if he wishes to offer him a drink.

The biggest hazard for the press officer who is seriously concerned with providing the *press* with a service is the material which the exhibitors bring to the press room. Some of it should be banned. In the interests of exhibitors, the exhibition promoters and the press, the press officer is entitled to demand that (a) news releases be brief; (b) photographs be captioned and (c) no press packs or wallets be supplied. The conscientious press officer acts as an intermediary between exhibitors and the press and this double duty has to be remembered since it can be crucial to the success of the whole operation.

Press room hints for exhibitors who do not employ professional public relations services

News releases

1. The release (50 copies for the Press Room please, with spares for your stand) must contain news of interest to the press reviewing the exhibition. The first paragraph should summarise the complete news story.
2. Releases should be as short as possible, the ideal being a story restricted to one side of one sheet of paper, complete with stand number and the exhibitor's full name and address.
3. In addition to supplying the Press Room, exhibitors are advised to send news releases direct to special correspondents and specialised magazines likely to report the exhibitor's participation in the exhibition.

Photographs

1. Please supply 25 half-plate glossy black-and-white prints.
2. Each picture must be fully captioned and

bear an address and telephone number for further information. Captions should be attached to the backs of prints, preferably with Sellotape.

3. Pictures must not be stapled to news releases, or attached with paperclips.
4. Colour prints or transparencies are not required in the press room, although their supply can be arranged with editors who request them.

The Press do not want:
(a) Press packs or wallets
(b) House journals
(c) Picture postcards
(d) Timetables
(e) Sales literature
(f) Company histories
(g) Free gifts or samples

During the exhibition, the staff of the press room will be delighted to receive new stories.

One of the abominations of all kinds of public relations events is the over-elaborate so-called press kit, and in the press room there is even less excuse for its use than at the press reception or on the factory visit which is at least restricted to one organisation. When asked why these monstrosities are put in the press room, the excuse is made that this is what the client wants.

This is nonsense. When consultants do what clients want they should stop pretending to be consultants. Does a doctor obey his patient? A consultant's job is to advise: he is paid to know better than the client.

The only way to put a stop to this, which merely helps to encourage the press in their disrespect for public relations, is for exhibition press officers to agree on a form of standard procedure which can be distributed by all press officers prior to all exhibitions.

The *Press Room Hints* quoted here should be universally applied.

EXHIBITIONS IN DEVELOPING COUNTRIES

When population is scattered and largely agricultural as in the villages of many African, Asian and South American countries, the mobile show with dancers, singers, puppet shows and films shown on a screen erected on the roof of a Land Rover, or videos shown on TV sets, is an excellent medium. Sometimes these travelling shows seek to win the sympathy and support of the chief, headman, or elders who act as the innovators and then convert adoptors among their people. Mobile shows have been used to introduce topics like banking, husbandry, birth control, child welfare, census procedures and many other subjects, some commercial and others promoted by the government. The puppet show is a good method where there are language problems and the message may be conveyed very enterprisingly in mime. These more direct forms of communication have much greater penetration than radio. In fact, they can go to places never reached by radio, for there are large areas of the world where communication is still by the traditional methods of the drum, the gong and morning and evening official court messenger.

However, there are problems. In some Muslim communities, the women may not be permitted to see the shows and exhibitions, while there is seldom anyone more resistant to new ideas than an ill- or uneducated villager who follows traditional life-styles. One of the basic obstacles to education in illiterate populations is the lack of parental literacy. This is a handicap little known in Western society. Moreover, in developing countries, lost literacy occurs among teenagers after they leave school and cannot find employment requiring literacy. Media that involve demonstrations and presentations are therefore very important among these millions of people.

Special exhibition centres have been built in countries such as Indonesia, Malaysia and

Singapore. In hot countries, trade fairs and other exhibitions are often held outdoors.

PRIVATE EXHIBITIONS

The private exhibition can be combined with other public relations media already and about to be discussed, and we must not overlook the small, portable exhibition arranged on hardboard, peg-board or Marler-Hayley display stands, or even simply laid out on tables.

Private exhibitions may be large permanent ones like the Legoland children's park at Billund, Denmark. In London, there is an interesting exhibition at the Thames Barrier, while in Portsmouth harbour there is the *Mary Rose* exhibition. Many companies have exhibitions on their premises.

Mobile or touring exhibitions are also possible, and all kinds of vehicles, such as caravans, buses, trains and even aircraft are used. Or an exhibition can be mounted temporarily at a library, hotel, railway station forecourt, airport or other appropriate venue.

CHAPTER 11

Sponsorship

WHY SPONSOR?

Sponsorship may be undertaken for advertising, marketing or public relations purposes, or for a combination of two or three of these purposes. There can also be public relations spin-offs from sponsorships which are conducted mainly for advertising and marketing objectives. This is therefore a complicated subject and different people in an organisation may want a sponsorship to achieve different ends. Occasionally, financial aid may be given for purely philanthropic purposes, and we have seen monies donated and causes supported when a company has had a social conscience and felt impelled to make a contribution to society. There are also occasions when a business leader has had a personal interest in a subject, and has persuaded the board to indulge in a sponsorship.

In the last two instances no reward is sought or expected. However, most sponsorships today are not quixotic, and they are funded for very deliberate business reasons. Two important questions need to be answered before committing the organisation to a sponsorship: (i) what rewards are likely to be gained? and (ii) what will be the total cost? The cost depends on the nature of the sponsorship, and could range from no more than prize-money to supporting advertising and various forms of hospitality and socialising.

Before considering purely public relations reasons for undertaking sponsorships, let us look at some of the advertising and marketing reasons for *investing* money in sponsorship, bearing in mind that both can enjoy public relations spin-offs and other rewards.

ADVERTISING OBJECTIVES

One advertising purpose is to use sponsorship when regular forms of advertising are denied, and a typical example is the tobacco company which is banned from commercial TV in the UK. By sponsoring major sporting events such as motor-racing, motor-car rallies, golf, tennis and cricket, a company is able to include its name in the name of the event (e.g. Benson and Hedges International Open) so that it is quoted repeatedly by commentators, reporters, spectators and the public at large. In the course of the event, perimeter boards and banners can be exhibited, and racing cars (e.g. Marlboro, Players Special) and motorcycles (Rothman-Honda) can be painted with the sponsor's name. This also applies to other sponsors who have not been banned from commercial TV. All these visible representations will be picked up by TV and press photographers' cameras, whatever limitations may be applied from time to time over exploitation of such coverage. Sponsors can also refer to their participation in poster and press advertising.

Many organisations can use sponsorship to ally their brands with appropriate activities, and Coca Cola, for instance, have supported a number of young people's sports such as swimming and athletics.

MARKETING OBJECTIVES

Louella Miles, writing on sponsorship in the CIM journal *Marketing Business* (June 1991), said that

> 'to be a successful sponsor you have to fulfil certain requirements. You need to be:
>   Clear headed about your marketing objectives.
>   Certain that these objectives can be met by sponsorship.
>   Sure that you carry the rest of your company with you (nothing destroys a sponsorship more swiftly than various departments squabbling over its relevance).
>   Provided with a watertight contract, vetted by your lawyer and a specialist in this area.
>   Prepared to work hard to make it a success. The launch is the easy part, the hard graft comes in years one and two.'

Sponsorship may well be used to position products in the market, and there are marketing as well as advertising implications in some of the examples given. If a company changes its policy and wishes to appeal to a different segment of the market it can sponsor something which is popular with that new market segment. For example, a company predominant in the female market may introduce lines of interest to the male market, and by sponsoring an interest of predominantly male appeal it could establish its new marketing strategy. At one time Yardley, the perfumers, did this when they introduced male toiletries and sponsored motor sport.

Sponsorship may be used to counter competition, as Canon did versus Olympus, in adopting the Football League for three seasons with all its spin-off advertising opportunities at local (92 teams), national and even international level. The sponsorship also made known Canon's range of office machines. The international aspect is a bonus since English football has followers world-wide. But the Canon Football League also had major public relations implications, and at the end of the three years the managing director claimed that hardly an office in the UK did not have a Canon machine.

DEFINING PURPOSE AND SUITABILITY

There are plenty of cultural, educational, sporting and other interests which would welcome financial aid, and there are commercial organisations which see sponsorship as a means of achieving their advertising, marketing or public relations aims. In between, there are specialised organisations such as the Association of Business Sponsorship of the Arts which seek sponsors, and specialist consultants like Alan Pascoe Associates and CSS International Holdings which are skilled at negotiating and organising sponsorship.

An interesting development has been the increasing cost of TV advertising (with diminishing audiences due to satellite TV and alternative TV uses and programmes including time-switching to watch recorded programmes) to the extent that beyond a certain point, conventional advertising has ceased to be cost-effective. Some advertisers have therefore turned to sponsorship with its additional public relations advantages. In spite of the large sums of money spent on sponsorship, these expenditures are often cheaper and more effective than commercial TV, and may even gain TV coverage anyway, although in a different way, since sponsorships cannot include specific and persuasive sales messages. At most, it is reminder advertising, which may, of course, be little different from outdoor advertising for mass market brands. A further development has been the sponsoring of actual programmes, first on BBC and then on ITV in 1991 with the new ITC.

Should one sponsor a book prize, museum exhibition, the raising of a sunken treasure ship, awards to journalists, expeditions or other feats of endurance, research fellowships to graduates, racing yacht or power-boat, race-horse or show jumper, golf tournament or cricket series, tennis player or marathon runner, racing-car team or motor cyclist, or maybe the local brass band or cycling club? The choices and opportunities are longer than your arm.

The extent of sponsorship can be seen from the section in *Hollis Press and Public Relations Annual* and the publication in 1992 of a new annual, *Hollis Sponsorship and Donations*.

The right sponsorship must be selected. It needs to have a character in keeping with that of the sponsor, appeal to a sufficiently large number of the potential sponsor's customers, and be capable of attracting the interest of the media or in some other way have public relations possibilities. A number of opportunities may have to be compared on a cost-benefit basis, until all but the most profitable are eliminated. Sponsorships have to be assessed just as critically as media when planning a media schedule. It would be perfectly reasonable to come to the conclusion that no sponsorships were worth supporting!

It is essential to define objectives clearly, and it may be that sponsorship will be a medium through which the public relations message can be addressed to a particular public in order to achieve a specific objective. This is a sensible, practical approach to the subject, making it possible to assess the advantages and disadvantages of the various forms of sponsorship which are available. Thus, we match suitability with objectivity, remembering what we said earlier about the expectation of rewards and the total cost.

If one wishes to develop knowledge about an industry, a sponsored technical book may be useful; a company associated with motoring (as Esso, Shell and Michelin have done) may find it appropriate to sponsor road maps and tourist guides; to enhance community relations, a company may support a local theatre; because supporters are mostly customers, it may be a good idea to sponsor the local football team (e.g. by providing strip as Sharp have done, the players wearing shirts bearing the name Sharp); and to encourage wider and more efficient use of a product, prizes may be put up in contests and shows as sewing-machine makers and horticultural suppliers have done. Matching purpose and kind of sponsorship is very important, as is resisting invitations to enter into sponsorships which may be mainly philanthropic and offer no material rewards.

At the same time, it is only fair to say that a sponsor must be worthy of the sponsorship. To be able to sponsor generally implies that one has arrived: no one wants to benefit from an unknown or disreputable sponsor! There have been British interests which have rejected foreign sponsors because it was considered that such an association would not enhance the reputation of an interest with long-standing British traditions. Athletes have resented sponsorships by brewers.

As will be realised, sponsorships can cost a fortune as in the case of a motor-racing team or be modest ones such as giving products as prizes at local flower shows. It all depends on the size and kind of market. A multi-national selling a product world-wide could find it highly profitable to sponsor a motor-racing team engaged in international Grand Prix racing, whereas a manufacturer of garden insecticides could find the provision of prizes at local flower shows an ideal way of enhancing its reputation with amateur gardeners. The costs are relative in each case.

An example of a global sponsorship is the Whitbread Round-the-World Yacht Race, which for the 1993–1994 race attracted 82 yacht syndicates from 25 countries. Individual yacht sponsorships, such as Panasonic's, have the name blazoned on the sails, to be seen by 750 million people during the nine-months 32 000 miles race.

KINDS OF SPONSORSHIP

The range of subjects for sponsorship can be defined under certain headings, the most exclusive and most popular, but also often the most costly, being sport, but there are others which may interest a potential sponsor. Japanese companies sponsor almost every kind of sport.

Educational. Under this heading we have bursaries, scholarships, fellowships and other awards which can be made to encourage study and research, possibly producing results or potential recruits of value to the sponsor. There may also be sponsorship of colleges, chairs and professorships, and of equipment. These financial aids may help to enhance the reputation of the company among students, either as a future employer or in a more general sense of establishing understanding, respect and a corporate image among potentially influential people.

Another form of educational sponsorship is the provision of video tapes such as those financed by Eli Lilly for the British Diabetic Association which have been shown to patients at diabetic clinics. They have featured the famous diabetics Harry Secombe and Elaine Stritch.

Cultural. Here we have a form of sponsorship which resembles the historic patronage of artists and musicians by wealthy benefactors. A company may strengthen its reputation by financing art exhibitions, symphony orchestras and concerts, libraries, theatres, players and operas. For instance, the Midland Bank has sponsored promenade operas at Covent Garden. This may be seen to be a service to customers as well as subsidising the very existence or survival of cultural events and institutions.

Marks and Spencer have sponsored the London Philharmonic Orchestra for more than 17 years, and invest nearly £50 000 a year on LPO's concerts for children which are held three times a year at the Festival Hall on London's South Bank, and appeal to school-children, their parents and teachers.

Awards. To encourage interest in their subjects perhaps achieve greater accuracy and better coverage, a number of companies offer annual awards to journalists and press photographers. Food companies may offer awards to the best food writers, camera manufacturers may do likewise to press photographers. Newspapers themselves are sponsors of awards to architects, businessmen and other groups.

An original one is Toshiba's Year of Invention Award, which costs in all £500 000 spread over prizes, advertising, fees and administration.

Books. Technical and educational books, sports annuals, guidebooks, road maps, and other publications may be not only sponsored but sold as legitimate publications under recognised publishers' imprints.

The sponsored book is usually arranged with a reputable publisher who includes it in his list and retails it through bookshops. But in order to justify a specialised book and to illustrate it properly, production costs are shared by the sponsor who also undertakes to buy perhaps half the number of copies printed. The author is usually a company expert on the subject. In this way an excellent book is often published which would not otherwise be economic as a normal commercial publishing proposition. Thus, there is a service to all concerned, reader, publisher, sponsor and perhaps the industry itself if the book is authoritative and a general contribution to the literature on the subject. A long-established example of this is the Rentokil Library which consists of 17 useful books on pest control and timber preservation written by the company's scientists.

The above refers mainly to specialised technical books with limited circulations, but there are also best-sellers like the popular sports annuals and, of course, the *Guinness Book of Records*, the *Guinness Book of Advertising* and an enterprising publishing division. We must not forget McDougall's famous cookery book, new editions of which are advertised on bags of flour and sold by direct response.

Expeditions and feats of endurance. Expeditions, mountain climbs, voyages and other feats of endurance rely on generous contributions of funds and equipment. Sometimes these activities may be used to test products, and the results can be publicised afterwards. Other sponsorships may have less obvious value, and no benefit may accrue to the suppliers. It depends how the sponsorship can be exploited, or what publicity is achieved. A whole enterprise may be funded by one sponsor such as a bank. A vehicle or boat may carry the name of the sponsor. If the venture is successful, great credit may befall the sponsor; if the venture meets disaster the sponsorship could be a total loss. One of the Himalayan climbs was sponsored by a bank which was criticised for so doing because of the economic situation but when the climb was successful the bank won praise for its confidence and support.

Sports. This is by far the largest area of sponsorship. Large audiences can be reached, there are numerous major and minor sports, and particular sports may be sufficiently specialised to provide a direct route to a certain public. Darts sponsorship has been used to encourage more people to visit pubs; tennis has been used to introduce new racquets; and golf has been used to promote golf trolleys.

In recent years, sponsorship has helped to popularise sports especially when this has been coupled with TV coverage, two interesting examples being snooker and bowls. Both now enjoy greater public interest, and make good television. Large numbers of people who previously had no interest in either sport now watch these sponsored contests. If TV is involved, the visual impact has to be understood. *Will it be good or bad public relations?*

Snooker has proved to be sufficiently exciting to claim big audiences, with the added advantage of some colourful snooker stars who may even appear on other TV programmes. But the burly darts champions may have discouraged some viewers who saw beer-drinking as the cause of the players' obesity!

Sports sponsorship can also include the supply of essential equipment such as clothing, balls, bats and racquets, and time clocks and computers for producing results. They may be visible on TV or in press photographs, perhaps referred to in advertising.

Sports sponsorship may be of events themselves, or of prizes and trophies awarded; or of teams or of individual participants; or in the provision of clothing and equipment used. Thus, in any one event many sponsors may be involved, as is seen in Grand Prix motor-racing, show jumping and the London Marathon.

PUBLIC RELATIONS ADVANTAGES

We have looked briefly at the advertising and marketing values of sponsorship, but what are the special public relations advantages which are of interest to readers of this book? Why has sponsorship become a primary medium in so many public relations programmes? In fact, this is almost the opposite to the situation in some developing countries where sponsorship is seen to be the sole expression of public relations. In Britain, sponsorship has existed for a very long time, but today it is big business. One of the reasons for its popularity is that it has sometimes taken over from less cost-effective media advertising. Another is the way in which TV has popularised so many sports, so that sponsorship of these sports provides a direct communication link with their audiences. Moreover, sponsorship provides association with popular interests.

The following are some of the public relations purposes of sponsorship.

Corporate image. Sponsorship can help to show the organisation as one which is socially responsible or makes a contribution to society, thus building goodwill and reputation. This can be at local community, national or international level.

Japanese companies have often used sponsorship to overcome prejudice, especially in countries which they had occupied during the Second World War. In Britain, Japanese companies have monopolised sports sponsorship.

Some of Britain's most famous sports events are now sponsored, very largely with corporate image effect, most noteworthy being the Ever Ready Derby which helped to re-establish the image of a company which had gone through a series of changed names and ownership.

Corporate identity. Because the organisation's logo, house colour or typography can be associated with the event, it is possible to increase awareness of the physical identity of the organisation. This familiarisation process can be a communication asset, so that the organisation is easily recognised and distinguished from its competitors.

Name familiarising. An organisation or a product can gain name familiarity through sponsoring, particularly if it is a new, difficult to spell or pronounce, or foreign name. The Japanese have made very effective use of sponsorship for this purpose. It is not just name-plugging in an advertising sense, but of familiarising people with names so that they know what they represent. Cornhill Insurance has benefited greatly from sponsoring test cricket, becoming well known to many thousands of potential buyers of household insurance who had never heard of the company before it sponsored the Cornhill Tests.

Understanding. Coupled with name familiarisation can be the use of sponsorship to create understanding of what an organisation does or what products or services it supplies. The range of Canon office machines has become far better known as a result of football sponsorship; Yamaha organs have been distinguished from Yamaha motor-cycles as a result of snooker sponsorship; and bank services to young farmers has been developed through local show-jumping sponsorships.

PUBLIC RELATIONS SPIN-OFFS

The principal spin-off of all sponsorships is usually *media coverage*, and the greater the public interest in the subject the greater the volume of press, radio and TV coverage. An event like the London Marathon produces media coverage before, during and after the event, with hours of coverage on the day. Test cricket matches go on for days; when *The Sun* sponsored the Grand National, it gave the event sports page coverage for months leading up to the race, which also had international TV coverage.

The event can also be videotaped for showing to future audiences, such as on exhibition stands and at sales conferences, or to customers. Photographs can be placed in the photo library and used to illustrate articles and books.

Some sponsorships lead to sales of body media such as hats, visors, T-shirts and sweaters. There may also be sale of souvenirs. Even toy cars bear the names of sponsors to give them realism.

CHARITY SPONSORSHIPS

Charity events can be sponsored, one example being the British Gas hot air balloon, shaped like a rugby ball, which has competed in cross-Channel balloon races. On one occasion the British Gas Balloon raised £75 000 for the Paul O'Gorman Fund for Children with Leukemia and contributed towards a new centre at Great Ormond Street Children's Hospital in London.

HOSPITALITY AND PARTICIPATION

Another substantial benefit is the opportunity to invite company guests or staff members to the event, and to provide hospitality for friends, reporters and commentators. A sponsor may take coachloads of employees to, say, a sponsored horse-race or show-jumping event. Canon salesmen took customers to see local football matches. These costs need to be considered when budgeting the total expenditure for a sponsorship: it may not stop at the direct cost of the sponsorship itself.

At some events, hospitality is the main form of sponsorship, Glyndebourne, Henley Regatta, Royal Ascot and Wimbledon being examples and there are specialised firms such as Letherby and Christopher who handle corporate catering.

However, this can be a touchy subject and guests may be cautious about accepting invitations which seem to occupy unwarranted office time or look like bribery. Sainsbury's have a rule that freebies should be refused.

Nevertheless there is one form of hospitality which has caught on (and it usually occurs at weekends) and this is hot air ballooning. Aerial Promotions offer champagne flights and hospitality days can be incorporated with accommodation and sporting activities. Wicker's World Hot-Air Balloon Company give guests 1½ hour flights, travelling 15 miles at 4000 feet.

Participatory sponsorships are also popular, either on their own or combined with ballooning. These include karting on indoor circuits, driving Honda powered Frazer Nash rally karts; clay pigeon shooting at Scottish venues; laser clayshooting; driving or riding in military vehicles; or driving exciting vehicles such as Honda Pilot dune racers or Yamaha quad-bikes.

SPONSORED PROGRAMMES ON TV AND RADIO

Until fairly recently, the distinction was made in Britain between commercial broadcasting in which commercials appeared in brief spots or segments (commercial breaks) in the course of programmes for which the broadcaster was responsible, and sponsored broadcasting as adopted widely overseas in which whole programmes were sponsored and often produced by advertisers. Soap operas originated in this way in the USA, being series or serials sponsored by advertisers of soap and other products. Commercial broadcasting was introduced into Britain in the 1950s on the understanding that programmes would be produced independently of advertisers. Sponsorships, particularly of sports, were undertaken in the hope of getting media coverage, especially on TV, and hence the Cornhill tests, Canon Football League, Ever Ready Derby and the Mars London Marathon.

Subtle changes began to occur with BBC Television accepting sponsorships such as British Gas cathedral concerts, Lloyds Bank Young Musician of the Year (for several years), and the Lloyds Bank Fashion Awards, Clothes Show Live Exhibition and the Lloyds Bank Fashion Challenge.

The real impetus to programme sponsorship arose out of the financial problems of the ITV companies. World events like the Gulf War were so costly to cover that it was said that British television had no funds to cover a major Royal event for five years! In 1991 a number of programmes were put up for sponsorship but there were few takers, either because companies were sceptical or because of the recession.

A problem seemed to be to decide what if

any benefit was likely to be derived from an announcement of the sponsor's name at the beginning, in the middle and at the end of programmes. Among the first sponsors was PowerGen's sponsorship of ITV's national networked weather bulletins. This was a static logo and name which appeared at the end of the weather forecast (although it now appears at the beginning and the end). People questioned its value, but it was a new name and as a result of the sponsorship, awareness of it rose in seven months from 3 percent to 37 percent between September 1989 and March 1990 according to research conducted by The British Market Research Bureau. The original contract for a year commencing September 1989 was renewed after only six months to run to the end of 1992, at a cost of under £4 million. Awareness created by this sponsorship helped with the privatisation share flotation. This original sponsorship complied with the IBA ruling at the time and occupied 5 percent of the screen and appeared for about five seconds at the end of each bulletin.

A feature of this and the various sponsorships which followed was that there were various tie-ins and sponsorship spin-offs. The novelty of the PowerGen sponsorship created media and public interest. It was linked with charitable activities and work in education and the environment. Within the company itself, ITV weather presenters took part in corporate videos and internal presentations, hosting the celebrations on March 31 1990 when Power-Gen became a plc.

The other and larger power generating company created by privatisation out of the original Central Electricity Generating Board (CEGB) under the Electricity Act 1989, was National Power. This, too, needed to create awareness about itself and chose sponsorship of ITV's World Cup football series. It was given four credits an hour with a full on-screen logo credit before and after each commercial break. During the opening titles the commentator verbally credited the company by stating 'Brought to you in association with National

Power', this verbal credit being repeated at the end of each match.

There were also reminder press advertisements, plus special inserts and programme page credits in *TV Times*, and Oracle teletext. In all, National Power sponsored 69 hours of ITV World Cup football. During the World Cup, total adult viewing of ITV increased by 23 percent, and the average match audience was by 7.5 million. Research conducted by BMRB showed that 71 percent of adults thought National Power a suitable World Cup sponsor.

However, the most spectacular of early sponsorships was Sony's £1m awareness sponsorship of the 70 hours of ITV's Rugby World Cup in the Autumn of 1991. This was the largest sporting event in 25 years. In the run-up to the World Cup, Sony also sponsored ITV's coverage of the Summer Tours, and in addition backed the networked trailers leading up to the World Cup matches. During the Summer Tour programme, Sony was given credits in the opening titles, break-bumpers and end sequences. For the actual Cup broadcasts, Sony negotiated a 10 second voice and visual credit at the beginning of each programme, culminating with 'Sony, Broadcast sponsors of ITV's Rugby World Cup coverage — You won't get a better view.' The last phrase was also seen on screen with Sony's logo. There was also a specially commissioned introductory film showing a rugby match from the ball's point of view, while many of Sony's 10-second outgoing break-bumpers concentrated on trivia questions such as 'What was Twickenham used for before it became England's HQ? (a) a public house; (b) a bus depot; (c) a cabbage patch?' The answer was given at the beginning of the incoming break-bumper, coupled with the phrase 'Makers of . . .' finishing with a Sony product such as a Walkman.

The broadcast sponsorship was linked by Sony's biggest in-store promotion, with point-of-sale display materials carrying the Rugby World Cup theme.

Finally, Sony Music recorded the World Cup

theme song, *World In Union*, sung by Dame Kiri Te Kanawa, plus the England squad's *Swing Low Sweet Chariot*.

The sponsorship ran from September 28 to November 3 1991 and was a highly skilled use of sponsorship on ITV. On January 31 1992 the Independent Television Association (ITVA), which represents all the UK ITV companies, published a 25-page qualitative research report on the Sony sponsorship.

BMRB conducted a workshop survey for the ITVA study based on eight discussion groups, representing 20–35- and 35–55-year-old male and female groups and different social grades in London, Gloucester, Swansea and Edinburgh. All respondents claimed to have watched three Rugby World Cup matches, and half the respondents had watched eight or more matches. In addition a face-to-face quantitative survey of 600 adults who had purchased consumer electronic products in the last six months, or intended to purchase in the next six months, was conducted by RBL (Research International). This survey tested awareness of Rugby World Cup/interest in rugby; awareness of sponsors of Rugby World Cup; awareness of specifics of sponsorship; attitudes to Sony's sponsorship activity; effect of broadcast sponsorship of Rugby World Cup on Sony's brand awareness and brand image; and the effect of broadcast sponsorship on maximising impact and effectiveness of Sony 1991 advertising campaign. (N.B. In these summaries we have concentrated on sponsorships as public relations media, but there were also associated or subsequent advertising campaigns.)

BARB recorded a cumulative total audience to ITV's Rugby World Cup coverage of over 173 million viewers nationally, with 82 percent of the population watching some coverage — equivalent to 34.4 million adults. Of the RBL Research sample 56 percent claimed to have watched at least one whole match or highlight programme. Rugby leapt from the fourth to the second most watched sport on television.

On awareness, 24 percent of the sample were aware of Sony's sponsorship of a recent major TV event, and among regular rugby viewers the figures rose to 43 percent. When the qualitative groups were questioned, Sony was the first name mentioned as sponsor of the Rugby World Cup, and in some cases was the only name mentioned. Of regular rugby watchers, 60 percent recalled the trivia game and 55 percent the Sony sequences. The conclusion from the RBL field research was that 'Sony's broadcast sponsorship of the Rugby World Cup generated awareness equivalent to (or greater than) other major sponsored events such as football, tennis, snooker, cricket, golf or darts. Many of these are much longer established and have cost the sponsoring company much larger amounts of money cumulatively.' The report however made no comparison with motor sport or horse racing.

Viewers' opinions of the business of sponsorship were very favourable, and Sony's involvement was seen to be appropriate and credible. On attitudes, there was praise for ITV, considering the BBC was more closely associated with rugby. There was generally good recall and reaction to Sony's involvement. Sony's brand image was enhanced, and there were good trade relations resulting in record sales in December. Generally, the research showed a perfect match between Sony and the Rugby World Cup, showing Sony to be innovative, there was the right audience (ABC1 with a male bias), good timing for product sales, and good associations such as music and song.

Two things begin to emerge from this new form of sponsorship in spite of the limited time given to credits. The right product or service needs to be matched with the subject sponsored, and creative ingenuity can exploit the occasion. If we now look at some of the sponsored programmes which followed Sony's in 1991 and 1992, these two points become clear.

Croft Port sponsored *Rumpole of the Bailey* before Christmas 1991, good timing for a little known port compared with the long-established sherry of the same name. Barclaycard sponsored the holiday programme *Wish You Were Here*, which was appropriate. Beamish stout sponsored the repeats and new *Inspector Morse* series, Morse being a beer drinker. And very cleverly the French beer Kronenbourg sponsored the Inspector Maigret series. Media Dimensions, with increasing ingenuity produced the credit sequences for Croft Port, Beamish stout and Kronenbourg. Most ITV sponsorships are handled by the sponsorship division of Granada Television. Let us review each of these more closely, but first let us also consider a change in the rules.

In 1991 the Independent Broadcasting Authority (IBA) was replaced by the Independent Television Commission (ITC) for commercial television and the Radio Authority (RA) for independent local and national radio. Both published codes of practice for the now permitted sponsorship of programmes, setting out how and when credits could be introduced. Thus, the sponsorships since that of PowerGen conform to the new permits and rules.

The first sponsored drama on ITV was International Distillers & Vintners' Croft Port's sponsorship of *Rumpole of the Bailey* in which Leo McKern starred. The Thames TV series of six one-hour programmes ran through October, November and December 1991 and was Croft's sole major pre-Christmas promotion, supported by a Rumpole book offer on bottle-neck tags. Rumpole, in this and earlier series, is seen as a wine drinker although in compliance with the code the actual sponsored brand may not feature in the programme. Sound effects were used very effectively in the credits, the first being the sound of a cork being extracted, the second of the port being poured, and finally the credit featured an empty glass. IDV is said to have paid rather less than £300 000 for the sponsorship, and as a first-comer secured a bargain. The distributors, Morgan Furze, reckoned they could not previously afford to advertise Croft Port on television. For £300 000, they could have bought an advertising campaign covering only London.

ITV's top rated Chart Show has an average weekly audience of 2.2 million, and its sponsorship of Pepe jeanswear was the first sponsored ITV youth programme, the first music independent ITV programme, and the first networked ITV programme. Starting on December 7 1991, the sponsorship was for 13 months with 56 weekly programmes and repeats. The programme was re-designed with the Pepe logo on space invader machines which opened the show. An off-screen tie-up was the free *Music File* monthly which was distributed through retailers. Product and programme were a good match.

The popular *Wish You Were Here* programme presented by Judith Chalmers, was a natural for Barclaycard who used the message 'Barclaycard and Wish You Were Here welcome you around the world'. There was a strong association between the card and holidays. Back up included reference in the Barclaycard house journal for card holders, a Holiday Facts booklet offered to viewers and a roadshow which visited railway stations and shopping malls.

Courage's Beamish stout sponsored the top rating ITV drama *Inspector Morse* for about £600 000, this covering the repeat series on Saturdays and the new series on alternate Wednesdays, from January 5 to April 22 1992. Of the 14–15 million audience, 40 percent are in the ABC1 social grades. Inspector Morse, played by John Thaw, is a beer-drinking man. The Beamish stout logo is dusted with a fingerprint brush in the credits. The producers of the credits sought empathy with the programme to the extent of shooting the credits on film, like the programme, and using music by the composer of the Inspector Morse theme music. It was a subtle use of programme sponsorship at a time when Beamish was endeavouring to compete with its long-established rival Guinness.

Legal and General have made great play of their multi-coloured umbrella — a metaphor for protection and cover — in its sponsorship of regional ITV weather forecasts, shown in regions other than Thames, Scottish and Ulster. The sponsorship began in August 1991, making great use at the beginning and end of the bulletin of its red, blue, yellow and green umbrella.

The Kronenbourg £500 000 sponsorship of Granada's *Chief Inspector Maigret* series on Sunday evenings was a very clever idea. Based on Simenon's novels the new version of *Maigret* (played by Michael Gambon) revived memories of an earlier series. Like *Morse*, the audience was ABC1, but here we had a French beer supporting a series about a French detective. Movement was given to the credits by a foot stepping into a puddle which was reflecting Kronenbourg 1664 in neon lights.

In all these examples there is a mixture of advertising and public relations. There is no direct advertising in the persuasive sense, but certainly brand awareness is stimulated, and the public relations aspect comprises association with programmes in character and of merit, while contributing to the pleasure of viewers.

Answering a call in the press office (reproduced by courtesy of British Gas North Thames).

PART TWO

Organisation of Public Relations

In-house Public Relations Department or Outside Consultancy

PUBLIC RELATIONS VERSUS ADVERTISING SITUATION

Although there are more than 1000 public relations consultancies of various sizes in the UK, the situation cannot be likened to that of the advertising world. There are two reasons for this.

First, when a company's advertising reaches a volume when (a) more expert creative and media services are required and (b) it is economic for an advertising agency to accept the account, an advertising agency will be appointed. The opposite happens in public relations. When little public relations is undertaken, it will be economic to appoint a consultancy until the volume of work justifies setting up an internal department. Very large organisations may also employ consultancies for special services such as counselling, corporate and financial public relations.

Second, whereas the majority of advertising personnel are employed by advertising agencies, the majority of public relations personnel are engaged in-house. This is demonstrated by Figure 12.1.

The report by Cranfield School of Management (1989) stated that 19 500 people held professional public relations positions, and that they had 15 000 support staff. Expenditure by the top 1000 companies was approximately £500m.

Again, there are two reasons. Advertising calls for the skills of specialists such as artists, copywriters and media planners and buyers, and in most cases it would be uneconomic for an advertiser to employ such people full-time but economic to share the services of the agency team. Public relations is more intimately concerned with the whole organisation and is a continuous process, thus justifying the employment of full-time staff.

But the second reason is one which really differentiates public relations from advertising. Not only is public relations to do with the *total* communications of a business or commercial company, and not merely with its marketing and advertising, but it is conducted by numerous non-commercial and public sector organisations which are not (or very seldom) involved in advertising. They include central and local government, voluntary bodies, public services, educational establishments, health services, the armed forces, the police, religious and political organisations, trade unions, and so on, which collectively employ a very large number of the country's public relations men and women.

This is an interesting situation, especially when a certain glamour seems to attach quite mistakenly to consultancies, and people seeking public relations careers tend to think in terms of consultancies only. Moreover, the advertising and marketing trade press tends to

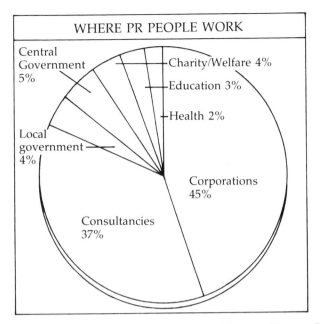

Figure 12.1   Breakdown of employment of public relations practitioners. (Source: Report by Cranfield School of Management, 1989, on behalf of the Institute of Public Relations.)

think mainly in terms of consultancies (perhaps they are the only likely advertisers!), and to confuse public relations with advertising by referring to consultancies as agencies, which they are not since they are not commission-earning agencies of the media as the name 'advertising agency' really means.

We therefore have to consider both the internal public relations department and the external consultancy. Each has its advantages and disadvantages, each is different and neither is necessarily better than the other. As already said, it is possible for an organisation to employ both, and without any conflict between the two, provided the division of roles is understood and used to advantage.

POSITIONING OF AN IN-HOUSE PUBLIC RELATIONS DEPARTMENT

The positioning of the public relations department unit will affect the pros and cons of the in-house operation. If, under some perverse Kotlerian decision, it is positioned within the marketing department, its role will be limited and could be restricted to the 'Four P's' concept of mere 'publicity'. However, in more enlightened organisations or ones where it is recognised by top management, the public relations department will be independent, servicing all functions of the organisation, the PRO being answerable to the chief executive and possibly serving on the board.

As discussed further in Chapter 14, there are many variations on this theme. Much of this confusion derives from business training, with marketing students being mis-taught about the role of public relations, and management students seldom being introduced to the subject at all. Significantly, while the holder of the CIM Diploma can gain exemptions from CAM Certificate subjects, it is necessary to take the public relations paper at Certificate Level if the candidate wishes to take the CAM Diploma in Public Relations. Consequently, the able PRO has to fight from a position of strength, and earn the status required to do a proper job for his or her organisation.

ADVANTAGES OF THE IN-HOUSE DEPARTMENT

The following are the main advantages of the in-house department.

1. *Full-time service*. It functions full-time, and in some organisations, it operates 24 hours a day. It is not limited to the time-bank of labour represented by a consultancy fee.
2. *The PRO belongs to the organisation*. The staff PRO is part of the organisation, and it is his or her business to know everyone and to be known by everyone. Lines of communication can be established throughout the organisation locally, nationally and internationally, and thus information can be obtained. The outsider may have few direct contacts beyond the client representative. The PRO will enjoy this advantage all the more if responsible for the staff house journal.
3. *Permanency*. In-house PROs are more likely to stay with the organisation longer, whereas consultancy staff change jobs more frequently in order to further their careers. This again helps to create confidence between the PRO and executives, managers and directors.
4. *Economical*. It is easier for the in-house PRO to cope with a variety of jobs, since sources of information and resources are close-at-hand. It is possible to switch from one task to another more easily than the outsider can.
5. *Easy co-operation*. Many people can contribute to public relations — it is not the private domain of the PRO — and the insider can work closely with other people who can contribute to the total

public relations effort, including the chief executive, marketing, sales, sales promotion, advertising, works and personnel managers.
6. *On-the-spot when needed*. When the organisation is in the news, or there is a crisis, the PRO can usually deal with the media more quickly than the consultant who may not know what has happened nor be able to get quick approval for a statement. Modern crisis management nowadays means that there is a drill for emergency action, with the PRO and the chief executive well informed and able to work together.
7. *Familiar with the industry*. The PRO usually understands the particular industry, either because he or she was trained in it originally, or because trouble has been taken to become familiar with it. This gives the in-house practitioner authority when dealing with the media, or with people inside the organisation.

DISADVANTAGES OF THE IN-HOUSE DEPARTMENT

Ideal though the above seven points may seem, there can be weaknesses in the internal set-up.

1. *Bias*. There is always the danger that the staff PRO will be uncritical, either through loyalty or because he or she does not enjoy a sufficiently high status to withstand the demands of management. Much depends on the extent to which the PRO is respected as a professional adviser. If buried in the marketing department the PRO's influence could be very weak, especially when confronted by the typical marketing manager's misunderstanding of public relations. But the PRO may just be too close to the organisation to see its faults.
2. *Limitations of the industry*. It may be that

the industry is so specialised, e.g. motor-car, textiles, publishing, tourism, that the PRO's experience is too narrow to have the breadth of consultancy experience. Only certain areas of the media and certain techniques will be known. When new demands are made, as when the company broadens its activities and enters another industry or trade, the in-house PRO may have problems.

3. *Limited background*. Sometimes people within the organisation are transferred to public relations even though they have no knowledge of the subject. There may be a sideways promotion of a fairly senior person who does not relish undergoing professional training. Lack of experience and training can be a serious handicap.

4. *Seldom independent*. A distinct disadvantage is that it is sometimes difficult to be independent, and to be able to criticise management's policies and decisions, whereas the outside consultant can be more candid.

5. *Lack of respect*. There is a saying that it is difficult to be a prophet in one's own land, and it is easy for the inside PRO to be taken for granted. Outside consultants are often regarded as oracles!

Now let us consider a similar set of advantages and disadvantages for the outside consultant, after which different kinds of consultancy will be discussed.

ADVANTAGES OF THE CONSULTANCY

The consultancy may enjoy and offer advantages different from those of the in-house PRO.

1. *Independence*. The consultant is an independent adviser, and being paid to give professional advice, this can be candid. The consultant is often in a different position to the advertising agent who might lose the account if too critical!

2. *Experience*. The consultant has wide experience gained from servicing a large number of different accounts over a number of years. Many new ideas can therefore be offered based on this experience which might not occur to the in-house PRO with more limited or specialised experience.

3. *Media knowledge*. Because of the range of accounts serviced, the consultant will be familiar with more media than the staff PRO, including the creation of special media.

4. *Resources*. The consultant will have more facilities and resources and access to specialist services such as photographers, printers, film and video makers plus knowledge of venues for events.

5. *Specialist staff*. The larger consultancies will have specialist staff experienced in different areas of public relations such as sponsorship, house journal production, research, financial public relations or Parliamentary liaison. Specialist consultancies are discussed later.

6. *Centrally located*. Many staff PROs operate from remote locations or provincial towns: the consultant is often more centrally located, close to the media and creative services. However, with modern communications and the dispersal of publishing houses this has become less of an advantage.

DISADVANTAGES OF THE CONSULTANCY

From the above list of advantages, it may seem that the consultancy has much in its favour, but there are also the following disadvantages to be considered.

1. *Fee limitations*. The consultant can do only what the fee permits on peril of going out of business. Peter cannot be robbed to pay Paul in the sense of borrowing time from a big-spending

client to subsidise a smaller client. The staff PRO is a company man who seldom has fixed working hours. The client is buying only a share of the consultant's time, a point not always realised by greedy clients.

2. *Remoteness from client*. While it is a big advantage to be centrally located, this has its drawbacks since it means the consultant may be remote from the client. Either the client or the consultant has to spend time travelling to meetings. Unlike the staff PRO, the consultant cannot talk to people 'just down the corridor' or on the next floor. Regular liaison is less easy.

3. *Few client contacts*. The consultant will have fewer contacts and access to people in the client organisation, and may deal with only one person representing the client's interests.

4. *Limited knowledge of industry*. While the consultant enjoys broad knowledge of public relations techniques, intimate knowledge of clients' industries or trades is unlikely.

5. *Shared loyalties*. Loyalties have to be shared between clients, and unlike the in-house PRO, the consultant cannot devote entire attention to one organisation. This may be inconvenient to a client when the consultant is engaged on someone else's account and is not available.

6. *Lack of skills*. While the top consultancies employ highly skilled staff (and charge accordingly) many of the smaller ones can afford to employ only inexperienced staff and can offer only meagre training facilities.

These comparisons are interesting and emphasise the point made earlier that the staff PRO and the consultant are different but can complement each other. The point may be reached when the client feels the fee has reached a stage when, for the same money, an in-house PRO can be appointed. But it has to be remembered that fee and salary cannot be equated. The PRO will be working full-time for the organisation, whereas the consultancy fee probably represents only a certain volume of time and includes the consultant's operating costs. In addition to the PRO's salary, it will be necessary to supply this person with an office, staff, equipment and various other services.

TYPES OF CONSULTANCY

There are basically four types of consultancy.

1. *Department of an advertising agency*. Some years ago, many advertising agencies offered public relations as an additional service, but they rarely understood that it incurred special costs, and they were unfamiliar with charging fees based on labour. They lost money and dropped public relations. In any case, they usually offered little more than press relations to supplement advertising campaigns, and had no knowledge of the broader span of public relations. More recently, to satisfy client demand as public relations has developed, many advertising agencies have now created public relations departments. But again, the service may be limited as advertising people rarely understand the subject beyond augmenting advertising campaigns with product publicity.

2. *Subsidiary of an advertising agency*. This is a more practical proposition, the subsidiary operating as a proper consultancy, usually under a different name and as a separate company. It may accept agency clients or ones that do not use the agency.

3. *Independent public relations consultancy*. Unrelated to an advertising agency, the independent consultancy may be a one-person affair or employ a large number of staff and have specialist departments and regional or even overseas offices.

4. *Public relations counsellors*. These consult-

ants specialise in assessing communications problems and making recommendations, but do not conduct campaigns for clients. Counsellors are also employed by the larger independent consultancies.

SPECIALIST CONSULTANCIES

A number of consultancies offer specialist services, either in particular subjects such as high-tech, travel and tourism, fashion, foods and drinks, 'green' products or motoring, or in certain areas. The latter include Parliamentary liaison and lobbying, financial and corporate public relations, house journal editing and production, and crisis management.

SERVICES OF A CONSULTANCY

When invited to make a presentation for a new account, the consultant should apply the Six-Point Planning formula as described in Chapter 3 if he or she is to offer *a cost effective service and make a profit*. The italics stress the need to act professionally.

Increasingly, clients are being asked to invest in preliminary research, otherwise a realistic scheme cannot be presented. This does not always happen, and plans are often based on very rough-and-ready assessments of the situation. It also has to be costed realistically, otherwise the client does not know what is being bought, and the consultant cannot recover costs and make a profit.

Very important to the efficient running of the service are regular progress meetings at which the consultant and the client can discuss work in progress and make any changes that may be necessary from time to time, including revisions of the budget if extra work is required.

And if both client and consultancy are to be satisfied about the achievement of objectives, there should be a system of assessment, perhaps again involving research, as described in Chapter 8.

The account will be serviced by an account executive as in the case of the advertising agency, except that his or her time will be covered by the fee, not commissions on the purchase of advertising space and air-time. Everything the consultant does for the client has to be paid for, since the consultant has no other source of income, and that includes talking to the client.

FREELANCES

A development in the 1990s has been the arrival of freelance practitioners who offer *ad hoc* services. A directory of freelances appears in *PR Week*. Very often they offer services in specialised areas of public relations.

The Public Relations Consultants Association, the consultancy trade body, has an Independent Professional Consultants Group for experienced freelance practitioners. The membership criteria stipulates (1) 10 years experience in public relations at a management level; (2) 5 years in business as an independent consultant; (3) 2 years audited accounts; (4) fee-income less than £100 000; and (5) full member or fellow of the IPR. This is of course an elite body of professional independents, compared with some of the inexperienced freelance operators mentioned in the previous paragraph, and may well consist of retired practitioners or senior practitioners who have been made redundant through no fault of their own, and have valuable experience to offer.

CHAPTER 13

The Press Officer and the Press Office

ROLE OF THE PRESS OFFICER

The press officer may be a specialist in the in-house department and not, therefore, be a fully fledged PRO. However, many a PRO or consultancy account executive will incorporate press officer duties in their general work.

The press officer's job is not to write and distribute material as directed and authorised by an employer. If employers of press relations services merely want to say what they like when they like they should use a direct mail agency. It is the press officer's place to reason why, and that is a testing responsibility. Although the press officer is employed by the purveyor of news, that employment can be followed successfully on an employer's behalf if it is recognised that he or she must behave responsibly to communication media. The press officer is a professional, not a hired hack writer.

Advertising agency people can seldom understand this, perhaps because they work in much more prescribed circles, or even because it is their experience that having booked an advertisement space they can sometimes lean heavily on the advertisement manager to obtain a write-up out of the editor. This does happen, of course, and being neither genuine editorial nor sincere press relations, they are looked upon as just another part of the advertisement.

But genuine press relations efforts are publishable on their merits, not because advertisement space has been purchased. In fact, the best public relations story is generally one that appears nowhere near an advertisement for the same thing.

Nevertheless, as was pointed out in Chapter 2, there is an adversarial situation between the public relations and media worlds, simply because they are motivated differently. Neither is altruistic. Herb Schmertz of Mobil was not entirely cynical when he wrote in his book *Goodbye to the Low Profile* (Mercury Books, 1986) 'If there is something you want to hide, but are required to disclose, put it in a press release . . . most journalists find it hard to take seriously what you give them willingly.' Another version of this in Britain was the notorious 'Friday night drop' when an awkward financial story was released when it was too late to do any harm.

TEN RESPONSIBILITIES OF THE PRESS OFFICER

The competent press officer should:

1. Establish internal lines of communication so that there is ready access to sources of information within the organisation.

2. Collate information and pictures for future use, building a comprehensive fact and picture library.

3. Issue material in a form acceptable to various media so that the organisation is made known and understood, its achievements are appreciated and its reputation is deservedly enhanced.

4. Maintain a press service so that all enquiries from media are dealt with quickly, efficiently and honestly.

5. Be impartial to the extent that media will trust the press officer to supply ungarnished facts.

6. Be able to judge the news value of information supplied for distribution and be prepared to reject a story that is not suitable for release.

7. Be constantly aware of the danger of issuing false or misleading information even though it may be supplied by an apparently reliable source.

8. Feed back information, such as external attitudes or news about rival organisations, so that the press office service provides a two-way liaison.

9. Be so organised that a fully competent press relations service can be provided, on a 24-hour basis if necessary.

10. Record the results of press office efforts and report accordingly to superiors.

To some readers these ten responsibilities — the ten commandments of press relations — may come as a bracing surprise. Certainly, a good many cynics in both advertising and the press world do not expect a press officer to be so meticulous or fastidious. But scruples are the strength of press relations and these responsibilities are taken very seriously by those who adhere to the Code of Professional Conduct of the Institute of Public Relations, not purely for moral reasons but out of economic necessity. It is only when such responsibilities are accepted that the press officer can operate effectively and deserve the respect that is accorded to any other professional practitioner.

TO WHOM IS THE PRESS OFFICER RESPONSIBLE?

This is a difficult question to answer because media relations practice is seldom clearly defined as an organisational function. Strictly speaking, the press officer should be responsible either directly or through the PRO to top management. In actual practice, this may not be so.

In a voluntary body, the press officer is likely to be a member of a small team of permanent officials headed by a general secretary or director. In industry, as already mentioned, the press officer's status and supervision can vary tremendously. He or she may be the only public relations person, and his chief may be a promotional executive handling marketing, sales or advertising. Again, the press officer may be a specialist assistant to the PRO whose status will depend on the extent to which the board is public relations oriented.

This assumes that media relations are conducted by a full-time press officer, but this is not always the case and this book is also intended for others who may have to deal with the press, having no journalistic experience or inside knowledge of publishing house operations and requirements. Marketing, sales, advertising, personnel, works and shop managers may well have to deal with the press from time to time.

Unfortunately, a good many news releases are issued by people completely unskilled in this work and often utterly unaware that any special skill is required. Since the number of organisations issuing stories is large, whereas the number employing press officers is comparatively small, it is not really surprising that so many releases received by editors are unpublishable. Only a proportion of the blame for poor news releases can therefore be directed at the professional press officer. In fact, the best news releases are usually from in-house public relations sources.

From these remarks, it will be seen that a large number of people dabble in media relations, with or without ability, knowledge and experience. For successful media relations, however, a competent trained press officer is necessary.

HOW ARE PRESS OFFICERS RECRUITED?

The answer is directly related to the quality of press relations practice. What are the methods of recruiting press officers?

They are many and diverse, and there is serious need for a more direct entry to press relations with provision for trainee facilities, day release for training and possibly some form of specialist qualification as distinct from the all-round qualification of CAM. But at present, we find press officers recruited from the following fields: newspaper and magazine journalism, advertisement copywriting, transfers from other jobs in the same organisation and trainees.

The latter category is almost non-existent in any real sense of the word. There are some instances of trainee public relations executives who include press relations in their training, but as yet there is very little attempt to recruit trainee press officers from among graduates as happens in the advertising world. It is a very unsatisfactory state of affairs, but undoubtedly one of the most potent reasons for the absence of trainees is the lack of employer appreciation of the need for training. Employers tend to think that all one has to do is employ a journalist, forgetting that he or she knows nothing about public relations.

Do journalists make good press officers?

Far too often management, needing to appoint a press officer yet knowing little about the subject, will take a short cut and appoint a journalist, assuming that any journalistic experience is sufficient qualification for a good press officer. This assumption is seldom valid. The average journalist knows little about media outside his immediate and usually narrowly specialised experience and consequently has practically no knowledge of media relations from the outside. He probably knows very little about how a newspaper or magazine is printed.

Some of our leading practitioners were, of course, very fine journalists. Newspaper experience is not only writing experience, but includes familiarity with the wider aspects of life, the way in which the world earns a living and the manner in which we are governed. It may also include managing a publication with all its business and labour relations implications. Not every journalist, however, enjoys such broad or senior experience.

A journalist working on a paper presents copy in a very different way from that required of an accomplished press officer. The staff journalist is often working to meet a deadline and tends to type imperfectly on small pieces of paper. With single-stroke keying in modern newspaper offices, the journalist will not even use a typewriter and paper but 'file' stories from a computer keyboard. The journalist's job is to complete an assignment, and stories do not have to be marketed in competition with others. Nor does more than one editor have to be pleased. A conscientious press officer, however, is aware that a release has to compete with scores of others and that extra trouble is necessary to produce a release that sells itself through its clarity of heading and content, neat setting-out and legible presentation. This becomes even more essential as computerised newsrooms become common.

Moreover, the press officer has to understand readership profiles, know by which process each journal is printed, and be aware of copy dates, otherwise editors will be irritated by receipt of irrelevant stories. The working journalist has to understand the needs of one paper only.

If a practitioner is being recruited to service a motor-car account, or to work in a motor-car public relations department, it may be sensible to appoint a motoring correspondent or a journalist on a motoring journal not because he or she is a journalist but because of their knowledge of the motor-car industry.

It is fairer to say that the abilities and character likely to produce a first-class journalist will equally make a first-class press officer, but that is very different from saying that ex-journalists make good press officers; a good many people other than journalists are capable of excelling as press officers provided that they can match up to the requirements listed in the next section.

What makes a good press officer?

The simple answer to this question is that anyone who can write concise, precise English; is a thorough, methodical and imaginative organiser; likes, understands and gets on with people; has wide interests and experiences; is in every way an intelligent, adaptable, broad-minded person with an infinite fund of curiosity; is always willing to recognise personal limitations yet maintains a zest for learning; who above all has a tenacious, persistent nature and never gives up, is never fobbed off, nor falls victim to disappointment but is always enthusiastic without being boastful about expected achievement; anyone who fits that job specification will make a first-class press officer. This is very different from the typical advertising agency idea of someone who is merely able to 'con' the press: the press officer has to be a person of distinct attributes and integrity. This job specification may surprise some readers and suggests that the press officer has to be a miracle person, but then we are aiming at perfection, not black magic.

News sense

There is, of course, one attribute that a trained journalist does have that is indispensable to a press officer, and that is 'news sense'. In the past, journalists have been favoured recruits to public relations because they alone have been expected to possess news sense, but if others can acquire this ability to detect what is certain to interest other people, they will be well equipped for the job. Looked at more closely, what is this 'news sense'? Is it not exactly the same as the marketing man's ability to produce and sell goods that will satisfy a need?

News sense is not so much creating news as recognising what aspects of a piece of information, or what manner of presentation of this information, will most succeed in interesting the media. It is really a piece of elementary motivation research.

For example, a company may obtain an export contract for the supply of a given quantity or value of goods. This item may rate a couple of lines in a business column or magazine. Similar stories are published, practically listed, daily. Often, the two or three lines printed have been subbed down from dull, wordy releases of practically no news value.

The press officer with a nose for news will delve deeper for a real story. Call this creating news if you like, but you cannot invent what is not there to be discovered. If someone has the wit and the will to look into a contract and find out, say, that this was the first time such a contract had been awarded to a British company, and then go on to find out how this British company — the company or client — had in fact beaten foreign competition, then we are approaching a story of 'hard' news importance. This story need not be just an item for the business section but may possibly be worth space on the front page, a story of interest to radio and TV, the DTI and the BBC World Service at Bush House. But it all began with a dull-seeming two-line admission by an unimaginative export manager who could not really be expected to have 'news sense'.

With this introduction to the role of the press officer, let us now consider the necessary qualifications and abilities.

The media are sometimes cynically disposed towards PROs and press officers because they mistake them for press agents. The whole aim of press agentry is to get pictures and stories into print by one means or another that will publicise the press agent's client, and clients are usually personalities such as entertainers — people who have to be in the news to exist. Press agents are sometimes more frankly called publicity agents. Their work is akin to advertising in effect, but the method of operation is often dubious. It should not be confused with public relations.

The difference between press relations and press agentry is clear when the principle is accepted that the press officer aims to issue material that is first and foremost news of reader interest and value. Publicity must accrue from this basic value, but the news will be issued with proper regard for the integrity of the press.

This difference is reasonably well understood when the source of the news is an official information service, and now that news distribution is becoming a very important branch of marketing, this commercial aspect can be more help than hindrance.

Advertised goods and services are openly advocated, whereas personalities rely upon publicity gained by whatever means may be within the ingenuity, power and purse of the press agent.

Advertising takes the risk of publicly making claims, and it is nowadays so hedged about by both legislation and voluntary control that most advertising is highly trustworthy and reputable. It has to be, and companies stake reputations worth millions of pounds on their advertised claims.

DESIRABLE QUALITIES OF A PRESS OFFICER

Now let us be analytical and consider the four most desirable and important abilities of a press officer. These are the ability to:

1. Obtain facts
2. Write journalistically
3. Market stories
4. Time distribution of stories

1. Ability to obtain facts

The press officer must be able to interview people, prepare a questionnaire, or carry out either field or desk research to get the information for news stories. In this, it is necessary to be politely persistent. The ability to investigate calls for more than inquisitiveness. It requires wide experience and catholic tastes, for with these attributes, points of sympathetic human contact are possible. No one wants to talk to another who appears narrow, selfish, ignorant and unsympathetic.

Above all, in the search for facts, there must be consciousness of the value of these facts from the point of view of the ultimate reader. An employer or client may wish to present facts that are important to this person: the press officer must assert the unquestionable right to demand and to issue only the facts that are publishable and readable. If such facts are withheld, the press officer is bound to declare there is no story that can be released. If asked to decorate the facts more favourably, the press officer must dissent. And if it is suspected that the information is not all that it seems, the facts must be checked before editors are asked to take material on trust and publish to their disadvantage.

Without integrity, any person engaged in public relations work must fail, and this applies particularly to the press officer whose stock-in-trade must be trust. The press officer must be above suspicion, no matter how cynical the media may be. Unless an employer understands this position, the press officer will be unable to function properly. All this may sound very purist, but would a surgeon permit the patient to direct an operation?

There is no doubt that at the present time there are PROs, consultants, press officers and others holding associated positions who, through fear of dismissal, permit misguided users of their services to abuse them. To enjoy respect for integrity, the press officer must argue from a position of strength given by superior experience, training, qualifications and not least of all by ability to deliver the goods.

When a consultant excuses poor work on the grounds that 'the client insists' that a story be written in such a way, or that it must be embargoed, or that elaborate press packs must be put in an exhibition press room, that consultant is incompetent to the point of wasting the client's money. That such a dim state of affairs is all too common only goes to show the lowly state of our business and the ineptitude of certain practitioners. *In public relations the customer is seldom right*. The practitioner should be paid to be right.

2. Ability to write journalistically

As we shall discuss this in more practical detail in Chapter 15 on how to write news releases, the subject is only briefly touched on here. A poet or novelist might make a poor press officer. We are not writing to impress or entertain. Our words must interest and inform, briefly and clearly. Every word must count, but superlatives have no place since we cannot put words of praise into editors' mouths. A news release contains no comment. We have to write as we might expect a journalist to write, given the same facts, and we cannot express the journalist's opinions. Thus in a news release, we do not write of a 'famous' company.

Journalistic writing is the opposite of essay writing. There is no introduction, development and conclusion. Instead, in a news story,

the gist of the story is told in the first paragraph, and then expanded in the paragraphs that follow. This can be seen at once in any newspaper. The easiest way to learn to write news releases is to read newspapers and study how reports are written. The same method is used world-wide. Unfortunately, most news releases appear to have been written by people who never read newspapers!

3. Ability to market stories

The press officer must know where to place stories. This is very much a selling operation even though the stories are submitted free of charge. But more than this, releases must be sent only to the editors most likely to be interested in them. The marketing of press releases requires a thorough knowledge of media, and the acquisition of this knowledge is a painstaking business. The press officer who writes a story and then does a blanket mailing of all the journals covering that subject is an amateur compared to the one who knows media and selects the right publications for each story.

Sometimes clients ask consultants what mailing lists are used for their stories. A good press officer does not keep lists because there is no permanent set of publications that is suitable for every story issued by a particular organisation. This point must be emphasised since it is seldom appreciated. The constant study of media is therefore imperative because changes are so frequent. The market for any given story must be known and understood.

Reference to the building-up of mailing lists, or use of distributing services from which addresses can be selected, follows in the section on the press office, while Chapter 6 is devoted to communication media.

Media selection is a question of knowledge, not contacts. Addresses in a press officer's library are only useful if something is known of the publications they represent. There is plenty of published information, to mention only *Benn's Media Directory*, the *PR Planner* and the *Editors* series.

In other words, the press officer has to be his or her own literary agent.

4. Ability to time distribution of stories

This ability derives chiefly from knowing how publications are produced, printed and distributed. The printing process is the most important of the three: is it flexography, letterpress, lithography or photogravure? An elementary knowledge of printing is essential to anyone engaged in public relations. If the press officer understands the process by which various journals are published, the time to release stories will be known and releases will not be sent to publications which have already gone to press or have been printed already. Some journals, such as women's magazines, may have a lead time of three months. A morning national is printed at night, and with contract printing, outside London copies will be printed about 10pm. Only something dramatic like a front page murder story will interest an editor after early evening, and even a 'hard' news story from a public relations source is unlikely to be of much use to such an editor after lunch-time. Nowadays, front page news in the nationals is seldom later than *News At Ten* on ITV.

A women's weekly printed by photogravure or offset-litho may go to the printer six weeks before publication, and its planning, writing and illustration will have been done over a period of three to six months before publication. Other monthly journals need material before the middle of the previous month, while a weekly magazine may want material as early as the previous Friday if published on a Wednesday.

A provincial weekly newspaper sold on Friday is often made up on Tuesday, set and proofed on Wednesday, and printed and delivered on Thursday, which means that copy is required on Monday at the latest. Thus, stories to the provincial press should be posted on Thursday or Friday, or hand-delivered on Monday (perhaps following a telephone call to say the story is on its way).

For example, certain work was to be done to a parish church, but by the time it had been completed and photographed, the story would have been too late for that week's issue and stale news for the next. A photograph of the exterior was taken on the Thursday. The story was written up from the job specification and approval obtained for the draft. The picture, caption and release were delivered to the newspaper office on the Monday morning. By the time the story appeared in print on the following Thursday, the work had been completed as reported.

But writing before the event can have its snares if plans change at the last minute after the story has been written. There have been some luckless stories about events that never happened!

THE PRESS OFFICE

The department run by the press officer is known as the press office, and journalists making enquiries are as likely to ask the telephone operator for the press office as the press officer. Consequently it should be organised and equipped so that it can operate efficiently and with expert understanding of how the press works and what it wants. It should have good intercommunication or direct-line facilities so that the press officer can communicate quickly within the organisation. There should be a first-class secretary who knows exactly what to do in the absence of the press officer, and in a large organisation there will be assistant press officers. In some organisations with scattered locations, it may be necessary to have press officers in the field who can be contacted instantly.

Two things are essential to the successful running of a press office: first, access to information internally; and second, access to

translated, to editors worldwide with whom they have established excellent contact over a great many years. See also Chapter 24.

Visnews have a documentary film and video archive dating from 1896. They have film and video production facilities and interview studios, and provide a world-wide distribution service to TV stations by satellite, landline or air freight. This includes video news releases as described in Chapters 21 and 24.

In addition, the press officer should acquire the various official booklets that are issued from time to time by the Department of Trade and Industry, which list the facilities provided by these official means of communication with the overseas press, radio and TV.

If the press officer has to mail stories to the overseas press, he can obtain quite good information from the directories listed above; more complete directories are published in the larger countries, although these can be expensive to buy.

PRESS CUTTING SERVICES

It is important to know the results of press relations work, and since it would be impractical to subscribe to every journal to which stories are submitted, the services of a press-cutting agency are valuable. In London and certain other parts of the UK there are agencies which will supply cuttings at a fee for so many cuttings per subject. Some agencies also charge a search fee irrespective of whether cuttings are actually found. Cutting agencies exist in most countries with a large press. Addresses of press-cutting agencies are given in *Hollis Press and Public Relations Annual*.

These agencies receive a certain amount of criticism because they seldom succeed in finding more than about 50 percent of the cuttings that exist. There are many reasons for this failure, but they are not entirely the fault of the agencies. For example, a story might appear in only one edition of a newspaper.

Moreover, cutting agencies do not necessarily search every publication issued in the country. There are also stories which refer to the organisation or product without actually naming it, and such items are likely to escape the press-cutting staff unless they are searching under a general subject. On the whole, the fees charged by these agencies are not high. The most satisfactory service results when a broad subject heading can be given to the agency rather than just the name of an organisation. It pays to send the agency a list of the journals to which a release has been sent. Press cuttings as a means of recording results are fully discussed in Chapter 8.

THE DOS AND DON'TS OF GOOD PRESS RELATIONS

To conclude this chapter, here are twelve points worth remembering as a guide to good press relations.

1. *Understand the press.* Do not expect editors and reporters to be out to trick you, but remember that publishing is a highly competitive business. Be realistic. If you try to hide facts you are asking for trouble. The press can be ruthless. Do not favour one paper more than another, and do not give unfair exclusives. Let every paper have the same chance with the same story and pictures. And do not give different pictures to competing journals in the same category. However, unless syndicated, feature articles must be exclusive.
2. *Tell the truth.* Do not issue half a story, or try to gild a story in your organisation's favour. Press people will usually respect confidences. Put newsmen in the picture as much as you can but avoid giving stories 'off the record'.
3. *Always be accessible.* Make sure the press can reach you at any time. When you leave the office say where you are going.

Put your address on your news releases and on photo captions. Give your private telephone number as well as your office number if your business has 24-hour demands. Respond quickly to requests for information written or phoned.

4. *Be prepared*. If a story is likely to break, check policy and have the facts ready. Know what you are talking about. This can be very valuable if you have to refute false statements or correct misunderstandings.

5. *Regard press people as fellow practitioners*. Respect their calling and invite them to respect yours. Remember, you can only argue from a position of strength. Do not try to teach them their job. Do not try to tell them what is news. Be patient with the cynical reporter who sneers at public relations. Go out of your way to tip him off about a possible story. Press officers and journalists should work as a team.

6. *Show visiting pressmen around*. Turn calls into memorable visits. Take visiting pressmen behind the scenes. Open their eyes. Let them meet people. Make them feel welcome. Make them feel they can drop in whenever it pleases them.

7. *Provide facilities*. Make it easy for reporters to get their stories away. Find them a quiet room, a desk and a chair, a typewriter and a telephone or fax machine, a company car if necessary. Do not begrudge them any assistance. Observe every courtesy, hospitality and respect due to a guest.

8. *Maintain a friendly relationship*. Keep on good terms with the press, but do not exploit friendship. Think of occasions when you can be nice to press people. Do not try to buy their favours with too many drinks or lunches. Try to remember names. Keep a personal book of names. You will meet hundreds of journalists and remembering all their names is not easy.

However, from harsh experience Herb Schmertz in the book mentioned earlier in this chapter warns 'Don't try to make friends with reporters, but do try to establish a real relationship.'

9. *Do not get a reputation for stopping stories*. Sometimes you will not want them to print a story, but always try to have a replacement story if you can. Remember, the reporter is expected to come back to the office with a story.

10. *Do not expect coverage because your organisation advertises*. Keep the two separate. Do not get involved in advertising. Avoid the blackmail of write-ups *if* you advertise, and vice versa. Our work must be publishable on its own merits.

11. *Be careful over corrections*. Errors do occur. Take them up, the editor may be genuinely unaware of the true facts. But do not antagonise editors. A tactful way of dealing with mistakes is to write to the editor, expressing thanks for publishing the story and then mention that if any readers' enquiries are received the correct details are so and so.

12. *Remember deadlines, copy dates, publishing days*. Do not waste reporters' time with stories too late to catch the right or next edition. Watch out for Saturday stories — Sunday papers carry little news and by Monday a Saturday story is cold. Do not give evening papers a story at five o'clock. Remember that monthlies need stories six weeks ahead, and that many popular magazines work months ahead. If space has been promised for a feature article, make sure you supply the manuscript by the agreed copy date.

The twelve points offered above provide a workmanlike basis for good day-to-day press relations. They should be remembered, together with the reasons for the rejection of news releases given in Chapter 15. The simple philosophy is good relations in all directions, within and without one's organisation. Nothing is perfect. The press officer will work most efficiently when there are no illusions about the press world. People are often irrational, exasperating and human. Moreover, the media are in business to stay in business: the best way to maximise news coverage is help the media to build and keep readerships and audiences, remembering that the media are under no obligation to use public relations material.

CHAPTER 14

Public Relations as Part of Other Duties

OTHER PEOPLE'S JOB SPECIFICATIONS

To what extent should public relations be part of the duties of other people in an organisation, whether or not there is a full-time in-house PRO or an outside consultant? Should public relations duties be the monopoly of a professional practitioner? These questions pose both problems and solutions. The answers range from executives who are virtually part-time PROs to those who should include public relations in their job specification.

There are therefore three aspects to consider: (i) executives who include public relations (or its equivalent) in their job title; (ii) executives who embrace public relations without specifying this in their job titles; and (iii) those whose work inevitably involves public relations even if they do not necessarily call it that.

These considerations recognise that inevitably public relations reaches into every area of an organisation's operations, and this invites a broader view of our subject. It is not limited to the marketing function. Let us discuss each of the three groups mentioned above. In so doing we accept the world as it is in which there may be varied, loose or important acceptance of the role of public relations. The fact is that every organisation has public relations, whether this is admitted or not, and many of its personnel have some sort of public relations role to play. They have to communicate, and they have to deal with human relations which all amounts to creating knowledge, understanding and confidence. This is what public relations is all about. It is sometimes said that the CEO should be the first PRO.

COMBINED JOBS AND JOB TITLES

The public relations profession is bedevilled by an array of job titles that extend beyond the simple public relations director, officer or manager, while a press officer handles only a minor side of public relations (and actually only press relations duties). Thus, we have information officers, external relations officers and public affairs officers, although the latter may specialise in corporate public relations. All this can be confusing enough, but then we have advertising, publicity and other executives who incorporate public relations in their titles. Is this a workable combination?

In the case of a government chief information officer, it is common practice for this official to incorporate advertising, public relations and propaganda in his duties. But what of the advertising and public relations manager, or one with some such title? When these two activities are so different, how can such a person combine both effectively? And why are they combined?

Much depends on the kind of organisation. An industrial company may conduct little advertising but much public relations, while a consumer product company may engage in heavy advertising and comparatively little public relations. The same person may therefore have responsibility for both. But generally, there is an inadequate use of public relations, otherwise the duties would be split, and there may be a misunderstanding of the full meaning and use of public relations. Because more money is usually spent on advertising than on public relations, the former may be regarded as the more important when in fact the latter is, because it concerns the total organisation, and not only its promotional or marketing activities.

Consequently, a dilemma arises, which may not be appreciated, especially by management in making appointments. Advertising and public relations are different activities applied to different purposes. Public relations is not a form of advertising. Much depends, therefore, on the ability of the so-called advertising and public relations manager to wear two hats, and to do mental somersaults in the effort to handle two entirely different roles.

Problems of credibility can arise. A news release, or an invitation to a press reception or facility visit, issued by a person with such a title, may arouse the doubts of editors and journalists. Moreover, can a person responsible for advertising, and with an advertising mentality, write a news release or feature article, or produce any other public relations material, such as photographs or videos, which do not contain puffery or attempt to gain free advertising? Necessarily, the two styles of communication are completely different, and they would not succeed if this were not so.

Unless the advertising and public relations manager is trained and experienced in these two very different practices, the company's relations with the media could be disastrous. It would be like a bookmaker trying to double as a jockey. Unfortunately these disasters do occur. It is one of the reasons why publishers are able to blackmail companies into buying advertisement space to support editorials, and why so many alleged news releases are rejected by dismayed editors. To put the two jobs in the hands of one person is to invite both delusion and confusion.

Of course, there may be good reasons for the doubling up of these two responsibilities. It may be a small company, and two separate executives may not be justified financially. Or it may be significant that the need for public relations work is recognised at all. Even so, it is essential that the executive understands the distinct nature of each task, and that calls for a blend of study, training and experience in both subjects.

OTHER EXECUTIVES

There are other executives whose normal job titles obscure a possible public relations function for which they may be responsible, and they include advertising, marketing, sales, sales promotion and especially marketing services managers. In the absence of any separate or defined public relations responsibility, these executives either deal with public relations or should have an awareness of it. There is a distinction. Although marketing managers may take a poor view of public relations, it can enhance their work during most phases of the marketing mix. It can concern branding, pricing, packaging, distribution and after-sales service.

The antipathy between marketing and public relations may seem hard to explain and accept, but unfortunately it exists and persists, and it starts with marketing writers and teachers and even reaches into the syllabuses of marketing examinations and the curricula of marketing courses. This is not difficult to understand when we find public relations relegated to mere 'publicity' and diverted to the Promotion 'P' of the misleading 'Four Ps' concept so popular with marketing students. The world over, they are familiar with Philip Kotler's books and his unhelpful definition which says:

> Publicity is non-personal stimulation of demand for a product, service or business unit by planting commercially significant news about it in a published medium or obtaining favourable presentation of it upon radio, television, or stage that is not paid for by the sponsor.

This is a spurious mockery of public relations, and any member of the British Institute of Public Relations who subscribed to such a perverted view would deserve to be suspended from membership. When such a dreadful definition exists in a popular book written by an eminent marketing writer read by most of the world's qualified marketing executives, it is not surprising that public relations practitioners find it difficult to make themselves understood and to work successfully in a marketing environment. It is one very good reason why the PRO should not be positioned in the marketing department. It is like putting a virgin in a harem.

Let us analyse Kotler's words to see why they are wrong, remembering that he is misnaming public relations (if only press relations to be more accurate) as *publicity*.

Publicity is a result of something being made known, and it may be good or bad publicity according to the nature of the announcement.

Public relations is not necessarily *non-personal*, even in the confined field of press relations. Much of it is very personal such as dealing personally with journalists, advising management, conducting seminars and conferences, and communicating on an eyeball-to-eyeball basis. We are not only dealing with mass audiences and with publishing or broadcasting. We use micro- as well as macro-media in public relations.

Stimulation of demand is the responsibility of advertising and selling, not of public relations, which aims to create understanding through knowledge. That understanding may then enable advertising and selling to stimulate sales.

Planting suggests underhanded manipulation of the media, and is at variance with the IPR Code of Professional Conduct which rules that 'a member shall not disseminate false or misleading information'. The word 'planting' in a definition of public relations is obnoxious, and cannot be excused as a case of American-English semantics. It represents what has now become a marketing attitude to and an abuse of public relations.

Commercially significant is another warped phrase, and for two reasons. First, public relations is concerned with the communication of non-commercial, such as government departments and voluntary bodies, as well as commercial organisations. 'Significant' suggests bias, and above all public relations requires credibility, and that depends on impartiality. Bias kills credibility.

Published medium, etc. The definition refers to only the mass media, as if it is a kind of advertising, and fails to recognise that many public relations media are private or created media such as house journals, slides, videos and the personal kind mentioned earlier.

Favourable is an unwise choice of words, since public relations has also to deal with the unfavourable when accuracy of information is necessary.

Not paid for by the sponsor overlooks the fact that even press relations incurs costs of labour, materials and expenses and that media coverage involves space and air-time which is priceless, and there is no question of it being free because it was never for sale.

From this analysis it will be seen that the definition is dangerously misleading, but its influence can be seen in the unfortunate attitude towards public relations which is common in the marketing world. Therefore, if marketing, sales and marketing services executives are to enjoy the real benefits of public relations they should adopt the definition given in Chapter 2 of this book, which not only contradicts the Kotler one, but declares a different and broader frame of reference.

There is every reason why marketing should adopt a different view and can enjoy the benefits of public relations, since there are many similarities between marketing and public relations which both have to do with communications and human relations. This is best achieved if the 'Four Ps' concept of the marketing mix is forgotten so that public relations can be seen to be related to most, if not all, of the elements of the marketing strategy. If this more far-reaching application of public relations is accepted, the marketing executive has a considerably stronger role. This does require a revolution in marketing thinking, and it leaves no room for the antipathy which so often exists between the two practices.

This theme has been developed more fully in other books by the author, but a few examples are useful here. The concept of a new product (or an innovation) may benefit from feedback from the media and the market which has been monitored or received by the public relations department. The name of the company or product has public relations implications in its ability to be pronounced, spelt and memorised, and this can include the conversion of long business names into acronyms like Fiat, Sabena and Toshiba. Packaging, especially modern convenience packs such as aerosols, blister packs, lightweight plastic bottles, dispensers and sachets, creates customer goodwill compared with bulky or unhelpful conventional packages. Some aspects of the marketing mix can cause good or bad public relations, especially if the marketing manager is so zealous about maximising profits that good customer relations are sacrificed in the process. How do people react to price? Is it too low to inspire confidence, or is it unfairly high? Sales force relations can be a special form of management–employee relations. Distributor relations must not be neglected, and well-informed, well-trained retail sales staff can enhance customer relations.

There is a public relations element in advertising and sales promotion which should neither offend nor disappoint. Finally, there is the after-market which embraces guarantees, service, spare parts and the maintenance of customer interest.

All this implies a more thorough application of public relations than its derisory relegation as mere publicity under the heading of promotion. Moreover, it shows that public relations is not a form of promotion or advertising, but enters into the marketing manager's total strategic thinking. Regarded in these broad terms, public relations can enjoy a legitimate place in the marketing manager's function. Similarly, this can apply to the sales and marketing services manager.

The situation is somewhat different in the case of the advertising, publicity or sales promotion manager who is conducting a specialist function within the marketing framework. In many organisations, the designated responsibility is doubled with that of public relations. The difficulty here is for this executive to remember which hat is being worn. For instance, it will be necessary to understand that the writing of advertisement copy and public relations material requires totally different literary styles. Sales promotion, being a form of marketing, should not be confused with public relations. Nevertheless, there are public relations implications in the way customer expectations are respected. The advertising manager will deal with media advertisement departments, and has to remember to address public relations material to editorial departments. It would be unwise to expect the advertising agency to handle public relations assignments since it is rarely that agencies have an understanding of the subject. It would be wiser to engage a consultancy.

In contrast to the above remarks, a publicity manager (as in the holiday resort business and entertainment industry) may be more engaged in public relations than in advertising. The title is often loosely used, and the efforts of this person may be more publicity-seeking than advertising-controlling. The aim will be to keep the resort 'in the news', and media relations will therefore be an important part of the work.

PERSONNEL MANAGEMENT/HUMAN RESOURCES MANAGEMENT

Inevitably, public relations occurs in employee relations work, and this can be a contentious subject. Should the personnel manager be responsible for internal public relations, or should the PRO be responsible for both internal and external relations? Who should bear responsibility for the production of induction material for new recruits, for house journals, and for keeping employees informed about company affairs such as trading results, pension schemes, Christmas bonuses and participation in share issues? In some organisations, especially in the developing world, internal public relations is seen as the responsibility of the personnel or human resources manager. However, in some large companies, particularly in the USA, the house-journal editor has developed into an internal communications manager. In other companies, the in-house public relations manager may handle internal as well as external relations, and work in close cooperation with the personnel manager. This is probably the best arrangement.

There are many variations in operation, but whatever the division of duties, personnel management — covering recruitment, welfare and training — calls for an understanding of public relations. As suggested above, the most satisfactory division is one in which the personnel manager confines himself or herself to recruitment, welfare and training (if there is no separate training officer) plus industrial relations so far as they concern union relations. This leaves the public relations manager to concentrate on all forms of internal communication. In so doing, the work of the

personnel manager can be supplemented and supported, and industrial relations can be assisted by creating harmonious management–employee relations. The latter is important because industrial disputes are often the product of rumour in the absence of information.

MANAGEMENT

The chief executive officers of the most successful companies are often business leaders who understand public relations and fulfil the ideal that the CEO should be the company's first PRO. But this is not always so. MBA studies rarely teach prospective managers anything about public relations. On the whole, few people who rule the boardrooms or directors of companies have had any training in public relations, and consequently they regard the PRO as hired help, taking the attitude 'why keep a dog and bark yourself'.

Yet one of the skills of successful management is surely communication, and a poor communicator makes a bad leader. A primary cause of industrial disputes is not intransigent trade unions but uncommunicative management. Public relations should therefore be written into the job specification of any manager from the CEO down.

There is another aspect to this. Management may have to play the role of company spokesperson, perhaps in press, radio or television interviews, at press receptions and during facility visits. On these occasions, the CEO should not be aloof from the media but should understand how the media operate, and know how to work with editors, reporters, interviewers, producers and presenters. To conduct this partnership with the media, the CEO needs to understand public relations techniques.

It is significant, and a compliment to public relations, that it is becoming increasingly common in large public companies for those being groomed for top management to have to spend up to three years in the public relations department. As a measure of their status they are often given the title of 'public relations' or 'public affairs' manager, even though they have no experience with which to fulfil the role. No doubt such people are ably assisted, but it is some recognition of the importance of public relations that a future chief executive is expected to have had first-hand managerial experience of public relations.

Also significant, and in a more practical way, is that some of our more important PROs are board directors, and some of them have actually advanced to becoming managing directors of their companies.

*Checking the proofs of a house journal (reproduced
by courtesy of British Gas North Thames).*

PART THREE

Creativity

CHAPTER 15

How to Write a News Release

A SPECIAL LITERARY FORM

In this chapter, the technique of writing a news release is based on a seven-point formula, but before this is considered a few other points should be discussed. We refer to a 'news' release rather than a 'press' release because it may be sent to broadcast as well as print media. We do not use the expression 'handout' which is a derogatory one used by some journalists.

The first thing to make absolutely clear is that a news release is just as much a specialised literary form as an essay, poem, short story, novel, textbook, letter, report, feature article or a piece of advertisement copy. Moreover, it has to be marketed.

According to the importance of the journal, every editor is confronted every morning with scores and perhaps hundreds of news releases. The majority of releases — often from famous sources — go into the bin directly the first few lines have been scanned.

NO PUFFERY

Puffery is the editor's word for advertising. It resembles the puffer fish which creates a bigger image of itself by puffing itself up. When advertisements first appeared in newspapers, well-known writers were engaged to puff up products. Editors will not print advertisements in their columns. The news release writer must therefore avoid self-praise, favourable comment, and adjectives.

A large number of news releases are discarded simply because they are obvious puffs, have been sent to the wrong publications or are too late. Many are too long and the subject is not apparent in the very first few words. The editor is not going to wade through three or four pages of turgid paragraphs to find out what the story is all about. We have only to read any newspaper story to discover how news is written, yet editors are invited to believe that the senders of news releases have never read a newspaper story. If one looks at any news report in any newspaper it will be seen that the first paragraph is a digest of the whole story.

Here is an example of puffery from a news release issued by Exel Logistics:

> Leading retail multiple BhS has awarded Exel Logistics a five year multi million contract to handle its total warehousing and distribution operation.

The media dislike puffs such as 'leading' and *International Freighting Monthly* printed:

> British Home Stores (BHS) has awarded Exel Logistics a five year multi mullion contract to handle its total warehousing and distribution operation.

A news release requires its own particular writing skill. It needs to be terse, factual, explanatory, and totally free of superlatives or self-praise. It is the most 'unlearned' aspect of public relations, and the one that is most responsible for the antagonism towards public relations that is expressed by so many editors. A news release is not a short article, nor is it a kind of advertisement. It is no exaggeration to say that 70 percent of the releases received every morning by editors should never have been posted. There are two reasons for this miserable state of affairs. First, very few people employed in public relations have ever had any training in the writing of news releases, let alone in public relations itself. Second, the writers of news releases are the victims of clients and employers who insist that news releases should contain what they would like to see in print, not what editors are likely to print or readers will enjoy reading. The difference is enormous. There is only one answer to this: the writer must be so well trained and qualified that he or she has the status to be respected as a professional. This is what the CAM Diploma and membership of the IPR is all about.

The worst releases come from consultancies probably because they are too anxious to please their clients. In-house releases tend to be more professionally written.

discern the merits of the story and act as referee between the original sender and the final reader.

It is therefore the job of the press officer to supply communication media with material which will help them to produce publications and programmes of *interest and value* to readers, listeners or viewers. This is the primary task, the one for which the press officer should be trained and qualified. Interest and value were the criteria enunciated by the American consultant Ivy Ledbetter Lee in 1906, but it has been generally ignored. Of course, if the client or employer prefers to keep a hired hack to send out stories that please vanity, complaints are not justified if press cuttings are rare or non-existent.

The onus is on the press officer to service the press and to create a two-way relationship so that editors seek stories because the source is reliable and professional. It is the press officer's responsibility to be accurate, and he or she enjoys the privilege of being better informed than the media.

Sometimes people ask why the IPR does not do a better job for public relations. That is a non-question, for the only people who can earn it an enviable reputation are its practitioners. Public relations is judged by the people in it and the way they practise. Consequently, it gets the criticism it deserves.

THE EDITOR AS REFEREE

News release writing has to inform in such a way that the information is seen by editors to be worth passing on to their readers. That implies a *double* communication, to and from the editor, so that a news release is not even a news story such as a reporter might produce. It has to compete with rival stories, and it has to be marketed on the strength of its news value and relevance to the journal concerned. The good presentation of the story, as explained in Chapter 17, is also part of this marketing process. The editor must be able to

A BAD EXAMPLE

An example of bad press relations can be taken from the news agency world. The London news agency which supplies news to the UK national and regional press is the Press Association. By its very nature, it is supplying mostly important 'hard' news stories, the kind that will appear on the home (that is, UK) news page of nationals and the front page of regional dailies. It has to be a very big public relations story of national importance to be sent out by the PA wire service. Yet the PA is frequently put on the mailing list of, by PA standards, trivial product publicity stories. Ideally, the PA journalist would like to sub down from a maximum of 100 words. Also, very few people go to the trouble to write a special brief story for the PA; instead, they send the PA the same voluminous three-page release that has gone elsewhere. The PA fills two six-foot dustbins daily with the rubbish that reaches them every morning from consultancies, in-house departments and especially Whitehall PROs. Most of this is written by ex-journalists who have obviously never had any training in public relations.

JOURNALISTS NEED TRAINING

Even the experienced journalist needs further training to write good news releases, and often graduates with no journalistic experience have become better press officers or PROs than ex-journalists. There are lots of reasons for this, if only that it depends what sort of press experience the journalist has had. More often than not the best experience that a journalist can bring to public relations is a wide knowledge of the world at large rather than writing ability. The great anomaly of public relations is that a great many journalists have been recruited by the profession, yet their standard of news release writing is extraordinarily poor.

WRITING FOR PARTICULAR JOURNALS

A singular problem does confront the news release writer. Seldom can an individual story for each separate publication be written. We have to avoid giving exclusives, and so the story has to be broadly pleasing and valuable to a number of editors. However, the mistake is sometimes made of trying to make a single version of a story all things to all men, spreading it over many pages in the vain hope that different editors will go to the trouble of extracting the bits they want. It is the press officer's job to write what editors want, a technical story for the technical press, a much

less technical story for the popular press. Studying the market and supplying what it is most likely to publish is what is meant by marketing a news release. It is this meticulous approach to press relations that makes public relations so time-consuming, but it is the way to maximise press coverage.

Again, the writer should remember (or observe) two peculiarities of the press. Only certain parts of a newspaper or a magazine are devoted to each subject, and the limited space of this section, page or column dictates that the release must be brief if it is to compete successfully for a portion of this space. In addition, some publications, such as most of the weekend newspaper magazines and the TV/radio listings magazines, print no releases at all.

A TYPICAL EXAMPLE

Let us take a simple example. A common story is that of a new appointment. If one looks at the 'new appointments' columns in *The Financial Times*, *The Times* or *Campaign*, it will be seen that most announcements are confined to a single sentence. It will be noticed too, if other papers are studied, that *The Guardian* and *The Independent* and quite a number of others do not print these announcements at all. Yet extensive biographies, accompanied by photographs, are sent to a long list of publications! Why? Simply because the market for such stories has not been studied and understood, and the senders are ignorant of media needs. The stories, and beautiful salon portraits, may well please the subjects, but that is immaterial to a press relations exercise.

Different versions of the story can be sent to other journals, more about the appointee's career for the professional journal perhaps, more about the life story and personal details for the local paper, and perhaps a whole article for the house journal.

There are occasions when one-off stories are necessary, or when the mailing list is limited to two or three local newspapers. Stories about prize-winners are often sent to their local papers.

It would be wrong to suggest or expect that every release is intended for publication. The press officer will sometimes issue background information to which journalists may refer when writing about the subject. Releases sent to nationals may need to offer a number of story leads which can be followed up according to the policies of individual editors since rival newspapers will not wish to print exactly the same report. On the other hand, product publicity releases may well be printed as submitted, sometimes because trade and other specialist magazines are short-staffed and the editor is glad to print a well-written piece as it stands. But whatever the intention or fate of the news release, the literary standard should be a *publishable* one, either because it makes it easier for journalists to extract the facts, or because it saves the editor time if subbing and rewriting do not have to be performed. Extensive rewriting of verbose stories can lead to the unintentional introduction of errors.

While emphasis will be placed on the application of a seven-point formula for the writing of a news release that is publishable as it stands, the facility to write in such a disciplined fashion will enhance the ability to write any other kind of press story.

So, before proceeding to the formula let us first look at the various kinds of news release that the press officer may be called upon to write.

QUOTATIONS

Should a release contain quotations? 'Yes' if the person quoted has authority and the remarks add useful information to the story. 'No' if mere platitudes such as 'This is a remarkable breakthrough' or 'We are very proud of this development'. 'No' if the person quoted has no top management authority. 'No'

if the quotations are overdone as in the example given in Chapter 17.

SIX KINDS OF NEWS RELEASE

1. *One-sentence releases*: announcing new appointments, promotions, retirements, change of company name, and change of address.
2. *Publishable as it stands seven-point formula release*: as detailed below.
3. *Background story*: general information for filing and use when the journalist is writing about the subject.
4. *Summary and full technical story*: When a long detailed release is justified, it is helpful to editors to precede the main story with a short summary of perhaps a hundred words. To separate the summary from the actual story it can be indented more generously on each side, or boxed.
5. *Extended picture caption story*: A good picture may be the most publishable aspect of the release, and attached to it will be a story of perhaps half a normal sheet of release paper.
6. *Digest of a speech or a report*: Rather like the summary and full technical report, this kind of release is helpful to the editor in highlighting or summarising the most important contents of an accompanying document such as a speech, annual report, brochure or catalogue. For instance, a very newsworthy announcement may be contained somewhere in a speech of several pages, but it can be quoted in an accompanying release.

THE FRANK JEFKINS SEVEN-POINT FORMULA FOR WRITING PUBLISHABLE NEWS RELEASES

The following seven points form a logical sequence for the presentation of facts in a news release. The formula is also useful as a guide to the sort of information without which a story cannot be written, and as a check list to ensure that a story contains all the necessary factual elements. With the aid of this formula, a rough draft release can be produced very quickly. Inability to base a release on this formula will immediately reveal the inadequacy of the material on which the writer is trying to produce a story. Woolly stories, using many words to say very little, are the result of not using a formula or plot. Here, then, are the seven points to follow:

1. The *subject* of the story.
2. The name of the *organisation*.
3. The *location* of the organisation (which may be different from the address for further information).
4. The *advantages* of the policy, scheme, action, product or service.
5. The *applications* to which the subject may be put.
6. The *details* of specifications, prices, colours, sizes and so on.
7. The *source* of further information, samples, price lists, or address of showroom, information centre or the maker.

These seven points can be memorised by the seven key words: Subject–Organisation–Location – Advantages – Applications – Details – Source. The initial letters give us the mnemonic, SOLAADS.

It is usual for press officers to give their name, address and telephone number for 'further information', but it is also useful to close the story with a paragraph which says 'XYZ is made and marketed by the ABC Co. Ltd of 112 Orchard Way, New Hoxley, Exshire, EX4 7MA.' Use of such a closing paragraph also provides the means of stating the full company name so that there is no need to clutter up the opening paragraph with some long-winded monstrosity such as 'The XYZ Company Limited, a member of the OMS

Group, Inc., of Chicago', which no-one is going to print. Moreover, it gets in the way of the story and obscures the subject.

While this may look like the framework for a release of seven paragraphs this is not so. The formula represents the possible *sequence* of information, even of a long release running to more than one page. The secret of a good release, however, is that the opening paragraph should summarise the whole story. (Look at any newspaper report and it will be seen that the essence of the story is given in *the first paragraph*, succeeding paragraphs providing amplification.) It also tells the editor immediately what the story is all about. Editors dislike teasers. The opening paragraph is therefore the most important part of the news release, and will be dealt with separately in the next chapter as it is of supreme importance.

There is nothing difficult about writing a publishable release when this formula is used, for it imposes the discipline of representing, in a logical sequence, a coherent assembly of facts expressed in the fewest necessary words. There is no requirement for dramatic prose, although apt words and correct terminology call for a first-class vocabulary and understanding of the subject matter. While an advertisement may demand superlatives and repetition, a news release does not. Adjectives should be expunged. Brief statements such as 'in three popular shades' which may be all right in an advertisement must be detailed as 'in shades of pink, blue and green'. In other words, a good news release is one that states cold-blooded facts without comment.

The seven-point formula in use

To explain the use of the formula in practical terms here are two demonstrations, one for a building society story and the other for one about a new air-travel service. The SOLAADS mnemonic is set at the side of the breakdown of information, and this outline provides a useful guide to the facts required before the story can be written.

A building society savings scheme Let us assume that this is a fairly simple story about a new savings scheme whereby the lender who leaves a minimum sum in an account for six months receives a higher rate of interest. The seven-point formula is applied like this:

1. S New savings scheme — leave minimum sum for six months, earn higher rate of interest.
2. O Name of building society.
3. L All large cities, towns, branches and agents.
4. A Higher interest. Hedge against inflation. Easy withdrawal.
5. A Saving up for special occasions, holiday, wedding, anniversary, new furniture or to meet accounts that fall due such as rates or school fees.
6. D Details of scheme — how to join, interest rates, when and how paid.
7. S Head Office address for details.

An air-travel service In this case, let us assume that an airline is announcing a new route which is time-saving and cheaper.

1. S Air travel using route.
2. O Name of the airline.
3. L Airport from which the new service operates.
4. A Shorter journey — fewer stops — cheaper.
5. A Business travel.
6. D Aircraft, times, days, fares, services (e.g. meals).
7. S Airline office in London.

Both examples provide a plan or plot for the writing of the release, and neither release can be written until the writer has researched all the necessary facts. Afterwards, the draft can be checked to make sure that all these points have been covered.

WHAT IS THE SUBJECT?

When one tries to apply the seven-point formula, it is necessary to determine the subject. Editors often complain that they cannot find the subject! The subject could be different according to the journal. If, for instance, the press officer was working for a central heating firm the stories could have a variety of subjects such as the company, the equipment it manufactures or the fuel or fuels used, according to the type of story and the class of media. To take this instance still further, if oil suddenly became the cheapest fuel and the company made an oil-fired boiler, the boiler would be the primary subject.

However, it is not merely a question of topicality: the subject should be chosen for its reader interest and reader value. Company names are pretty dull subjects, and that is why they need to be pared of their 'company limited' frills. 'Ford's new Mondeo' is infinitely better than 'The Ford Motor Company's new Mondeo', and those three short, sharp words combine as a total subject which is impossible when the full company name is recited.

What, then, is the subject? No doubt the managing director would plump for the name of the building society. But that is not the subject: it is the new savings scheme, and better still it is the extra rate of interest. In the case of the air-travel story, the subject is not the name of the airline but the new route. The mistake is often made of beginning news releases with the name of the organisation. Nearly all the releases submitted for Chapter 16 began with the company name, although it was not the subject. Editors usually put such names at the end of the sentence, unless it is a dramatic story such as 'Ford has gone bankrupt'.

Here is a good example of an opening paragraph which puts the subject in the first words of the first paragraph:

The formation of a Scottish Shippers' and Transport Users' Group representing companies using road, rail, sea or air transport was announced today by Freight Transport Association President.

To combine the advice given in Chapter 17 on presentation and the above on the actual writing, the plan of a model news release is given in Figure 15.1.

A PRACTICAL EXAMPLE

Now let us look at the creation of a real example written by the author. The object of the story is to inform readers of suitable English-language journals in many parts of the world about the next international summer school run by his School of Public Relations.

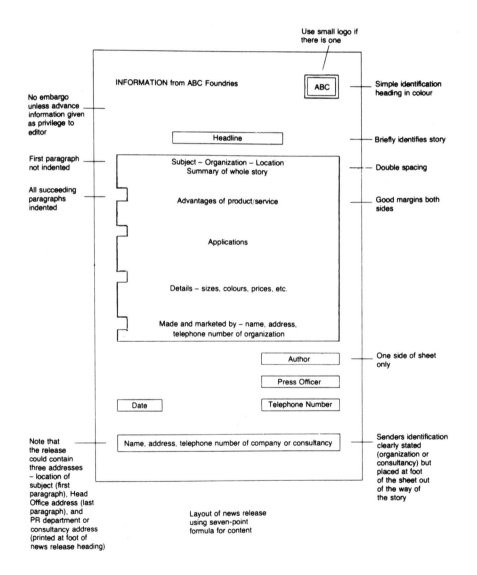

Figure 15.1   Plan of a model news release

Let us first apply the seven-point formula as already demonstrated for a building society and an air-travel service.

1. S An annual international Summer School on the subject of Public Relations Management.
2. O The Frank Jefkins School of Public Relations.
3. L London.
4. A Regular course, well supported. New topics in revised programme.
5. A Public relations managers from overseas.
6. D Fees. Closing dates for bookings and fees.
7. S Prospectus and timetable available. Address, telephone, fax, telex numbers.

When all the necessary facts were assembled, the following news release was written. Because there are many new topics there is substantial reference to advantages. The order of the seven points has been slightly changed to suit the story. But, first, what is the subject? It could be the event itself, its title, the location, the date or the name of the school. Permutations of these five items could produce at least five different opening paragraphs, and this first paragraph (which may be all that gets printed) is the most difficult part of the release to write. The final following example is the final result, but the first lines took the longest time to write.

FRANK JEFKINS' 1992 SUMMER SCHOOL

The 13th annual international Summer School on Public Relations Management will be held in London on July 6–24 by the Frank Jefkins School of Public Relations.

The previous 12 Summer Schools have been attended by PR managers from some 160 organisations in nearly 50 countries.

A new and topical programme has been planned for 1992. New topics include international news release distribution by satellite, video news releases, political lobbying, local government PR, psychology of public relations, launch of Philips CD-I, the Japanese approach to marketing and corporate communications, marketing quality assurance, the European Parliament and the Single European Market, corporate culture and mission statements and pre-testing and post-testing advertisements.

These are in addition to the regular sessions on planning PR campaigns, writing press material, advertising, marketing, marketing research and management.

The non-residential course fee is £2250. Bookings close on June 8 and fees must be paid by June 22.

A pictorial prospectus and timetable is obtainable from the Frank Jefkins School of Public Relations, 84 Ballards Way, South Croydon, Surrey, CR2 7LA, England. Telephones: 0689 847282 or 081–657 2911. Fax: 081–681 2864. Telex: 915393 SSOS–G.

January 1992

The release states essential facts which will interest potential participants. It makes no boasts, but sets out the facts without comment. However, the copy for the prospectus will be different in style since it has to advertise, persuade and sell. Alternative versions of the first paragraph are discussed in Chapter 16 on the Opening Paragraph.

The Opening Paragraph

In the previous chapter, a seven-point formula — or model — was set out for the writing of publishable news releases, and great importance was placed on the opening paragraph. Two important statements should be emphasised.

1. The secret of a good release is that the opening paragraph should summarise the whole story.
2. If all that is printed is the first paragraph, the message has been published.

The subject should be stated in the first paragraph, but preferably in the first sentence and ideally in the first three words, if not the first word. The opening paragraph should 'blow' the whole story.

In most cases, the opening paragraph should contain the subject, organisation, location and brief highlights of the story. By making use of the seven-point formula, the form and content of the opening paragraph becomes a natural discipline. When editors make their rapid appraisal of releases, a glance at the opening paragraph will be sufficient to tell whether the story has a possible use or whether it will join the great majority that are discarded. This is so whatever the subject matter.

Moreover, it may be that the full story is printed in an early edition of an evening newspaper, when news is scarce and more space is available for our story. As the day progresses, more news comes in and later editions are published, our story is likely to be cut to make room for other stories. In the final edition, the story may have been reduced to no more than the opening paragraph which is still capable of conveying the message because it is a summary of the whole story. *A good news release is therefore capable of being cut from the bottom up.*

A great mistake with some releases is that they open with a rambling sentence, even a rambling paragraph, and nowhere in these hundred or so words is there any mention of the subject of the story, let alone the substantial introduction recommended in the preceding paragraph. This is no exaggeration. It happens all the time.

With modern newsrooms, where stories are subbed on screen, it is common for journalists such as special correspondents (e.g. motoring) to set their computers to record the first paragraphs of stories relevant to them which arrive while they are out of the office.

The author received many releases in response to his appeal, others came from editors, or from exhibition press rooms (the ideal place in which to find bad news releases), or were received direct as the author is on certain mailing lists. While the attempt has been made to select some of the more interesting examples, the overwhelming experience was that most releases were incredibly dull. Not only were they dull, but few of them had anything to say that was worth reading. No wonder editors despair of public relations.

Two mistakes predominate in a large number of releases received by editors, the first one occurring in the majority of releases considered for this book.

The first fault is that many releases commence with the name of the sender, which is not the subject of the story. The subject is what the sender has done, will do, has produced or whatever the story is about. It is journalistic practice to put the name of the organisation at the *end* of the sentence, for example: 'A new route to Japan is announced by British Airways', and not 'British Airways announces a new route to Japan'. There may be occasions when the company is the subject of greatest reader interest, but this is rare.

A simple demonstration of the importance and content of the opening paragraph can be seen by reading the 'introductions' to all the reports in a newspaper. It is possible to read *only* the first paragraphs of each report to obtain a complete digest of all the news in a newspaper.

The second fault, so common with releases written by students (and by others unfamiliar with the technique of writing news releases), is that they begin with a preposterous statement such as 'We are proud to announce . . .' One has only to look at a newspaper to see that no story ever begins like this, if only that the pronoun 'we' would not be used since it is the newspaper which is doing the reporting (even if it prints a release without alteration), and the statement belongs to an advertisement or a sales letter. The story should be aimed at the eventual reader in the style used by an editor, and not addressed to the editor.

As was stated at the end of the previous chapter, before giving an example of a complete release, the first paragraph is the most difficult part of the release. Let us go back to that example and see how many different ways that opening paragraph can be written, beginning with the one adopted which was:

The 13th annual international Summer School on Public Relations Management will be held in London on July 6–24 by the Frank Jefkins School of Public Relations.

It contains seven possible subjects: '13th', 'international', 'Summer School', 'Public Relations Management', 'London', 'July 6–24' and 'Frank Jefkins School of Public Relations' are all possible subjects with which the paragraph could begin. The variations or permutations are as follows.

An international Summer School, Public Relations Management, will be held in London for the 13th year run by the Frank Jefkins School of Public Relations on July 6–24.

July 6–24 are the dates of the 13th international Summer School, Public Relations Management, to be held in London by the Frank Jefkins School of Public Relations.

Public Relations Management is the subject of the 13th international Summer School to be held in London on July 6–24 by the Frank Jefkins School of Public Relations.

London is the venue of the 13th international Summer School, Public Relations Management, to be held on July 6–24 by the Frank Jefkins School of Public Relations.

The Frank Jefkins School of Public Relations announces its 13th international Summer School, Public Relations Management, to be held in London on July 6–24.

The above exercise demonstrates that while the rest of the story, which develops and substantiates the summarised statement in the opening paragraph, is comparatively easy to write, the opening paragraph can result from a very self-critical rewriting until the best version is achieved. Note that in none of these examples is there any comment or puffery. There is just a bold statement of indisputable facts.

Now let us look at some other examples taken from releases which were kindly supplied to the author for use in this book.

Here is the opening paragraph from a Co-op news release produced by Countrywide, who were not identified on the release, nor for that matter was any author stated or date given.

In September 1990, the Co-op was the first UK retailer to sign the Whale and Dolphin Conservation Society undertaking, aimed at eliminating unacceptable risks to marine animals associated with certain forms of fishing practices.

This is a clear positive statement. To explain its purpose, it was headed 'Background Information' and it provided background to the Co-op's involvement with Project Dolphin Alert (The Moray Firth 1991 Trial).

The next example is from a release produced by Roger Haywood Associates on behalf of Ecowater Systems, which permits expression of some niggles. The brief opening paragraph read:

The first ecologically advanced domestic water softener with an environmentally conscious mind of its own has been launched by Ecowater, the world's largest residential water treatment company.

While the ecological mumbo jumbo is presumably an attempt to jump on the 'green' bandwagon, it does not explain how a water softener is ecologically friendly. Nor is this substantiated in the following three-page story

which merely implies that the system prevents furred pipes, but with more efficient use of salt and water. Thus this opening paragraph is unable to stand alone as a complete comprehensible summary.

However, our principle niggle lies in the use of the word 'largest', and we shall return to the vocabulary of this story in Chapter 18. It is all too easy to slip into the glib usage of a word such as 'largest'. Largest for what reason? Volume of production, value of sales, number of plants, number of employees, or is it the largest in financial terms of assets or profits? Such a vague generality needs to be explained. It is the sort of emotive language that one can get away with in advertisement copy, but it is not objective journalism. If an editor asked the managing director why his company was the largest could he give a coherent answer? He was probably delighted to see the word used in a news release about his company.

Another story from the same stable shows how the same writer can use the opening paragraph to tell the story in a nutshell, but this time for a different client, Cargill PLC. It reads:

Completion is announced of the next step of a comprehensive programme aimed to reduce the odour from the Cargill Milling Division's Tilbury plant. The filter used to extract oil from the maize or corn germ, a process which can give off an odour, has been moved into the main processing area from a building outside the plant. This has eliminated the need to transport part-refined maize products around the site, as well as ensuring that odours are kept inside the plant building.

This paragraph really tells the whole story, and it was the first of six paragraphs of a short release, needlessly taking up two pages because the heading and headline occupied half the first page. The lot could have been printed on one page. It was padded out with a quote from the general manager which added nothing significant to the story.

Here is an example of unwillingness to accept that a good story can be told with relatively few words. As anyone knows who has experienced the smell from such a plant, this story is good news and very much to the credit of the company. The main fault with this otherwise good opening paragraph is that it takes thirteen words to arrive at the subject which is 'Odour from the Cargill Milling Division's Tilbury Plant has been reduced by moving the filter'. Now we have the sort of report normally found in the press.

The next example from the Retail Motor Industry Federation has the distinct merit of being short:

Motorists seeking help and advice on the new exhaust emission requirements of the MoT test from 1 November should consult their local RMI MoT test station.

The whole release, which explained the benefits that motorists could obtain from the service occupied only four paragraphs on one sheet of paper. Admirable! But one quibble remains: what is the RMI? Nowhere in the story does it say. Royal Motoring Institute? Road Mechanics Institute? Whenever initials are going to be used in the story the full name — in this case Retail Motor Industry Federation which is probably unknown to the majority of motorists — should be spelled out in full followed by the initials in brackets. Afterwards, the initials can be used. This is the problem of knowing what you mean if no-one else does.

From the Midland Bank comes a story in which, at first glance, the opening paragraph seems to be excellent.

Thirty-five jobs have been created in Cleveland as a result of the Cleveland County Loan Fund, launched in March 1990 by Midland Bank, the Cleveland Action Team and the Hartlepool Task Force.

This appears to be a good arrangement of the details, summarising the story very nicely. 'Thirty-five jobs' makes a topical subject. However, this did not satisfy the various newspapers in NE England, perhaps because they sought a local subject. The *Hartlepool Times*, *Hartlepool Mail*, *Middlesbrough Evening Gazette* and the *Darlington Evening Echo* all led with 'Cleveland Action Team', the *Newcastle Journal* preferred 'The Cleveland County Loan Fund', and only the *Hartlepool Star* led with 'Thirty-five jobs' and printed a slightly subbed version of the first three paragraphs of the release. The lesson here, of course, is that if you write a story for the local press, it has to have a local subject. This may be overlooked when such a story is written by a central public relations office in London.

The following is from a Bass release. A curious thing about all Bass releases is that they start with 'Bass PLC' which is rarely the subject of the story, and smacks of advertising or some management edict. Here is a typical example:

Bass PLC today announced the closure of two of the 13 breweries operated by Bass Brewers, with a loss of some 480 jobs. Production at the two plants at Preston Brook near Runcorn and Springfield, Wolverhampton, will transfer to other Bass breweries. The plants will close on 2 August 1991.

Presumably it is company policy to try to plug Bass PLC in the first instance, but it is rather obvious. The subject here is the closure of two of the 13 breweries operated by Bass Brewers. Does the reader care about the business distinctions that Bass Brewers brew beer for Bass PLC? There are too many internal politics here which get in the way of telling a story.

CHAPTER 17

Presentation

WHY PRESENTATION IS IMPORTANT

There are two important aspects to the production of a successful news release. One is the way it is presented and the other is the way it is written. Although the presentation is largely a matter of designing and reproducing what has been written by hand or on a typewriter, the author should have the final appearance in mind at the creative stage. Discipline can then be applied to techniques that are logical, and therefore essential, if a publishable release is to be produced. Capital letters will be restricted to proper names and full points eliminated. It will be known that good secretarial practice is seldom good printing practice, and secretarial staff will need to be instructed in what, to them, may well be strange typing techniques and styling. A news release (or an article) has to be set out as a manuscript and not like a business letter. Judging by the appearance of many news releases, this is unknown to most public relations secretaries and typists.

Therefore, in this chapter the basic presentation is analysed and discussed very carefully. A first-class press officer will be meticulous over these details. How a news release should and can be written is explained in the other chapters.

THREE PURPOSES OF PRESENTATION

The purpose of good, correct presentation is threefold: (i) to achieve legibility; (ii) to make the release attractive to read; and (iii) to minimise editorial work so that the release is capable of publication as it stands. The less a story is re-written, the less likelihood there is of its meaning being changed. But having said that, it must be admitted that while a trade magazine may print the story exactly as submitted by the press officer, the national newspaper will inevitably do a rewrite job to suit its own style, and may well use the news release merely as a piece of information on which to base a story resulting from further investigation. In both cases, however, it is essential that the press officer issues information in a thoroughly professional manner, and this really boils down to presenting the facts as an editor would like to receive them.

These three requirements therefore imply a knowledge of human psychology and an appreciation of editorial needs. Unfortunately many news releases fail to meet these three elementary requirements. The presentation of a news release is as much a piece of marketing as the packing of a shirt in a plastic bag and a nice box.

MODERN EDITORIAL NEEDS

In the modern computerised paperless news-room, editorial amendments and subbings will not be made on the original release so that it can be sent to foundry for setting. With direct input, the story will be keyed so that it appears on the screen of the visual display unit (VDU). Sometimes the original appears on the left-hand side of the screen and the subbed version appears on the right-hand side. This makes it all the more imperative that the opening paragraph contains the subject and is a sum-mary of the whole story. The original paper release is then discarded.

ESSENTIAL ELEMENTS OF PRESENTATION

The presentation can be divided into the following ten elements:

1. The basic sheet
2. Length, ending and authorship
3. Headlines, subheads and paragraphs
4. Typing, style and punctuation
5. Embargoes and dating
6. Picture availability
7. Layout
8. Running-off
9. Assembling
10. Envelopes

1. The basic sheet

Sheet size. A4 (297 mm × 210 mm) has become the universally accepted paper size for news releases. An advantage of this size sheet is that it makes it very easy to restrict the majority of news stories to the ideal of one piece of paper, a distinct advantage from the point of view of a busy editor. It is always psychologically easier to induce someone to read what is presented to them on one side of one piece of paper.

The printed heading. A news release that is merely reproduced on to plain paper without a printed heading looks dull and amateurish. A printed news release heading should quickly establish the identity of the sender. When a reputation has been won for good, interesting and accurate press stories, instant recognition by means of a distinctive heading will be a desirable asset, since the editor of even a small trade paper may receive as many as fifty different news releases of varying length in a single morning's post. The best headings are fairly simple and do not occupy too much space. A news release heading should simply distinguish that it is not a business letter or an advertisement heading. The wording should clearly state the name, address, telephone number and telex or fax number (if there is one) for further information, and a night or home telephone number can be helpful. Use of the organisation's house colour and logo create immediate identification.

A consultancy has the problem of declaring the identities of both itself and its client, but from the editor's point of view it is the *client's* identity which matters, even though further information is to be had from a consultant. It is therefore wrong, if common, for the consult-ant's name to predominate.

In fact it is best if the sender's identification is printed discreetly at the *foot* of the sheet, the only print at the top being perhaps a single word such as NEWS or INFORMATION or possibly NEWS RELEASE. The story should appear as high up on the sheet as possible.

The effect is to give emphasis to the story, and since the story is reproduced in black it will contrast very legibly with neat, informa-tive but unobtrusive coloured print. Moreover, since the subject of the news release will be clear from the headline and the opening words, this style of release heading is self-identifying so far as the client or organisation is concerned.

The majority of news release headings are bad. They are over designed, look too much like sales letters, and the printed headings occupy far too much space. Keep it simple! Do not let a garish heading get in the way of the news. Do not annoy editors before they have a chance to read the release.

And do not use other silly and irritating devices such as putting a box round the story, printing vertical coloured rules in the margin, or typing the whole story in italics or in capital letters. Nor should the release paper be decorated with pictures or fancy effects. The printed heading should not get in the way of the story, but simply identify and locate the sender.

2. Length, ending and authorship

The question of length occurs many times in this book. The more concise and precise the release, the more readable and acceptable it is likely to be. Space is scarce and there is competition for this space from staff writers, news agencies, stringers, freelancers and other news releases. Sometimes it is wise to estimate how many words are given to the average story and write no more. Nevertheless, with very technical products it may be proper to cover the subject in sufficient depth to make the story worth publishing. Discretion must be applied according to the topic and the media.

However, in this chapter we are concerned with length from the point of view of presentation, and length can sometimes be determined at the typing stage because if a second sheet is going to be required to carry a continuation of only a few lines it is usually possible to cut the story in order to keep it on one piece of paper.

Again, there is the question of extra work and extra costs. A public relations department or press office in industry is seldom overstaffed and a few words running over on to a second sheet means an extra reproduction operation and an extra job in stapling the two sheets together. Time is money, especially in a consultancy where the fee is based on the consumption of time.

Similarly, the consultant who charges his clients for the consumption of unnecessary reams of paper, as can happen over a period of a year, is not acting very responsibly if paper is wasted, so length of releases can be a matter of strict account management. In a consultancy, it is essential to be cost-conscious. There are only two people who can pay for wasted paper, the client or the consultant. Wasted paper can consume profits.

Finally, there is the question of editorial time and editorial needs. Editors receive so many hundreds of public relations stories every week that they simply do not have the time to wade through pages of verbosity. The news agencies, which generally put out on their wire services stories of no more than 80 words, despair at the daily arrival of long-winded news releases which condemn themselves on sight.

Thus, when the facts are presented as briefly as possible, and the story can be read almost at a glance, there is seldom any need to go beyond the ample space provided by a single A4 sheet. It can take 300 words which is a lot of words.

The *ending* of the release, and its *authorship* are related to the length and particularly to the more detailed release which does run to more than one sheet.

All news releases should close with the name of the writer, the telephone number and the date, and a serial number will be useful if releases are issued frequently. This is important when the story has originated from a consultancy, less necessary when it has come from an organisation whose press officer is named on the printed heading. Closing the story with the author's name is a clear way of finishing and a good way of establishing personal contact and responsibility for the facts.

There is no need to write 'ends' at the close of the story, as this is apparent from the closing details of the author's name and so on mentioned above.

The curious use of 'ends' is a relic of the newsroom practice when journalists wrote on a series of small pieces of paper, each one concluding with 'more' and the final one with 'ends'. This was essential because in the composing room, the copy was often set by different Linotype operators. Eventually, the type was assembled on the 'stone' and it was necessary to know where it ended. This no longer happens with web offset printing so use of the word 'ends' tends to age the writer, or suggest ignorance of modern newspaper production.

3. Headlines, subheadings and paragraphs

Here we have three elements of a news release on which there seems to be hardly any agreed standard practice, yet when ordinary editorial needs are considered there can surely be no question about the *required* practice if good press relations are to be maintained. Let us examine each one in turn.

Headlines. Although it is tempting to invent clever, alliterative headlines, no-one will use them. Each editor likes to write his own, unless he is lazy or there is no better alternative to yours. The purpose of the news release headline is to quickly *identify* the story. The headline, which is not to be confused with the printed heading already discussed, has a practical purpose to perform, but it may never be printed if only because editors do not want to print the same headlines as their rivals. Sometimes employers and clients try to insist that the press officer should word the headline in some dramatic or persuasive manner, but the press officer must dissuade them from doing this, as an advertisement-type headline suggests to some editors that the content will be the same. Editors hate 'puffery'. The headline should therefore create the right impression that what follows is a genuine, factual, news story.

From a Retail Motor Industry Federation release the following headline is taken. It identifies the topic very well.

UK CAR PRICES COULD BE LOWEST
IN EUROPE

Subheadings. Again, it is tempting to insert subheadings to add interest to a story, but they may be a nuisance to the editor who either does not use them, or likes to put them in where they suit best. Subheadings are usually used for typographical effect, providing artistic contrast to make the page attractive, especially in magazines. So it is best not to use subheadings, except in a very long release which has clearcut sections dealing with separate items such as a number of different models. Even then, it may be better to write individual releases on each subject rather than bury the various items in an omnibus story.

Common sense must prevail to some extent. In all these matters, the press officer has to remember that the story is going to many editors who will each have distinctive styles of presentation, and therefore it is wise to present the basic story as baldly but as clearly as possible, leaving each editor to set it out as he or she pleases.

Paragraphs. The use of paragraphs and their presentation is imperfectly understood by some press officers, but the lesson can be learned very quickly by studying the columns of daily newspapers. Modern journalism calls for short paragraphs. They help people to read quickly, and to absorb the message clearly. Short paragraphs can be deliberately used to keep the interest flowing.

Indention of paragraphs. The setting out of paragraphs is not limited to their length, however. Most releases are set out in block paragraphs, like a business letter. This is wrong. Most publishers and printers use what is known as 'book style'. The first paragraph is *not* indented: all succeeding paragraphs *are* indented. The style derives from handwritten Bibles which had decorative drop capitals at the beginning of chapters. This book follows 'book style', as do most newspapers and magazines. Secretaries should be instructed to type releases in this accepted way.

It is also wrong to use extra double spacing

between paragraphs although this is common practice, possibly because typists are used to doing this when they do not indent paragraphs. It serves no purpose in a properly indented release, as will be seen if one looks at a newspaper or magazine.

Some publications open stories with a drop capital, as already mentioned, and a lesser form is to set the first word or two in caps. This should never be aped in a news release since different publications use different styles.

4. Typing, style and punctuation

A release should be typed in ordinary typewriter characters and the editor will decide whether he wants to set the story in medium or bold type and also whether words are to be set in capitals or italics. It is not the writer's job to do this, or to try to emphasise parts of the story in any way. Consequently, the typist should never use any of the special effects that are possible with a word-processor such as using bold type or italics. The example quoted here from Cobourne Co. Film and Video is an excellent example of what not to do!

NEWS RELEASE — FOR IMMEDIATE USE

CBI AWARD FOR EFFECTIVE COMMUNICATION
A series of video programmes produced by Cardiff-based Cobourne Co Film & Video has been awarded the **CBI AWARD FOR EFFECTIVE COMMUNICATION**.

Sir John Banham, Director General of the **CBI** said, "*Most progressive companies have a total communications policy, and this should include visual communications. Senior management will give serious consideration to any method of communication that can be shown to produce outstanding business results. It can be done — as the winner of this year's CBI Award has shown*".

The CBI Award is given, "*for the communciations project which best demonstrates a positive effect on client's business. Programmes from businesses, organisations and institutions all over the world have competed to win this award. To win is to achieve a status that is recognised throughout the world as a guarantee of the highest standards of creativity, production values and effectiveness*".

The judging was led by **John Dunkley, Director of Public Affairs at the CBI**. Another judge, **Michael Beard, Director of Corporate Communications at Taylor Woodrow plc** said that the programmes, "*clearly demonstrated tangible effects on the profitability of client companies. A striking combination of the effective and innovative use of visual communications*".

The winning programmes, starring **Simon Bates, Paul Heiney, Alison Mitchell** and **Joanna Lumley**, explain the protection afforded by the Consumer Credit Act to potential purchasers of home improvements and double glazing.

Cobourne Co Film & Video is a TV production company that specialises in marketing, advertising, sales and PR programmes. Cobourne Co is based in **Llandaff, Cardiff** and was formed just two years ago by Richard Cobourne. Cobourne Co's clients include Bayer Pharmaceutical, Ford, Jaguar, GKN and McCann-Erickson.

The winning team led by Richard Cobourne includes Alison King (Producer/ Researcher), Jane McCabe (Administrator) and Gareth Walters (Business Development). "*Our success*", said Cobourne, "*is based on the talents of our small team. Alison and Gareth both have good degrees in sales and marketing, they have both worked in British industry as well as TV, sales, PR and advertising agencies — so client's can be assured that they receive proper marketing skills based on real experience of the market place. Jane's computer and admin skills ensure that clients are given a first class business back up. My BBC TV and radio background ensures high professional standards — we can now called ourselves the winning team!"*

Most companies at some time or the other have made a corporate video. Measuring it's effectiveness has been difficult. Often the basics, such as setting a proper objective and evaluating the viewers, have been ignored. Cobourne Co's programmes are based on three levels of proper research — research the objective; research the potential audience; research the effectiveness.

"Research is vital", said Cobourne, *"but too many film and video companies are too interested in the art! Corporate TV companies must balance creativity with business objectives. All our programmes are business led. Our client's ultimately make programmes for one reason only — to increase the bottom line. Winning the CBI Award for Effective Communication supports our beliefs."*

The winning programmes are currently being used by over fifty home improvement and replacement window companies to promote sales — and improve the reputation of their industry. Home Improvement industry specialist USP has calculated that as a direct result of Cobourne Co's programme, sales have increased by over £20 million. Furthermore one-in-ten replacement windows are being sold after the potential customer has viewed the programme in their home.

END

Picture

b/w photograph of Richard Cobourne receiving CBI Award.

More information, interviews and for details of full length features please contact:
Alison King,   Cobourne Co on
Telephone   0222 567593
Fax   0222 578496

If you use this story we would be most grateful for a copy. Please send **FREEPOST** *to:*

Cobourne Co Film & Video
FREEPOST
Bush House
39 Cardiff Road
Llandaff
CARDIFF
CF5 1ZZ

In most respects it is a bad release, although the opening paragraph is quite good in summarising the story. There is no point in saying it is for immediate release. It is in single space typing. Whole words are in capitals. Some words are in bold type. The quotations are in italics. The left-hand margin was cluttered up with a logo. The whole piece is too long and the quotes are overdone so that instead of a news story it is pure puffery. It also contains two mistakes. And one never asks to be sent a press cutting!

Capital letters. Capital letters belong to titling or to proper and geographical names. Indiscriminate use of capital letters can be the bane of an editor's life. A company or product name should never be written *entirely* in capitals, nor should initial capitals be used for nouns as they are in German.

'The new range of Central Heating equipment made by ABC Ltd includes Solid Fuel, Gas-fired and Oil-fired Boilers' should be like this:

'This new range of central heating equipment made by ABC Ltd includes solid fuel, gas-fired and oil-fired boilers.'

Far too many news releases are written with needless capitals and it is plain to see the extent of editorial correction that is necessary.

Technical people are apt to refer to Cocoa, Radar, Timber, Steel, business people to Directors, Boards, Annual General Meetings and Dividends, but these capital letters are wrongly used and must not appear in news releases.

Only very important people such as the President, the Queen, or the Archbishop are given capital letters. Managing directors, chairmen and other business leaders are not — not even in *The Financial Times* — while *The Economist* has almost eliminated capital letters altogether.

Nor should emphasis be given by typing whole passages in capitals. All emphasis should be left to the editor since, as we shall see in the next chapter, it is not the place of the press officer to comment or invite testimony. The author of the news release must be content with supplying factual material free of bias. Otherwise the news release becomes an advertisement. This distinction is sometimes, and understandably, difficult to appreciate by advertising people when they are employing press relations services. You can use as many capital letters as you like in an advertisement where they are used for persuasive effect.

The opening word or first few words should not be typed in capitals, even though some editors may occasionally use this style, as already mentioned, in place of a drop capital.

Underlining and quotation marks. No underlining should appear anywhere in a news release, and preferably not even in the headline, because whereas to the writer, underlining means a rule or line set there for emphasis, to the printer an *underlining is an instruction to set in italic type*. It is no business of the press officer to stipulate which words should be set in italics, except in the case of foreign words or Latin names in scientific matter. The academic style of italicising book titles does not apply to news releases.

Similarly, quotation marks can generally be avoided. The time to use quotation marks is when actual speech or material from another source is being quoted, always remembering that it is necessary to place quotation marks at the beginning of each paragraph and to conclude the entire speech or quotation with quotation marks. Otherwise it is not absolutely clear where the quotation starts and finishes. Single quotes are usually used.

The following quotation comes from a Retail Motor Industry Federation release.

'If motor manufacturers sold cars to retailers at the same price throughout Europe then UK pre-tax prices to the customer would undoubtedly be the lowest.'

These comments were made by Alan Pulham, Director of the Franchised Retailer Division of the Retail Motor Industry Federation at Motorfair today (Wednesday 16 October).

Rather cleverly, these were the opening two paragraphs of a release from which we have also quoted the headline and the embargo.

Numerals and symbols. A paragraph should never begin with a numeral unless a list of points is being made, and if the sentence cannot be recast satisfactorily the numeral should be spelt out. Except in special cases such as dates, measurements and prices, numbers from one to nine should be spelt out, after which numerals such as 59 and 101 should be used until the numbers become so unwieldy that it is clearer to spell out many thousands and certainly millions. Five million or £5 million is more readily understood that 5 000 000 or £5 000 000. The actual numerals should be given in dates, June 1 and not June First, and 1970, not one thousand nine hundred and seventy, and definitely not nineteen seventy. Similarly we write the 20th century as we do the 19th hole. The press officer has to be extremely careful that accurate and easily understood figures are given in news releases. An error can be disastrous once it is printed, and little can be done by way of correction. If the story has been widely distributed, the error may be perpetuated for weeks, months, even years.

The same applies to measurements and signs where there is any risk of a mistake. It is advisable to avoid the signs and write 90 degrees and 100 percent. Percent is usually printed as one word, and the % sign is not used in sentences.

While on the subject, it is all too easy to be slapdash about the use of figures, signs and punctuation, and inconsistencies such as 'four wheel' and '4-wheel' are surprisingly frequent in the same press release. In the short space of a few hundred words the press officer should be capable of repeating numerical facts in the same way.

A sign that is badly abused is the ampersand (&), which should never appear in a sentence unless it is part of the normal way of spelling a company name. At best, it is a lazy device, sometimes resorted to by those who write quickly in longhand. The ampersand has its special uses where space is scarce, that is in headlines and tabulated matter such as lists, catalogues and accounts.

Full points or full stops. Full points should not be used between initial abbreviations such as BSc, BBC, MCC and so on. If they were inserted viz: B.Sc., B.B.C., M.C.C., the effect would be a spotty mess. A study of the press will show that the *Financial Times* index is abbreviated as the *FT* Index, the Institute of Public Relations as IPR, the United States Army as the US Army and Member of Parliament as MP. This absence of full points in abbreviations is common to all types of publications, and although exceptions can be found, the appearance of the text is always improved when the full points are omitted. There are, however, two regular exceptions: i.e. and e.g..

Full points remain a vital form of punctuation, and the so-called letter-writing style

which omits all punctuation must not be used when typing a news release.

Punctuation generally. The clarity of a news story can depend upon use of punctuation, and commas, semi-colons, dashes and brackets are the signposts of written communication. The pedantic use of punctuation can impede reading, but the lack of essential punctuation can cause misunderstanding. Sometimes punctuation is omitted through carelessness, and releases must be scrutinised to see that parentheses are completely punctuated. A parenthesis, an aside, should have a comma before and after the aside, but the second comma is often forgotten.

5. Embargoes and dating

The date when a story may be published, the use of dates in stories, and the date when the release is issued are three things of great consequence to the recipient of press releases.

Embargoes. An embargo is a request to the press that the story should not be published before a certain date and perhaps even a certain time on that date. There are many genuine occasions when an embargo is vital, and this is often so in financial public relations or when stories are being issued in different parts of the world where disparity in times could cause embarrassment if publications took place literally at the same time. The announcement of price changes or the publication of a speech are typical examples where it can be very helpful if an editor can have the copy well in advance provided the privilege is respected and the speech is not printed before it has been delivered.

Having admitted the necessity for embargoes, it must be emphasised that embargoes should be used sparingly and sensibly. Long embargoes, however, are bad and hardly ever justified. They usually have the effect of killing interest in the story. An embargo should be a privilege, enabling the editor to have advance knowledge or information which it would be foolish or improper to publish before the stipulated date and time. For example, lobby correspondents receive advance copies of white papers, the contents of which they must not divulge prematurely. However, if an embargo is unexpected and irrelevant it may even get overlooked.

Most stories should therefore be for immediate release, and if that is so it is pointless to print *for immediate release* across the top, unless it comes from one of those rare organisations which seldom issues a story without a stringent embargo. One suspects that some of the releases from commercial sources which bear dramatic embargoes or permissions for instant publication are produced by somewhat amateurish writers who are trying to capture some of the supposed glamour of a hectic newsroom.

Here is an example of an embargo from a Retail Motor Industry Federation release:

Embargo: Not for publication before 15.30 hours Wednesday 16 October.

The embargo was used because the release referred to a statement which coincided with the Motorfair.

Dates. If a date is important to the story it should be included in the narrative, and the month should read first and be spelt out in full thus: November 12, 1985 (not November 12th). The month, which is generally more significant and memorable than the day of the month, should be placed first. Vague references to 'today', 'yesterday', 'tomorrow' or 'recently' must be replaced by the actual date. Reliance should not be placed on the date of the release itself. Nor should dates be given 'th', 'st', 'rd' or 'nd' endings.

However, since the appearance of *The Independent*, this newspaper and some others put the date before the month, e.g. 12 November. As a result, both styles are now in use, although it is surely clearer and more logical to put the month first.

If the release describes a stand at an exhibition, the headline should state all the relevant details about name of exhibitions, venue, *dates*, hall and stand number. In London or Birmingham, there are two or three exhibitions taking place every week and editors cannot be expected to know when and where every exhibition is being held.

It should not be necessary for an editor to have to ring the press officer and ask 'when did it happen?'. Moreover, dated stories should be issued promptly so that their news value is not lost, and this implies knowing the last date or even time for copy for different types of publication. It may be that it is too late to write, reproduce and distribute a news release and that the story must be despatched by telephone, telex, Two-Ten, PA or Reuters.

Dating releases. Apart from dates that are part of the information supplied, releases themselves should be dated. Some press officers insert the date at the beginning of the first page, others at the foot of the story.

6. Picture availability

It may not be feasible to send photographs with every news release issued as this would be costly and wasteful. But the availability of pictures can be stated on the release, and since this is not publishable information these details should be set apart from the body of the story, that is, below the author's name. (Alternatively, the pictures can be identified and described on an accompanying order form.) Photo captions should not be incorporated in releases: they must be attached to the actual prints. Pictures should not be pasted down on releases.

7. Layout

Spacing. All manuscript work should be double or one-and-half spaced in proportion to the size of the typewriter typeface.

Machines with very large typefaces should

not be used for news release work since they will spread the story over more pages than, say, Elite type. Nor should a typewriter with italic face or all capitals be used.

Margins. A right-hand as well as a left-hand margin is needed in a news release. Both margins should not be less than 1.5 inches (4 cm).

Continuations. When the news release consists of more than one sheet this should be clearly indicated at the foot of the page, and all succeeding pages should be numbered. The word 'more' or 'continued' should be typed in the bottom right-hand corner. If this is done, more elaborate continuation references are redundant, but some people do put the title of the piece at the top of each page to make absolutely certain that scattered pages can be reassembled safely.

8. Running off

One side of the paper. All manuscript work must be typed or reproduced on one side of the paper only, and anything on the reverse side will be ignored. Editors and publishers always work from material on one side of the paper only; it would be awkward for the keyboard operator if there was copy on the reverse side too.

9. Assembling

As we have already said, the ideal news story is one that is confined to one sheet of paper, but there are times when a story does run to two or three pages. Separate pages should be stapled together in the top left-hand corner. When folding the release for insertion in the envelope, the stapled end should be enclosed within the folds, otherwise there is risk that the metal will rip the envelope during its passage through the post, or damage accompanying photographs.

It is also important to fold cleanly to avoid

unnecessary bulk which can spring open a poorly-sealed envelope. If mailings are frequent, a folding machine is a good investment, and there are several makes on the market which handle work of various complexities.

This is possibly a good point at which to warn the press officer that secretaries are not always aware of the rough handling that postal packages have to suffer. Unless items for the post are securely packed and sealed they will stand little chance of surviving the hazards of the postal services. The onus is on the sender to protect whatever is mailed.

10. Envelopes

The release should be folded as few times as possible so that it is as presentable as possible on arrival. An A4 release needs to be folded only twice to fit a DL or 9 × 4 inch envelope. A bulkier release, or a feature article, is best folded only once and posted in a larger envelope.

However, when accompanying a half-plate photograph (the size of print least likely to get damaged in the post by the string or rubber bands which postmen put around bundles of letters for any one address), the release has to be folded once each way for insertion in a suitable envelope. A single sheet news release is preferable with photographs so that there is no danger of damage from the metal staple.

It is a simple matter to draw up a brief version of these recommendations and to see that every member of the press office staff has a copy to learn by heart, and stick on the wall if need be.

In this chapter the author has not hesitated to slaughter some of the sacred cows of press relations, such as embargoes, and the use of expressions such as 'for immediate release' and 'ends'. Most of these terms were derived from journalistic practices but the habits of the newspaper office are not necessarily applicable to individually produced news releases.

It is a mistake for press officers to add a note

at the end of the story requesting a cutting if the story is printed, and it is unnecessary to enclose a covering letter urging the editor to print the story. Many editors are generous about sending cuttings, or better still actual copies of the journal, but it is rather tactless to ask editors for favours. An exception, however, may be when the story is sent overseas and it is doubtful whether a press cutting will come through a press cutting agency. When despatching news releases, a copy of the story and, if possible, a copy of the mailing list should be sent to the press cutting agency.

The best advice on the presentation of releases is to look at actual printed stories and see how they are presented. When the release closely resembles a printed story, the editor will not have to waste time making amendments to the presentation itself. When there is no composing room to instruct, and copy is keyed straight into the computer, even more time is saved if the release is in a form ready for keying.

Good presentation looks professional, encourages respectful attention, and saves editors a lot of work. Bad presentation looks amateurish, and suggests that the story itself is equally poor.

CHAPTER 18

Some News Releases Analysed

WHY ARE SO MANY RELEASES DREADFUL?

It is easy to be critical and to be a perfectionist. However, when writing a news release, the object is to get it published. It is not therefore being pedantic or idealistic to say that if a news release is to stand any chance of getting published it not only has to be sent to the right journal at the right time but it should resemble what the reader expects to read in a journal for which he has paid good money. It cannot be repeated sufficiently that the great majority of news releases bear not the slightest resemblance to what one reads in any journal in any part of the world. In his travels, the author has wearied of editors asking him why public relations people send them such rubbish.

Is it the fault of public relations practitioners? The writing of news releases has little place in the CAM examinations, and the author's experience is that few CAM students even at the Diploma stage have the slightest idea how to write a publishable news release. It is perhaps the tragedy of public relations that he or she generally lacks the one skill the practitioner should possess, which is the ability to write a news release. It should be the most elementary skill — it is not difficult if one takes the trouble to read newspapers — but the situation is as serious as if a book-keeper cannot add up or a typist cannot type.

The only excuse one can suggest is that even if the public relations practitioner is capable of writing a news release it is mutilated by superiors, and especially by marketing managers. This is a fundamental weakness with the consultancy system which requires that clients be pleased. We should be professionals who do not permit the destruction of our work so that it earns the contempt of editors.

A number of releases are now examined, but their faults may not be the responsibility of their authors. The first was produced for the Co-op by Countrywide Communications London Ltd.

EMBARGO: NOT FOR PUBLICATION OR BROADCAST BEFORE 10.30 HOURS TUESDAY 1 OCTOBER 1991

SCIENTISTS NEARER TO SAVING DOLPHINS

British scientists demonstrated a new deep sea "traffic system" today (1 October 1991) which they believe could prevent thousands of dolphins being needlessly killed each year.

A team of scientists from Cambridge, Loughborough and Aberdeen Universities reported the results of trials of a "cat's eyes" type reflector device which will help avoid dolphins' capture in fishing nets.

The reflectors when attached to fishing nets, will work like cats eyes on the road and enable the dolphins' built-in sonar to detect their presence and avoid the nets.

The dolphins — and porpoises too — die when they are caught up in commercial fishing fleet nets, including the "wall of death nets" of the tuna fishing industry.

Following the trials of the reflectors in the Moray Firth, Scotland, sponsors are being sought to enable the scientists to continue their work and develop prototype designs for practical use by the fishing community world wide.

This summer's trials were backed by Britain's biggest retail group, the Co-op, whose 4000 stores sell over 1500 tonnes (10 million cans) of tuna each year.

The Co-op is campaigning with the Whale and Dolphin Conservation Society for a ban on fishing methods which harm dolphins.

It has pledged not to market its tuna as "dolphin friendly" until an international system is in place to monitor the tuna fishing industry.

David Bellamy, the Co-op's environmental advisor speaking at the launch of the appeal for funds said:

"This is the most promising piece of research yet to safeguard the dolphin from mass destruction.

"It is an approach which should be enthusiastically welcomed by conservationists world wide. We must all work together to stop indiscriminate fishing methods which every year claim the lives of perhaps one million dolphins.

"Anything that can prevent the wholesale slaughter of these beautiful animals must be given every chance of success", he added.

The scientists need a minimum of £150 000 over the next three years to continue their work.

– ends –

Note to News/Picture Desk Editors:

1. Grace Drury and Martin Henderson will be available by mobile telephone on 0836 389045 and 0836 325719 respectively on 1 October.

2. Barry Leggetter will be available at Countrywide Communications on the telephone number below.

Issued on behalf of:

Martin Henderson
Public Relations Manager (Food)
CWS Ltd
New Century House
PO Box 53
Manchester
M60 4ES

Tel: 061–834 1212
Fax: 061–832 2715
Home Tel: 0772 690690

by:

Grace Drury/Barry Leggetter
Countrywide Communications (London) Ltd
Bowater House East
68 Knightsbridge
LONDON SW1X 7LH

Tel: 071–584 0122
Fax: 071–584 6655
Home Tel:
(Grace Drury) 081–881 6409

1 October 1991

First of all it is not clear why the story has an embargo, except that it has been issued in advance of the event which may or may not take place. This is a dangerous practice. It invites the editor to do one of two things: to ignore the embargo and write about the intentions of the British scientists to introduce their new 'traffic system' or to ignore the story until it had actually happened and await a report. Why could not the story have been released on October 1? Embargoes such as this are confusing and best not used. Editors dislike frivolous embargoes.

The subject is 'cats eyes' type reflectors, but this does not appear until the middle of the second paragraph.

This is not an easy story to put across because it operates on two levels — the preservation of dolphins and the fact that the Co-op sells large quantities of tuna, the fishing of which is a hazard to dolphins. Not particularly clear in this story is the origin of the tuna sold by the Co-op. The tuna sold in the author's local Co-op Late Shop comes from Thailand and the Philippines, and the label makes no claims about protection of mammals. However, the labels on tins of Prince's tuna on the same shelf claim 'Tuna must be caught without unacceptable risk to marine mammals.' A similar claim appears on the labels of John West tuna sold in other shops.

Nevertheless, the story is informative and interesting, uses short paragraphs and straightforward language free of puffery, although the second page begins to ramble with its quotation from David Bellamy and the ineffectual last-minute appeal for funds with no indication as to whether or not its donors may be the Co-op. Really, the first six para-graphs of the release are adequate. That would make it a good one-page story.

An in-house release from Kent County Council provides the following amusing short story which, together with 'before and after' sketches, achieved considerable coverage in the Kent press. This particular release read:

TAKE SIX BUILDINGS ...
Kent-based artist Graham Clarke is helping to launch Kent Design Initiative — a pro-gramme to raise design standards, organ-ised by Kent County Council and the RIBA SE Region, and sponsored by Costain Con-struction and Ibstock Brick.

Today (Wednesday 11 September) Graham Clarke will unveil his tongue-in-cheek look at 'alternative' designs for six Kent buildings. Each of the buildings will undergo a drastic transformation — on paper at least!

Although intended as a light-hearted review of the anything-is-possible ap-proach, Graham Clarke's 'transformations' reflect one of the Initiative's important aims — to make people stop and think about their views on design, especially of buildings.

The serious side of Kent Design Initiative starts on 8 October with the first of a series of six lectures given by top architects and designers to raise awareness of, and encour-age, good design in the county.

... END ...

In the chapter on the opening paragraph, we quoted from the release about Ecowater. The release is too long to reproduce here — it reads more like a feature article! — but the eighth of eleven paragraphs is worth quoting since it descends into pure copywriting. Incidentally, it is the second time that the word 'unique' appears, a word all public relations writers should avoid as it is a meaningless cliché. Nothing is unique. Here is the paragraph:

The Permutit Sensatronic is easy to programme and boasts an exclusive at-a-glance
back-lit LCD display, readable in all lighting
conditions, which shows the time, flow
rates, regeneration time and water hard-
ness setting, as well as the average daily
water usage. A unique electronic charge bar
shows precisely how much capacity is left
in the system.

Now this is a muddle of factual information
and advertising bombast. 'Easy to programme'
is an emotive generality; 'boasts' belongs to
copywriting; and 'a unique electronic charge
bar' cannot be unique and from this description could be anything. In the middle are some
technical details, but it all reads like the leaflet
you get from the retailer. You do not understand it, but you are expected to be impressed.
A good question is whether any editor is likely
to understand what this is all about.

From Taylor Woodrow comes the following
happy release, all in short paragraphs, and a
commendably neat printed heading permitted
the story to begin high on the first page. Why
do so many releases have deep headings
which force the story to begin low down the
page so that extra pages are necessary, even
for a fairly short story? If the heading occupies
minimum space most releases need not fill
more than a single sheet, which is easier to
produce and easier to edit.

Taylor Woodrow helps to relaunch Daphne's childhood memories

Grandmother Daphne Young today stepped
aboard the Thames sailing barge which
bears her name — for the first time since
she launched the historic vessel as a small
child nearly 70 years ago.

Today, 68 years after naming the Lady
Daphne, she was back to crack another
bottle of champagne across the bows of one
of London's few remaining traditional sailing barges at the invitation of her current
owners, Taylor Woodrow.

A delighted Mrs.Young said, "This is a
wonderful day for me. I can't believe that
almost 70 years after first naming the
Daphne, I'm now back here to launch her
once again."

There to greet Mrs.Young and her husband,
George, was the first man to sail single
handed non-stop around-the-world, Robin
Knox-Johnston CBE and the vessel's skip-
per, Derek Ling, who welcomed her aboard
the recently overhauled Lady Daphne,
berthed at Taylor Woodrow's premier
Thameside development, St.Katherine by
the Tower.

Robin Knox-Johnston, the managing director of St.Katherine's Haven, said, "We are
delighted that Mrs.Young could be with us
today to celebrate 70 active years for both
her and Taylor Woodrow."

Mrs.Young, now living in Salisbury, was
joined by family and friends for a reunion
party aboard the vessel, which had been
originally built by Shorts, the world-
renowned marine and aviation company, in
1923 for her grandfather's shipping company at Rochester in Kent.

The Lady Daphne, which spent most of her
commercial life hauling grain, cement and
china clay throughout the south of England,
was the first of three Thames sailing barges
built for Mrs.Young's grandfather. In 1975
the vessel, bedecked with its distinctive red
sails, was bought by Taylor Woodrow and
given a new lease of life as a unique venue
for corporate entertainment.

History Note: In 1923, the year that little
Daphne launched her namesake, the first
Cup Final at Wembley was held, Stanley
Baldwin was elected Prime Minister, Calvin

Coolidge was sworn in as president of the USA and Adolph Hitler started his Munich Putsch.

Note to Editors: The Taylor Woodrow Group operates worldwide in construction, house-building, property and trading.
ENDS
For further information contact Taylor Woodrow Corporate Communications: David Brooks or Matthew Moth on 071 488 0555.

Generally, this is a well-written story, but with a human interest story like this, one should avoid being too gushing with expressions like 'a delighted Mrs. Young'. It depends on the class of media to which it is sent, but a localised version (with 'Salisbury' in the first paragraph) would be necessary for the Wiltshire press. It is rather difficult to identify the sort of media to which this story might have been written. Sailing barges have their particular fascination for some people, but this story has a mixture of topics, local interest, plus Taylor Woodrow's interests. A little puffery slips in with the expression 'world-renowned' which invites deletion by a sub.

It is therefore worth considering another Taylor Woodrow story which is closely related to the company's business, and there is no problem about possible titles to include in the mailing list. It is, however, a story for which no standard mailing list would apply, and one would need to be created which covered the different readerships for such a story. Again, there are nice short paragraphs which are difficult to sub or re-write.

Further road work boosts Taywood's Ghana operation

Taylor Woodrow's operations in Ghana have been boosted by the start-up of a £30m road reconstruction project and the successful completion of the first four-star hotel in the capital of Accra.

At Tamale, in northern Ghana, Taylor Woodrow's associate company, Taysec Construction Ltd, has begun work on 51km of road within the township, including service diversions and rebuilding associated drainage.

This latest project is part of a continuing programme to upgrade Ghana's north–south highway linking the southern seaports with the north of the country and landlocked neighbours, Mali and Burkina Faso.

Since 1985, when Taysec Construction began work on the Yapei–Morno stretch of road for the Ghana Highway Authority, it has improved nearly 200km and has work in hand for another 190km.

Taylor Woodrow International, in association with Taysec, has also just completed the £13m renovation of the Continental Hotel in Accra, uprating it to a full four-star standard hotel.

This fast-track design and construct project was completed on time in under a year. The newly transformed building now offers 167 bedrooms, plus 16 separate chalets, a large swimming pool, 150-seat restaurant, casino and various leisure and business amenities. The hotel will be operated by the Dutch Golden Tulip International Group.

The Taylor Woodrow Group operates worldwide in construction, housebuilding, property and trading.
ENDS
For further information contact: Taylor Woodrow Corporate Communications; David Brooks or Matthew Moth on 071 488 0555

Sometimes an opportunity can be exploited,

and the following Girobank story is a cheeky one.

EVERCREECH POST OFFICE FILLS THE GAP

The recent decision by the Nat West Bank to close its sub branch in Evercreech at the end of October is causing many residents to complain that this will leave the village without a bank.

Local traders, in particular, are saying that there will no longer be anywhere to pay in their takings and that they will now have to travel to Shepton Mallett or Frome, a journey of several miles which will take up valuable business time and increase the security risk.

But local sub postmaster Geoff Lawson is keen for all villagers to know that his post office can fill the gap left by the departure of the Nat West and other banks which have already closed.

He says: "Girobank offers both personal and business customers, through post offices, a comprehensive banking service which matches that offered by the major banks, and they're open long hours during the week and on Saturday mornings."

Small businesses can use post offices for paying in their takings and drawing change at very competitive rates through its Fixed Tariff Account. These funds can then be used to make payments or be transferred to another bank account where they may have credit facilities.

—ends—

More information from:

David Hide
Girobank plc

Tel: (0272) 277474 Ext 2353

Once again there are short paragraphs. The first paragraph does not quite summarise the whole story, nearly falls into the trap of being a teaser, but is acceptable in making a point on which to base the story. The Geoff Lawson quote is good since it adds information to the story.

The following Mercedes-Benz story makes the ultimate use of the short paragraph, but are they too short, are there too many of them, and would the apparent length of the release be reduced if some of these paragraphs were concertinaed?

The main trouble with this story is that something went wrong with the writer's brakes and he could not stop writing. The opening paragraph, brief as it is, succeeds in summarising the story, although the subject is in the wrong place. Mercedes-Benz is not the subject, which is the reduced price of airbags. A curiosity of this story is that it is taken for granted that the reader knows what an airbag is, and how it contributes to safety. One should always explain as early as possible.

Quotations can be useful, but Mr Hans Tauscher says nothing that adds to the information and merely offers some sales talk. This sort of quotation should be avoided.

Five paragraphs are devoted to identifying Mercedes-Benz models which have airbags, but all this could be condensed to one paragraph stating that all models now have driver airbags while some also have front seat passenger airbags.

Having criticised the story for not explaining how airbags work, we are told in the 16th to 21st paragraphs how the system operates! The writer has been so busy boosting Mercedes-Benz cars that the real interest in the story is brought in as an after-thought. This is silly, and can only infuriate an editor. How an airbag works (in half the words) needs to be the second paragraph on page one. But this is not the end, for the story takes a third direction and lists the history of Mercedes-Benz safety developments since 1931! This has no place in a story about a price reduction for airbags. Is it really part of a major safety initiative? The cynical journalist could conclude that they cannot sell them. Business firms do not usually reduce prices for saintly purposes.

So, here is the press release which occupied five typed pages:

MERCEDES-BENZ REDUCES PRICE OF LIFE-SAVING AIRBAGS

Mercedes-Benz today reduced the price of life-saving airbags as part of a major safety initiative.

And from today airbags will be fitted as standard equipment on 11 Mercedes-Benz models, including the new S-class.

Mercedes-Benz (United Kingdom) Ltd has reduced the option price of driver airbags by almost 50 per cent in a move which will help to improve safety on Britain's roads.

It means more than 3000 Mercedes-Benz cars, with airbags fitted as standard equipment, will go on to British roads every year.

In addition, the decision to drastically reduce the option price of airbags is designed to see an even higher take up of the important safety device.

The option cost of the driver airbag will now be £750. It was £1433.15.

Mercedes-Benz also offers front seat passenger airbags on all 200–300 mid-range saloons, estates and coupes; on all SL sportscars and on all new S-class models.

The option price for both driver and front seat passenger airbags has also been reduced from £2493.13 to £1500.

All seven new S-class models, which have their British debut at Motorfair Press Day on October 16, have driver airbags as standard.

Driver airbags also become standard equipment on the 300SL, 300 SL-24, 500SL and 500E from today.

The flagship of the Mercedes-Benz range, the 600SEL, has, in addition, a front seat passenger airbag as part of the car's comprehensive standard specification.

Mr.Hans Tauscher, Managing Director of Mercedes-Benz (UK) Ltd, said: "We are very pleased to be able to make this announcement today, particularly as it was Daimler-Benz who invented the car airbag.

"Mercedes-Benz has always been at the forefront in all matters of safety and we will continue to be so. The inclusion of airbags as standard equipment on these models extends even further the excellent value for money which Mercedes-Benz ownership represents."

Airbags were introduced by Mercedes-Benz in 1980 following a £9-million development programme and nearly 700 000 have been fitted in cars sold around the world.

They have been optionally available in Britain since 1984 and front seat passenger airbags have been offered on most models since 1987. More than 3000 customers in Britain have ordered cars fitted with airbags since they were introduced.

HOW AIRBAGS WORK

Electronic sensors automatically trigger the airbag in an accident. It inflates within 25 milliseconds and quickly deflates after doing its job of protecting the head and chest of the driver or passenger.

The whole cycle is complete within a fraction of a second.

The driver's airbag is housed in the central boss of the steering wheel and the front passenger airbag is contained in a compartment on the front facia.

An extremely small pyrotechnic charge triggers a reaction that produces the harmless gas — mainly nitrogen — which inflates the airbag.

Sensors will only activate the airbag if crash forces are equivalent to the car hitting a wall at 12 mph. This means that the airbag will not be fired in low-speed bumper-to-bumper crashes.

All Mercedes-Benz cars are fitted with automatic seat belt tensioners as well as the normal inertia-reel system. They are also activated by sensors firing a small charge. Within 12-milliseconds any slack in the seat belt is taken up, giving even greater protection to the occupants.

SAFETY FIRSTS FROM MERCEDES-BENZ

Mercedes-Benz spends the equivalent of £1-million A DAY on research, much of it in active and passive safety.

Seventy-five per cent of the safety testing carried out by Mercedes-Benz is to meet the company's exacting standards. Only 25 per cent of the work is actually required to meet legislation.

Mercedes-Benz has been developing safety features on cars and trucks since the 1930s, including many important safety firsts.

1931 — independent suspension — greatly improved roadholding
1949 — safety door lock — will not jam or burst open in an accident
1951 — safety cell and crumple zone patented
1959 — first company to introduce roll-over crash tests
— first production car with interior designed to reduce injury to passengers — energy absorbing surfaces
1961 — servo-assisted disc brakes introduced — better brakes requiring less effort to use
— anchor points for safety belts standard
1967 — collapsible steering column with impact absorber
1968 — Mercedes-Benz safety head restraints introduced
1973 — front seat belts and head restraints fitted as standard
1978 — ABS brakes option on production cars
1980 — airbags introduced
1984 — seat belt tensioners fitted to all Mercedes-Benz cars
1985 — unveiling of £6.6-million driving simulator in Berlin
1987 — passenger airbag introduced
1989 — automatic roll bar on SL sportscar

ends ...

For further information please contact:
Doug Wallace on (0908) 668899

In spite of the above criticisms, this story did receive wide coverage in local newspapers throughout the UK, stressing the price cut and printing much of the relevant detail, but ignoring the history of Mercedes-Benz developments. Most papers combined some of the short paragraphs, while others printed the story as written and set out. No doubt the reputation of the car, the topicality of a price cut, the safety angle and the novelty of the airbag all contributed to the story being welcomed. It was a story which needed subbing only for space reasons, not because it was woolly or verbose. However, all the press cuttings seen by the author came from the regional press, none from the national or motoring press whose subbing could have been more stringent. Even so, the following show how a five page release can be reduced to a single paragraph.

MERCEDES-BENZ has cut the price of its life-saving airbags by almost 50 per cent. They will now cost £750. The airbags will be fitted as standard equipment on 11 of the 1992 Mercedes-Benz models including the new S-class. (*South Wales Evening Post*).

MERCEDES has dropped the price of fitting a steering wheel safety airbag from £1433 to £750 and they are standard on 11 models. The bag inflates instantly in a crash to cushion the driver against injury. (*Northants Evening Telegraph*).

The above both prove the point that if the opening paragraph summarises the whole story, and only that gets printed, you are home and dry. Also, the bigger the paper, the fewer words it is likely to print. The paragraphs reproduced above condense the content of several paragraphs in the original story, and are a perfect object lesson for news release writers.

Comment has already been made on the opening paragraph of the following story, but here it is in full.

BASS BREWERS RATIONALISATION

Bass PLC today announced the closure of two of the 13 breweries operated by Bass Brewers, with a loss of some 480 jobs. Production at the two plants at Preston Brook near Runcorn and Springfield, Wolverhampton, will transfer to other Bass breweries. The plants will close on 2 August 1991.

Over the past five years Bass has achieved considerable improvements in efficiencies and capacity in many of its breweries, such that substantial cost benefits can now be achieved from a concentration of production.

The decision follows a rigorous review of each brewery and the production requirements of Bass Brewers.

A Bass Brewers spokesman said:

"In a beer market that is changing rapidly in the aftermath of the Department of Trade and Industry Orders, cost efficiency is even more vital and scale economies are becoming increasingly important.

Having evaluated the range of options, we have concluded that the best solution is achieved by the closure of the Preston Brook and Springfield breweries.

We very much regret the impact of this decision on the employees affected. A substantial support package will be made available to those facing redundancy."

For further information, please contact:
Ben Hanbury, Director of Corporate Affairs, Bass PLC

Tel.071–486–4440
Robert Humphreys, Director of Public Relations, Bass Brewers

Tel: 071–486–4400

NOTES FOR EDITORS

Bass Brewers is the Division of Bass PLC which brews the Company's beers and distributes, markets and sells these drinks throughout the UK and Eire.

Bass are to be commended on their frankness, although 'rationalisation' is a euphemism for 'redundancies', and the story offers no genuine explanation why 480 people are to be sacked. How loss of trade can be converted into improvements in efficiency is something of a deceit. Have the Department of Trade and Industry Orders got anything to do with the fact that there is a recession, large numbers of people are out-of-work and they cannot afford the high price of beer? Moreover, traditional beer drinking has had its day, partly because the drinking of alcohol is discouraged, while the drink-and-drive campaign has had its effect. It might have been more honest if this story was related to reality. The sackings are a sign of the times for which Bass can take no credit.

The next example, from the Abbey National Building Society (although by going public in 1989 it became a bank) is an attractive story in which, for a change, advertising itself becomes news. The opening paragraph sums it up very well. Is there any connection between the Abbey and an abbot's habit?

WHY CHANGE THE HABIT OF A LIFE-TIME?

Abbey National plc has returned to its 'Abbey Habit' slogan for the company's first corporate advertising campaign since flotation in July 1989.

The 'Habit' tune, which was composed by Jeff Wayne, best known for The War Of The Worlds, is one of the three most popular advertisement jingles of the last fifteen years. Despite an absence of almost seven years, the famous tune is still fondly remembered and instantly recognised by people across the country.

The 'Habit of a Lifetime' campaign was devised by the newly-formed advertising agency, Barker and Ralston, and was put together in less than ten weeks. Abbey National surprised the advertising world when it became the agency's first major client earlier this year.

Commenting on the launch of the new campaign, marketing director John Berry said:

"The campaign focuses on the Abbey National brand, rather than its individual products. It positions Abbey National as a provider of a wide range of personal financial services: for life. I'm confident that, once again, most people will immediately associate the famous "Habit" tune with Abbey National."

Contacts:
Yasmin Encer, press officer
Tel: 071–612–4567
Simon Kearney-Mitchell, press officer,
Tel: 071–612 4234
Erica Harper, press officer,
Tel: 071–612 4363

Here is a release which says it all in four paragraphs on one piece of paper. It is brief and forthright.

Disappointment at new EC speed limit

The Freight Transport Association is disappointed that the EC Council of Transport Ministers has agreed today to limit the maximum speed of heavy goods vehicles to 90kph (56mph) as from 1 January 1994.

This measure forms part of a new agreed EC Directive on the fitment of speed limiters to coaches and lorries. FTA has no argument with the introduction of speed limiters but, given there has been no harmonisation of speed limits in Europe, sees no reason for adopting a common limit.

Whilst there is no justification for reducing the UK speed limit from the existing 60mph to 56mph, only a vigorous campaign by this country's transport industry prevented the worst excesses of the EC's original proposal, based on 80kph (50mph).

In terms of road safety, the change at best can only be described as neutral.

ENDS

Unlike the one quoted earlier from the RMI, the full name of this organisation is spelled out at the outset, afterwards being referred to as the FTA.

This one from the Open University gets down to business immediately, its purpose being to chase up late applications for single courses rather than the longer-term degree courses.

STILL TIME TO TRY

There is still time to apply to study a single course with the Open University next year — the application period for the University's associate student programme closes on 7 October.

More than 130 courses are available on a 'one off' basis in the Arts, Social Sciences, Mathematics, Science, technology and Education. They include new courses on 'Third World development' and 'Issues in women's studies'. Among others are 'Fundamentals of computing' (for which a home computer is needed), an 'Introduction to psychology', 'Elements of music' and 'The Environment'.

Associate students of the Open University study at home in their spare time from correspondence texts and audio-visual material, often including television. Some courses carry the opportunity to go to summer school.

Although no formal educational qualifications are required these courses are more demanding than the OU's first-year foundation courses which start the student on the road to a degree.

Most associate student course credits or passes count towards a degree if the student later decides to become an undergraduate. Courses start in February 1991.

A prospectus is available from the Central Enquiry Service, Open University, P.O.Box 625, Milton Keynes, MK1 ITY (telephone: 0908 653231).

Press enquiries   Simon Newton,
                  Deputy Director,
                  Public Relations
                  Telephone: 0908 653212
                  Home 0908 566352

Perhaps the epitomy of how not to write a news release comes from Hollis Directories. They, of all people, should know better. It reads:

NEW DIRECTORY PROVIDES INSIDE TRACK ON £325 MILLION SPONSORSHIP MARKET

A major new reference work is to be launched by Hollis Directories Ltd, Europe's leading public relations publisher, in November 1992.

The new book, called **HOLLIS SPONSORSHIP & DONATIONS**, will provide a unique link between sponsorship/donation seekers and Britain's top sponsoring companies, and will span all organisations and governing bodies in Britain which have dealings in the sponsorship and donations sector. Other Hollis publications are **Hollis Press & Public Relations Annual** and **Hollis Europe**.

According to the latest report from Mintel, corporate sponsorship in 1991 was estimated to have reached £325 million, with sporting events taking a total of £250 million, the arts taking £345 million, and other areas receiving £30 million. Mintel highlighted new sponsorship areas as being broadcasting, education, social and environmental sectors. The Association for Business Sponsorship of the Arts (ABSA) has revealed that an additional £12.5 million was spent by UK businesses on corporate membership of the arts.

The new Hollis publication, already tagged "Spons & Dons" within the Hollis editorial office, will cater for sponsorship seekers who need to present their case to potential funding organisations as well as servicing specialist consultancies retained to advise on appeals and opportunities.

The key contents of the new directory will include a unique matchmaking section where potential sponsoring companies can outline projects they are interested in supporting and list details of major sponsorship ventures. They are also given the opportunity to reveal budgets, and the names of executives responsible for sponsorship and donations. In-depth information on those seeking funds with details of audience, timing, support required and benefits accruing; a comprehensive list of sponsorship consultancies; client/consultancy links; events calendars of both sponsored and non-sponsored events and new sponsorship research by Hollis are also included.

Editor of **HOLLIS SPONSORSHIP & DONATIONS** is Alexandra Pawson 25, who has been with Hollis for the past two and a half years where she worked on the first and second editions of Hollis Europe, the reference book for the European public relations industry.

Publishing director, Rosemary Sarginson, said "We will be developing a totally new thoroughly researched and comprehensive database in order to create a product which

will enable us to offer other services to the sponsorship industry in the future."

—ends—

For further information:
K. Rosemary Sarginson — Publishing Director, Hollis — 0932 784781
Phyllis Oberman — PR Consultant — 081—455 1711
13th January 1992

First, the dreadful headline is too long and reads like an advertisement. *Second,* the opening paragraph has no subject. *Third,* the opening paragraph fails to summarise the story. *Fourth,* it contains the self-praise expression 'leading'. *Fifth,* there is unnecessary double spacing between paragraphs. *Sixth,* the succeeding paragraphs after the first are not indented. *Seventh,* the subject does not appear until the second paragraph. *Eighth,* it uses the word 'unique'. *Ninth,* it uses all capitals for the title of the new book. *Tenth,* it puts other Hollis titles in bold type. *Eleventh,* 'unique' reappears in the fifth paragraph, *Twelfth,* it closes with 'ends' which is a redundant throw-back. It is not a news release: it is an advertisement. Finally, the personal puff at the end is overdone. Out of scores of releases which were read for this chapter this was the worst. The irony is that whereas editors complain about the inability of public relations people to write news releases we have here an editor who cannot do so.

This bad release merits closer examination. An excuse is probably that the writer seldom writes releases, and so does not know the difference between an exuberant puff and a straightforward piece of news. Unfortunately, editors receive many such releases and do not make excuses but take them as being typical of the public relations world. They are, after all, common enough with releases from those consultants who aim to please their clients.

But why was this release written? If it was to announce publication of the new directory, it was 10 months premature. If it was to attract advertisements it had nothing to say on this score. If it sought entry material, it did not say so. Probably the ideal medium for such a story was *PR Week*, but it could extract only the following 10 lines:

> Hollis Directories is to launch a reference guide in November aimed at those seeking sponsorship. Called Hollis Sponsorship and Donations, it will include a 'matchmaking' section listing details of both sponsorship ventures and potential sponsors. Publishing director Rosemary Sarginson, also editor of *Hollis Europe*, said: 'We will develop a totally new database to create a product which will enable us to offer other services to the sponsorship industry.'

An object lesson lies in why this story was printed. We often criticise journalists for re-writing news releases and getting the facts wrong. No doubt the excellent Hollis reputation helped, but here is a case where the journalist has gone to the trouble to hunt for something worth publishing. If only the writer had saved him the trouble. The secret lay in the opening paragraph as can be seen by comparing the release with the printed version.

The author, reading the report in *PR Week*, was curious to know more so that he could refer to the new directory in the Sponsorship chapter of this book, but all his enquiry produced was a copy of the news release! Clearly the news was premature. One should never play games with the media, nor invite enquiries which cannot be satisfied. Either you have a full factual story, and a purpose for releasing it, or you don't.

Finally we have a very nice one from Midland Bank which earned an accolade in *Sussex Business Times* where John Nixon commented 'I am delighted to reproduce one that is, in my view, almost perfect, received recently from Anne Morton of Midland Bank.' Shorn of all unnecessary words, this is a tight story which deserves publication.

Midland Bank appointment

Peter Green has been appointed manager of Midland Bank's branch at 4 Robertson Street, Hastings. His predecessor, Tom Wiggins, has retired.

Previously Mr Green was manager of Midland's St Leonards on Sea branch.

Aged 44, he was born in Tenterden and joined the bank in Ashford in 1963.

Mr Green and his wife, Rita, have two children, Lisa, 19, and Christopher, 16. The family lives in Hastings.

In his spare time Mr Green enjoys gardening, DIY and sport. He is treasurer of the 1982 Luncheon Club and an associate of the Chartered Institute of Bankers.

—END—

Issued by: Anne Morton
            Tel: 071–260 8478

In this chapter we have given a selection of releases from a variety of consultancy and in-house sources. On the whole, give or take a few criticisms, they are professionally written. For the reader who does not see actual releases, these samples should be of special interest.

There are, however, some oddities of presentation on which comment is invited. Some of the releases follow 'book style', the first paragraph not being indented but succeeding paragraphs being indented. This is how most books, newspapers and magazines are printed. But many of the releases use slab (unindented) paragraphs throughout which is wrong and in no way resembles a printed press report. It is a lazy secretarial habit.

Another curiosity is that the quoted releases have double spacing between paragraphs. Why? Books, newspapers and magazines, and professionally written typescripts, do not have double spacing between paragraphs, especially since the paragraphs are indented. This is a peculiar habit which serves no purpose, but can extend a story over more than one page and make it look unnecessarily long drawn out. Perhaps it is thought that editors need the space in order to make amendments or write printing instructions? That is years out-of-date. Today there are paperless newsrooms, and journalists compose and sub stories on their computer visual display unit (VDU). They can even display a release on one side of the screen and produce a subbed version on the other side. Perhaps the producers of releases with double spacing between paragraphs have not caught up with the technology of direct input? Perhaps public relations practitioners do not teach their secretaries how to type copy for the printer?

However, a welcome feature of these releases is the use of short paragraphs. They suit the narrow columns of modern newspapers, are easy to read by the editor, and minimise subbing beyond the needs of space. A long woolly paragraph invites subbing, and this is where the information can be accidentally distorted.

CHAPTER 19

Feature and Syndicated Articles

NON-SPECULATIVE ARTICLES

A news release is broadcast, but an article is written specifically for one publication. It should bear an author's name and be exclusive to a single publication, although other articles on the same subject can be written by the same author for other journals and may appear concurrently. For example, the subject of holidays in Spain could form the theme of any number of original articles, each one being exclusive to a particular journal.

Such articles are not written speculatively. Editors do not sit back and wait for articles to appear out of the blue. Issues are planned and contents are commissioned. They may be written by staff writers, freelance contributors or by PROs and press officers. An editor may go to a literary agent in search of a suitable author. This means that there is no point in a press officer sitting down and writing an article and then offering it to an editor. The press officer is unlikely to be very successful in placing one of those articles which someone within the organisation has decided to write without being invited to do so.

There is a very substantial market for good articles from public relations sources, but chiefly for technical articles for trade, technical and professional journals which do not have large staffs. On the whole, national newspapers, women's magazines and other big circulation journals prefer to have articles written by their own staff writers, or by commissioned professional contributors, and will rarely publish features from public relations sources unless perhaps they are written by well-known or authoritative writers. In this chapter reference will be made to 'the press officer' but this can be taken to cover the PRO or consultant who may write feature articles.

The press officer can therefore achieve publication of feature articles in one of three ways (the third can be subdivided into a further three sections).

1. They may be written by staff writers.
2. They may be written by outside contributors.
3. They may be supplied by the press officer, either written by himself, or by a freelance author specially engaged, or by people within the organisation.

Let us consider each in turn.

ARTICLES BY STAFF WRITERS

Regular feature writers working on newspapers and magazines usually have to produce at least one article a week, and it is no mean feat to write interestingly on fifty or more different topics in a year. If a press officer can succeed in giving a staff writer a first-rate idea for an article it will be very welcome, but it must be an idea worthy of the writer, feature and journal.

The press officer should study the press and collect the names of writers who either write about the organisation's subject, or could be interested in some aspect of it. Thus, the press officer will be aware of the staff writers to approach when appropriate topics occur.

Similarly, special correspondents will be noted who have columns to fill, the motoring, industrial, gardening, property, shipping, aviation, science and other correspondents whose contributions may appear in many publications. For example, writers on gardening topics may write for scores of publications such as national newspapers, women's magazines, local newspapers and even parish magazines. They may also write under pseudonyms. It is not unusual for the editor of a specialised journal to be a special correspondent and contributor on the subject to other journals such as national newspapers. All these people are constantly seeking ideas and subject matter.

The more the press officer knows about the needs of these staff writers, the more usefully can they and the organisation be served. There are some very real press relations to be cultivated here in the realm of ideas for articles. Of course, it may entail rather more than just handing over an idea: the press officer must be willing to devote time to escorting the staff writer to the scene of the story which may be a factory, site or installation, and it will be necessary to get permission and make arrangements for such visits.

For the press officer commencing in a new post it will be a long and painstaking task to get to know all the staff writers who may be interested in material about the organisation, but the most satisfactory state of affairs is when staff writers know that the press officer is a valuable source of material and seek subjects to write about. The press officer who provides a service and does not look for

favours will have this service used and be given the favours.

ARTICLES BY OUTSIDE CONTRIBUTORS

Outside contributors are more numerous and less easy to contact because they may write less frequently for the same journals, and correspondence will have to be forwarded to their private addresses. But as the various publications are studied, it will become apparent that there are writers who specialise in certain subjects and that they should be kept supplied with information and possible themes for future articles. Freelance writers of all kinds abound, and if the press officer bothers to offer them information facilities they will tend to write about the organisation and its services or products simply because the trouble is taken to feed them with facts. The enthusiastic press officer will seek out these writers and make a point of offering to help them with facts, ideas, pictures, samples, facility visits, interviews or whatever may be of use to them.

There are some press officers who regard freelance writers as time wasters, nuisances to be put off and ignored. Provided they are not amateur writers producing speculative articles, they can be extremely valuable. It does pay, however, to check that their work has in fact been commissioned and will be published.

In addition, there are also textbook authors, compilers of encyclopaedias, handbooks and part-works, and script writers for radio, films and television who work independently and are glad to know of reliable sources of information.

SUPPLIED ARTICLES

Here we come to the kind of article which is most satisfying to the press officer because there is more complete control over its content and publication. When helping staff and free-lance writers one has to concede the treatment to them, and it may not necessarily be as the press officer would wish. But if the press officer writers or edits the piece, more responsibility can be taken for what is published.

There is no reason why a press officer who knows the subject and writes well should not become an established writer. Press officers, and practitioners generally, should be big enough to be able to put their own names to articles.

But the press officer may be too busy to write every article personally, or it may be a subject requiring an expert on the subject, and then a file of freelance writers can be referred to. The careful creation of a file of specialist writers on appropriate topics who can be commissioned to write articles is an important part of the organisation of a press office.

NEGOTIATING PUBLICATION

There is a false idea that public relations articles are published by taking editors out to lunch. Hospitality will not publish a bad article, and if a press officer aims to publish many articles he or she will be too busy conducting research and interviews, and writing the articles, to have time to entertain editors. The author used to publish at least 50 articles a year, in addition to other duties, doing so for more than ten years without meeting any of the editors concerned. There were also staff who wrote their quotas of articles. The author still writes articles. How is it done?

If the PRO, press officer or consultant has access to material which promises to make a publishable article, the procedure for negotiating publication is not unlike that of a textbook author approaching a possible publisher. A publisher is selected by studying the kind of books published. Then outline proposals are submitted to the chosen publisher, and if the idea is accepted the author receives a contract

and is commissioned to write the book. The author does not write the book first, nor is it necessary to take the publisher out to lunch or buy drinks, although publishers sometimes take their authors out to lunch. Fiction does have to be written speculatively, but textbooks and feature articles should not be.

The writer of a public relations feature article has one big advantage: there is usually access to material which is unknown to the editor, and so a good proposition will be welcome. The author's experience — and very often he or she is unknown to the editor — is that public relations articles are seldom refused if the proposition is a good one, and is made in the following businesslike way.

In a letter or telephone call (confirmed in writing afterwards) the writer should set out the theme of the proposed article to which access has been agreed, and ask the editor — if the proposed article is accepted — the following questions:

1. How many words are required.
2. The date of the issue in which the article will appear.
3. The date when the editor requires the article.
4. Whether any special treatment is required.
5. Whether illustrations are required such as black-and-white or colour photographs, charts or maps according to the subject.

The writer should assure the editor that commercial references will be kept to a minimum: editors do not want articles full of plugs for the organisation, product or service. The writer will also promise that the article will be checked for accuracy before being submitted for publication. It will be supplied free of fee.

If the editor accepts the proposition, the editor will virtually commission the article, saying what is wanted and when it is wanted but probably adding the rider 'subject to sight of copy', just in case it turns out to be a bad article. Normally, articles will not be edited, unlike a news release which could be totally rewritten. A good article should be publishable as it stands subject to minor sub-editings, perhaps to make it fit the space.

Now, when researching or conducting interviews, the press officer can say that the article has been commissioned for a certain issue of a certain magazine, which should be sufficiently positive to get the information required.

It is also possible to paraphrase a basic article and produce a number of exclusive articles for different journals, using the same information but varying the applications and case histories according to the readership of each journal. Here is an example of how it has been done.

A manufacturer of louvre windows enjoyed a very useful series of articles in journals read in local government, confectionery production, and laundry and dry-cleaning circles. The technicalities of how the windows were made and how they operated were identical, but the applications to various kinds of building and the interviews with people working in these buildings were quite different.

It does cost more to write an article than a news release, but when a series of articles results, the cost of fares and hotel expenses as well as the press officer's time becomes a very good investment. Sometimes the work cost can be diffused even more cleverly when the field research and pictures provide further material for house journal articles, picture-and-caption stories, annual reports, training manuals, and slides for training programmes and client presentations.

From this general list, it will be seen how a single press relations effort can contribute to the entire public relations programme for an organisation, entering right into the functions of finance, production and marketing. Within the press officer's own sphere, the material for one article in a specialised journal may be used later on together with the material on other subjects in a comprehensive article which reviews the achievements of the organisation in many different fields.

When commencing work on an article, the possibilities of using the same facts and pictures for other public relations purposes should be considered. For instance, 35 mm colour slides may be taken because these will be useful for future activities such as exhibitions or seminars, even though there is no immediate use for colour pictures for press relations purposes.

SYNDICATED ARTICLES

Just as newspapers and magazines sell or 'syndicate' their contents to other publications, especially overseas, so a public relations article can be syndicated, provided it is offered to journals with *non-competing circulations*. These could be regional evening newspapers or company house journals. Articles should not be mailed like news releases, but editors should be sent synopses and invited to request articles for publication. This method is more likely to secure publication.

In this way, it is possible to publish the same article in perhaps 50 local papers in the same week. For this purpose, short pieces of about 800 words are preferable.

Another method is to use the Two-Ten Communications feature article system. They will write the article, put it on disk and offer it with a basket of titles and intros to regional newspapers. If accepted the article can be supplied by computer.

Yet a third method, if one is a member of the British Association of Industrial Editors, is to offer a standard article to fellow house journal editors if it is of interest to their readers.

As will be repeated in Chapter 24 on Overseas Public Relations, syndicated articles can be distributed world-wide (or to selected countries) by EIBIS, who will also translate them.

ARTICLES AND ADVERTISEMENTS

Public relations techniques can be employed to

do all that is required to get the product off the ground in an economic and beneficial way.

An example of this occurred with a company supplying the hospital service. A certain hospital in Kent had a hygiene problem, but traditional methods of finance meant that only a small sum of money was allocated to deal with this problem. No one had really considered whether the expenditure achieved anything, and year after year the same ineffective work was carried out, having been put out to tender with a budgeted limit on cost. The fact that the hospital had suffered this problem for 90 years had not struck anyone on the management committee as being stupid.

An enterprising company, convinced that it had a method of totally eradicating the nuisance for ever, and not merely for a year, put up a scheme costing far in excess of the annually budgeted sum, won the contract and carried out the work successfully. At the time, this was a phenomenal achievement in the British hospital world. The press officer published an article in the leading hospital journal which brought hospital administrators from all over the UK to see the miracle in Kent. Articles about solutions achieved in other hospitals with the same or similar problems were later published in other journals.

By press relations methods, a service of great public value was made known to those responsible, and the company's reputation was notably enhanced as it became recognised by the health authorities as the specialist firm for this particular kind of work. The cost of producing the articles was negligible compared with the cost of inserting display advertisements which could not have told the story with anything like the same degree of authenticity and conviction. Later, this success in the hospital field was included in the company's advertising to the municipal and health authorities.

Enough has been said then, in this chapter to show that the signed exclusive article is not only a major part of press relations practice but a major medium of public relations practice in general.

There is, however, one other aspect of advertising in relation to public relations articles which needs to be discussed here. It has been shown that articles can, in special circumstances, do a better job than advertising, perhaps serving as the vanguard of advertising. Sometimes an alert advertisement manager will discover that an article from a public relations source is to be published, and there will seem to be an opportunity to sell advertisement space.

It happens all the time: companies in all foolishness buy such space and have advertisements facing their articles. The advertisement is unnecessary and a waste of money. But worse than this, the advertisement looks as if it is there because of the article, and the article looks as if it is there because of the advertisement. It looks like a double blackmail. The advertisement, *in that issue and in that position*, must destroy much of the authenticity of the article which depended so much on its editorial independence. A totally unnecessary and irrelevant element of commercial bias is introduced by the advertisement at a time when the content of the article is novel and acceptance is bound up with faith in the statements of the technically qualified author, a very different matter from being persuaded and convinced by the claims of an advertiser who is entitled to put the best face on things.

However, there may be times when an accompanying advertisement is justified. This is when the advertisement can do what the editorial cannot, giving more information, making persuasive sales appeals, offering catalogues or samples, and inviting response by means of a coupon.

Unfortunately, some marketing people cannot see the validity of this argument because they regard press relations as no more than an extension of advertising. But *the average reader makes very clear distinctions between the two* and rightly or wrongly it is the reader's point of view which matters here.

HOW TO WRITE FEATURE ARTICLES

Article writing is utterly different from news release writing. An article is not an extended news release. Instead, it is an original piece of writing based on carefully researched material, in which the personality of the writer can emerge and a much richer vocabulary can be used. There should be no plugging of company or product names, except that such names may be introduced where they fall naturally into the account that is being written. Once again it is necessary to market this piece of writing. A copy of the journal should be studied so that the article is written in the appropriate style. Even among journals of a similar kind, it is seldom that exactly the same article will be equally suitable for all of them. This often applies to length, one magazine running long articles, another preferring short ones, one using lots of pictures, another having few or none. Human interest may be required, perhaps with quotations from people interviewed. One journal may require a very technical article with all the accepted jargon and formulae: another will want very simple technicalities. The required style or treatment should be discussed with the editor before commencing the article, and it is a good reason for not preparing speculative articles.

Here are five reasons why an article may fail:

1. The identity of the reader (or market) has not been defined.
2. There is no plot or coherent sequence of information.
3. The article is woolly because the writer lacks sufficient information to be selective and so write concisely and precisely.
4. The vocabulary is poor and there are too many clichés and stock phrases.
5. The writer lacks the facility to write easily so that the article is pleasant to read (but this facility is the result of practice).

However, the PRO or press officer is a literate communicator who should not find it difficult to write a feature article. The main problem is having enough to write about. In practice, it is easier to write an article than a news release. Very few people can write a good news release, partly because they tend to write short articles!

Ideally, the writer should have so much material to work on that it is necessary to be selective. This in turn encourages the writer to be concise, and that gives pace to the piece and makes it easy to read.

PLOTS FOR ARTICLES

The writing of articles is made easier if the writer follows a certain plot or formula. An essay is not being composed with an introduction, a development and a conclusion. The following are some suggested plots, of which the first is often particularly applicable to the public relations article because it contrasts a superior situation with an earlier inferior one.

However, first it must be emphasised that before offering either an idea or an article to an editor, the press officer must make sure that permission to write and publish the article has been obtained if other people's interests are involved. For instance, an enthusiastic salesman may report a sale or contract to the press officer, believing this would make a good article, but the press officer must first check with the customer or client (either with someone in authority or with the customer's or client's PRO) to make sure that such an article may be written. The editor will expect that the final article, if it refers to people other than the press officer's own organisation, has been approved. It does happen that people do not wish to appear to be giving a testimonial, or may not wish to admit in public that they have made such an expenditure.

On one occasion, the author wrote articles about the total electrical installations for a new brewery, and the final draft had to be checked by 12 people representing the owners, architects, consultants, builders and a number of suppliers and subcontractors.

Plot No.1: Then and Now Method. This is the kind of article described in more detail later in this chapter, and it has a Seven-Point Plotting Formula. It depends on finding out the previous situation before the present successful situation occurred. It could apply to a new appointment, a new building, or the use of new equipment, and is ideal for what is known as the 'application story'. For example, an article could be written about a modern newspaper publishing house now equipped with single-stroke keying computerised newsroom and offset-litho printing, and this could be contrasted with the old method when journalists wrote stories on typewriters, copy was set on Linotype machines using hot metal, stereos were made and newspapers were printed on letterpress machines. The contrast between the old and the new would enhance the economy, efficiency and superior result of the new.

Plot No.2: Now and Then Method. This is often a good method when there is an historical story which would be boring if presented chronologically. The article could begin with the present situation, and then revert to how it all began a long time ago. Or the contrasts could be introduced throughout with historical flashbacks.

Plot No.3: Hybrid Method. Some articles will not require any sort of before-and-after treatment, and will describe a number of different things to do with the topic. This might apply to an article on cookery, DIY, holidays, insurance, savings and so on, which would set out a variety of ideas or recommendations.

Plot No.4: Interview Method. This is the question and answer or biographical article based on a personal interview with the writer describing and perhaps commenting on the results of the interview.

Thus, different styles of article may suit certain topics, but in the author's experience of writing many hundreds of articles on all kinds of subjects over a great many years, Plot No.1 is the favourite. This is because whereas a news release gives a straight account of a product or service, Plot No.1 introduces dramatic contrast which helps to make the piece compelling and convincing reading. It helps to sustain the greater length of the article yet, because the writer now has a wealth of researched information, it is necessary to be selective and concise.

This calls for shorter paragraphs, sentences and perhaps words so that the article is tightly written and made more readable. An experienced writer will automatically write like this, but a less experienced one needs to prune the piece. Fluency comes with practice. Bad articles usually result from the writer lacking a rich store of information, and writing too much about too little, using voluminous phrases when a single word would suffice.

SEVEN-POINT ARTICLE PLOTTING AND RESEARCH MODEL

As a guide to the writing of articles the following is a useful seven-point model:

1. The opening paragraph.
2. The problem or previous situation.
3. The search for the solution.
4. The solution.
5. The application of the solution.
6. The closing paragraph.
7. Check sources and obtain approval.

Concentrating on items 3, 4 and 5 for the moment, we have the basis for a mental or written questionnaire with which to conduct our research. This will probably require a visit to, for instance, the factory where our machine has been installed and is working, and this will entail one or more interviews. The interviews must be by appointment and with people who have the authority to give reliable information.

We have suggested that a customer has

made successful use of some equipment, and this case study is to be the substance of the story. There was a problem, which has now been solved. Presumably some effort was made to seek a solution: how did the customer find out about our product or service? Was the advice of a consultant, a friend or the trade association sought, or was a visit made to an exhibition or trade fair, or was an advertisement read?

We already know quite a lot about the solution since it is our firm's or our client's product or service, but we still need to know how it has been applied by the customer and with what results. For example, a new kind of dish-washing machine was bought by a hospital which had problems of labour shortage, needed to maintain high standards of hygiene, and needed to protect large utensils which became battered under ordinary scouring methods. The machine, with its nylon brushes, proved its worth and at the end of a year there was a very good story for the manufacturer's PRO to write for the hospital press. There was a happier kitchen staff, and shining, perfectly hygienic utensils, their shape retained and costly replacement made unnecessary.

Researching a feature article is a matter of discovery, and often the information is unexpected, fascinating and ideal for a feature article. But the writer has to probe and probe, politely but insistently, showing interest in an industry or business which may be foreign to him. People are flattered when a stranger takes an intelligent interest in their jobs and problems, their plans and achievements. It is essential to collect all the relevant details at the time of the interview because the writer may never have the chance of a second visit. Much has to be gleaned in a short time, maybe only an hour or two.

We have now reached the point where a lot of interesting information is required about the results that have been achieved with the product or service. It may be statistical or the statements and views of individuals. On one

occasion, the author was visiting a sugar refinery to write an article about the control of wasps. When introduced to the manager of the packing room he asked: 'What has been the effect of the wasp control service?' Overhead was a glass skylight, and the manager pointed to it and said 'Last year that was black with wasps. This year you can see the sky.' Then the manager produced the Red Cross book and turned the pages to the previous year showing the large number of treatments recorded for stings. Then he turned to current pages and showed that none of the staff had been treated for stings.

Before setting out to visit this plant in Norfolk the author had no idea what he was going to find, but when talking to people the facts were volunteered. So when researching material for feature articles it is a common experience to start with a more or less blank mind, perhaps wondering if there really is anything worth writing about, yet by adopting the discipline of hunting for the *problem*, *solution* and *results*, the article begins to create itself around this simple plot.

The word *problem* may not seem to fit every kind of topic, but in practically every case there must have been a very different situation before the product or service was bought and used successfully. For instance, before the university was built there was only a small technical college. Before the Channel Tunnel was built Channel crossings were subject to the vagaries of the weather. Before we had central heating we had fog from coal fires. And so on. The past reveals the benefits of the present.

Now we have to top and tail our piece, that is write the opening and closing paragraphs, and this is best done when the heart of the article has been composed. Unlike the news release, the opening paragraph of a feature article must *not* summarise the complete story. Instead, it has to grasp the reader's interest and propel the reader on. A question may be posed, a quotation used, an anecdote related or some other device employed to make the reader curious and anxious to know more. Ideas for the opening paragraph may come from the main part of the article. The closing paragraph has to finish the article on a note that satisfies the reader, and again an original touch may be applied.

Finally it is not only courteous but a sensible precaution to invite those who have supplied information to check the piece for accuracy. There is a deadline to meet, so return of the article must not be delayed. A simple method of expediting return is to say that unless the draft is returned by a certain date, approval will be assumed and the article will be despatched to the editor. It is important to have this cooperation so that everyone is happy with the published article. The writer can also keep faith with the editor by giving assurance that the contents have been checked.

One last consideration: if any other organisation, product or service is mentioned care must be taken to see that no objection can be taken to these references. For instance, if the article was about a repair service, and a well-known product was the subject of a repair, the inference could be that this product had broken down and was inferior. Naming names, without permission, could lead to legal proceedings if it could be shown that the reference was harmful to business. However, an article may be made all the more interesting and comprehensive if other products can be mentioned because they are complementary to one's own or a natural part of the story as long as no risk is involved. For example, an article about a new dock would make more realistic reading if the names of cranes, fork-lift trucks and straddle carriers were given as well as the identity of the computer system which was one's special interest in writing the article.

PRESENTATION OF ARTICLES

Articles should be typed in the same style already recommended for the presentation of

news releases, except that in a piece running to several pages subheadings may be justified. Some information may be set out in list or tabular form that is usually wrong in a news release which calls for paragraphs and sentences.

Thus, the article should be typed with double-spacing, and good margins on one side of the sheet only; capital letters should be used sparingly; sets of initials should not have full points between them; numbers should be spelt out one to nine; dates should be month first; but editors are unlikely to object to the occasional word being underlined for setting in italics.

SPECIAL ADVANTAGES OF PUBLIC RELATIONS ARTICLES

While it is true that a public relations article costs far more to produce and only one press-cutting will result, it does have many advantages over the news release:

1. Unlike a news release, it will not be rewritten by the editor.
2. It occupies more space.
3. It may be indexed, even announced on the cover, so that attention is drawn to it.
4. It is likely to carry more authority than a news release.
5. It may be retained and filed for future reference.
6. It could become part of the literature on the subject, referred to in the future, perhaps quoted from (like some of the articles mentioned in this book).
7. Reprints can be made for use in showrooms, as give-aways on exhibition stands, distributed by salesmen or used as direct mail shots.

The following is an example of a feature article written by the author, and it will be noted how the style differs from the author's news release quoted in Chapter 15.

WHY DISTANCE LEARNING?

Three years ago I would not have dreamed of marketing a distance learning course for the CAM Diploma in Public Relations, although I had been running such courses world-wide for the LCCI exams for some ten years. Why the change of mind? Years ago I had offered to organise such a course for the IPR free of charge but they were not interested.

A combination of marketing opportunities has coincided. Moreover, an old dog has to learn new tricks. To survive in business it is no good doing the same old thing, and my main activity was running public relations seminars which I pioneered in 1968.

First, the Institute of Public Relations planned to insist on the CAM Diploma as part of their membership requirements. But where were these candidates coming from? The annual number of new Dip CAMs was minimal.

Second, many public relations people — especially in the consultancies — were working long hours and could not attend classes.

Third, there were constant complaints about the standard of teaching in colleges.

Fourth, outside London and a few regional cities, evening classes were rare.

Fifth, even when students were able to take the Certificate subjects at evening classes, there were very few Diploma classes.

Sixth, on top of this there was a general cry for training, among both employers and employees, but no training resources existed other than limited in-house training (often the blind leading the blind) and expensive short seminars.

Seventh, short seminars, because of catering, overnight accommodation, travel, administrative and other costs, were becoming disproportionately expensive.

Eighth, CAM itself has been re-organised and revitalised and has more appealing syllabuses.

Here, then, was a market which was not being satisfied. Moreover, the Cranfield Study had revealed that there were thousands more people working in public relations than anyone had ever realised. The success of *PR Week* was proof of the existence of this market. It was a virgin market for a good distance learning course.

The first step in March 1989 was to produce an outline course and discuss it with the chief examiner and general secretary of CAM, putting all cards on the table and inviting criticism. CAM were not asked to sponsor or recommend it: only to fault it if they could. It was a commercial proposition and no favours were asked. However, it did promise to increase the number of registered students and examination entries, and this CAM naturally welcomed.

The components of the courses for the nine subjects were two-fold. Some thirty books were selected, read and Reading Notes written for every chapter against a 26-week timetable. (The courses were based on a minimum of 26 weeks study enabling — for instance — a student to take three subjects in June, three in November and the Diploma in the following June). This was more realistic than the muddle of options at different colleges.

The second component was the personal input and this consisted of a combination of experiences in advertising, marketing and public relations practice; teaching and especially distance learning; examining; textbook authorship; and voluntary work on educational committees, plus academic and professional qualifications. Nobody else offering a CAM course could surpass this.

Investment was then made in printing the prospectus, press advertising, a direct mail campaign, and the stocking of quantities of the 30 books. The courses were launched in September 1989. I was about to go to Hong Kong to set up an agency for the LCCI courses, in addition to Singapore, but the CAM courses were not to be offered overseas as the exams were too UK-oriented. So, the gamble was on and I am always a pessimist about new ventures. Our first students enrolled, and it was a race against time to get courses away before I went abroad.

We made our mistakes, perhaps because I like to keep things simple. It was expected that students would enrol in the autumn or early winter for the June exams, and in the summer for the November exams. The course was planned as a succession of three sets of three subjects. But candidates enrol all the year round, they start with us in the middle or the end (having studied other subjects elsewhere, or having exemptions), and they often want different subject groupings. All this has been coped with, and in the Autumn of 1990 enrolments were coming in daily, sometimes five or six a day.

It has become an exciting and demanding new business and, except for the annual international Summer School and a few overseas courses, I have stopped running seminars in London. Now I have students in every corner of the UK, and even in France and the Channel Islands, and although it is a home study course we are in touch with most of them by phone or letter and of course through our two sets of mock exams per subject which require very detailed and frank appraisals.

I have had to study every exam question set under the new syllabus, and be able to answer them in order to mark the mock exam papers. One thing that has been discovered is that through lack of strict moderating, some CAM questions are non-sense, the examiners in at least three subjects not knowing their subjects. One wonders on what basis candidates were passed or failed! What happens if a candidate tells the examiner he is wrong? I quoted a number of these absurd questions at the recent CAM Conference of examiners and lecturers at Rugby.

Perhaps one cannot expect CAM to have reached the perfection of the LCCI examinations procedure where examination papers are written two years in advance, moderated, and re-moderated by a committee of examiners, moderators and officials. Probably because of the new syllabuses, CAM have been working too close to their examinations, but even so there should be sufficient scrutiny to protect candidates from the mistakes and ambiguities of examiners who may know little about examining techniques. The new chief examiner has promised to look into this problem.

One encouraging feature is the number of employers who are paying the fees of our students. This, I think, demonstrates that employers are not only recognising the need for training but also the value of the CAM qualification.

CHAPTER 20

Photography for Public Relations Purposes

PUBLISHABLE PICTURES

The standard of public relations photography is often poor, and this is another aspect of public relations which is criticised by editors. They want pictures: good pictures enhance their pages and increase reader interest. While they may commission most of the pictures they print, or use their own staff photographers, editors welcome the good public relations picture if, like the good news release, it is of *interest and value* to their readers.

The weak excuse is sometimes made that there is insufficient money to spend on good photography, unlike advertising. That is poppycock. Most readers of this book could take a good public relations picture if they knew how, and with modern cameras it is not difficult.

There are two simple ways of producing publishable pictures. The camera should be regarded as yet another tool of communication, like the pen, typewriter or word processor. When using such a tool it is essential to know what message needs to be communicated. In other words, the camera should be used to *tell a story*, not just to take a picture.

Many public relations pictures are no more than dull record shots. Or they may contain blatant name displays, and are advertisements. Or, again, the wrong people are in the picture, such as a bikini-clad model driving a fork-lift truck in a picture sent to *The Financial Times*. Sometimes people do not try hard enough, and sometimes they try too hard — and try the patience of editors. Here the fifth attribute of a good PRO, imagination, comes into play.

Before taking pictures for public relations purposes, or commissioning a professional photographer to do so, it is necessary to decide what story the picture has to tell, and how best it can be told pictorially. That is rather different from sending a photographer to take some pictures, and hoping that the right pictures will be taken. Photographers are not mind readers.

This leads naturally to the second way to obtain publishable pictures. The practitioner must work with the photographer. This needs to be done in two ways, first by briefing the photographer on the story the pictures should tell, and second by being present when the pictures are being taken.

Some practitioners are shy of doing this, thinking the photographer being an expert should be left to get on with the job. The photographer may be a technical expert but he cannot guess what message the PRO wishes to convey, or what will be done with the pictures. Are they to be black-and-white or coloured pictures, or are both wanted? Are they going to a newspaper, are they to illustrate the annual report, or are slides required? Consequently, the PRO or consultant — who is the client — must instruct the photographer on exactly what is wanted.

It is also essential to accompany the photographer whenever possible, being helpful, acting as stage manager, preparing the scene if necessary by clearing away debris or making sure that people who are to appear in the pictures are appropriately dressed. The photographer will not necessarily know what may be right or wrong. For instance, it will not be obvious that only one and not two people should be operating a labour-saving machine, or that people should be wearing protective gear such as helmets or goggles. But the PRO should know what is required, and can help the photographer to produce pictures that are correct, credible and acceptable. The photographer can use the best skills and equipment to obtain interesting, well-lit, sharp and publishable pictures, even on comparatively dull subjects. Good photography results from a sympathetic relationship between the practitioner and the photographer.

QUALITY OF PICTURES

It is necessary to make sure that pictures will not only tell an interesting story, and convey the desired message, but that they are of the highest quality. Not only is quality of content important — and we shall examine some typical faults — but photographs must be sharp (that is, in focus), prints should be glossy and not matt, and they should suit the printing process by which they will be reproduced.

The latter is necessary to the briefing given to the photographer because it will help determine the lighting requirements, and the extent to which pictures may be detailed or close-up. If the picture is to be reproduced in a newspaper printed by letterpress, the effects of a coarse half-tone screen and absorbent newsprint call for boldly black-and-white ('soot and whitewash') pictures with a mini-

mum of detail. But if the process is offset litho, using much finer half-tone screens and better or different paper and ink, more detailed pictures with more grey middle tones can be printed successfully. Nowadays, the majority of newspapers and magazines are printed by offset-litho, using fine screens, so that a detailed landscape picture with varied tonal values can be reproduced very well, and even in small sizes.

Knowledge of these printing requirements is therefore necessary if editors are to be supplied with pictures that will reproduce well. If there are large white areas they may be ruined by show-through from darker print on the reverse side of the page, as can happen with mass circulation tabloids which are printed at great speed, destroying picture quality.

Some magazines are printed by photogravure which tends to give pictures a soft, blurred effect.

KINDS OF PHOTOGRAPHER

There are different kinds of photographer just as there are different kinds of artist or writer. Most photographers specialise in particular kinds of photography such as portrait, animal, fashion or industrial. There are also those who can supply prints quickly, which may be vital in public relations, and others who work more slowly and take a week to supply contact prints. The buying of photography therefore needs understanding of what services different photographers offer and provide.

USE OF PUBLIC RELATIONS PICTURES

Photographs have numerous uses in public relations apart from illustrating news releases and feature articles. They can be used in house journals, annual reports, educational literature, on calendars, as blow-ups in showrooms and on exhibition stands, or as slides. When photography is being commissioned, it is wise to consider the range of uses to which pictures can be used so that the fullest advantage can be taken of the photographic session or assignment. It may be a good idea to use two cameras and take black-and-white as well as colour pictures. Although well-equipped printers do have cameras which can convert colour pictures to black-and-white, it is best not to send coloured pictures to journals which print in black-and-white. Picture editors want to look at black-and-white prints. On the other hand, if pictures are being supplied for TV purposes they must be in colour.

When a film or video is being made, it is a good idea to take stills at the same time as the subject being shot may well provide opportunities for photographs.

The opportunities for taking photographs are numerous, often unexpected, and may occur at times, on occasions or in places where no professional photographer is present. The alert PRO should therefore carry a camera whenever possible, and be professional in its use. Modern cameras are almost foolproof so far as speed and aperture are concerned, but two skills are also required. The first is the ability to focus and produce sharp pictures. The second is the ability to compose a picture, that is plan or design the content of the picture artistically. For instance, a picture should not be divided into two halves by a horizontal line such as the horizon; something in the foreground can give a sense of depth; people should be behaving naturally and not grinning at the camera.

FAULTS TO AVOID

1. *Record shots*. Avoid taking uninteresting record shots. Introduce something that provides interest. A very simple device is to create a three-dimensional effect by taking the picture from an angle. This can be demonstrated by taking a box or tin and looking at it face-on, and then turning it so that three sides are visible. The method can be applied to many subjects such as a package, a building, a ship or an aeroplane. A much more interesting picture is achieved very easily. It can even be applied to a portrait.

2. *Busy pictures*. Concentrate on the subject, and avoid or remove extraneous items which interfere with the subject of the picture. For example, a plain background is often best, and devices for this could be a plain wall rather than wood panelling, decorative wallpaper or patterned curtains. Out of doors, the sky may provide a neutral background. If an interior shot is being taken it may be necessary to hang a white sheet, or use a roll of white paper, to eliminate backgrounds.

3. *Dress*. Make sure people are wearing the right clothes and look natural, and also make sure they are tidy and do not have pocket flaps turned in, or have ties askew. Perhaps they should have their sleeves rolled up, or be wearing a special overall or protective gear, or it should be a *clean* overall. Perhaps jewellery should or should not be worn. A common mistake is that a subject is smoking when this would be improper, or objectionable nowadays.

4. *Presentations*. If a presentation of a prize is being made, avoid taking pictures across a table with outstretched arms and an empty space in the middle. It may be better to get the subjects together later and photograph them standing closer together.

5. *Drinking pictures*. Try to avoid the hackneyed pictures of people on a social occasion standing with glasses in their hands.

6. *Tramline effects*. Avoid pictures in which shop counters, work benches and similar objects extend into the distance like converging tramlines.

SOME USEFUL HINTS

1. *Comparative sizes.* Try to give an indication of size when this is not obvious. Small objects can be posed with something which demonstrates smallness, such as the human hand. The large size of objects can be shown if associated with the human figure. Thus, a micro chip could be held in the hand, while a person could be standing next to a huge wheel. Hackneyed uses of coins and matchboxes should not be used with small objects — try to be more original.

2. *Colour pictures.* When taking colour pictures, make sure that they are colourful! Many subjects and scenes contain dull shades of blue, green and grey and lack yellow, orange and red. In fact, red is often missing altogether and it pays to look for something red to make a colour picture colourful. Street scenes, for example, can be colourless.

3. *Human interest.* If appropriate to the subject, have people in pictures, provided they look natural, interesting, and are in the right place at the right time, and preferably doing something which helps the picture. A picture of a hotel or restaurant looks more realistic if there are guests, a shop if there are customers, an aircraft if there are crew or passengers. Be careful about the use of professional models who do not look genuine: sometimes employees make better models. There is a saying that people like looking at people, which may be worth remembering when setting up public relations pictures. Children and animals often attract more reader interest than pin-ups.

4. *A little can tell the whole.* It is often better to take part of a subject so that it gives an impression of the whole. Part of an audience can look more effective than the whole audience.

5. *Name displays.* Avoid blatant name displays. Part of a name can suggest the whole.

CAPTIONING

Another complaint from editors is that public relations pictures are rarely captioned. The author receives many photographs, often on request, but they are seldom captioned. It is difficult to believe that public relations people can ever send out uncaptioned pictures, but it is a normal if stupid practice. Captions are important and imperative because they say what pictures cannot say for themselves, and they identify the sender. How can an editor write a caption if he has no information; how does he know who owns the copyright; and how does he know who to telephone if he wants more information or another or a different print? There are also inadequate captions which say too little, and captions written at the end of news releases which are in the wrong place.

It should be remembered that the caption will usually remain as a permanent attachment to a picture, and will not be removed for printing purposes. The picture editor will write a caption to appear with the printed picture, using the information given in the photo caption.

Editors cannot be expected to extract captions from the body of a news release. The release and the picture may be handled separately by a news or feature editor and by a picture editor. While releases are rejected, pictures may be retained in the photo library and referred to in the future.

If a caption names people in a picture their sequence should be clearly stated, e.g. 'picture shows from left to right', or 'picture shows back row from left to right', and so on if there is more than one row of people.

The caption should be brief, but it should state essential details which are not apparent from the picture itself. It is a good idea to have printed caption forms, bearing the name, address, telephone number and perhaps the logo of the sender. If many pictures are issued, the negative number should be stated. The caption should be attached safely to the back of the picture, and positioned the same way round as the picture. A simple way to attach a caption to a picture is to use a strip of adhesive tape top and bottom. Gums and glues may tend to corrugate pictures. Flapped captions are sometimes used, but they run the risk of being torn off. Photographers should be asked not to rubber-stamp the backs of prints, but the PRO may add a rubber stamp as well as a caption.

COPYRIGHT

The copyright should be owned by the sender, and this means that the editor may print the picture without fee, otherwise he will be expected to pay a reproduction fee to anyone else (e.g. a photo agency) who owns the copyright. There is no need, therefore, to state in the caption of a public relations picture that it is copyright and must not be reproduced without permission since this will inhibit the editor from printing it, and the whole object of sending it will be defeated.

However, when commissioning photography, the practitioner should make sure that the photographer (who owns the copyright in the first place unless he is an employee such as a staff photographer) assigns the copyright to the commissioners. If the photographs are commissioned by a consultant, to whom the copyright is assigned, the copyright remains that of the consultant until such time as it may be assigned to the client. Copyright is not automatically owned by the client unless the client (e.g. an in-house PRO) commissioned the pictures direct from the photographer and assignment was agreed. Ideally, in a contract of service with a consultant, all such copyrights should be assigned to the client, but a consultant may (as an advertising agency may well do) retain copyright until the client has paid his final bill at the end of a contract period.

Under the original Copyright Act 1956, the photographer (unless he was an employee) owned the copyright of negatives. However, under the Copyright Designs and Patents Act 1988, the photographer (unless he is an employee) owns the copyright of both negative and prints. When ordering photography the PRO or consultant must have these copyrights assigned so that the pictures may be offered to the media free of copyright restrictions, that is the sender owns the copyright.

There are also rights of 'intellectual property' and 'moral rights' which protect the photographer. For instance, a picture must not be altered so that it can be construed as being derogatory of the photographer's work. Nowadays photographers' names are usually credited, as are all those concerned with the production of a film or video.

CHAPTER 21

Video

For some fifty years the documentary film predominated as one of the most effective private mediums for public relations messages. Its main strengths were its element of entertainment — the appeal of the movies — and the fact that standard 16 mm projectors were universally available. Its weakness lay in the bulky cans of film, projectors were noisy, and films could break. Nevertheless, splendid public relations films were made and the Shell Film Unit's 1930s film of an Imperial Airways airliner refuelling — *Croydon Airport* — remains a classic which is still shown today. But the video camera, the videotape and the video-cassette recorder have revolutionised the documentary film and made possible many other forms and uses of this kind of medium.

First let us consider the video which has replaced the standard documentary film and consider the three essentials which should be defined in advance.

THREE ESSENTIALS OF DOCUMENTARY VIDEO MAKING

When making videos, it is essential to define their *purpose*, *production* and *distribution*.

Purpose

There should be a clear purpose, which should be related to its place in the planned pro-

gramme to achieve specific objectives. How can a documentary video fit into the total programme as an essential use of private media, or is it perhaps the wrong medium to use? Can it augment other public relations activities such as seminars and press receptions? Does the budget permit video production and will the likely result justify such expenditure? This type of video can serve many purposes such as staff education (including induction material), or for showing to distributors, customers or shareholders; or to recruit staff; or to secure business. Each purpose may need a very different kind of video regarding treatment, content and commentary. A general purpose video is seldom satisfactory. So, the precise purpose needs to be established when the initial 'treatment' is being written and agreed before a shooting script is written, casting and locations are decided, and shooting begins.

Production

Careful decisions are necessary regarding the production of a video. This is a much more versatile and flexible medium than film production. At its simplest, a video can be shot on a domestic camcorder and edited by using two VCRs, playing the original and deleting frames in the course of transferring to cassette. A voice over can be made while shooting, or the commentary and music can be dubbed in afterwards. Special electronic effects can be added. At the other extreme, the subject can be first shot on film (as often happens with TV commercials) and then transferred to video-tape for post-production computerised graphic effects including use of systems such as Quantel Paintbrush. In between there can be a straightforward video without special effects. Yet another form is the video made from still photographs or slides with added music and vocal commentary, this resembling slide-on-film.

Some of the original considerations of film-making also apply to video-making. Will it be made by an in-house or an outside production unit? Some large companies do have their own in-house video studio which is justified because it makes a number of programmes for training and promotion purposes apart from the production of a video house magazine and documentaries.

What will be the length? A documentary should rarely exceed 20 minutes, and for other purposes such as explaining a relocation venue, it could be as short as 8 to 10 minutes. Length affects cost, but it also concerns the ability or willingness of people to watch and maintain interest and attention. Crisp editing can often heighten audience attention.

Where will it be made? Studio production is the least expensive but it can lead to static scenes. Outside locations can be attractive and realistic, but if they are too distant they can involve costly travel for crew, equipment and actors. An outside location may mean that the whole team will have to stay at the location on different occasions, weather and other conditions permitting.

Will sound be recorded while shooting or dubbed in afterwards, perhaps with a well-known commentator? Will original or hired 'library' music be used? For international showing it can be a good idea to have no speech, make good use of mime by the actors, and use characteristic music which fits the scenes or the action. All these considerations will affect the cost.

Distribution

At the outset it is essential to define likely audiences, and then produce a video which suits them, with planned distribution that will reach these viewers. This links with purpose, but there is no point in making a video which is not intended to do a particular communication job. It may be necessary to advertise availability of the video (as occurs with those offered to schools), place it with organisations which arrange film showings, invite audiences to see it (one of the best forms of distribution), and generally make sure that it achieves its objectives. Videos do not date quickly and they can be made to live and work for the organisation for many years.

SYSTEMS AND FORMATS

Two basic systems are used in Britain, the Sony U-matic industrial system, and VHS (to which Sony U-matic system tapes can be transferred). Nowadays domestic VCRs are mostly VHS, this system having superseded the Betamax and Philips systems. They are also intended for PAL television transmission. In other parts of the world such as the USA and the Far East, other formats exist so that European-made cassettes are incompatible. However, television monitors are available which will accept all formats.

TYPES AND USES OF VIDEOS

In discussing the three essentials, purpose, production and distribution, we have concentrated on the documentary which has replaced the old 'industrial' film, with occasional references to complementary uses. Now let us consider particular types of video and the variety of uses which make this such a versatile and flexible medium.

1. Documentary

This kind of video, like the former 16 mm film, can have a variety of uses but even more so than the clumsier film which required a special projector. With VCRs and television sets widely available, the video documentary can be screened at more locations and on more occasions. It can be shown at induction meetings of new recruits; shown to invited groups of potential clients or customers; used as part of the programme of a press reception; shown on exhibition stands, thereby giving movement if exhibits are static; included in permanent exhibitions; and loaned to prospective customers. The latter method is commonly used in the holiday and travel industry, videos about holiday venues being loaned to interested clients. These examples indicate how video has become more versatile than film.

International Video Network Ltd has a Video Travel Library containing more than 80 videos about foreign countries and cities, which may be purchased.

2. Annual report and accounts

Two versions are possible, one for shareholders who cannot attend the annual general meeting, and a more popular version — sometimes presented as a discussion between the company chairman and an actor or TV commentator — for showing to employees. The latter is particularly useful with large organisations which have staff at various locations, including overseas ones or aboard oil rigs or ships.

3. House journal

The video house journal resembles a newsreel or TV news bulletin. The items are usually linked together by a professional commentator who may also conduct studio interviews. Video house journals can introduce management and employees to one another and demonstrate company activities. They can be shown at company locations or by staff in their homes. They can be useful in integrating staff in conglomerates or when there are acquisitions. A development of this is the corporate or business video which will be discussed separately.

4. Relocation

This is a popular use of video to help overcome the problems of relocation. When an organisation plans to move to a new location, it is not always easy to induce employees to move with it. A short video of perhaps 8 to 10 minutes can describe the amenities of the new location, and carry a message from the CEO. This can be shown in employees' homes so that the whole family may see it, important since the decision to move concerns not only the employee, hence the expression 'trailing spouse syndrome'.

5. Market education

Videos can be made to explain or demonstrate a product or service. They may be screened at a retail outlet, such as a motor-car showroom, or offered in advertisements as in the promotion of investments such as unit trusts, or for demonstrations by food manufacturers and supplied to women's clubs.

CORPORATE VIDEO: SATELLITE BUSINESS TV

This is the more sophisticated form of video house journal, although the name is something of a misnomer since it is sometimes applied to the documentary video, the modern counterpart of the 'industrial' film which public relations films used to be called. But unlike video house journals which are put on video cassettes for showing at different locations, the corporate or business video is sent weekly, fortnightly or monthly as the case may be by satellite to receiving locations.

The method was first introduced in the USA in the mid-1950s, where it was known as a private satellite network. The first systems were those of Merrill Lynch which cost $8 million and was addressed to retailers. J.S. Penny used such a system to show samples to buyers. Ford created an internal news service, and Wang installed one to train salesmen in the USA, Europe and Asia.

They are produced by one of three methods: (i) Satellite managers with associated production units; (ii) independent production units; and (iii) in-house production units. In the USA there are more than 300 private business satellite TV networks, and they are growing in Europe. Here are some examples:

(i) *Ford Europe* has its Ford Communications Network. Its satellite TV operation in the UK covers some 40 000 employees at 18 receiving stations using a British Telecom network, for a fortnightly news programme. An outside production team is used to make the 12 minute programme which contains three or four news items plus a couple of longer features. The same presenters are used and employees are used as often as possible to give credibility to scenes. Americanisms and management preaching are avoided. The fortnightly programmes are given repeated broadcasts in order to reach as many employees as possible. In the USA, there are daily broadcasts. A European network has been developed.

(ii) *Unipart Channel 5.* This monthly corporate video shows that corporate video is not such a new idea as this one was first launched in 1985, and it has a rather different audience to most, the customer audience of mechanics at service garages. However, the method of dis-

tribution became new in 1992 when it went out on satellite. It is produced in-house and runs for 30 minutes, most of it being shot on location. An occasional 30 minute employee video, *Grapevine* is also produced.

(iii) *Nuclear Electric* at Sizewell uses the Interchange Group's cabled message system which is useful for single locations. In this case, 10 receiving sets are installed to communicate with 550 staff. Messages are quickly put on screen, supported by graphics and rostrum camera visuals facility. The programme is shown frequently and items can be company news, information about working conditions, personal contributions from employees, or the menu in the canteen.

Similar systems are used by other companies. British Aerospace at Prestwick has a phone-in system whereby employees can submit items for a cabled message system, but sets can also run videos, tune in to channels or satellite programmes. Body Shop has a weekly programme via satellite. Business television is a growing medium and Maxat Satellite Communications, a leading satellite operator, expected the satellite business TV market to be worth £55 million by the end of 1992, according to a report in the February 1992 issue of *Televisual*.

A number of suppliers produce and/or distribute corporate videos. Maxat Satellite Communications work with Visage Productions. Maxat and BT have their own production units but also work with others such as the in-house Ford Communications Network. They also work with Corporate Television Communications which produces Digital programmes, while Visnews puts out programmes made by production units such as Cobourne Co and others mentioned later in this chapter.

Merrill Lynch the American accountants and investment bankers, are quoted as saying 'products or services introduced by video programmes increased sales by 30–40 percent, substantially reduced learning and training periods whilst at the same time improving product or service understanding. Business television programmes are possibly the most effective method of communication currently available.'

Video Press Release Ltd not only make VNRs (discussed later), but produce business satellite TV of various kinds ranging from BMW's weekly programme to dealers and Radio Rentals programme to staff. Other programmes have been made by VPR for Bayer, Wessex Water, Ford, Jaguar, GKN, British Coal, DEC, MoD, Jefferson Smurfitt, and McCann-Erickson. Live programmes can be delivered by satellite on a single point to multi-point or multi-point to multi-point basis. While many corporate news videos are pre-recorded, live programmes are possible and are becoming increasingly popular so that they represent an internal news bulletin not unlike one on public television. The application to British, pan-European, trans-Atlantic and international conferences may be expensive, but could be less expensive than having to attend conferences in person as a speaker. We shall move on to the allied subject of video-conferencing.

VIDEOCONFERENCING

There are several methods of videoconferencing but usually they involve use of either British Telecom ISDN2 digital lines or Megastream digital circuit, or of a satellite operator. BT offer a number of types of equipment which compress and digitise TV picture signals for transmission by standard digital telecom lines. The systems allow people in different locations within the UK and overseas to meet face to face as if in the same room. The conferencing can be conducted from the client's own premises, or a BT videoconferencing centre can be hired by the hour. The basic components are a colour camera, large screen monitor, microphone, loudspeakers and control system. Presentation material such as a whiteboard, computer graphics, flip chart, slides or videos can all be incorporated.

There are some 450 public videoconferencing centres plus in-house facilities around the world. To hold an instantaneous conference with colleagues at different locations is clearly cheaper and quicker than having to assemble them at one centre. There would be great savings in air-fares, hotel accommodation and loss of working time. The only problem with international videoconferencing is the time differential between different parts of the world.

VIDEO NEWS RELEASES

The video news release (sometimes oddly called a video press release since it is not sent to the press but only to television) is produced and distributed very differently from a news release addressed to the press. Nor does it resemble a documentary video. It is usually a kit of news shots or short sequences which can be used by the producers of news bulletins, magazine and current affairs programmes. A typical example is that when a news reader is reading a news item, it is supported by pictures. It is unlikely that the news service will take such pictures itself, it could hire a sequence from an archival source such as Visnews, but it is better if the pictorial background has been shot recently. For instance, the story may be about a strike, redundancies or falling sales at a motor-car plant, but public relations for the company are better if the pictures show a modern robotised factory.

An article contributed by WTN Productions in the *IPR Handbook 1992* (Kogan Page) says that 'in the USA an estimated 2000 VNRs are sent out every year', and that 'this figure is expected to grow by 20 per cent in the 90s'.

American use of VNRs was discussed in IABC's *Communication World* (October 1991), the point being made that while VNRs are sometimes attacked as being 'advertising parading as news' . . . 'Video releases look like TV news in the same way that press releases read like newspaper articles'. The writer, Emil Gallina of Hill and Knowlton, said 'The video news release was developed by press relations experts to answer the broadcast reporter's cry, "Give me something I can use" '. Nevertheless, the US Food and Drug Administration (FDA) decided to scrutinise VNRs distributed by pharmaceutical companies, and one company responded by banning them. This only goes to make the essential point that VNRs (like any other material submitted to the media) must avoid puffery and be of interest and value to their audiences.

It is significant that the American pharmaceutical companies used VNRs as part of their marketing efforts, and once again we experience the clash between marketing people who regard public relations as free advertising, and public relations people who are concerned with legitimate company news. Let us hope that the abuse of VNRs in America does not cross the Atlantic, and that simple principles are applied such as Emil Gallina's important argument that 'they are merely one source of raw material from which news reports can be created. When provided with a video news release, a responsible journalist checks the facts, attributes material to its sources, and digs for opposing views.'

WTN explain that the comparatively slow uptake of VNRs in Britain 'has been mainly due to two factors: firstly, broadcasters' distrust of news material in Britain that has been commercially produced, and secondly, the lack of understanding of the VNR at the commissioning end.'

However, Video Press Release Ltd offer an explanation in their literature when they point out that the economics of television make VNRs attractive. 'Why should TV stations use our footage?' ask VPR. 'Surely they have crews of their own?' Wrong. At the last count ITN were £9.8m over budget *before* the Gulf War.

The BBC and ITV have shed over 1400 jobs in 1990 and up to April 1991.

'A typical BBC region two years ago employed seven or more news crews — now there could be as few as two or three. A typical ITV station might have had seven or eight documentary and drama crews — now they might not have any at all!'

Generally, the move is towards independent programme production, and this was intensified by the licences awarded to contractors by the ITC in 1991. Moreover, 1992 was the year when it became necessary for 70 percent of programmes shown on EC television to be produced within the EC. Thus, the attitudes towards outside material have changed fundamentally, and if VNRs are produced to broadcasting standards, they are likely to be welcomed. Perhaps the point to emphasise is that whereas a paper news release can be distributed freely to many editors, it is necessary to discuss usage of a VNR with producers of news and other programmes. It may even be necessary to discuss in advance what scenes should be shot. On the one hand, production costs can be minimised if a corporate video is being shot at the same time, and frames from it can be extracted for a short VNR.

As VPR point out, VNRs are not limited to news bulletins. They can be used by the producers of daytime, women's, science, financial, business, ethnic, motoring, farming, children's, magazine, and other programmes including those which cover current affairs, and special events such as exhibitions and trade fairs.

Another supplier of VNRs is Bulletin Television News Service. They state that 'if broadcasters are not aware of the story, do not have the resources to shoot it, or cannot shoot all aspects of it, they still get the relevant television news pictures together with a script in the form they would produce themselves'.

Bulletin have a long record of successes. On regional TV, they secured 13 separate broadcasts totalling over 12 minutes airtime for client Option One for the Kenco London to Brighton

Veteran Car Run. Ten national and regional broadcasts totalling 11 minutes were obtained for their client Help The Aged's launch of telephone help services, Helpline. And internationally for Burson–Marsteller/US West, 23 separate international broadcasts were obtained reaching an audience of over 50 million, on the start of the first cellular phone network in Eastern Europe.

Examples of WTN productions are those of Peaudouce/Barbara Attenborough and British Telecom. Peaudouce and their public relations consultancy sought UK television exposure of their 'Childminder of the Year' awards, presented by the Duchess of York. A 3-minute VNR was made focusing on the regional finalists and the overall winner who came from Sheffield. Delivery was by hard copy cassette, Red Star delivery and London courier. The VNR was broadcast by BBC News, Thames and Yorkshire ITV.

The British Telecom 9-minute VNR showed all the implications arising from changing the London area code, and included shots of public telephones and faxes, and letter headed paper bearing the new code. Both domestic and international coverage was required. It was distributed via WTN's daily satellite feeds and hard copy cassette, with different versions for particular audiences. The UK, Australian and US versions were voiced. This VNR was broadcast by BBC Breakfast News, 6.00 News, 9.00 News; ITN News at 10.00; repeatedly on Sky News; EBC Germany; CBS Network in the USA; Ch 9 in Australia; Hong Kong TV and various other UK and overseas broadcasters.

WTN has a combined production and distribution set-up with two studios, a master control room with eight incoming and eight outgoing vision circuits to the BT Tower and ITN plus direct down and up linking satellite coordination, three machine component edit suite, three machine multi-format edit suite, seven two-machine edit rooms (PAL), two two-machine edit rooms (NTSC) and full standards conversion plus support facilities such as satellite news gathering.

WTN offer many other services including satellite conferencing and *Satellite Media Tours*. The latter enables an interviewee to 'tour' a country, or series of countries, without moving from a single studio. To quote from WTN's booklet *Television Public Relations — Some Useful Hints*, 'An example would be an author of a new book, who wants to gain exposure in many locations. TV stations are contacted and are each given a 5–10 minutes interview "window" at a certain time of the day. The interviewee is placed in a studio and a video of them is fed onto the appropriate satellite. Each participating station then has the opportunity to ask specific questions of the interviewee and to record the responses. At the end of their timeslot, another station takes up the questions and the interviewee effectively "tours" either a country or the world without leaving their seat.'

The largest distributor of VNRs is Visnews, an organisation famous the world over for news film coverage, originating as British Movietone News many years ago, set up in its present form in 1957, and now owned by Reuters.

It supplies 650 broadcasters in 84 countries. Its head office is in West London, and it has 34 bureaux all over the world. With affiliate stations in networks such as NBC, TV Globo of Brazil and DDI of India, Visnews have more than 1600 client stations. In the UK they supply the BBC, GMTV and Sky News. Visnews is particularly well known as the supplier of archival film, and their name will be frequently seen among the credits of documentary programmes. Visnews therefore has a professional reputation which it will not risk by distributing disguised advertising material.

Before producing a VNR, Visnews will conduct basic research to discover possible users of the VNR which is usually about 5 minutes long and without commentary. They will quote for a single European country, a Europe-wide service or world-wide distriibution. Most TV subscribers take a daily satellite feed of news material. Visnews has its own satellite over Europe, transmitting news as it breaks for 13 hours a day. Feeds are also made daily to the Americas, Japan, the Asia-Pacific-Rim, Australasia and the Middle East. VNRs are distributed along with other news material so it is imperative that they too are legitimate news.

Users of the Visnews Corporate Television VNR services include Euro Disney, Drambuie Liqueur Co, Saab Scania, Hong Kong Trade Association, P & O, and many other organisations. Production is by associated units, Visnews having the distribution network as described above.

One 6-minute VNR, which obtained 21 individual airings on UK television, was produced by JQ Films to describe the research to save dolphins from being caught in tuna driftnets. This was sponsored by the Co-op and was part of a campaign organised by Countrywide Communications (see the news release in Chapter 18). In addition to shots in the Moray Firth, library footage was included from Greenpeace, and from film by Partridge Films of dolphins in Mexico. Here was a typical example of a very acceptable VNR being supplied by Visnews which the BBC, ITN and Sky were unlikely to send out crews to cover.

Another example comes from Sea Containers who sought news coverage for the presentation of the Hales Trophy for the record-breaking trans-Atlantic crossing of their Sea Cat passenger catamaran. The production company, Upstream, took aerial pictures of the craft coming up the Thames and under Tower Bridge to the presentation by former Prime Minister, Lord Callaghan. Visnews secured nearly 6 minutes coverage on national and regional television.

The 25th birthday of British Telecom's tower was covered in a VNR made by Corporate Television Communications and distributed by Visnews. This required the use of archive pictures of various historical events including the aftermath of 1971's terrorist bomb blast and the fireworks, laser and light landline and cassette. The VNR received over 4 minutes' coverage.

In this section reference has been made to what may seem to be only a few minutes' coverage, but news bulletins are not lengthy and several topics are covered in a comparatively short time. Nevertheless, the impact of sound, colour and action, and its association with a well-known news reader on a popular station, and an audience which may run into

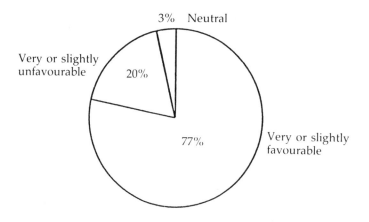

Figure 21.1   Attitudes towards VNRs. (Source: Frank N. Magid Associates.)

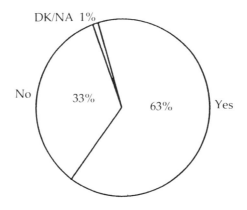

Figure 21.2   *Stations which use VNRs in broadcasts. (Source: Frank N. Magid Associates.)*

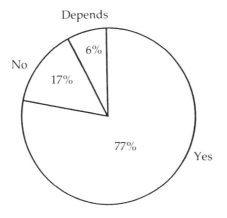

Figure 21.3   *Stations which wish to continue receiving VNRs. (Source: Frank N. Magid Associates.)*

millions has to be compared with column inches of cold black print.

Do broadcasters want VNRs? Visnews Corporate Television commissioned Frank N. Magid Associates to research the attitudes of European broadcasters towards VNRs and their usage. Of European broadcasters interviewed, 63 percent said they used VNRs and 40 percent wanted more each month. At least one VNR was used in a typical month by 58 percent of broadcasters at 30 television stations, and 84 percent of the material was aired on daily news bulletins. The charts shown in Figures 21.1–21.3 are derived from this study.

In this chapter we have recorded one of the most important and versatile advances in the means of communicating public relations messages. It is especially interesting in the way it spans both the mass commercial media and serves as a private created medium. With the move away from the production of television programmes by the contractors to their supply of independent producers, there are excellent technical facilities available to the public relations world, and with the greater use of videos for a variety of purposes, there is greater justification for setting up in-house video production units.

CHAPTER 22

House Journals

INTERNAL AND EXTERNAL HOUSE JOURNALS

House journals are one of the most frequently used forms of privately created public relations media, and are sometimes known as house organs or company newspapers. They represent the oldest form of created public relations activity, the first house journal being introduced 160 years ago, and many still in existence today were first launched in the 19th century. Charles Dickens quoted the *Lowell Offering* in his *American Notes* published in 1842. This gives the lie to the impression that public relations is a new or a young profession. Moreover, house journals are popular throughout the world, and are often the first attempt made by organisations to undertake public relations, in which case they may be the responsibility of the personnel manager in the absence of a PRO.

Internal house journals may be issued in-house to employees (very often including pensioners); to members of a voluntary organisation; or to subscribers to a charity.

External house journals may be issued to specific groups of readers such as customers and clients; distributors; specifiers and formulators; hotel guests or airline passengers or other outside publics.

Internal and external house journals should not be confused, and it is seldom a good policy to distribute internals to outsiders, beyond perhaps special friends and maybe the trade press, since their domestic subject matter is not really intended for outside readership. Similarly, a periodical aimed at an outside readership is seldom intended for employees.

DIFFERENT KINDS OF HOUSE JOURNAL

1. Newsletter

The simple newsletter containing a digest of news items in a few pages, perhaps no more than a four-page folder, is useful for the following reasons:

(a) When the budget is very limited.
(b) When it is desirable to convey information in a quickly-read form.
(c) When a brief digest is required for management, as distinct from the general house journal.
(d) When a house journal is being published experimentally for the first time, and a full-scale publication has not yet been contemplated or approved.

2. Newspaper

Usually tabloid, this style is popular when there is a large staff, particularly a working-class labour force which requires a popular content. It coincides with the facilities offered by web-offset printing. To be realistic, it should be printed as a typical newspaper on newsprint, but the mistake is often made of printing a tabloid on better-quality paper so that it no longer resembles a newspaper.

To be credible, a house journal should look like the commercial publications with which readers are familiar. For example, the very successful *Ford News* is not unlike *The Daily Mirror*, *The Sun* and *The Daily Star*, the kind of newspaper mostly read by Ford employees. In fact, the editor maintains that the journal should be as good as those newspapers, and credibility would be lost if better paper was used.

Ford News looks like a normal newspaper. It goes to all employees and has to appeal to all. It tries to communicate company news before it is read about in other newspapers. The 'Take It To The Top' feature prints readers' letters, with answers from management. There are three pages of classified advertisements, plus outside commercial advertisements. Well-known professional writers are commissioned to write on sport, DIY, money matters, motoring, and other topics, and there is a prize crossword. It is published regularly at 11am on the last Wednesday of the month. Copies are sent to company locations throughout the UK, and copies are distributed not only to employees but to thousands of pensioners and to the national and regional press.

3. Magazines

Because web-offset can nowadays print from webs or reels of better-quality paper, such as super-calendered, some editors have reverted from tabloid to A4 magazine format. There has been a considerable growth in the publication of A4 magazines. However, this format is more suitable for the more serious periodical, that is one containing articles rather than news items.

4. Wall newspaper

This is an attractive medium for premises such as a factory where the staff are confined to one location. It is easily produced and printed, and can be displayed like a poster at convenient points where it can be read, provided there is a sufficient number of displays for everyone to see it. Each issue can have a different coloured heading or masthead to indicate each new edition.

5. Electronic newspaper

One version is that distributed via personal computers fitted with printers to produce hard copies.

6. Video magazine

A number of companies, especially those with their own video studios, produce monthly or quarterly video magazines which are rather like company newsreels. They can be shown at company locations, usually as and when convenient to view rather than to assembled audiences. While the original is usually produced on Sony U-matic format, it is possible to make VHS cassettes for home viewing.

Video has the advantage of audiovisual impact and realism. A video magazine can include interviews so that employees can 'meet' management, or see what other employees do, and there can be features on new company developments, financial reports, introductions to companies which have been acquired, and generally it can bring alive topics which come across less effectively in print.

7. Corporate video

Several large companies operate private TV networks with video news bulletins transmitted by satellite throughout the day to their premises. The Interchange Group produce such programmes. Corporate videos are discussed again in Chapter 21.

CONSIDERATIONS FOR PRINTED HOUSE JOURNALS

When producing a printed house journal the following considerations are important:

1. Readership

This must be carefully defined so that material is carried which will be of interest and value to readers who should look forward to each succeeding issue. The in-house journal should be a medium of mutual communication, upwards, downwards and sideways. If it is only a platform from which management preaches to the staff, it will soon lose reader interest. The best house journals are those where the editor enjoys independence and is allowed total editorial control. Such an editor can then produce a journal that employees are willing to read.

2. Title

The journal should have a distinctive but credible name. Clever titles are unnecessary and many titles are simple ones which resemble commercial titles, e.g. *Ford News*, *Rentokil Review*. More fanciful titles, like that of Malaysia Airline's in-flight magazine *Wings of Gold*, are suitable for special external purposes.

3. Frequency

A journal should be issued as frequently as possible in order to maintain continuity of reader interest. Some are issued daily, weekly, fortnightly, monthly, two-monthly or quarterly. After that it really ceases to be a 'periodical'. The frequency may depend on the need to communicate, the budget and possibly quantity.

4. Method of distribution

Unless a journal is reliably distributed, copies will be wasted, and this is therefore a vital consideration since there is no point in going to the trouble and expense of producing a journal if readers do not receive it. The nature and structure of the organisation may decide the method of distribution, but it can be fatal just to send large bundles to different locations hoping that someone will distribute individual copies. Distribution must be properly organised. The best, although obviously the most expensive, is to post copies to employees' home addresses, but other methods such as distribution by hand, or from 'automatic newsboy' stands, may be used provided they are controlled responsibly. An advantage of postal distribution is that the journal is likely to be read by members of the employees' families.

5. Cover charge

Should employees have to pay for copies? Generally, it is thought that there should be free distribution, but there are some employee newspapers which command such high reader interest that employees are willing to buy copies as they would commercial newspapers and magazines.

6. Advertisements

Should advertisements be carried? Reader advertisements of the 'sales' and 'wants' variety are very popular, and they improve the readership of journals. Usually, they are inserted free of charge. If the readership is valuable to outside advertisers, space can be sold and the presence of commercial advertising can help to make the periodical look more like a commercial publication. A house journal with a large circulation can be a good advertising proposition, and the income will help the production costs.

PLANNING ISSUES, OBTAINING MATERIAL

If the editor just sat and waited for material to arrive he or she would find it very hard to sustain publication. The editor has to operate just like the editor of a commercial journal, planning future issues, running regular pages or features, and organising the supply of news, pictures and articles.

In large organisations with several locations, local correspondents can be appointed to send news to the central editorial office by specified dates. If articles are to be published, they must be commissioned in the sense that writers are briefed on what to write about and when copy is required. Interviews and photographic sessions have to be arranged. Outside material such as articles, cartoons, pictures and crosswords may have to be bought from specialists and agencies. All this has to coincide with strict time schedules so that the journal can be designed, copy can be subbed, copy can be sent to the printer on time so that proofs are received, corrected and returned, and the journal is printed, delivered and distributed to meet a regular publication date.

EXTERNAL HOUSE JOURNALS

Most of what has been said already applies to the staff journal, but the 'external' may be an important element in the public relations programme. Many of the items already considered will apply to the external, but the content and the readership will be different and, except for journals provided for, say, hotel guests or airline passengers, distribution will be by post. The content and the correctness of the mailing list will be important.

Once again, the journal — whatever its format — must be authentic, and the design should not be that of brash sales literature. Yet again, the more closely the journal resembles a commercial journal, the more readily it will be accepted. Too many externals fail in this respect — weight and quality of paper being too extravagant, or the pages looking more like promotional material — and yet the external is becoming increasingly popular.

The classy prestige journal has tended to disappear in favour of the one which has to do a job of work in creating understanding or educating readers. The journal that sets out merely to impress is a worthless luxury, but the one that helps retailers to sell products, or helps technicians to specify or formulate, or maintains customer interest, performs a positive public relations task.

A valuable use of the external is as a means of communication with customers and other influential people in countries which have little trade, technical or professional press. One journal (with translated editions if necessary) can then be mailed to interested readers in many countries throughout the world. This can overcome the problem of press relations in countries with few newspapers or magazines, and where there is probably resistance to publishing news releases.

However, when several language versions are produced it has to be remembered that sufficient space must be allowed for translations which sometimes occupy more space than the original English version. If Arabic versions are printed, it should be realised that publications in Arabic read from last page to first page.

Externals have tended to be more popular in the USA than in the UK. Some of the earliest house journals were externals such as the Singer magazine for buyers of sewing machines and the Travelers Insurance magazine for brokers, both appearing over 100 years ago.

PRODUCTION OF HOUSE JOURNALS

There are two main methods of producing house journals. First there is the traditional method of drawing page layouts by hand, casting off copy, and sending layouts, copy and pictures to the printer. The modern way of producing journals, especially ones with large circulations, is by desktop publishing (DTP), using computerised systems such as Apple Macintosh (using software such as PageMaker and Quark Xpress), IBM and other hardware.

An example of a journal produced with drawn page layouts is *The House Magazine* which is the house journal of the Palace of Westminster. It is an A4 weekly with a glossy cover, and its circulation of 2500 is said to have 20 000 readers among MPs, peers, British MEPs and journalists.

A DTP magazine is very demanding because the editor has to be writer, sub-editor, editor, designer and typographer so that the journal can be produced up to printing stage on disk. Norwich Union, Peugeot and Racal magazines are produced like this. There are also outside firms such as Dewe Rogerson Ltd with their Screenplay service who are equipped and staffed to produce house journals by DTP electronic systems publishing methods.

The advantage of DTP is that there can be fast on-screen make-up from copy on most disks, and there is no necessity for galley proofs, processing or paste-up. Numerous typefaces are available in sizes from 2 pt to 500 pt in quarter point variations. Headlines can be enlarged, reduced, expanded or condensed. While this occupies more time at the editorial end, the finished job goes to the printer so that the time normally spent on setting, make-up, proofing and corrections is eliminated, and it lends itself very well to offset-litho printing and excellent print quality.

Another public relations consultancy which offers a DTP house journal production service is Daniel J. Edelman, whose group director of Edelman Publications explained in an article in the March 1992 issue of *Public Relations* how it produces *Rockwell News* on an international basis. Produced in Edelman's London office on an Apple Mac system with Quark Xpress software, proofs used to be couriered to Rockwell International's Pittsburgh headquarters for approval but not now.

To quote Bob Wells, 'It involved acquiring a communications software package called MicroPhone 11 which allowed Edelman's Apple Mac system to link up through a telephone link with Rockwell's Macs in Pittsburgh. . . . The pages of the complete newspaper — text, pictures, graphics, colours and tints — were transmitted across the Atlantic, allowing Rockwell to make on-screen corrections and then send the pages back to London. The whole process took a few hours instead of days.

'Now the only time paper is involved with *Rockwell News* is when it is printed; copy is written on word processors and transferred electronically to the Macs; pages are designed and made up on DTP; complete pages are transmitted by telephone line to Rockwell in the USA for approval and correction, and film for the printer is generated by the DTP.' The whole is put on disk and sent to the printer.

Designing and laying-out a publication using a desk-top publisher (reproduced by courtesy of British Gas North Thames).

PART FOUR

Practice of Public Relations

CHAPTER 23

Professional Codes of Conduct

VALUE OF PROFESSIONAL CODES

Codes of practice set standards for the profession, but they are limited to those who are members of organisations such as the Public Relations Consultants Association (whose members are consultancies) and the Institute of Public Relations (whose members are individuals). To be a member of these bodies requires acceptance of their codes, thus enhancing the reputation of these members in the eyes of outsiders including clients or employers and the media, while requiring professional conduct between members. The PRCA and IPR codes are similar in setting out what is permitted and what is not. The PRCA has an additional Investor Relations Code of Practice which has arisen since the deregulation of the London Stock Exchange, problems over sensitive financial information and the need to avoid 'insider trading', that is profiting from confidential financial information. The IPR and the Investor Relations codes are reproduced in this chapter.

The basic IPR code has not changed very much, except in clarification, but there has been a substantial change to 'Clause 9' which used to rule against payment by results. However, because consultancies handling privatisation flotations and take-over bids may be paid by results, e.g. bonuses if a programme is successful, this clause was reversed as Clause 3.9 to read 'A member shall not guarantee the achievement of results which are beyond the member's direct capacity to achieve or prevent.' Thus the clause still forbids guaranteeing a successful outcome of a campaign — which could include, say, promise of a certain volume of media coverage for a given fee — but it does not preclude payment in respect of genuine results, the word 'payment' now being deleted. The code is under constant review and the version published in this chapter is as amended by the Annual General Meeting in 1992.

COMPLAINTS PROCEDURE

Complaints about breaches of the IPR code should be made in writing to the Executive Director who will place them before the Professional Practices Committee which, if considered appropriate may refer the matter to the Disciplinary Committee. If the complaint is upheld it could result in suspension or reprimand without reference to Council. While complaints about members from non-members may be considered, it is not unusual to consider complaints from members about non-members. In practice, serious offences are rare, and complaints are often comparatively trivial matters which can be settled amicably.

A national code can have teeth, and in at

least three cases, the IPR Code has been applied rigorously. This may be a costly business if the defendant produces a legal defence, and the Institute has to employ counsel costing thousands of pounds. Again, a suspension could imperil a member's career and provoke a libel case which could bankrupt a voluntary body. On the other hand, a code has no power of law and cannot impose a fine or imprisonment.

An international code is difficult to impose since conditions will vary from country to country. There are, for example, certain countries in Europe where staff journalists can be paid to write public relations articles. In some African countries bribery is not unknown, e.g. the notorious 'envelope' containing money and given out to journalists at press receptions, 'taxi' money, donations to the Press Club, and banknotes blatantly pinned to news releases.

THE IPR CODE OF PROFESSIONAL CONDUCT

In addition to the Code, the Institute has issued guidelines to assist members to interpret the Code. These guidelines are inserted in italics after each clause.

Conduct towards the practice of public relations.

A member shall:

1.1 Have a positive duty to observe the highest standards in the practice of public relations and to deal fairly and honestly with employers and clients (past and present), fellow members and professionals, the public relations profession, other professions, suppliers, intermediaries, the media of communications, employees and the public.

This clause emphasises the fact that the Code applies to a member's relationships with many different 'publics'. The list may not be comprehensive.

1.2 Be aware of, understand and observe this Code, any amendments to it, and any other codes which shall be incorporated into it; remain up to date with the content and recommendations of any guidance or practice papers issued by IPR; and have a duty to conform to good practice as expressed in such guidance or practice papers.

The Code is not a piece of window dressing; members have a positive duty to observe the Code, follow any changes made to it and conform to any guidance or interpretation that may from time to time be agreed by the Institute's Council and promulgated to members.

1.3 Uphold this Code and cooperate with fellow members to enforce decisions on any matter arising from its application. A member who knowingly causes or allows his or her staff to act in a manner inconsistent with this Code is party to such action and shall be deemed to be in breach of this Code. Staff employed by a member who act in a manner inconsistent with this Code should be disciplined by the member.

Responsibility for upholding the Code and the principles it embodies does not apply solely to members' own behaviour, but also to the extent to which they can exercise influence over others, especially their staff and fellow members.

A member shall not:

1.4 Engage in any practice nor be seen to conduct him or herself in any manner detrimental to the reputation of the Institute or the reputation and interests of the public relations profession.

This is a 'catch-all' clause. If, for example, a member is seen to be drunk or found to be dishonest, such behaviour may be detrimental to the Institute or the public relations profession. Whether such behaviour is actually in breach of this clause would have to be judged on the particular circumstances of the case.

Conduct towards the public, the media and other professionals.

A member shall:

2.1 Conduct his or her professional activities with proper regard to the public interest.

This emphasises the importance of responsible behaviour by public relations practitioners. The public interest is not easy to define; a product may be in the interests of one section of the public but contrary to the interests of another. The Code calls for a responsible attitude to all sections of the public.

2.2 Have a positive duty at all times to respect the truth and shall not disseminate false or misleading information knowingly or recklessly, and take proper care to check all information prior to its dissemination.

This clause applies whether the member is an employer or an employee.

2.3 Have a duty to ensure that the actual interest of any organisation with which he or she may be professionally concerned is adequately declared.

A member representing a client or employer must make the client's interest known when making representations and in a manner which is straightforward and does not mislead. The use of a 'front' organisation or name suggesting an objective different from that of a member's client or employer is not permitted. An example would be a (hypothetical) 'Paint Advisory Service' whose title would suggest the availability of 'neutral' advice on any paint problem, but whose ultimate objective is the sale of a particular make of paint.

2.4 When working in association with other professionals, identify and respect the codes of those professions.

Unlike some professions, public relations work is not done in isolation. A member may be working closely with, for example, a journal-

-ist, accountant or lawyer and must take care that they or their professions are in no way compromised.

2.5 Respect any statutory or regulatory codes laid down by any other authorities which are relevant to the actions of his or her employer or client, or taken on behalf of an employer or client.

This is a warning about the many regulations or codes, voluntary and statutory, that may be relevant to an intended course of action. Where appropriate, members should familiarise themselves with these regulations and should not only avoid offending against them, but should also warn their employer or client against so doing.

2.6 Ensure that the names of all directors, executives, and retained advisers of his or her employers or company who hold public office, are members of either House of Parliament, Local Authorities or of any statutory organisation or body, are recorded in the IPR Register.

Members have a positive duty to declare, in the register, any public office holder retained by them or their employers. The register is maintained by the Institute and is available to members or non-members on request.

2.7. Honour confidences received or given in the course of professional activity.

Members can only work effectively if they have the confidence of their clients or employers. This clause emphasises that respecting such confidence is a professional duty and applies even if the connection with that employer or client has ended.

2.8 Neither propose nor undertake, or cause an employer or client to propose or undertake, any action which would be an improper influence on government, legislation, holders of public office or members of any statutory body or organisation, or the media of communication.

The purpose of public relations is to promote better mutual understanding and this should be the keynote in trying to impress on the media or on representatives of the government any need to effect changes in the law or the rules laid down by such organisations. It is for individual members to judge whether payments, gifts or other 'inducements' given to holders of public office other than those declared under 2.6, are in contravention of this clause. Though, in the event of a complaint, such judgement would fall to the Professional Practices Committee.

Conduct towards employers and clients.

A member shall:

3.1 Safeguard the confidences of both present and former employers or clients; shall not disclose or use these confidences to the disadvantage or prejudice of such employers or clients, or to the financial advantage of the member (unless the employer or client has released such information for public use, or has given specific permission for disclosure), except upon the order of a court of law.

This is an extension to clause 2.7, applying specifically to confidential information gained from past or present clients or employers. For example: a member may not give confidential information about one client to a competitor of the client, or provide information about a client to a third party in return for some sort of reward. There are various other ways in which this clause could be contravened, but the clause could be over-ruled by a Court of Law.

3.2 Inform an employer or client of any shareholding or financial interest held by that member or any staff employed by that member in any company or person whose services he or she recommends.

This safeguards employers or clients from possible undisclosed interests a member may have when recommending the use of a third party.

3.3 Be free to accept fees, commissions or other valuable considerations from persons other than an employer or client, if such considerations are disclosed to the employer or client.

This permits, for example, a percentage of printing costs being taken by a member, but only if this is disclosed to the client or employer. Although not specifically stated, it is implied in the Code that this disclosure should be at the time fees are agreed.

3.4 Be free to negotiate, or re-negotiate, with an employer or client terms that are a fair reflection of demands of the work involved and take into account factors others than hours worked and the experience involved. These special factors, which are also applied by other professional advisers shall have regard to all the circumstances of the specific situation and in particular to:

(a) The complexity of the issue, case, problem or assignment, and the difficulties associated with its completion.

(b) The professional or specialised skills required and the degrees of responsibility involved.

(c) The amount of documentation necessary to be perused or prepared, and its importance.

(d) The place and circumstances where the work is carried out, in whole or in part.

(e) The scope, scale and value of the task and its importance as an activity, issue or project to the employer or client.

Public relations work varies greatly in complexity and this clause sets out five factors to be taken into account in negotiating fee or salary. There may well be others. If circumstances change during the course of an assignment, a re-negotiation could be in order.

A member shall not:

3.5 Misuse information regarding his or her employer's or client's business for financial or other gain.

This clause refers to the misuse of any information about an employer's or client's business to a member's advantage whether or not the information is confidential.

3.6 Use inside information for gain. Nor may a member of staff managed or employed by a member directly trade in his or her employers' or clients' securities without the prior written permission of the employer or client and of the member's chief executive or chief financial officer or compliance officer.

'Inside information' is information about an employer or client obtained during the course of a member's employment which would not be fully available to outsiders. The clause applies particularly to information concerning the financial status of the company concerned. Statutory and regulatory provisions place strict conditions on the conduct of financial communications and on trading in the company's shares or other securities as required by the Stock Exchange's listing requirements.

3.7 Serve an employer or client under terms or conditions which might impair his or her independence, objectivity or integrity.

This clause is designed to protect members from unfair conditions being imposed that might impair their judgement or compromise their integrity. For example, members should not accept a condition seeking to cause them to publish false information, thus breaching clause 2.2.

3.8 Represent conflicting interests but may represent competing interests with the express consent of the parties concerned.

Example: it would be a breach to represent both Coca Cola and Pepsi Cola, but provided both parties agreed, a member might represent one of them and also a brewer or a retailer. If a member is in doubt about the possibility of two clients being in conflict, the clients' views should be sought before agreeing to represent them.

3.9 Guarantee the achievement of results

which are beyond the member's direct capacity to achieve or prevent.

In most of the campaigns which a public relations practitioner undertakes, the outcome is influenced by a number of factors only partially or not at all under the control of the practitioner. For example, a member acting for a company making a hostile bid for another would be quite wrong to guarantee success. Similarly it would be wrong to guarantee a specific amount of favourable press coverage.

Conduct towards colleagues.

A member shall:

4.1 Adhere to the highest standards of accuracy and truth, avoiding extravagant claims or unfair comparisons and giving credit for ideas and words borrowed from others.

All public relations work is concerned with ideas, which may come from various sources. Practitioners naturally want to lay claim to their successes, but must stick to the truth in doing so, give credit where it is due and not plagiarise other people's ideas.

4.2 Be free to represent his or her capabilities and service to any potential employer or client, either on his or her own initiative or at the behest of any client, provided in so doing he or she does not seek to break any existing contract or detract from the reputation of any member already serving that employer or client.

A member is, of course, free to seek new clients or a new employer but in doing so must not in any way denigrate another member who may be already working for the prospective client or employer. If a member is making a presentation to a prospective client it is usual and courteous to inform any existing member concerned, or at least to ask the 'prospect' to ignore the approach where PR needs are already being satisfactorily met.

A member shall not:

4.3 Injure the professional reputation or practice of another member.

This clause scarcely calls for further comment. It is not difficult to damage a person's or a corporation's professional reputation. To do so where a fellow member is concerned would contravene the Code if not the libel laws.

Interpreting the Code.

5.1 In the interpretation of this code the Laws of the Land shall apply.
Even the IPR Code is not above the law!

THE PRCA INVESTOR RELATIONS CODE OF PRACTICE

1. DEFINITION: 'Investor Relations' is defined as the specialist application of communications techniques and skills to the development and management of communications between a company or other entity, whose securities are publicly traded, and the holders are potential holders of its securitised capital instruments.

2. THE REGISTER:
   2.1 The PRCA will maintain a register of Investor Relations practitioners.
   2.2 All PRCA Members who practise Investor Relations must record this fact by placing themselves on the PRCA Investor Relations register.
   2.3 Each such consultancy so registered must also supply a copy of its current compliance and confidentiality policy to the PRCA.

3. LODGEMENT OF THE REGISTER:
   3.1 The PRCA will lodge a copy of the Investor Relations Register with the International Stock Exchange or whichever UK regulatory agency as from time to time be most appropriate.
   3.2 The PRCA will hold the copies of Members' compliance and confidentiality policies available for inspection by the International Stock Exchange or other appropriate regulatory agency.

4. DEALINGS IN SECURITIES: Every Member Firm registered as practising Investor Relations shall ensure that:
   (a) The Member Firm or its employees does not misuse confidential information for gain.
   (b) The consultancy, its members, staff or their next of kin do not deal in clients' securities without the prior written consent of the Compliance Officer or other senior officers designated by the Board.
   (c) Where the consultancy's own securities are publicly traded, no member of the staff may deal in these shares thout prior written consent of the Compliance Officer or the Chairman.

5. ADMINISTRATIVE ARRANGEMENTS TO SECURE ENFORCEMENT OF THE DEALING RULES: Every firm registered as an Investor Relations practitioner shall:
   (a) Designate a senior member of the organisation as the Compliance Officer, whose duty it shall be to enforce compliance with the Code hin the organisation.
   (b) Have a written compliance and confidentiality policy which must be incorporated into every employee's employment terms and conditions.
   (c) Ensure that the Compliance Officer requires all employees to lodge details of any client shareholdings or nominee holdings in companies publicly traded within the UK on joining the company.
   (d) Ensure that all details of acquisitions and all transactions in such companies by employees subsequent to joining are declared to the Compliance Officer.

6. CONFIDENTIALITY — GENERAL: Every Member Firm shall safeguard the confidence of both present and former clients and shall not disclose or use these confidences, at any time, to the disadvantage or prejudice of such clients or to the financial advantage of the Member Firm,

unless the client has released such information for public use, or has given specific permission for its disclosure; except upon the order of a court of law.

7. CONFIDENTIALITY — PRICE SENSITIVE ANNOUNCEMENTS: Every Member Firm registered as an Investor Relations practitioner shall ensure that:

(a) All members of its staff retain confidentiality regarding price sensitive items relating to clients companies listed on the International Stock Exchange until they have been officially released in the manner required by the ISE regulations.

(b) All members of staff must retain confidentiality regarding price sensitive information relating to other client companies not listed on the ISE (whether domestic or overseas) until the appropriate announcements have been made public.

(c) Their clients fully appreciate the requirements of the current regulations relevant to the particular case regarding the release of price sensitive information and that they are informed that, under the PRCA Charter, a Member Firm is not permitted to serve a client under terms or conditions which might impair its independence, objectivity and integrity and that this covers the acceptance of instructions that are in breach of the ISE or other relevant regulations regarding the release of price sensitive information.

8. SCOPE OF THE CODE:

8.1 All Member Firms registered as Investor Relations practitioners shall uphold this code and cooperate with fellow practitioners in seeing that this is done. This code applies to the staff of Member Firms individually as well as to the organisation.

8.2 Member Firms shall see that the Compliance Officer ensures that existing and future clients are made aware of the compliance and confidentiality procedures.

OTHER CODES

Many public relations bodies around the world also have their codes, often based on the IPR Code but reflecting national situations. The International Public Relations Association has its International Code of Ethics (Code of Athens) which reiterates the Universal Declaration of Human Rights and expresses the following four stipulations:

'Each member shall refrain from subordinating the truth to other requirements; circulating information which is not based on established and ascertainable facts; taking part in any venture or undertaking which is unethical or dishonest or capable of impairing human dignity and integrity; using any "manipulation" methods or techniques designed to create sub-conscious motivations which the individual cannot control of his/her own free will and so cannot be held accountable for the action taken on them.'

IPRA also has its charter which resembles the Code of Professional Conduct of the IPR.

CODE FOR COMMUNICATION ON ENVIRONMENT AND DEVELOPMENTS

Ratified at the IPRA Council meeting in Nairobi in November 1991 was the following very topical new code which has nine clauses:

1. IPRA Members accept that they have a responsibility to ensure that the information and counsel which they provide and products or services which they promote, fall within the context of sustainable development.

2. Members shall endeavour to encourage their organisations, companies or clients to adopt policies which recognise that

careless use of resources and disregard for the environment can lead to severe limitations for economic growth, grave social disruption and serious health hazards.

3. Members shall, where appropriate, counsel their companies, clients or organisations to undertake regular environmental assessments of products and operations and to produce and communicate environmental codes of practice or guidelines for their employees and other publics.

4. Members shall not publicise or promote products, organisations or services as having environmental benefit unless these benefits are demonstrable in the light of current science and knowledge.

5. Members shall endeavour at all times to promote openness and dialogue which fairly handle both facts and concerns related to the environment and development.

6. Members shall not seek to raise or respond to unrealistic environmental expectations but shall generally support organisations, products or services which are provably taking steps to improve environmental performance in a timescale which takes account of community concerns and government requirements as well as technological and economic constraints.

7. Members shall seek to develop programs which counsel and communicate on the benefit of a balanced consideration of environmental, economic and social development factors.

8. Members shall provide a free flow of information within and through IPRA concerning environmental and development issues on an international level.

9. Members should be familiar with, and encourage the organisations they work for to support, and abide by, Codes of Practice of other internationally recognised organisations such as the United Nations and International Chamber of Commerce.

CHAPTER 24

Overseas Public Relations

SOME PROBLEMS DISCUSSED

Overseas public relations — no matter which is the PRO's home country or operating base — offers attractions concerning exports and problems regarding comprehension and the physical ability to communicate. It can be a total waste of time to undertake a blind mailing to overseas publications whose addresses have been taken from a directory, especially if the story is sent out untranslated on the assumption that everybody speaks English. If the exporter has no overseas subsidiaries or selling agents with public relations staff, it will be wise to appoint overseas consultants who are either nationals operating in their own countries or ones who are familiar with the media and the methods in a particular area such as the Single European Market. Such people will not merely translate, they will rewrite stories in the necessary languages.

Before examining the various ways in which the press officer can extend his efforts overseas let us first begin with the PRO whose main task is to do with the home market. The chances are that with very little extra effort, present work can be made to gain greater recognition for the organisation. First, the sales department must be asked whether overseas sales are wanted, or whether because of restricted franchises or because of import restrictions in certain countries it is not desired

that effort be squandered where it can do no good. Policies must be clearly understood by the press officer.

A few examples of these problems may be helpful to the reader. A company selling chemical products found it wise to avoid the South American markets because home production was encouraged in those countries. A UK company, marketing a German-made machine, had to avoid press coverage in the German-speaking parts of Europe. A British company producing a very specialised machine for the printing industry was faced with the problem that there was only a handful of potential buyers in the UK and that sales could only be made on a world basis. Consequently, when a machine was sold to Brazil, and then another to Greece, these sales made ideal stories for overseas distribution, and both the COI and the World Services of the BBC at Bush House made good use of this information.

Particular problems are therefore worth analysing at the outset.

1. Translations

It is not merely a matter of translating English into a foreign language, or a number of languages, but the translation must be intelligible. If jargon appears in the original, it must be explained in a translation. Some words such as 'pig', 'stone', 'blanket', 'plate' and 'sample' have precise technical meanings in English, but a literal translation could be rude, funny or incomprehensible. Countries in the Far East and in Australia may be used to American terminology, and a British expression could be misinterpreted. The terminology of the motor car industry is quite different and so are some of the spellings, e.g. gear lever (shift), boot (trunk) and tyre (tire). A story sent to North America needs to be translated into American. There is an American translation of one of this author's books!

Moreover, while it may be true that a foreign editor speaks English, the journal will be written and read in the national language, so the news release needs to be translated.

Translators should be familiar with the current idiom of the country into whose language material is being translated. Ideally, the translator will be a national. If technical jargon is used, a definition should be supplied to the translator. One of the best ways to secure accurate translations is to re-translate a foreign version back into English to see if there are any errors of meaning. Some languages have very limited vocabularies and it may be necessary to use an English word. Problems occur with Malay and Indonesian languages, which are similar, and have no plurals.

Care also has to be taken with words which have offensive or double meanings in other languages. This can apply to brand names which cannot be translated and could cause problems. Or the same name may be used for a totally different product.

The writing also needs to be kept as simple as possible, otherwise strange or unfamiliar words may be leap-frogged and a different meaning can be applied, even when material in English is supplied to English-speaking countries but where, once again, the vocabulary is limited. An example can be taken from an examination paper in public relations. The question asked was 'why do editors seldom want colour pictures'. The word *seldom* was unknown by some African students who read

the opposite meaning into the question. Consequently, it pays to write in simple Anglo-Saxon English, using words like live instead of *reside*, and house rather than *residence*.

Whether material for overseas publication is in English or a foreign language, it is imperative that nothing is taken for granted. Simple words have different meanings in some parts of the world, or different words are used. For example, exhibition language can vary. In Britain, we may refer to a 'stand', but in some countries the word is 'booth'. We may 'exhibit' while others may 'expose', and 'exposition' is used rather than 'exhibition'. It is necessary, therefore, that any word used must be readily understood and incapable of a different or a double meaning. Similarly, care has to be taken over addresses which must state the country since there are places with British and other national place names all over the world. Care also has to be taken to distinguish the sex of people, and which is the surname and which is the forename. In many Eastern countries the surname is given first, as the author has frequently discovered on his travels where he has been addressed as Mr Frank.

2. Public relations and Europe

The Single European Market promises to become a communications monster of between 17 and 24 nations as the remaining EFTA countries (Austria, Norway and Switzerland) are admitted plus possibly Cyprus, Czechoslovakia, Finland, Hungary, Malta and Poland. Where will its boundaries end? The Balkans, Turkey, Russia?

Two contradictory trends are at work in Europe. First, there is the unifying of the industrialised nations to form the equivalent of the USA. Second, there is a complexity of nation states, ethnic groups, languages and religions. We are being enticed into both camps which means that we have to relearn the communications process which was comparatively simple in Britain with its highly urbanised, physically well communicated, virtually one language society serviced by mass and national media.

As Janie Jeffreys of EIBIS (see later section) says, 'You can't take 10 000 editors out to lunch. That's roundly the number of good industrial, technical, business and special-interest publications in the Community countries.' That's only in those EC members, at the time of writing, whose language is not English.

3. Media of overseas public relations

As will be discussed in the following section on 'Means', media in overseas countries vary from those in Britain where we enjoy a great variety of printed and broadcast media, much of it national, because Britain is a compact, highly urbanised, well educated, literate, and prosperous country where most people speak the same language. Even in North America some of these conditions do not apply: media tend to be more localised or regionalised and other languages such as Spanish are becoming common. The sheer size of some countries such as Australia, India, Indonesia and the USA creates differences between their media and the British.

To conduct overseas public relations does require an open-minded approach to geography and wholly different economic and social situations. Much can be learned from the notes which precede country sections in *Benn's Media Directory* (Europe and World) editions, and the very useful *Royal Mail International Business Travel Guide*, while country-by-country reviews are published by *The Economist*, several banks and the Department of Trade and Industry.

The DTI has a number of *Hints to Exporters* booklets relating to particular countries which are published at £5 per country by DTI Export Publications, PO Box 55, Stratford on Avon, Warwickshire, CV37 9GE. The DTI also publishes a useful monthly journal, *Overseas Trade*, which may be obtained free of charge from DTI

Overseas Trade Services at Room 802, Bridge Place, Eccleston Square, London, SW1V 0PT.

MEANS OF CONDUCTING OVERSEAS PUBLIC RELATIONS

(i) British journals with overseas circulations

In many industries, trades and professions, American and British journals have international circulations, partly because they are accepted as world authorities on their subjects, partly because it would not be economic to produce similar journals in some countries, but also because it would be uneconomic to publish such journals in America and especially Britain unless there was not a circulation beyond that possible in the country of origin. Yet another reason is that the English language is not limited to the Americas and Commonwealth countries, but is commonly used in foreign countries such as Indonesia and in much of Europe.

A number of newspapers are published internationally, making use of satellite facilities to print overseas, the *Financial Times* and the *Economist* being examples. The *Economist* is unusual in having two-fifths of its circulation of 400 000 in North America.

(ii) Overseas news agencies

In addition to Reuters, Belgian, French, German, Italian, Spanish, Swiss, Bulgarian, Czech, Slovakian, Hungarian, Polish, Romanian, Russian, Canadian, United States, Egyptian, Israeli, Ghanaian, Pakistani, Chinese and Australian news agencies are located in London, and their addresses can be found in the *Hollis Press and Public Relations Annual* and *Benn's Media Directory*.

(iii) Overseas press correspondents

There are also London representatives of leading foreign and Commonwealth newspapers and magazines, some being full-time staff but others part-time correspondents who probably have a full-time job elsewhere and so are rarely free to attend press receptions.

(iv) Freelance writers, press services

According to the country or topic, there are many freelance writers and news services which specialise in supplying certain types of material. Once the press officer begins to send material overseas he or she is likely to be contacted by them, but a number are well-known in their fields, and most of them prepare reports on British exhibitions for overseas journals. Since they operate permanently in Britain and do their own translating, they are very useful to know.

(v) Overseas press mailing lists/services

English-language and translated public relations material can be sent direct to overseas editors. Addresses can be selected from the Europe and World volumes of *Benn's Media Directory*, or from *Advertisers Annual, Willings Press Guide*, and *PR-Planner Europe*. Or they can be selected from the lists offered by PIMS and Two-Ten Communications who will despatch stories. Two-Ten (formerly UNS/PNA) have a computerised satellite service which can distribute press material to 3 500 publications in 138 countries, supplementing this with translation services. Instantaneous satellite transmission can be done in minutes.

(vi) External house journals

These may be one of the most practical methods of communicating direct with overseas government buyers, importers, agents, franchise holders and so on. In some cases, when the market is mostly among English-speaking countries, an English language magazine will be adequate, but otherwise it will be necessary to print in, say, French, German, Italian, Spanish and Portuguese if the journal is to be read in Europe, South America, the Middle East and former European colonies in Africa. The Dutch and the Scandinavians will accept journals in English, but elsewhere such as Japan, other languages will be necessary. For Gulf countries, alternate pages in Arabic and English are possible because in these countries there may be a hundred or more immigrant nationalities for whom English may be a common language.

One advantage of an international house journal is that the contents can be taken from overseas sources, pictures and articles showing British products in use by different nationalities. This makes them more directly relevant to overseas readers than if the material was purely British-based. Stories and pictures can be invited from overseas agents and customers. The author once edited an international house journal in which every item came from a different overseas source, each one describing how the company's products were used for different purposes the world over. For example, a combine harvester can be built in various versions to suit the particular crops and conditions in different parts of the world. An international house journal which described and illustrated local uses would be much more interesting than one in which the contents were limited to British or even European uses.

In Britain we are extremely fortunate in having a number of printers who are highly skilled at producing foreign-language print, having special design, translation and foreign typesetting facilities.

The external house journal is an impressive form of overseas public relations work, and it could become very valuable in communicating with Single European Market countries and also those of the prospering Pacific Rim countries.

(vii) Overseas public relations consultancies

There may be good reasons for using the services of overseas consultancies which can be relied upon to produce translations and know local media. There are networked consultancies such as Burson–Marsteller, Edelman, Hill & Knowlton and Shandwick which have offices world-wide, while smaller ones have overseas associates. Use of overseas consultancies may be necessary when a campaign is required simultaneously as with the global launch of a new product, or for some kind of world tour.

(viii) Video news releases

VNRs are discussed more fully in Chapter 21, but here it is worth mentioning a development of the 1990s which has borrowed from the American system of distributing VNRs to the continent's broadcasters by satellite. British firms such as Bulletin and Visnews can negotiate use of VNRs by foreign television stations. Visnews, with its ownership by Reuters, has a well-established international news service. With international satellite facilities, it is possible to use the edge of the tape to communicate messages to and from television stations in order to arrange supply of VNRs. Visnews supply 650 broadcasters in 84 countries, plus affiliate stations such as NBC, TV Globo of Brazil, and DDI of India, bringing the total of overseas users of Visnews services to 1600. Provided the public relations content does not offend the integrity of the news and information facilities Visnews has established since 1957, this is an excellent means of distributing material for use in news bulletins and other programmes. VCRs should not be confused with documentary videos. Rather, they are kits of action shots and scenes which can be screened in association with a news reader. Their subject matter and likely acceptance can be negotiated before shooting.

(ix) Overseas press conferences/receptions

As in Britain it is possible to invite journalists to attend press functions, but each country needs to be studied to learn its peculiarities and possibilities. Not many countries have as centralised a press as Britain does. Most European countries have press centres based on regional cities, and to deal with media nationally the main method may be through news agencies which distribute news to regional publications. In some countries, where the press is less free, it may be necessary to deal with state news agencies which will have power to censor material. In others a press function will be regarded as a great party occasion and could go on for hours with need for extensive hospitality. It is not unknown in some Third World countries for a press function to depend on some form of bribery such as a donation to the Press Club, or personal payments to journalists who take the view that they are poorly paid and are being expected to do favours for rich foreign companies. The habits and styles of some countries may defy normal ethics of public relations behaviour, and one does not have to do more than cross the Channel to discover this let alone chance one's luck in West Africa.

(x) DTI new products from Britain service

This is an international service run by the Department of Trade and Industry in collaboration with the Central Office of Information and British Embassy information staff in some 30 countries. It is a free Government sponsored service available to any British exporter, and may in itself be a simple way of conducting overseas press relations, especially by the smaller company with little to spend on public relations.

Clearly, the subject must be newsworthy and it can deal with a service as well as a product. It helps if the exporter has an agent or some other distribution service in the countries to which the story is sent. Photographs — and not just catalogue pictures — are welcome.

If the information and picture is sent to the DTI, and is accepted, a news release will be produced by the COI and this will be checked with the exporter. Translations will be made as necessary for the selected countries, and releases and pictures despatched to the embassies for distribution to local media.

Results can be surprising. One company received 100 enquiries from the ASEAN countries and was able to set up distributors in Korea, Indonesia and Singapore plus New Zealand. Another such story produced 200 enquiries and resulted in the setting up of distributors in Canada, The Netherlands, Japan and South Africa. As can be seen, this particular service can identify demand in perhaps unexpected places.

(xi) EIBIS International

For more than 30 years, EIBIS — the initials stood for Engineering in Britain Information Service but EIBIS is not confined to engineering — has built up a relationship with editors throughout the world who receive with respect news releases, feature articles and photographs supplied by EIBIS. Today, EIBIS has assembled an analysis of the world's technical, industrial and commercial press covering 27 000 journals, newspapers, news agencies and information services which are then divided into more than 450 subject categories and seven marketing areas. Thus, a client can decide exactly where a public relations story is to be sent.

The client sends information to EIBIS whose writers prepare releases, articles or photo captions, writing them in clear, simple prose, that is factual and authoritative and is readily translatable. EIBIS are experts at producing translations, using individual translators working in their own countries who are familiar with current idiom and the latest terminology.

This service is particularly valuable for those interested in the Single European Market, but EIBIS covers the world, and for those wishing to export to Pacific Rim countries. Janie Jeffreys, managing director of EIBIS has written a booklet *The Export Challenge of the*

Pacific. In it she points out that Japan has more than 1000 useful industrial publications, South Korea has around 100, and Taiwan, Hong Kong and Singapore between 20 and 50 specialist titles each, while China has more than 700 serious technical/industrial titles. English predominates in many Asiatic countries, except China, Japan and Korea.

(xii) BBC World Service

This is similar to the DTI/COI service described above, except that it provides the additional services of the BBC which is highly respected overseas. At the time of writing its most appropriate programme for exports is *New Ideas* (20 minutes on Monday afternoons) which is a vehicle for British products and services. It provides 'a window on the world of technology, innovation and new products', being ones which are a credit to Britain.

The BBC World Service broadcasts in 37 languages including English, with the addition of Ukrainian in April 1992. It publishes two books *Nation to Nation* and *A World in Your Ear* which describe the Service.

(xiii) Central Office of Information

The COI has been streamlined in recent years and no longer has a separate overseas department. Moreover it has become an executive agency, primarily acting on behalf of more than 100 central Government agencies but also able to act for other public sector clients. In so doing it is cost effective in recovering not less than the prime costs of all services other than those covered by other official funds. Figure 24.1 is an organisational chart of the COI's functions.

The work of the COI is thus more concerned with the publicity work of government departments and agencies, handling it like a national advertising agency and public relations consultancy, but contracting out 85% to advertising agencies. Consequently, it has become far less concerned with distributing private sector information to overseas media. An exception is

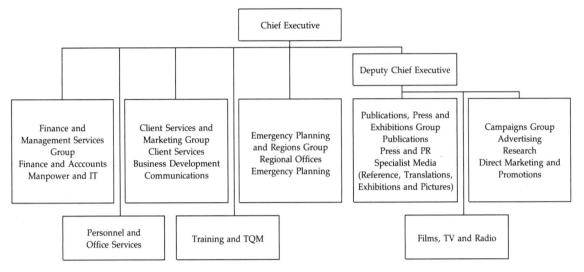

Figure 24.1   Departmental chart of the Central Office of Information

trade promotion publicity carried out on behalf of the DTI (see above), which includes some 2600 stories a year on new products, trade mission participants and UK exhibitors at overseas trade fairs.

Otherwise the COI concentrates on the issue of information about Britain as such (e.g. coverage of major conferences), or on national topics like the Channel Tunnel, research at the Royal Observatory in Edinburgh or the Farnborough Air Show.

Government department and agency topics can be of international significance, and for this purpose the COI runs a first-class translation and foreign print service. The Foreign Languages Unit translates, revises and proofreads in more than 30 languages, mainly for

the Foreign and Commonwealth Office but also for the DTI, MAFF and the Civil Service Commission. Work for the FCO, which includes the production of many foreign language magazines, runs into about £18 million a year. The COI has an overseas radio service supplying material to radio stations in more than 100 countries, doing so by satellite and telephone links.

While most of the overseas distribution is of government department or agency activities, or about major events in Britain which make good news about Britain, news about products for exports continues to be sent to some 140 overseas posts but should now be sent to the DTI on whose behalf they will be distributed by the COI.

CHAPTER 25

Academic and Professional Qualifications

The recognised professional qualification in public relations is membership of the Institute of Public Relations which in 1993 had more than 5000 members. The recognised academic qualification is the CAM Diploma in Public Relations, and in 1992 it became necessary to hold the DipCAM or an accepted equivalent plus the required length of practical experience to become a full Member of the IPR.

In recent years, degrees in public relations have been awarded by British and Irish colleges and universities. The first, a post-graduate MBA in Public Relations at Cranfield School of Management, proved to be a disappointing failure. Stirling University has been more successful with its MSc in Public Relations, probably because it did not rely on part-time British students but could take overseas students on either a full-time or distance learning basis. First degrees of a pre-entry nature are offered by a number of universities. The DipCAM is not intended as a pre-entry examination.

Of a more introductory nature is the Group Diploma of the London Chamber of Commerce and Industry which is popular world-wide, and is accepted as one of the entry requirements for the CAM Certificate in Communication Studies.

An interesting 1-year diploma course in International Public Relations is that run for

several years by the West Herts College (formerly Watford College).

From the following brief notes on available academic and professional qualifications it will be seen that education and training is now plentiful in Britain. There are excellent opportunities to become proficient in a communications career. Studies may be undertaken at many colleges and universities and by distance learning. In addition, there are many short seminars of from 1 day to 3 weeks duration. As the chapters of this book imply, public relations has become a very complex subject which demands considerable personal knowledge and skill. From the most untrained profession in the world it is becoming one where earning power means doing power. No longer will it do to be an ex-journalist with ability to read a menu and a wine list. It is significant that in a period of recession, the reason often quoted for taking the CAM exams was to gain security.

LONDON CHAMBER OF COMMERCE AND INDUSTRY

This is probably the oldest and largest independent business studies examining organisation in the world, and it has held examinations for more than 100 years. Of special interest to those interested in the marketing and communications business, there are Third Level Certificate examinations in Advertising, Marketing, Public Relations and Selling and Sales Management. A Group Diploma may be obtained in three or all four of these subjects if sat and passed at the same time. The Group Diploma in Advertising, Marketing and Public Relations is accepted by CAM in lieu of other educational awards, while Distinctions (75 percent) in these subjects will qualify for exemptions from the same subjects in the CAM Certificate in Communication Studies.

No entry qualifications are required and the LCCI Diploma is a good pre-entry qualification with use of the designatory letters (ALCC) for which an annual fee is necessary. LCCI examinations are held in the UK and in many parts of the world in April, June and November.

The Regulations, Syllabuses and Timetables may be purchased from the LCCI Examinations Board, Marlowe House, Station Road, Sidcup, Kent, DA15 7BJ. Telephone: 081 302 0261.

COMMUNICATION ADVERTISING AND MARKETING EDUCATION FOUNDATION

CAM is the vocational examining body for the British advertising and public relations professions, and its Diploma is of near degree status. Six subjects have to be passed to secure the Certificate in Communication Studies, and then three to obtain the Diploma DipPR(CAM). The Certificate subjects are Advertising, Marketing, Public Relations, Sales Promotion and Direct Marketing, Media, and Research and Behavioural Studies. The core subject for the Diploma is Management and Strategy, and two other subjects have to be taken according to the chosen option. For the CAM Diploma in Public Relations, the other two subjects are Public Relations Management and Public Relations Practice.

Examinations for the Certificate are held in June and November and for the Diploma in June. Entry requirements are a degree, or two A Levels plus three O Levels or GCSEs, one of which must be English Language, the LCCI Group Diploma, or an acceptable business studies certificate or diploma. Exemptions may be possible on a subject for subject basis. Holders of the CIM Diploma are exempt from the Certificate subjects with the exception of public relations. Senior candidates with 7 years practical experience may be awarded exemption from the whole of the Certificate. It is necessary to be a Registered student before being accepted for the Certificate examinations, and to be registered again for the Diploma examinations.

The average CAM student is a graduate, aged between 25 and 35 years, with 3 years experience. Although students may take the examinations overseas they have to show proof that they can follow a suitable course, and that local invigilation can be arranged. However, the examination questions are UK-oriented and it is difficult for students living abroad to cope with these examinations if they lack British working experience.

Since 1992, applicants for full membership of the Institute of Public Relations have to possess the CAM Diploma (or its equivalent). Syllabuses, Regulations and a registration form may be obtained from the CAM Foundation, Abford House, 15 Wilton Road, London, SW1V 1NJ. Telephone: 071 828 7506.

WEST HERTS COLLEGE/PRCA DIPLOMA IN INTERNATIONAL PUBLIC RELATIONS

This important diploma has been offered by the college (formerly Watford College) for many years, and has become well established. It is a 1-year course with a 3-week consultancy placement at the end of the second term, and a 1-week exchange visit with a French college is arranged in the final term. The Diploma itself is awarded on the results of the final term examinations in the main subject areas plus continuous assessment, and assessment/project grades in all other disciplines. In addition to college examinations, two external examinations are taken: these are the IPT print paper, and the RSA or LCCI foreign language paper.

Subjects covered are print, design, writing for the media, video, photography, broadcasting, public relations, public relations media, advertising, psychology, market research, international marketing, languages, law and management disciplines.

Address: West Herts College, Hempstead Road, Watford, Herts, WD1 3EZ.

BOURNEMOUTH UNIVERSITY

The Department of Marketing, Advertising and Public Relations at this university offers a BA(Hons) 4 year CNAA sandwich course in public relations, and was the first in Britain to do so. The first 2 years cover a range of relevant topics, the second year builds on this broad base, the third year takes students outside to placements, and the final year brings together what students have learned in college and on placement and deepens understanding, knowledge and skills. The course is augmented by visits from public relations professionals.

First year subjects are: mass communication and society, organisations: behavioural and communication, introduction to public relations, professional skills and perceptions, public affairs and introduction to marketing. *Second year* subjects are: attitudes, persuasion and influence, inter personal and group communication, corporate public relations, professional skills and perspectives, finance and accounting for public relations, commercial and media law for public relations, opinion assessment and campaign evaluation. *Third year*: professional attachment to a public relations consultancy and an in-house public

relations unit. *Fourth year*: specialist PR themes, project workshop, public relations strategies, public relations issues, public relations management, and a group project.

Basic admission requirements are five O Levels including English at B grade and mathematics, or two A Levels at B grade, or three A Levels at B, C and C grades. Certain other qualifications, and mature students, are considered.

Address: Department of Marketing, Advertising and Public Relations, Bournemouth University, Dorset House, Talbot Campus, Fern Barrow, Poole, Dorset BH12 5BB.

DUBLIN INSTITUTE OF TECHNOLOGY

The College of Commerce at this Irish Institute offers a 1-year course for its Diploma in Public Relations. Introduced in 1979 as a certificate course, it was the first of its kind in Ireland, and was redesigned as a Diploma, particularly in response to its graduate intake. The course consists of two 15 week semesters. Assessment is by a combination of continuous assessment, assigned practical work and written examinations.

Subjects covered are: (*First semester*) Public relations theory and practice, journalistic and public relations writing, management, print production and office technology, television and video in public relations practice, marketing, social psychology and interpersonal behaviour, the legal environment, modern European language. (*Second semester*) Public relations theory and practice, advertising, mass media, theory of mass communication, photography, public relations implications of current issues, the political environment, modern European language.

Admission is by degree, third-level diploma of three years full-time duration, third-level certificate of two years full-time duration with credit or distinction, or an equivalent educational or professional qualification.

Address: College of Commerce, Dublin Institute of Technology, Rathmines Road, Dublin, Ireland.

LEEDS METROPOLITAN UNIVERSITY BUSINESS SCHOOL

At Leeds Metropolitan University, the Business School offers a full-time or part-time BA(Hons) Public Relations Studies. The full-time programme runs for 3 years, but the part-time one is more variable. At the time of writing, it is the only degree level course in public relations available in the North of England.

The course structure has three levels and a number of indicative options. *Level 1* consists of introduction to public relations, public relations and the media, public relations practice, parts 1 and 2, people in organisations, IT for business, business context, quantitative business analysis, business economics, business accounting, language modules 1 and 2, and transferable business skills. *Level 2*: the graphics of communication, public relations and politics, public relations planning and management, public relations practice, parts 3 and 4, philosophy and the communications industry, business applications software, the sociology of work organisations, and marketing principles, language modules 3 and 4, and research methods. *Level 3*: corporate relations, public relations practice, parts 5 and 6, specialist public relations, group project: the public relations audit, dissertations, language modules 5 and 6, corporate strategy, and an option (e.g. international marketing, marketing management, organisational behaviour, power, society and the state, etc.).

Entry requirements include A Level CCC grades, BTEC full-time with three distinctions, four merits in final year, BTEC part-time with three distinctions, three merits over 2 years, and certain other qualifications plus mature students.

Address: Leeds Business School, Leeds Metropolitan University, Queen Square House, Woodhouse Lane, Leeds, West Yorkshire, LS2 8AB.

NAPIER UNIVERSITY, EDINBURGH

The Department of Print Media, Publishing and Communication offers a 3-year BA Communication. There are core modules for Communication plus elective subjects, the number of which will grow.

First year core modules are: communications modelling, mass communication, psychology, linguistics, research methods, media production and writing for the media 1, presentation 1, and integration project 1. *Two modules* elected from: European Studies 1, French 1, Italian 1, German 1, mass media 1 (newspapers and magazines), design 1 (visual communication), print production, accreditation of work-based learning 1.

Second year core modules: organisational communication, marketing, market research, media law, media production 2, presentation 2, and integration project 2. *Three modules* elected from: European studies 2, French 2, Italian 2, German 2, design 2 (graphic communication), mass media 2 (TV studies), literary codes, sociology of culture, business enterprise, and accreditation of work-based learning 2.

Third year core modules: professional communication, public relations, advertising, employee-communication, media buying, influencing attitudes, and integrative project 111. *Four modules* elected from European Studies 3, French 3, Italian 3, German 3, design 3 (media design), design 3 (advertising design), mass media 3 (film studies), modernism and accreditation of work-based learning 3.

Minimum academic requirements are: three SCE Higher passes, including at least a B pass in Higher English, plus O grade passes in at least two other subjects, or two GCE A Level passes, including at least a C pass in A Level English language or literature plus O Level passes in at least three further subjects, or a range of National Certificate modules, or other acceptable equivalent. Those wishing to take a foreign language as an elective subject should have at least an O grade pass in French or German.

Address: Department of Print Media, Publishing and Communication, Napier University, 219 Colinton Road, Edinburgh, EH14 1DJ, Scotland.

ST MARK AND ST JOHN COLLEGE, PLYMOUTH

This Church of England voluntary college, known as Marjon, offers a modular BA(Hons) in Public Relations as one of a number of options. The format is therefore different from that of the other public relations degrees described in this chapter. There is a special public relations subject handbook which covers theory and general practice, specialist skills and knowledge 1, theory and context, specialist skills and knowledge 2, ethics of public relations, public relations project, and advanced knowledge and theory.

Under a modular degree, students choose a combination of two subjects (of which public relations could be one), taken as major or minor routes. A major route consists of eight or more modules, and a minor route involves at least six modules. A typical plan is to take one major and one minor route to produce a total of 18 modules.

Entry requirements are passes in five subjects of which two must be at A Level and GCSE/GCEs must be graded C or above and include English language. Equivalent qualifications will be considered. Mature students must have passes in four subjects, of which one must be at A Level and GCSE/GCEs must be graded C or above, or an acceptable equivalent.

Address: The College of St Mark and St John Foundation, Derriford Road, Plymouth, Devon, PL6 8BH.

UNIVERSITY OF STIRLING

The School of Management at the University of Stirling offers a full-time MSc in Public Relations, and a Diploma and MSc in Public Relations by distance learning.

The 1-year post-graduate course has Autumn and Spring semesters. The *Autumn semester* covers public relations theory and practice 1, communications 1, economic principles of public relations, management and marketing, the media and society, working with the media, and design editorial management. The *Spring semester* has two options from subjects such as financial public relations, political public relations and audio and video production plus media practicals, advertising and promotion, business ethics, communications 2, and public relations theory and practice 2, followed by a dissertation project.

Entry requirements for both the full-time and the distance learning MSc are a first degree, but applications are considered from those with significant public relations experience.

The 3-year distance learning post-graduate course offers an MSc in Public Relations for 30 credits, a Diploma in Public Relations for 22 credits, and a Certificate in Public Relations for 16 credits.

The programme content is as follows: *Foundation year*: public relations and its environment, introduction to public relations, communication principles and practice, and general management and marketing. *Certificate year*: consumer and industrial/technological public relations, international communication and the media, corporate, financial and public affairs, public relations for governmental and non-profit-making organisations. *Diploma and MSc year*: business ethics and legal restraints, public relations management, public relations case studies, and a project consisting of an indepth study of an aspect of public relations. There are also 1-week residential schools, set up at Stirling, in North America and the Far East.

Addresses: (Full-time MSc). The Admissions Office, School of Management, University of Stirling, Stirling, Scotland, FK9 4LA. (Distance Learning). School Office, School of Accountancy, Business, Computing and Economics, University of Stirling, Stirling, Scotland, FK9 4LA.

INSTITUTE OF PUBLIC RELATIONS

This is the British professional body for individual public relations practitioners, and was founded in 1948. There are five main forms of membership, student, affiliate, associate, member and fellow. *Student* membership is available to those over 18 years of age who are studying on an IPR recognised examination course in public relations and lasts for 3 years. *Affiliates* are bona-fide practitioners in public relations or carrying out a specialist role in public relations but do not qualify for any other grade of membership. *Associates* must have 3 years substantial experience in public relations and may use the designatory letters AMIPR.

To be eligible for full *membership* it is necessary to have had at least 4 years substantial experience at operating executive level and to hold an acceptable academic qualification. The latter may be the CAM public relations diploma, a full-time degree in public relations or similar qualification approved by the IPR Education and Training Committee, or an approved overseas qualification. Membership is also awarded to those with at least 10 years experience in public relations of which not less than 4 years shall have been in a senior appointment, or who have at least 10 years experience in senior management and hold a senior public relations appointment in a major organisation. Members have full voting rights and may use the letters MIPR.

Fellowships are awarded in recognition of outstanding work in public relations. Fellows may use the letters FIPR and have the same voting rights as members. Fellows are elected by Council on the basis of a citation supported by two sponsors.

Address: Institute of Public Relations, The Old Trading House, 15 Northburgh Street, London EC1V 0PR.

INTERNATIONAL PUBLIC RELATIONS ASSOCIATION

Founded in 1955, this association consists of senior public relations practitioners in some 70 countries. It holds annual meetings in different countries, and world congresses every 3 years in major cities throughout the world. A notable activity has been the publishing of Gold Papers, two of which have been on education which have influenced university courses in Britain. The distance learning course at Stirling University is pioneered by IPRA. The association holds Golden World Awards for public relations programmes.

Address: International Public Relations Association, Case Postale 2100, CH–1211 Geneva 2, Switzerland.

INTERNATIONAL ASSOCIATION OF BUSINESS COMMUNICATORS

Formed by the amalgamation of US and Canadian house journal editors' organisations, and broadening its scope to cover internal and other communications activities, IABC has chapters in 14 countries including the UK. It has a Gold Quill Awards programme, and holds accreditation examinations permitting use of the letters ABC.

Address: International Association of Business Communicators, One Hallidie Plaza, Suite 600, San Francisco, CA 94102, USA.

BRITISH ASSOCIATION OF INDUSTRIAL EDITORS

This is an association of house journal editors founded in 1949. There are four categories of membership: *associate*, who is a person engaged in corporate communications; *member* (MAIE Dip or MAIE), who is a corporate communicator who has passed or been exempted from Part 1 and passed Part 2 of the Association examination; or who has given such proof of professional ability and competence as may be decided by the Association; *fellow* (FAIE), being a member who is considered to be of the highest professional standing and achievements, has had at least 10 years practical experience, and has been in membership for at least 5 years. *Affiliates* are those engaged in ancillary activities.

In 1954, BAIE established its annual Editing For Industry Awards, covering company newspapers, magazines, videos, annual reports and other publications.

Address: British Association of Industrial Editors, 3 Locks Yard, High Street, Sevenoaks, Kent, TN13 1LT.

CHAPTER 26

Special Areas of Public Relations

In this chapter we shall discuss certain areas of public relations that have not featured or been fully discussed in previous chapters but which reflect current trends and developments. They help to demonstrate the ever-changing demands upon communications processes, and also the ever broadening span of public relations involvement in the affairs of every kind of organisation.

THE GREY REVOLUTION

While many TV commercials are 20 years out-of-date in the family life they depict, or in their emphasis on youth, there is an increasing number which resemble the *One Foot In The Grave* comedy series. A revealing review of the ageing population situation appeared in Matthew Gwyther's two-page article in the business section of the *Independent on Sunday* on March 29, 1992.

The article pointed out that by 1995 'in Britain there will be more consumers over the age of 45 than under 30' and that by 2030 'deaths will exceed births and our population will start shrinking.' Already, the Period Total Fertility Rate for Europe was only 1.9 children per family when the figure for long-term replacement should be 2.1. Evidence of the impact of the grey revolution was shown by the fact that over-50s were being recruited by

McDonalds and B & Q for their reliability as well as because of the dearth of youngsters, while driving instructors were concerned about the diminishing number of young drivers.

The causes of the grey revolution are dietary, medical, social and economic. Wartime rationing introduced many civilians to healthy foods they had never previously bought, the National Health Service encouraged longevity, while the Pill and working wives ended the post-Second World War baby boom. Purchasing power has shifted from the young to the middle-aged and the elderly, these older people including many who have retired long before the nominal age of 65. Now, we talk of the over-50s as the market for packaged holidays, motor-cars, VCRs, camcorders, and investments. This changed situation needs to be reflected in public relations programmes and the selections of publics and media.

In recent years we have become accustomed to various life-style categories that have been applied to advertising, and we have seen the demise of the Yuppie and the rise of the empty nester, but now new psychographic groups are emerging. We now have, for instance, that of Mike Laming, managing director of Development Business, who has conjured up five phrases for the over-45s. These are (i) Retirement Aware; (ii) Wind-down, (iii) Lifestyle Adjustment; (iv) Leisure years; and (v) Inactive. The last category starts at age 75. Some people aged 75 do not consider themselves to be old.

One market that has become especially alert to the grey market is the financial one, and we have seen Eagle Star sponsoring Help The Aged advertising, while Northern Rock Building Society has admitted that 80 percent of its investment accounts are held by people over 55. Commercial Union has issued its 3rd Age Initiative healthcare policies for the elderly, while TSB has picked the 45-plus market as its target market. We have even had undertakers advertising insurance schemes on television.

NETWORKING

This is a term that applies to both advertising agencies and public relations consultancies, reflecting the international nature of business communications with satellites providing both the means of communication via the press and television, and the means of conducting business via markets, Stock Exchanges, fax and computer systems. A number of public relations consultancies, notably American ones such as Burson–Marsteller, Hill & Knowlton and Daniel J. Edelman, have operated international networks for many years, but British ones have been established which straddle Europe and link up with the United States and Japan. The British consultancy Shandwick has the world's largest network with 100 offices world-wide.

Networking will be particularly important as the Single European Market grows and it will provide opportunities for European consultancies to link up, either as single companies or as associates.

Experience of the recession in Britain may give preference to the looser arrangement of associateship since less capital will be involved. Already, we have seen the financial loss or collapse of those networks in which too much capital was invested in acquisitions. If one merely has a working arrangement with a consultancy in another country the whole does not suffer if one member fails.

The advantage of networking is that clients can be offered an international service of equal standard and with immediate facilities for translations and media coverage as available in each country. This is more practical than working with a number of separate, independent and uncoordinated consultancies in different parts of the world.

EFFECTS OF BAD ADVERTISING

Advertising and public relations mentalities can be perversely different, advertising campaigns sometimes being aimed at short-term targets and profits whereas public relations campaigns are more concerned with long-term reputation. The two can behave like an estranged couple.

A characteristic of the recession in the 1990s was brutal competitiveness that has sometimes resulted in the deliberate flouting of the law as has been seen with the attitudes of the supermarket chains to Sunday trading, and the holding of illegal free draws by the *Daily Express* and others.

The Advertising Standards Authority has never before received so many justifiable complaints from the public, the Benetton posters being an exceptionally disgraceful episode which involved criticism, not only of the advertiser but also of its advertising agency and the billposters. The Benetton advertising went from extreme to extreme. Subjects included a magazine advertisement captioned United Colours of Benetton which showed two children, one white with blond curls and the other black with hair in the shape of horns, suggesting one was an angel and the other a devil. It produced 60 letters of complaint to the ASA together with one from the Commission for Racial Equality. The complaints were upheld and the advertisement was condemned and withdrawn.

But worse followed with a poster of a bloodstained newly born baby, and other unpleasant subjects including one of a youth dying from AIDS. No doubt people who had never heard of Benetton very soon did know of the company, and the awareness rating was high. But what sort of awareness? And did it matter that millions of people of both sex who were never likely to buy a Benetton garment were now aware of the company's despicable abuse of advertising?

Sales promotion schemes can be too clever by half. The Office of Fair Trading (under the Control of Misleading Advertisements Regulations 1988 which is the British version of an EC directive) complained to the ASA about a Golden Wonder Ringos on-pack promotion which claimed FREE MONSTER IN MY POCKET and added in smaller type See back of pack for details. Twenty packs had to be bought to obtain the 'monster' whereas the larger wording could have been taken by children to mean that the 'monster' was inside the pack. The complaint was upheld and Dalgety Spillers Foods Ltd agreed that the wording was misleading.

The motor-car industry has never been shy of inviting criticism of its advertising. This used to be of knocking ads, but today it can offend against both British and EC rulings about promoting fast cars. Some 50 viewers complained in January 1992 about the Citroen commercial in which a blindfolded woman was abducted, this implying threat and menace according to complainants. The Independent Television Commission felt that the spy spoof treatment overcame the objections. However, the March 18 1992 ASA Monthly Report 10 contained four criticisms of motor-car press advertisements, these being for Citroen, Renault, VAG and Vauxhall. All were condemned for their unrealistic or dangerous claims.

Viewers are becoming increasingly critical about claims made in TV commercials, and complain to the ITC. Like the ASA, which handles complaints about print advertisements, the ITC issues a report on complaints received. In its January 1992 report, three famous brands provoked complaints: Kelloggs Golden Oatmeal Crisp, Persil Concentrated and Heineken Export Lager.

The Kelloggs commercial contained 'not the sliced almonds shown in the commercial but much smaller slices of almond'. The Persil commercial made over-ambitious claims and would not remove stains as claimed. The Heineken commercial said 'one import that the country's finding easier to swallow' but the lager was in fact brewed in Britain. While they were not necessarily deliberate attempts to mislead, and various excuses were offered, the ITC does act as a consumer's watchdog.

Bad advertising that produces adverse comment is bad public relations.

ENVIRONMENTAL ISSUES

Efforts to protect the environment and to reduce pollution are laudable, and a number of organisations have recognised the public relations value of this. When environment-friendly claims are sincere, this is fine, but some marketing people have exploited green issues to promote sales, regarding such claims as a public relations ploy. In America it is known as 'green bashing'. Public relations practitioners need to ensure that green claims are genuine.

In continental Europe, where green advocates are more politically successful than in Britain, there are systems of labelling which guarantee claims, while in Germany there is a system of returning packaging to manufacturers. The EC has become involved in more than 250 directives regarding environment topics such as packaging and waste management.

Typical objectives set by the EC on packaging and packaging waste are:

(i) To promote the use of returnable packaging by the avoidance of unnecessary packaging and its weight.

(ii) The vigorous promotion of recovery of

packaging waste so that a minimum of 60 percent by weight will be recycled.

(iii) To fully inform consumers about the environmental advantages of using returnable and recyclable packaging.

(iv) To stimulate consumers to participate actively in recycling systems for packaging.

Packaging is a public relations topic in itself since consumers often regard it as unnecessary and wasteful. True, packaging does provide the final advertisement, 'pack recognition' is often a vital part of advertising, and the cost of packaging is included in the price, but do consumers wish to revert to the unhygienic days when biscuits were weighed up from tins, sugar and rice from sacks and tea from boxes? Imagine Sainsbury's operating today as it did years ago when butter was patted up on a marble slab, eggs were sold in paper bags and sugar was shovelled into a conical spill. Consequently, packaging waste is a derivative of modern retailing and hygiene standards. There is therefore a public relations case for the actual packaging as well as for the avoidance of pollution caused by packaging waste.

In Britain, political action has been minimal, responsibility being left to manufacturers, but EC directives and devices such as Eco labelling will oblige governments to do more than mutter platitudes. An inevitable effect of serious efforts to curb environmental damage and pollution will be increased prices to cover the cost. This is a potential time-bomb since it could radically worsen the cost of living and heighten inflation. A public relations issue faces many industries: do they ignore the environment or do they put up prices? A healthy sign is that young people are very environmentally conscious, and may be willing to pay higher prices, but what about the vast grey market mentioned earlier in this chapter?

The Incorporated Society of British Advertisers (ISBA) has, in conjunction with the Department of Trade and Industry (DTI), taken the initiative and produced a booklet *Environmental Claims In Advertising*. This is a single guide to all the applicable advertising codes and refers to the Advertising Standards Authority (ASA) and the Committee of Advertising Practice (CAP), the Independent Television Commission (ITC) Code of Advertising Standards and Practice, the ITVA copy clearance guidelines, and the Radio Authority Code of Practice. For instance, it quotes the following example of an unacceptable and an acceptable claim. *'Our nappies are kinder to mother nature'* is unclear and thus unacceptable, but *'Our unbleached nappies are kinder to mother nature'* would be all right.

While the ISBA guide refers to advertising, many of the recommendations contained in the print, TV and radio codes can be applied to public relations such as in the writing of news releases about products with green claims.

Consciousness of environmental responsibilities is now being expressed in annual reports, while BP published *New Horizons* in 1991 in which it described its policy of improving health, safety and environmental performance. This includes the reduction of waste through prevention, recycling or re-use of waste products, and by seeking to protect the environment by seeking to minimise the impact of activities. This report was commendably frank and did not cover up the fact that some of its activities have harmed the environment and invoked fines, while at the same time describing its crisis management efforts as in the case of the 1000 tonnes BP Alaskan oil spill in 1990.

Many green products are more expensive simply because they do not yet benefit from volume production and sales, but it can be good public relations for a supermarket chain to be able to boast that its egg boxes are made of recycled paper. Recycling itself may not always be the answer since the recycling operation can consume more energy than if the waste was simply burned.

LOBBYING

In the USA lobbying is very much a political way of life, and elected representatives are better staffed and equipped to receive the attentions of pressure groups of which the 'gun lobby' is said to be the most influential. Lobbying is seen as a very respectable part of the political scene as a means by which politicians can communicate with those representing special interests. In Britain, there is a tendency to resent or suspect any attempt to influence politicians as if it was a kind of bribery and corruption which lobbying and other forms of Parliamentary liaison are not. It was the efforts of Des Wilson and his Clean Air campaign that persuaded the government to ignore the motor industry and support unleaded petrol, which was one of the rare occasions on which the British Government gave positive support for an environmental issue.

With the emergence of the European Commission in Brussels and the European Parliament in Strasbourg, lobbying has become a European activity and it is necessary to deal with MPs and civil servants at home, and MEPs and commissioners across the Channel. The European Parliament is a very different political animal compared with the British Houses of Parliament. Unlike the British situation with Government and Opposition dividing the House into two distinct opposing sides the European Parliament is a hemispherical chamber with (at the time of writing) 518 deputies representing eleven political groups from 12 member states containing 325 million people. There is no Government and Opposition.

This calls for a very different lobbying approach to that found in Britain, or in the USA, for there is a proliferation of representatives who take decisions. The European Commission in Brussels makes proposals that are discussed by the European Parliament in Strasbourg. The final decision is made by the Council of Ministers which is made up of representatives of each of the member states, but there are also special committees of experts that contribute to decisions. After that, directives are usually issued which are effective only if they become national law in the individual member states. It is a complex process with lobbying opportunities at many stages. Not all directives become national law as has been seen with VAT which the British apply more selectively than proposed by the European Commission.

Parliamentary liaison operates in three ways. Members of Parliament may be paid fees by companies for advising them on Parliamentary procedures, although they must register their commercial interests and declare their interests if speaking in the House. Then there are consultancies that advise clients on Parliamentary procedures. These procedures relate to the passage of bills through their series of readings and committee stages in both Houses; proposed new legislation; questions and replies at Question Time; and the holding of Royal Commissions (discontinued by Mrs Thatcher) and Select Committees at which evidence may be given by interested parties. The third method consists of direct lobbying by representatives (such as PROs) of bodies which are pressure groups for their particular interests, e.g. the National Farmers Union, the National Union of Teachers and the British Medical Association.

PRODUCTS VERSUS SERVICES

Throughout the industrialised world fewer people are now employed in making things, and the shift has been to service industries. This was first observed in the USA as long ago as 1959, but it became more pronounced after 1980.

The two main reasons for the switch are that as consumers have more discretionary income they tend to spend on services rather than on products, while it is less easy to get extra productivity out of services and so reduce staff whereas computers and robots can replace staff (and increase productivity and quality) in manufacturing. Thus, we have a demand plus labour intensive equation.

This has opened the door to the special public relations needs of service industries. At the same time there is the contradiction that the two countries which have the most successful economies are those which excel in manufacturing, namely Germany and Japan.

The demand for services is also linked to the ageing populations in industrialised countries (which has already been discussed in this chapter). The over-60s in particular are more likely to spend money on services that help them or which they can enjoy rather than on products to accumulate. It depends on the age of the person — the newly retired may need to buy a motor-car but people of most ages can enjoy restaurants, entertainments and holidays.

Consequently, prosperity depends on services and this is where public relations can make a great contribution by educating the market about available services.

An interesting difference applies, however, to public relations for products and for services. Products can be exported, and will be involved increasingly in special markets such as Europe and the Pacific Rim with its prospering Asiatic nations. But services are more national and less easy to export. Exceptions are possibly financial services and retail distribution, investment rather than banking and cross-frontier retail chains.

Government services, especially in the federalising Europe of the future, will have much to communicate, and so there will be new demands for skilled communicators. So too will public services such as health and the police.

Married to all this, since services (e.g. stores, hotels, airlines) are often scattered over many locations, and could be located throughout continents and the world, some of the new media and media resources described in this book will be especially valuable in conducting public relations for services. Three immediately come to mind: international distribution of news releases by satellite; similar distribution of video news releases; and the creation of large networks for pre-recorded or live corporate videos.

THE FAMILY REVOLUTION

Sociologists used to talk in terms of the extended and the nuclear family, but family units have been changing over the past 30 years until we have reached the stage when conventional ideas about the family are no longer relevant. This is not necessarily a worse or a bad state of affairs, but a sign of the times, perhaps of a long period without a major war in Europe which has permitted new norms to establish themselves. The word 'housewife' used to be a common expression in marketing, market research and advertising: now it is a term to be avoided. And this is not just feminism. Householder perhaps? It was almost poll tax payer!

This has been an evolutionary process, reflecting the changing nature of society. The extended family was natural in a rural, agricultural country where the family consisted of three generations and the young and the old were dependent on the earning adults who had purchasing power. It was a protective family, and in poorer countries the productivity of the family was self-sufficient and there was little or no excess which could be marketed so that purchases could be made. The extended family still exists in those European countries with large rural areas such as Ireland, Italy, France and Spain, although France has seen considerable industrialisation since the Second World War. Extended families are common in Third World countries, while in some societies the womenfolk may live in polygamous circumstances because so many menfolk are too poor to marry.

Transport, such as railways, led to migration and immigration, to urbanisation, small housing, the break up of rural extended families and the evolution of the small nuclear family comprising husband, wife and children. With far fewer dependants and greater earning power, the family income permitted a far richer variety of purchases. The housewife became the primary economic unit, the person who spent most of the weekly pay packet. The Friday evening newspaper carried the most advertising, and Saturday became the main shopping day. The supermarket became the housewives' domain, and the TV commercials were aimed at her almost exclusively. The housebuilder sold his house on the quality of the kitchen. The holiday brochures were requested by housewives for the family holiday. The housewife paid most of the bills. The husband was the worker bee who brought home the honey.

Not so any more. Nearly three-quarters of married women go out to work and are honey bees. Nearly two in three marriages result in divorce. Men and women cohabit with no intention of marrying. The single parent family has become common, either because the mother never married or the parents are divorced. There are now cheque books bearing the different names of two people of different sex. Most young women prefer to be called 'Ms'. Even the empty nest is vanishing and young people are returning to their original homes. While the conventional nuclear family is unlikely to disappear, the family institution is no longer the rock of society.

In this evolution from extended to nuclear to anything goes type of 'family', we see the influence of security. The family has hitherto been regarded as the foundation of civilised society, but the trend now is towards greater independence, freedom and self-reliance. It is challenging and, if it represents strength, commendable.

But for the marketing, advertising, public relations and even propaganda worlds, it is an earthquake. We have already commented on the grey revolution but this is a quite different one at the opposite end of the population. Public relations people have to cope with these new sociological complications. Very different publics now emerge. Very different media are necessary to reach them. Different people now buy goods and services for different reasons, ecological reasons for example, or for reasons of convenience (e.g. late night shopping) because of limited shopping time. This could even justify Sunday trading.

CHAPTER 27

Case Study: Making Friends for Rentokil

This case study is based on some observations by the author who was public relations manager for five years at Rentokil before it became a public company, and two reports by his successor Peter Bateman who is Director of Public Relations. The whole is based on 30 years experience, but the story originates some 60 years ago. Both the original companies, British Ratin Ltd and Rentokil were founded about the same time in the 1920s although Rentokil was not adopted as the group name until 1960. We will come back to Peter Bateman's piece on *What's In A Name*.

INTRODUCTION

This Rentokil story spans some 30 years, and is exceptionally relevant to this book, and a fitting conclusion to it, since Rentokil has been a continuous growth company throughout the period, has done very little advertising, but has used every kind of public relations technique and strategy. For most of that period, Peter Bateman has directed the company's public relations. It is an international company with a diversity of interests which has enjoyed innovative management, dedicated staff, good products and services, but the company's phenomenal growth (Britain's 'Company of the Year' 1991 according to the Confederation of British Industry) would not have occurred unless there had been a continuous programme of market education.

Rentokil's financial success is epitomised year after year with press reports such as the following in *The Independent* on March 19 1992:

RENTOKIL REMAINS ON TARGET AT £94m
Clive Thompson, chief executive of Rentokil, has again delivered on a long-standing promise to boost its profits by at least 20 per cent a year.

The pest control and environmental services group yesterday reported a 27 per cent surge in taxable profits to £94.6m last year, on a 26 per cent jump in turnover to £389m.

The result was better than market expectations. In the past 10 years Rentokil has improved profits and earnings by 21 and 23 per cent annually. In the same period the shares have advanced more than ten times ... .

That report appeared during a recession with many firms reporting multi-million pound losses, and during a General Election period when Labour was leading in the polls and depressing the stock market.

The author had an early experience of Rentokil's staircase-like progress. When he left to manage the technical public relations consultancy, Scientific Public Relations, Rentokil

was still a private company with predominantly Danish ownership under Sophus
Berendsen of Copenhagen. When he joined
the company — British Ratin as the holding
company was called — he became responsible
to joint managing director Bob Westphal. His
positioning could not have been better and he
enjoyed working for a man who was the best
public relations man he has ever met. He was a
true communicator, and this was the essential
ingredient of Rentokil's success. Westphal
knew that the company's products and
services could not be sold unless people knew
what problems they solved. Almost anyone
was a potential Rentokil customer.

Bob Westphal was an abrasive Australian
lawyer and ex-Second World War bomber
navigator, with a physical resemblance to the
late President John Kennedy, who had married the daughter of a Rentokil branch
manager. He began at the bottom as a field
salesman.

His idea of autocratic democracy was to let
his managers discuss his ideas until they
agreed on what he planned to do. He once said
'we'll try six things — three of them are bound
to work.' He also said about matters that
executives regarded as being very sensitive
'Tell them everything — we're sure to do 50
per cent of the business!' On one occasion he
told the author that as public relations
manager he should know more about the
business than anyone else in it, and Westphal
regularly rang him to keep him informed about
developments and future plans. On another
occasion, when the author refused to waste
money having photographs taken of a director
— who demanded his dismissal — Westphal
retorted 'If Frank says no photographs, no
photographs.' That sort of status, however,
had to be earned by performance.

During those early growth years in the 1960s
before flotation as a quoted company, some
seventeen companies were acquired or created
by British Ratin. They included Chelsea Insecticides Ltd, Disinfestation Ltd, Scientex Ltd,
Rodine Ltd, Associated Fumigators Ltd,

Woodworm & Dry Rot Control Ltd, Woodworm Insurance Ltd, and of course the little
retail products company Rentokil. It became a
confusing conglomeration and a single unifying company name was sought. This was a
public relations feat of great importance to the
future of the company. It was not an easy
decision because it meant that managing directors who were big fish in small ponds became
small fish in a big pond. But Bob Westphal and
the author were agreed that they already
possessed the best name in Rentokil which,
since it sold retail products, already had a
national reputation.

And so Rentokil Group was formed. It did
have one disadvantage, however, in that the
public associated Rentokil with woodworm
although that was only one of its numerous
interests, while today the company has medical, cleaning and hygiene services and is the
world's largest supplier of office plants. One
big advantage was that with one name, all the
company vehicles carried the same name, and
a national fleet of vehicles appeared which had
only previously existed under different names
and colours.

The name Rentokil risked being associated
with the habit nowadays of creating names like
Rentavan and Rentamob, but it is rarely taken
to mean quite literally Rent a Killing Service!
However, the origin goes back to the 1930s
when Professor Maxwell-Lefroy successfully
controlled death watch beetle in the timbers of
Westminster Hall, and was persuaded to bottle
and retail the insecticide he had formulated.
He was an entomologist so he wanted to call
his product Entokil. The name was unregis-
trable so he added 'R' to it, thus producing a
very pronounceable and easy to remember
brand name.

Bob Westphal also insisted on all the
vehicles being white to emphasise hygiene. He
also insisted on decorating them with the
Royal Warrant, which had been awarded for
rodent control and moth-proofing at Sandring-
ham and Windsor. He further insisted that all
40 branch managers should become public

Figure 27.1   Rentokil fumigation 'bubble' for 'green' pest control

speakers and organise talks and film shows for local clients.

Eventually Bob Westphal became chairman and later retired. In 1983 Clive Thompson was recruited as chief executive, coming from Schweppes where he had run the Jeyes company. In the past, the company's directors and managers had grown up with the company and were well known to the staff, but Clive Thompson (and the previous CEO, Brian McGillivary) were unknown outsiders. At the time, *Rentokil Roundabout* existed, a video house magazine, and the interview with the new chief executive Thompson enabled Rentokil employees world-wide to meet their new boss 'on screen'. Clive Thompson brought a new marketing style to the company, and this included developing the lucrative European and Pacific Rim markets, extending environmental services, and introducing the growing and supplying of tropical and other indoor plants.

The following case study is based on Peter Bateman's writings. A characteristic of Peter Bateman's work has been his sense of humour,

frequently expressed in Letters to the Editor which scores of journals have published. He once wrote a news release about Rentokil's bird control service (e.g. removal of pigeons and starlings from public buildings) with the headline PARLIAMENTARY PIGEONS LOSE THEIR SEATS, and for an article on house flies he wrote the headline IF YOU FOLLOWED A FLY FOR A DAY YOU WOULD NOT EAT FOR A WEEK. He also wrote a hilarious release about a flea circus, which the Press Association sent out on its wire service.

This case study is presented in two parts, first as a straightforward report on the company's public relations work, and second as a narrative of Rentokil's public relations philosophy. Combined, they demonstrate very forcibly what public relations can do for a company which has imaginative business leadership at the top and a solid foundation of public relations practice capable of exploiting every communication technique. Rentokil may be a public relations natural because it has never been short of a good public relations story, but nevertheless it has always been a business which could not succeed unless what it had to offer was thoroughly understood. It is a classic case of creating knowledge through understanding, and of overcoming prejudice, hostility, apathy and ignorance.

THE PUBLIC RELATIONS OPERATION: INFORMATION AND OBJECTIVE

A service industry thrives on the effective promotion of a deserved reputation to the public it seeks to influence, by means of well-informed media and well-informed staff.

Historically, the tradition of providing accurate information about pests, started by Professor Maxwell-Leroy the founder of Rentokil, Karl Anker-Petersen, managing director of British Ratin, Dr Norman Hickin and William McAuley Gracie, has been continued and amplified for 60 years, for more than 30 by professional in-house public relations staff.

1. The primary objective is to tell people about the company's services and products: to inform about the nature of the problems that can be solved by them safely and effectively.
2. By so doing, traditional markets are expanded, new markets may be developed, confidence in the industry is stimulated and goodwill for Rentokil is generated.
3. Well-informed media, government and other publics are also more understanding and sympathetic towards a company that is shown to act responsibly in the face of any untoward incident. The company does not claim to be infallible!

PLANNING AND STRATEGY

The director of public relations has executive public relations responsibility for all the company's UK environmental services and reports to regional managing director environmental services. Public relations for property care and products is undertaken by their own divisional marketing staff assisted by the director of public relations when necessary.

Effective public relations starts with a knowledgeable work force so internal communications receive considerable attention.

External public relations is directed at educating clearly defined publics and establishing Rentokil as the authority to which the media will refer on any matter relating to its areas of business.

PUBLIC RELATIONS SPECIFICATION

1. To act as Rentokil's information service and represent the company in order to obtain maximum favourable, truthful coverage in appropriate media.
2. To act as the source to which all media enquiries come and where they will be dealt with promptly and accurately.
3. To assist in the production of material such as leaflets, books, wallcharts, films, video tapes, direct mail, external journals and lecture material and speeches.
4. To provide adequate internal company communications by visits, lectures, noticeboards, newsletters, magazines and contributions to induction training.
5. To reinforce the corporate identity, maintain Rentokil as the authority in each of its chosen fields and to create a climate of goodwill to assist marketing, recruitment and investment.
6. To advise and help public relations programmes and communications systems for the overseas companies and liaise with the group financial public relations consultancy and corporate affairs manager. To liaise closely with divisional marketing executives and with R & D technical and information section staff.
7. To liaise with the creative services department and the company photographer.

8. To monitor and report on the results of agreed public relations policies and campaigns and the opinions and attitudes of various publics towards the company.

EXECUTION

In 1959, The Pest Advisory Centre (later the Rentokil Advice Centre) was opened at 16 Dover Street, Mayfair, where it remained until 1979 when its function of handling enquiries, arranging lectures, identifying specimens and issuing educational material, was transferred to Felcourt, the company's head office.

Each major Rentokil branch became a local woodworm and dry rot centre or a pest advisory centre giving free advice and housing a small exhibition of pests, during a period of 20 years.

FILM AND VIDEO

The Rentokil Film Unit was formed in 1959 and produced instructional films on rats, mice, cockroaches and beetles, the best of which have now been transferred to videotapes. *The Intruders* won an Industrial Screen Award for best in-house public relations film. In 1985, total borrowing of the 20 film titles reached 10 000 audiences for the year. Several films were translated and distributed overseas by the British Council and the Central Office of Information.

In 1977 Rentokil invested in its own video production unit, studio and branch network of video playing equipment. This creative services department now includes a stills photographer and display manager.

Over 160 video programmes have been produced for training, employee communications and as sales aids. Several have won awards from the International TV Association.

Rentokil films and videotapes have been used in BBC and ITV natural history programmes and by instructors on British Pest Control Association training courses, as well as by schools, colleges, and professional or voluntary organisations, from women's groups and Young Farmers Clubs, to environmental health officers.

PRESS, RADIO AND TELEVISION

Much of the company's public relations activity for more than 30 years has been aimed at raising the status of the pest control industry and achieving greater respect for its achievements through authoritative press articles, news items, background briefings, and the provision of articulate, knowledgeable broadcasters. This implies an effective news gathering system and News Lead forms are provided for branches to encourage the notification of interesting items.

The same strategy applies to obtaining greater awareness of the benefits of deep cleaning, sanitary waste disposal, tropical plants indoors, and all the other Rentokil activities.

On average, one press release is issued every week, some 450 press cuttings are received each year and as a direct result of this activity over 150 photographs and some 25 feature articles are published each year, and about 60 radio or TV broadcasts totalling nearly 20 hours of air time. The company is frequently consulted by the BBC Natural History Unit and other programme makers.

The public relations director has personally taken part in over 600 broadcasts, from local radio phone-ins to nationally networked TV news and documentaries, including *City Safari*, *Wildlife*, *The World About Us*, *Today*, most of the news and current affairs programmes, four 'Tuesday Calls' and a series of 21 'pest of the week' talks for John Dunn (Radio 2), and more recently *Newsnight*, *Sky News* and a 10-part *Pest*

Patrol series by Granada networked on ITV within the *This Morning* programme in May and June 1990. Local branch managers are also trained to take part in local radio programmes when appropriate.

BOOKS

In addition to The Rentokil Library series of 17 textbooks, material is provided to authors and researchers of other books in which pest control, hygiene or property care are featured and both Norman Hickin and Peter Bateman have published books of their own on pest control subjects and contributed to others.

PHOTOGRAPHS AND SLIDES

Extensive use is made of the company's own photographic library to provide material for publication or for bona fide lecturers to public health or institutional management courses.

LECTURES

Speakers are regularly provided for schools, technical colleges, professional institutions and voluntary organisations throughout the UK to the extent of at least 100 talks each year. Audiences include the Royal Institute of Public Health & Hygiene, The Institution of Environmental Health Officers, The National Trust, various women's groups, food hygiene technologists, public health students, hospital domestic services managers, food production staff, hygiene officers, Rotary, Round Table, warehouse-keepers, institutional management students and conservation groups such as Friends of The Earth, or local natural history societies. Public relations staff also contribute to customer seminars and the public relations director is on the Speak Out panel of The Chemical Industries Association.

WALLCHARTS AND LEAFLETS

A series of wallcharts on flies, cockroaches, rats and mice, woodworm and rot have been made available for schools and colleges.

Reprints of articles and leaflets are sent out in response to requests from the general public or students. Pest identification charts, preventive pest control booklets, and promotional brochures produced by the marketing departments are also distributed as part of the advice service.

RENTOKIL SERVISCENE

This news magazine describing Rentokil Environmental services is published twice a year, much of it devoted to seasonal or topical pest control subjects and other services of value to customers and potential customers. Twenty thousand copies are distributed via branch managers and sales staff and to a mailing list of some 4000.

Contents include updated information on relevant legislation, new techniques, pest-borne diseases and damage, unusual infestation problems and case histories, details of new services and authoritative short articles on anything from clinical waste disposal to Legionnaires' disease or office cleaning.

TRADE ASSOCIATION SUPPORT

Rentokil has always actively supported the British Pest Control Association since its formation in 1942, devoting not only money but the time of senior executives to helping it to raise and maintain the highest technical standards and to achieve recognition by Government, the public, and in new markets.

The Association has elected six Presidents from Rentokil, Stuart Hedgcock, A. Fraser McIntosh, Fred Hawkes, Peter Bateman, Graham Crowe and Tony Stephens.

Rentokil has been invited to provide mater-

Figure 27.2   Safe disposal of used hypodermic needles (Rentokil Medical Services)

ial for BPCA publications and played a leading role in their campaign *Hospitals Can Damage Your Health* which led to the lifting of Crown Immunity from NHS hospitals, thereby improving the hospital market for commercial pest control contractors.

Rentokil currently, at the Association's invitation, provides BPCA with the chairman of its public relations and conference committee, and members of other specialist committees.

The greater awareness of the BPCA as representatives of the non-agricultural pest control industry is reflected in the growing membership and in its recognition by government ministers in current discussions on the Food and Environment Protection Act, the

further abolition of Crown Immunity and other matters. Direct talks have been held with MPs of all parties, senior civil servants and with Ministers of the Crown. Company members of the BPCA board have also represented the industry in Europe and the USA.

Rentokil has also always played a leading role in The British Wood Preserving and Damp Proofing Association, providing a number of officers and technical advisors to the remedial, pre-treatment and environment sections.

Rentokil's public relations director has also been asked to act as honorary PRO for The Society of Food Hygiene Technology, has been a Council member and was elected a Fellow of the Society for his work in promoting it.

EVALUATION — SOME EXAMPLES

In 1960, 'pest control' was a term associated only with crop spraying and agriculture. Telephone directory entries were headed Vermin Exterminators. Rentokil had a Service Division described as a holding operation while the Woodworm and Dry Rot Division went ahead. It traded as Disinfestation Limited.

Today Rentokil is established as a respected leader within a recognised public health, commercial and structural pest control industry and is rapidly becoming acknowledged as a leading international servicing organisation.

THE LOCAL AUTHORITY MARKET

In 1962, local authorities virtually refused to recognise any commercial pest control activities in the public health field. Advertising in the municipal press was a waste of money.

During the next two winters, Rentokil ran seminars throughout the UK specifically for local authorities. By 1965, advertisements in local authority magazines were bringing in business. Subsequently — and recently helped by the Government's privatisation policy — pest control contractors have been able to obtain work from the public sector, to the benefit of the whole industry.

This experience has also helped Rentokil companies overseas to gain business with municipalities from Hong Kong to Hamelin.

Rentokil publications and the videos *Rentokil on The Rates?* and *The Manx Pied Piper* made a significant contribution to this change of attitude. By 1985, more than 30 authorities had completely privatised their pest control and others use contractors wherever necessary.

THE HOSPITALS MARKET

Apart from the effects of the NHS (Amendment) Act 1986, the whole tendering procedure for hospital contracts was discussed with the DHSS, model contracts being revised and advice given by Rentokil's own qualified environmental officer. This followed discussions between Peter Bateman, representing BPCA, with the Health Minister Barney Hayhoe and senior civil servants, with Rentokil public relations supporting the vigorous BPCA campaign.

This is already leading to more sensibly priced hospital contracts, to the benefit of the whole industry, and the campaign is being extended to abolish Crown Immunity from other government premises, under the Food Safety Act 1990.

As a result of the hospitals campaign, the BPCA won the Public Affairs Category of the 1986 Sword of Excellence Awards from The Institute of Public Relations.

THE WOOLLY BEARS PICNIC

A group of worried residents on a housing estate at Eastleigh sought Rentokil's advice about a bad infestation of carpet beetles.

Rentokil R & D sent an entomologist to address a meeting, practical advice and help were given, which included a recommendation to use a DIY mothproofer.

Public relations activity to inform the nation followed; readers, TV viewers and listeners began to look for 'woolly bear' grubs of carpet beetles, found them, and sales of Rentokil Mothproofer for the quarter rose by six times (in Hampshire by 12 times), plus pest control branches gained significant job work to deal with the pest.

NATIONAL CATCH A COCKROACH MONTH

To make people more aware of cockroaches as a potential health threat, to help assess the status of cockroach species, their distribution and preferred premises, a campaign was launched to gather live cockroaches from all over the UK.

Additional scientific value could be obtained by finding what disease organisms they carried and whether they were resistant to insecticides then in use.

The cooperation of Oxfam/UNICEF was obtained for an agreed minimum donation of £5000 and Rentokil offered 5p per cockroach to the charity (which helped improve sanitation for refugee boat people) with a certificate to each donor.

Hundreds of schools joined the project as well as workers who collected 1000 cockroaches in all types of premises from prisons to convents and from hospitals to distilleries.

Hundreds of requests were received for more details about cockroaches and about the Oxfam and UNICEF projects. Valerie Singleton accepted the cheque of £5000 from Rentokil's chief executive, and the national press, radio and TV coverage (over 20 hours of airtime) created the required degree of awareness, the laboratory got the information they needed and the boat people received some relief of their suffering.

THE MANX PIED PIPER

When the Isle of Man Local Government Board awarded Rentokil the contract for all the island's rodent control, they needed a considerable public information programme to ensure its success.

Many of the landowners and householders were sceptical, apathetic or curiously superstitious (the word 'rat' was taboo) and had been used to fairly casual waste disposal routines and cheap but ineffective DIY baits of warfarin in locally produced grain. There was also concern about local job losses to outside contractors. A press conference was held in Douglas, attended by the medical officer, the chairman of the board from The House of Keys, the environmental health officer and the Rentokil team.

The resultant Manx radio and newspaper coverage helped to dispel misconceptions, advised householders, property owners and farmers what to do to get the service, and a poster campaign ('If you see one, report it!') reinforced the message.

As predicted, requests for treatment rose dramatically, then fell as each infestation was dealt with.

The actual population of rats on the island had been seriously under-estimated, but Rentokil drafted in or recruited extra staff to meet their contractual obligations and the company's professionalism quickly won the respect of the sceptical as well as the public health staff. The medical officer had earlier been concerned about the spread of Weil's disease.

The contract ran for eight years.

CONSERVATION GROUPS/ANIMAL WELFARE/ANIMAL RIGHTS

Rentokil has supported other BPCA member companies in making representations where appropriate to the RSPCA and groups such as The Friends of the Earth, and the company has been instrumental in providing security guidelines following threats by animal activist extremists.

FINANCIAL RECORDS

In 1969, Rentokil Group became a public company with its shares quoted on the London Stock Exchange.

Despite a depressed stock market ('Shares Slide' and 'New Issue Indigestion' were typical headlines the same week), Rentokil shares were oversubscribed four times at a 50p (ten shillings) premium, largely because the company was known as a leader in its chosen field with a high reputation for quality and consistent performance.

In 1990, The Rowland Company, then handling Rentokil's City and Financial PR, won the Best Investor Relations Campaign award from *PR Week*. Between 1984 and 1989, the share price rose from under 80p to over 200p with a profit/earnings ratio of 20:1. In 1992, the shares reached over 400p.

In 1990, Rentokil also won The Best Service Company category in the Business In Europe Awards organised by *Management Today*. In 1991, it became one of the FTSE 100 top performing UK companies with a market valuation of £1.5 billion.

SUMMARY

During the past 30 years, the industrial, commercial and domestic pest control industry has become acknowledged, appreciated and respected as essential to the preserving of health, food and property, thanks in some measure to a deliberate planned and sustained public relations policy.

Within that industry, Rentokil has earned a reputation for integrity, reliability, discretion and expertise that has established it as an international authority on pest control and environmental services.

The current task of the company's public relations is to enhance that status and extend it to every one of Rentokil's activities in every market in which the company operates.

The extent to which this is being achieved was reflected in an *Economist* survey in 1991 of Britain's Most Respected Companies in which Rentokil was placed 11th overall, 1st in the Chemicals sector (above ICI), 6th equal with Unilever on the quality of its marketing and 9th equal with Wellcome in its concern for the community and the environment. The company has since been placed in the Business Support Services category of industry and in the CBI Business Enterprise Awards for 1991 was named Company of the Year.

The second part of this study is based on Peter Bateman's article, *What's In A Name?*

WHAT'S IN A NAME?

A squirrel is a rat with good public relations. This may be an over-simplification of the role of public relations but nevertheless it indicates how public relations can influence a person's viewpoint.

The practice of public relations is not only carried out by specialists who talk to the media as 'a Rentokil spokesman', it is carried out by company staff, every day. It is not an optional extra nor just a part of the marketing mix. Every employee is in this together.

The company's reputation is made or marred by the impression given by everyone in their work, and indeed beyond their working day. How is a telephone call handled? Is the surveyor knowledgeable and helpful? Is the correspondence or survey report neat, accurate and clear? Does the technician or serviceman arrive on time, look smart, drive carefully, have a clean van? *These* are the factors by which the company's services will be judged, just as much as by the skill with which the work is carried out. After all, who would have confidence in a company whose staff turned up late, unshaven, in filthy overalls, kicked the cat and could not explain what they were doing?

A great deal of Rentokil's business comes from recommendations, either directly or indirectly, from satisfied customers. It follows that reputation is indivisible and whether one works for property care, pest control, tropical plants or office machinery, to the client the employee represents Rentokil (and may be expected to know about any aspect of its services or products).

One of the company's great strengths is the belief, shared by the majority of clients, that *If it's from Rentokil, it must be good* (costly maybe, but good!). The other side of that means, if one service fails to meet a customer's justifiably high expectations *all* Rentokil services may be cancelled (which will unfairly penalise colleagues and undo years of goodwill).

Public relations is *not* 'How to wine friends

and get people under the influence'. It *is* concerned with providing accurate information (doctors bury their mistakes, ours get published!) to establish understanding, appreciation and recognition of what we do. This creates confidence and generates goodwill and this is the way we change the world. As Abraham Lincoln said, 'Public sentiment is everything.' It follows if you do not want it published, do not let it happen! Most of Rentokil's activities, however, deserve to be published, and that is where the company's professional own trumpet blowers come in. The practice of public relations is not only to present the face of the firm but to make sure that the face is clean, preferably smiling, has an effective voice and a sympathetic ear.

Yes, public relations is part of the marketing mix, creating a climate of knowledge, informed opinion, appreciation and respect, so that selling is easier and more cost-effective. But it is much more. It is the voice of conscience on the nature of the policies, the services and the product sold. It is the means of maintaining confidence among investors, of recruiting and holding staff, of influencing whatever bodies are relevant, from government departments to local chambers of trade, specialist associations or pressure groups. It is concerned with being a 'good neighbour' in the community.

THE NATURE OF PUBLIC RELATIONS

Those who specialise in public relations are expected to be infinitely patient, tactful, resourceful, imaginative and courteous, literate and articulate. There is craftsmanship in communicating the right message to the right people in the right form at the right time. The PRO needs to know more than anyone else in the organisation about its history, policies, services and products, and to be available to enquiring journalists at any time (usually when he is in the bath at home on a Sunday night!).

It may be necessary to talk to many publics, from government ministers and local authorities to shareholders, suppliers, trade associations, local voluntary groups, existing customers and potential customers.

Public relations work is planned to help with various marketing or policy objectives but the best laid plans are often dropped to deal with immediate requests for urgently needed photographs, comments on an alleged poisoning incident, reassurance on the safety of our techniques, information on our policy in South Africa, the life cycle of the German cockroach the number of rats in London's sewers, or the percentage of cooling towers infected by Legionella.

Lectures are arranged for Rotary, Round Table, Lions, Women's Institutes, Weight Watchers and Friends of the Earth. Technical Colleges, hygiene courses, catering students, all benefit from the knowledge provided by visiting Rentokil speakers.

Rare Bug Eats Fergie's Frocks screams *The Sun*. So who do the other editors come to for reliable information? Rentokil, of course! Over the years Rentokil has built up a reputation among the media so that they can be sure they will get a response, that it will be positive, and that it will be accurate.

NECESSITY OF A WELL-INFORMED PUBLIC

This reputation not only provides opportunities not given to others, but stands the company in good stead in the face of any unfavourable criticism or reports and ensures the chance to put forward the company's case. The business depends upon a well-informed public, and that can only be achieved through well-informed media.

Every day of the year on average, three or four stories appear somewhere in a newspaper or magazine about Rentokil; every week there is a radio or TV item relating to Rentokil and they add up to over 40 hours of broadcasting a year. Many are local, some are national, a few are on the BBC World Service and become international. In addition, about 100 feature articles and 300 Rentokil photographs are published each year.

The main point of Rentokil's public relations is that in today's competitive business environment, the company's products and services must not only *be* good but must be *seen* to be good. The 'halo effect' of reports and authoritative articles in editorial columns or news and documentary programmes provides a credibility far greater than is achieved by advertising. If a few sales leads are generated in the process, so much the better, but much of the effort is rewarded simply by customer's frequent comment, *'Well, I never knew Rentokil did that!'* First educate your market, then you can sell to it.

ACTIVITIES GENERATE NEWS

Rentokil is fortunate that the company's activities generate so many genuinely interesting, newsworthy stories. Keeping the rats out of Hamelin, shooing the starlings off the Forth Road Bridge, seeing that the Parliamentary pigeons lose their seats, saving priceless Norwegian churches, running a National Cockroach Month — these are just a few of the highlights. Behind the occasional ego-trip on *Clive Anderson Talks Back* (not forgetting the rat called Nora), *Women's Hour*, *Today*, *You and Yours*, or *Breakfast Time*, are the routine contributions to *Farming Today* or any other of the 89 local radio stations, 6623 trade and technical journals, 1478 consumer magazines, 195 paid-for provincial weeklies and 132 national and provincial daily or Sunday papers. And that is only the press relations part.

Occasionally it is more important to keep Rentokil or one of its customers out of the press or a hostile TV show; not because there is anything to hide but because the media will

not provide a fair hearing. Such occurrences are mercifully rare but again, the respect for Rentokil's integrity has been known to kill such proposed programmes. Accolades have been won from hard-bitten journalists for Rentokil's professional public relations.

Rentokil produce *ServiScene* for 20 000 UK environmental services customers, and environmental issues for the divisional staff, and help the *Rentokil Review International* editor with desk top publishing for this twice a year publication.

However many millions of listeners or viewers are addressed, the company will never ever have a more important audience than its staff. They *are* Rentokil. A dangerously parked van or a broken promise can undo years of goodwill, but the more they tell people about their work, the more they take an enthusiastic pride in their own skills, knowledge and the fact that their work is worthwhile, the more will the business thrive.

Whoever said *No news is good news* was not providing Rentokil's sort of service — and certainly did not understand public relations.

SOME ACHIEVEMENTS

Before the Rentokil Woodworm and Dry Rot Centre opened, nobody knew woodworm could be cured.

When Rentokil went public in 1969 in a depressed stock market, the shares were oversubscribed four times at a 50p premium because of its reputation and known expertise as well as its performance.

One news story about carpet beetles that became of national interest, increased sales of Rentokil Mothproofer by six times in one quarter.

No new Rentokil service or product launched in the past 30 years has had any significant advertising support other than direct mail and brochures. Public relations has told the story.

The NHS (Amendment) Act that lifted Crown Immunity from NHS hospitals was largely the result of a public relations campaign to Government, initiated by the British Pest Control Association and executed by Rentokil public relations resources. It won the Public Affairs Category in the IPR Sword of Excellence for 1986.

The Rentokil Library series of 17 hardback books is recognised as the definitive source of reference for each of the subjects covered by the titles.

The new Rentokil logo incorporates the new Royal Warrant which now applies to all Rentokil Environmental Services (whereas it had hitherto applied only to pest control and timber preservation services and products). The change reinforces Rentokil's status as a world class environmental services company.

CAM Diploma Syllabuses

All candidates must complete a 3 hour written examination in *Management and Strategy* plus *two* other related papers.

MANAGEMENT AND STRATEGY (COMPULSORY)

Business management, practice and strategy and its specific application in the communication and related industries.

Elements covered include: organisational structures, the financing of organisations, the management planning process including objectives, strategic audit, the use of matrices in portfolio management, positioning, uses of research, voluntary and legal constraints; the practice of management including financial techniques, human resource recruitment and development, resource evaluation, management applications in the communications industry e.g. PR, media independents, market research, advertising agencies.

PUBLIC RELATIONS — MANAGEMENT

The principles of public relations management in all types of organisations. Management of the function and its effective integration into the overall management of an organisation.

Elements covered include: the public sector, private sector, non profit sector; their management, opportunities and constraints, and public relations' contribution within them. Specific topics in public relations management including the use of research, strategic planning, issues management, managing external services and creative staff.

PUBLIC RELATIONS — PRACTICE

How the techniques of public relations management are applied within all types of organisations and in consultancy settings. All the specific topics learned in the PR Management syllabus will be called upon for this paper. It is essentially an applications module, using case studies.

CAM Diploma Past Examination Papers and Case Studies in Public Relations Practice and Public Relations Management

Communication Advertising and Marketing Education Foundation Limited

CAM DIPLOMA

Examination in

MANAGEMENT & STRATEGY

JUNE 1992

Time allowed: THREE HOURS.

The paper is divided into four sections. All candidates are required to answer FOUR QUESTIONS. Questions must be selected from at least THREE of the four sections.

All questions carry a maximum of 25 marks.

Candidates are advised that the examiners will be seeking evidence of ability to translate knowledge of facts and techniques into appropriate practical applications.

The examiners will also be impressed by legibility and clarity of expression.

Rough work should be included in the answer book(s) and ruled through, but it will not be accepted as part of the candidate's answers.

SECTION A

Question One

Small firms find it difficult to survive in some industries, particularly in manufacturing; yet in others, for example retailing, they trade side by side with large companies. Some industries - and particularly service industries - are dominated by small and medium sized enterprises.

Explain why there are such differences between industries (50%) and why firms of all sizes operate successfully in the marketing and advertising services fields (50%).

Question Two

You are managing director of a sizeable and profitable subsidiary of a publicly quoted but ailing communications group. Your board is considering undertaking a management buyout. (a) What are the chief considerations in attempting the buyout? How could it be financed and structured? What possible personal and corporate risks and rewards would be entailed? (50%). (b) What are the possible sources of finance and their relative merits? (50%).

SECTION B

Question Three

UK charities find themselves in an ever more competitive environment. There are many new fund raising ideas involving concerts, television and many relief initiatives such as Red Nose Day. Many large charities have appointed marketing directors to maximise their revenue opportunities.

1

Consider one of these listed charities and identify the key elements of a marketing plan with the objective of increasing income:-

Oxfam
Royal National Lifeboat Institution
Royal Society for the Prevention of Cruelty to Animals
Battersea Dogs' Home
Greenpeace

Imagine that you are the new Marketing Director and that you are writing an outline presentation to the Management Board.

Question Four

In the 90s a competitive edge will be gained by many companies working in close partnership with major customers in the development of new products and services. For example, FMCG companies might gain by a close developmental relationship with powerful multiple retail groups; similarly manufacturers of hi-tec components might succeed by working very closely with major customers for those components.

What factors of your customers' businesses would you need to take into account? (40%). What difficulties are likely to be encountered in implementation? (30%). How can the process be facilitated? (30%).

SECTION C

Question Five

British companies seeking to expand and trade in Europe would be greatly aided by a rapid movement to a single market. Construct a S.W.O.T. analysis for any company with which you are familiar on the basis of a single (EEC) market for their products/services over the next decade.

Question Six

You are the Chief Executive of a large PR company with six divisions addressing different marketplaces - Corporate, Pharmaceuticals, Hi-Technology, Financial Services, Consumer Products and Property & Construction. The Pharmaceutical Division is a star performer in terms of profitability and growth. It is becoming increasingly impatient with "under-performers" - the other divisions - and is developing its own way of doing things.

These tensions are becoming a major pre-occupation within the company. As Chief Executive you decide to draw up a programme to encourage the company to break down the barriers between the divisions and develop a stronger cohesion. What areas might this address? (40%). What options might you have to deal with this situation? (40%) Are there any ways of implementing any proposed change which will increase the likelihood of its acceptance and success? (20%).

SECTION D

Question Seven

You are the Marketing Research Manager of a manufacturing company that puts all market research out to external market research agencies. Write a report which demonstrates how your department adds value to your company's operation.

Question Eight

Within a company marketing business products, the Director of Marketing Services has been asked by the Board for increased efficiencies. Major expenditure is concentrated on external PR consultancies and on a wide range of sales literature.

What major issues would need to be considered? (50%). What are the practical considerations surrounding any change of suppliers? (50%).

**COMMUNICATION ADVERTISING AND MARKETING EDUCATION
FOUNDATION LIMITED**

CAM DIPLOMA
JUNE 1992

PUBLIC RELATIONS
MANAGEMENT

CASE STUDY

CAM Foundation, Abford House, 15 Wilton Road, London SW1V 1NJ

Aggro plc, a UK-based public company quoted on the London Stock Exchange, manufactures agricultural fertilisers. The domestic market accounts for 10% of its turnover with 80% from exports to other EC countries. One of the company's major specialisations is in support of beet cultivation - a crop which farmers are increasingly turning to and on which Aggro is pinning hopes for its own future. Over the past five years the company has spent £25 million on a research programme to develop a fertilizer to increase yields of beet by at least 50%. The outcome is Beetup - planned for launch in six months.

The European Commission announced yesterday its intention to introduce a draft directive which would ban the use of Notix - a substance widely used in the agrochemicals industry and considered by some EC scientists to be carcinogenic. Notix is also a key ingredient of Beetup. It is expected that the draft directive will be enforced within two years.

The Aggro directors have decided to delay the launch of Beetup for one year so that research can identify a non carcinogenic substitute for Notix. In addition, the Board has ordered, as a matter of urgency, a review of all its products to ascertain the extent of current use of Notix and the effect of a ban on Aggro's markets. Simultaneously a full-scale internal environmental audit has been implemented.

Communication Advertising and Marketing Education Foundation Limited
CAM DIPLOMA

Examination in

PUBLIC RELATIONS MANAGEMENT

JUNE 1992

Time allowed: THREE HOURS.

All candidates are required to answer QUESTION ONE and ONE OTHER QUESTION.

Question One carries 75% of the marks and the other question 25%.

Rough work should be included in the answer book(s) and ruled through, but it will **not** be accepted as part of the candidate's answers.

Question One (Mandatory, based on the Case Study)

You are the chief executive of Worldwide PR Inc, which advises Aggro on corporate and marketing communications. The Chairman of Aggro has asked you to provide him with a memo presenting an overview of the current and potential strategic issues which the company is likely to face as a result of the EC announcement. An outline of how these issues might be addressed, giving due attention to timescale and budgetary considerations, is also required.

You should write this memo and include five factors which, in your view, must receive priority. Bear in mind that you are addressing the Chairman as one senior businessman to another and at this stage he does not require details of how your recommendations will be implemented. However, pay attention to communications aspects, publics and commercial implications which might not have occurred to him, so as to ensure that the memo is coherent and a clear statement of the company's position from which decisions on public relations action can be made.

Question Two

The Cutie Cake Company plc was founded in 1912 to manufacture biscuits, pies, cakes and pastries and by 1970 had become one of the top three players in the biscuits market. It is publicly-quoted and the head office is in Stockport, Cheshire where the business was started.

The company added ranges of frozen foods, savoury ready meals and snacks in 1982 and also introduced artificial ingredients and additives (sweeteners and colourings) to some of the best-selling lines. However consumers considered that this compromised the CCC's reputation for quality and some activist groups began to pin-point the dangers associated with additives.

1

Sales began to decline in 1990 and, last year, a number of crises faced the company including the death of a child following an allergic reaction to an additive used in one product. A court case is pending on this issue.

Last week, the CCC board decided to examine the possibility of stopping the use of artificial ingredients in favour of natural products, some of which would have to be sourced from abroad.

Your Managing Director has asked you, as Public Relations Manager of CCC, to write a memo on the communications impact of the various options open to the board.

Question Three

The Blue Star charity was founded over 100 years ago to assist people at home and abroad. Its work covers all aspects of care and the relief of human suffering. It is involved in disaster relief and refugee support in Third World countries through to the operation of day care centres for the elderly and provision of volunteer medical services in the UK.

There are some 100,000 volunteer supporters in the UK who are organised in a branch structure based on large towns and cities. They include individuals who are trained in emergency medical support as well as fundraisers and welfare workers who help out in day care centres. Apart from those fund-raising activities which are the traditional hallmark of charitable giving in the UK, there is a file of 150,000 regular donors, both individuals and companies. Blue Star used to be the UK's leading charity but it has rather faded from prominence and has been overtaken by newer, more dynamic organisations. It is now 15th on the Charities Aid Foundation list which ranks charities according to donated income.

Although Blue Star has not always used aggressive marketing techniques, the trustees have agreed to spend £2 million over three years to increase the charity's profile and to boost funds needed for its caring work. From this budget, £500,000 has been allocated for public relations.

Your brief is to draw up a programme which addresses the key objective of progressively increasing and extending media coverage and the perception of the charity as a vibrant and progressive organisation. Write a paper for the trustees setting out the creative strategy on which this programme will be based.

COMMUNICATION ADVERTISING AND MARKETING EDUCATION FOUNDATION LIMITED

CAM DIPLOMA
JUNE 1992

PUBLIC RELATIONS PRACTICE

CASE STUDY

CAM Foundation, Abford House, 15 Wilton Road, London SW1V 1NJ

You work for an engineering company WIDGETS which makes specialist parts for the aeroplane industry. The company employs 3,500 people in the UK of whom 85% are men. There are no women in senior management positions.

As technology has progressed the skills required in the workforce have become increasingly electronics orientated.

The current demographic situation offers WIDGETS fewer graduates with the necessary scientific background you want. Of these graduates 55% are women. However the 'male' orientation of the company means that few female graduates perceive your company to be an attractive place to work. Also those already employed find the environment unwelcoming and unrewarding with few career opportunities for pregnant women or returnees and as such you are losing a valuable resource in whom the company has an investment.

The chairman and the board of the company have decreed that WIDGETS as a company must change its culture to make itself more attractive to female graduates and women employees.

The human resources department has now completed extensive research to establish what actions should be taken to achieve cultural change. They have an action plan which includes a review of the physical environment to ensure it meets women's requirements, intensive regular appraisals seeking to identify women who can be promoted, job share in selective instances, a creche for shift workers, career breaks for up to five years for female employees with young families, paternity leave and a childcare location service. They have also recommended that the normal working day should be from 8 am - 6 pm and that meetings should be held within this time-frame if at all possible.

2

Communication Advertising and Marketing Education Foundation Limited
CAM DIPLOMA

Examination in

PUBLIC RELATIONS PRACTICE

JUNE 1992

Time allowed: THREE HOURS.

All candidates are required to answer QUESTION ONE and ONE OTHER QUESTION.

Question One carries 75% of the marks and the other question 25%.

Rough work should be included in the answer book(s) and ruled through, but it will **not** be accepted as part of the candidate's answers.

Question One (Mandatory, based on the Case Study)

You have been asked to recommend a communications programme to accelerate this cultural change internally and externally. Please list your key target audiences, outline your message, suggest five high priority vehicles by which to communicate and make a recommendation as to how to measure your communications' success. (A budget and timetable are not required at this stage).

Question Two

A southeast harbour board is concerned about the impact the opening of the Channel Tunnel will have on cross channel ferry traffic. The board is worried that jobs will be lost, and that the number of visitors to the town will be severely curtailed. Having lost the battle against the construction of the Tunnel, the harbour board is concerned to learn that a vigorous campaign has been launched to abolish duty free goods. This would have a further negative impact on business. The campaign argues that 'duty free' runs contrary to the dismantling of trade and tariff barriers required under the Single European Act. It also charges that 'duty free' gives an unfair competitive advantage to the ferries and airlines over the Tunnel.

While acknowledging that 'duty free' will eventually have to go, the British Government is prepared to seek derogation of powers from The Community to retain 'duty free' for a transitional period. Given the harbour board's limited PR resources, outline your strategy for stiffening the Government's resolve in trying to secure as generous a transition period as possible.

Identify the clear message which you want to get across, your key target audiences and suggest some effective methods for generating public and political support for your case.

Question Three

You are the corporate affairs manager of Harrisons - a company which is fully listed on the London Stock Exchange. In recent years, there have been a number of management changes at board level that created considerable media attention, not least because of the size of the "golden handshakes". However, life has become easier during the past twelve months as a new management team has got on quietly with running the business and improving profitability.

You receive a phone call at home from the Chairman who explains that the Chief Executive (Bob Jones), brought in from another major company last year, was leaving the company forthwith. Following an investigation by The Stock Exchange, there was evidence that he had been involved in insider dealing whilst at his previous company.

Jones strongly denied the charges but had felt obliged to inform the Chairman since he was likely to be arrested and charged shortly. The Chairman had insisted upon his resignation which Jones had refused to provide, claiming that the company should stand behind him. After taking legal advice, the Chairman terminated his contract and escorted him from the building.

(a) Identify the key audiences.

(b) Draft a "bullet-point" outline of the announcement which will form the press release that would be issued in the morning.

(c) Draft a timetable of actions during the following day.

(d) Describe the tactics you would employ in handling the announcement, bearing in mind the requirement that price sensitive information is released simultaneously.

Bibliography

MAGAZINES AND PERIODICALS

Adline, Adline Publishing Ltd, Adline House, 361–363 Moseley Road, Birmingham, B12 9DE. Monthly.

BAIE News (Journal of the BAIE), 3 Locks Yard, High Street, Sevenoaks, Kent, TN13 1LT. Monthly.

Campaign, Haymarket Marketing Publications Ltd, 22 Lancaster Gate, London, W2 2LY. Weekly.

Communication World (Journal of the IABC), One Hallidie Plaza, Suite 600, San Francisco, CA 95102, USA. Monthly.

Conferences, Exhibitions & Incentives International, Haymarket Management Magazines, 30 Lancaster Gate, London W2 3LP. Monthly.

Exhibition Bulletin, London Bureau, 266–272 Kirkdale, Sydenham, London, SE26 4RZ. Monthly.

Exhibitor, The, Conference & Travel Publications Ltd, Media House, The Square, Forest Row, East Sussex. Quarterly.

International Public Relations Review (Journal of IPRA), P.O.Box 9588, Washington DC 20016, USA. Quarterly.

Marketing, Haymarket Marketing Publications Ltd, 22 Lancaster Gate, London, W2 3LP. Weekly.

Marketing Business (Journal of the CIM), Headway, Home and Law Publishing Group Ltd, Greater London House, Hampstead Road, London, NW1 7QQ. Monthly.

Marketing Week, Centaur Publications Ltd, St. Giles House, 50 Poland Street, London, W1V 4AX. Weekly.

Overseas Trade, Overseas Trade Services, Room 802, Bridge Place, 88–89 Eccleston Square, London, SW1V 1PT. Monthly.

PR Week, Haymarket Business Publications Ltd, 22 Lancaster Gate, London, W2 3LP. Weekly.

Public Relations (Journal of the IPR), The Institute of Public Relations, 4th Floor, The Old Trading House, 15 Northburgh Street, London, EC1V OPR. Monthly.

Sponsorship News. Charterhouse Business Publications, P.O.Box 66, Wokingham, Berks, RG11 4RQ. Monthly.

Televisual, Centaur Publications Ltd, St. Giles House, 50 Poland Street, London, W1V 4AX. Monthly.

UK Press Gazette, Maclean Hunter House, Chalk Lane, Cockfosters Road, Barnet, Herts, EN4 0BU. Weekly.

DIRECTORIES AND WORKS OF REFERENCE

Advance (monthly loose-leaf information about press features), Themetree Ltd, 2 Prebendal

Court, Oxford Road, Aylesbury, Bucks, HP19 3EY.

Advertisers Annual, Reed Information Services Ltd, Windsor Court, East Grinstead House, East Grinstead, West Sussex, RH19 1XA. Vol.1. Agencies & Advertisers, Vol.2. UK Media, Vol.3. Overseas Media.

Benn's Media Directory, Benn Business Information Services Ltd, P.O.Box 20, Sovereign Way, Tonbridge, Kent, TN9 1RQ. Annual. Vol.1. UK, Vol.2. Europe, Vol.3. World.

Blue Book of British Broadcasting, Tellex Monitors Ltd, Communications House, 210 Old Street, London EC1V 9UN. Annual.

Editors, Media Directories Ltd, 9–10 Great Sutton Street, London, EC1V OBX. Six volume media directory.

Europe Information Pocket Book, NTC Publications Ltd, Farm Road, Henley-on-Thames, Oxfordshire, RG9 1ES. Annual.

European Marketing Pocket Book, ditto.

Guide to European Business Media, Business Communications, Swallows Farm, Thaxted Road, Wimblish, Essex, CB10 2XP. Three times a year.

Hollis Press and Public Relations Annual, Hollis Directories, Contact House, Lower Hampton Road, Sunbury-on-Thames, Middlesex, TW16 5HG.

Hollis Europe, ditto. Annual.

Hollis Sponsorship and Donations, ditto. Annual.

Institute of Public Relations Handbook (IPR membership list and year book), Kogan Page Ltd, 120 Pentonville Road, London, N1 9JN.

Marketing Pocket Book, NTC Publications (as above). Annual.

Media Pocket Book, ditto. Annual.

PIMS Directories, PIMS House Mildmay Avenue, London N1 4RS. Media, Townslist, European (Trade and Newspapers), Financial, USA (Trade, Newspapers, Consumer) directories.

PR Planner-Europe and *PR Planner-UK*, Hale House, 290–296 Green Lanes, London, N13 5TP. Updated looseleaf.

Printing Reproduction Pocket Pal, Creative

Services Association, c/o R. Prior, 277 Torbay Road, Harrow, HA2 9QE.

Public Relations Consultancy (Public Relations Yearbook), (PRCA), Financial Times Business Information, 50–64 Broadway, London, SW1H 0DB.

Royal Mail International Business Travel Guide, Royal Mail International, 52 Grosvenor Gardens, London, SW1W 0AA.

Willings Press Guide, Reed Information Services Ltd, Windsor Court, East Grinstead House, East Grinstead, West Sussex, RH19 1BR. Vol.1. UK, Vol.2. Overseas.

Writers and Artists Yearbook, A & C Black (Publishers) Ltd, 35 Bedford Road, London, WC1R 4JH. Annual.

BOOKS

All About Public Relations, 2nd Ed, 1991, Haywood, Roger, McGraw-Hill, Maidenhead.

Business of Image, The, 1991, Jenkins, Kogan Page, London.

Company Image and Reality, 1984, Bernstein, David, Cassell, London.

Complete Spokesperson, The, 1991, Coulson–Thomas, Colin and Bartram, Peter, Kogan Page, London.

Communications in Industrialising Countries, 1989, Jefkins, Frank and Ugboajah, Frank, Macmillan, London.

Corporate Culture, 1991, Hampden-Turner, The Economist Books, London.

Corporate Image, 1990, Ind, Nicholas, Kogan Page, London.

Effective Employee Communications, 1990, Bland, Michael and Jackson, Peter, Kogan Page, London.

Handbook of Public Relations & Communications, 4th Ed, Lesly, Philip, Mercury Books, London.

How To Manage Public Relations, 1991, Stone, Norman, McGraw-Hill, Maidenhead.

International Public Relations in Practice, 1991, Ed. Nally, Margaret, Kogan Page, London.

Mission & Business Philosophy, 1991, Campbell, Andrew and Tawadey, Kiran, Butterworth-Heinemann, Oxford.

Modern Marketing Communications, 1990, Jefkins, Frank, Blackie, Glasgow.

PR Business, The, 1991, Bell, Quentin, Kogan Page, London.

Practice of Public Relations, The, 3rd Ed, 1988, Ed. Howard, Wilfred, Butterworth-Heinemann, Oxford.

Public Relations, 4th Ed, 1992, Jefkins, Frank, Pitman, London.

Public Relations Casebook, 1990, Capper, Alan and Cunard, Peter, Kogan Page, London.

Public Relations For Your Business, 1987, Jefkins, Frank, Mercury Books (W.H.Allen), London.

Public Relations in Action, 1989, Jefkins, Frank and Lowe, Vincent, Macmillan, London.

Public Relations in Practice, 1991, Ed. Moss, Danny, Routledge, London.

Public Relations Techniques, 2nd Ed, 1993, Jefkins, Frank, Butterworth-Heinemann, Oxford.

Sense of Mission, A, 1990, Campbell, Andrew, Devine, Marion and Young, David of Ashridge. Hutchinson Business Books, London.

Sponsorship, 1989, Sleight, Steve, McGraw-Hill, Maidenhead.

Addresses of Societies and Educational Organisations

British Association of Industrial Editors, 3 Locks Yard, High Street, Sevenoaks, Kent TN13 1LT; (0732) 459331. Membership: Editors of house journals. Entry by examination. *BAIE News*.

Communication, Advertising and Marketing Education Foundation (CAM), Abford House, 15 Wilton Road, London, SW1V 1NJ; 071–828 7506. Certificate and Diploma examinations. Vocational examinations for those working in British communications industry. Holders of CIM Diploma exempt from certificate, except PR, if they wish to take CAM Diploma in PR.

Institute of Public Relations, The Old Trading House, 15 Northburgh Street, London, EC1 0PR; 071–252 5151. Membership by age and experience plus CAM Diploma or its equivalent. Journal *Public Relations*. Annual Sword of Excellence awards.

International Association of Business Communicators, One Hallidie Plaza, Suite 600, San Francisco, CA 94102, USA. Membership, Accredited Membership (by exam). *IABC News, Communication World*. Annual Gold Quill awards. Chapters in UK and other countries.

International Public Relations Association. Case Postale 126, CH–1211 Geneva 20, Switzerland. Has members in 70 countries. Membership by election according to international PR experience, *IPRA Newsletter*, *International Public Relations Review*, international conferences.

The London Chamber of Commerce and Industry, Examinations Board, Marlowe House, Station Road, Sidcup, Kent DA15 7BJ; 071–302 0261. Third Level Certificate Examinations in Advertising, Marketing, Public Relations, Selling and Sales Management (with Diplomas for passes in three or four subjects taken at the same time). Diploma in Management Studies if three subjects passed at different times.

Public Relations Consultants Association. Willow House, Willow Place, Victoria, London, SW1P 1JH; 071–233 6026. Corporate Membership. *PRCA News*.

Services

BBC World Service, Bush House, P.O.Box 76, Strand, London, WC2B 4PH.

British Council, 10 Spring Gardens, London, SW1A 2BN.

Central Office of Information, Office of the Controller (Overseas), Hercules Road, London SE1 7DU.

Department of Trade and Industry, Ashdown House, 123 Victoria Street, London SW1 GRB.

EIBIS International, Chancery House, 53–64 Chancery Lane, London, WC2A 1QU.

PIMS, Pims House, Mildmay Avenue, London, N1 4RS.

Two-Ten Communications (incorporating UNS/PNA), Communication House, 210 Old Street, London, EC1V 9UN.

Index

Abbey National 204
above-the-line 49
academic qualifications 257–62
acronyms 167
Advance 50, 160, Appendix 3
adversarial situation, the 7–8, 52, 152
Advertisers Annual 50, 54, 58, 160, Appendix 3
advertising 11, 13, 30, 31, 44, 49, 60, 62, 68, 85, 90, 91,
133, 134, 164, 165, 172
  appropriation 66
  bad 265–6
  commission 65, 71
  free 15, 31, 65, 85
  how it differs from public relations 14
  manager 23, 28
  outdoor 134
  reminder 134
  weight of 90
advertising agency 6–7, 71, 76, 146, 147, 150, 152, 155,
255
  à la carte 66
  public relations department of 150
Advertising Standards Authority 265–6, 267
Aerial Promotions 139
after-market 167
ageing population 264–5
agent acts as principal 6
airbags 200, 201–2
Airbus 99
airships 64
Alcatel 99
alternative newspapers 54
American English 251
American Notes 235
ampersand 191
Anker-Petersen, Karl 274
annual reports 4, 37
  video 227
apathy 3, 12, 13, 18, 19, 21, 23, 35, 47
Apple Macintosh 238–9
appointments stories 174
appreciation of the situation 9, 10, 18, 19–20, 21
Association of Business Sponsorship of the Arts 134
Attenborough, Barbara 231
attitude study 24, 89
audio-cassette tape 34
Audit Bureau of Circulations 50, 85
Australia 49, 251
awareness 23, 24, 25, 89, 107–108, 141

B & Q 264
banks 30, 136, 137, 138, 142
Bar, A.J. 88

Barclaycard 142
Barnardos 38
Bass PLC 183, 203–4
Bateman, Peter 271, 273, 268, 280
Battle of Wapping 51
Bauer, H. 56
BBC 54
  External Services 60
  News 59, 111, 231, 232
  Overseas Services 40
  Radio 51
  TV 13, 39, 51, 139, 230
  World Service 104, 105, 155, 250, 282, Appendix 5
Beamish stout 142
below-the-line 49
Benetton 265–6
Benn's Media Directory 20, 50, 54, 58, 105, 158, 160, 252,
253, Appendix 3
Benson and Hedges International Open 133
Bernays, Ed 9–10, 15
bias 11, 25, 101, 148, 190, 213
Bibles 187
Bild 52
BMW 229
body media 138
Body Shop 228
bold type 188–9, 206
book style 187, 207
booth 251
Bournemouth University 259
BP 267
brainstorming 25
brand, product manager 28
brand awareness 143
break-bumpers 140
bribery 139, 243
British Aerospace 228
British Airports Authority 37
British Airways 33
British Association of Industrial Editors 57, 212, 262–3,
  Appendix 4
British Caledonian 33
British Diabetic Association 136
British Gas 94
  cathedral concerts 139
  hot air balloon sponsorship 138–9
British Home Stores 172
British Market Research Bureau 140, 141
British Overseas Trade Board 40
British Pest Control Association 276–7, 279, 283
British Rail 88
British Rate and Data 54
British Ratin Ltd 271, 272, 274

British Sky Broadcasting 51, 54
British Telecom ISDN2 229
  London area code 231
  Megastream 229
  videoconferencing 229
  25th birthday of BT Tower 232
British Wood Preserving and Damp Proofing Association
  277
Broadcasters' Audience Research Board 50, 85
broadsheets 50
budgeting 18, 19, 20–21, 59, 65–83
  skeleton budgets 74–82
  value of 83
building societies 30
Bulletin Television News Service 230
Burroughs 88
Burson–Marsteller 231, 254, 265
Bush, President George 12
business video 69, 188–89, 227–29

cabled message system 228
calendars 61
Callaghan, Lord 232
Calor Gas 88
camcorder 225, 264
Campaign 50, 174, Appendix 3
Canada 49
Canon (UK) Ltd 134, 138, 139
capital letters 184, 188–9, 190
  drop 187, 188
caption, photo 175, 223–4
car ferries 30, 89
Cargill PLC 182–3
catering 75–6, 76–78, 110, 113, 116–17, 119
CBS network 231
Central Office of Information 250, 254–5, 255–6, 275,
  Appendix 5
  department chart 256
Central Statistical Office 23
Chalmers, Judith 142
Chambers of Commerce magazines 53, 57
change, effecting 3, 85
Channel 9, Australia 231
Channel Tunnel 30, 90, 99, 216, 256
characteristics 25
charities 12, 29, 37, 38, 62, 100–1
charity sponsorships 138–9
Chart Show 142
Chartered Institute of Marketing 10, 36, 134, 147, 173
chief executive officer 28, 168–9
Childminder of the Year Awards 231
China, Chinese 49, 104
circulation 50, 51, 52, 56, 85
Citroen 266
City, Business, editors 4, 33
civic newspaper 54
clay pigeon shooting 138
Clean Air campaign 268
cliché 197–199, 214
CNN 5
Cobourne Co Film and Video 188–9, 228
Coca Cola 134

Code for Communication on Environment and
  Developments 248–9
Code of Athens 9, 248
codes of practice 242–49
colour photographs 52–3, 111, 223
Commercial Union 265
Commission for Racial Equality 265
commission system 7, 66
Communication, Advertising and Marketing Education
  Foundation (CAM) v, 10, 11, 14, 97, 147, 154, 195,
  218–9, 257, 258, Appendix 4
  past exam papers Appendix 2
  syllabuses Appendix 1
Communication World 229, Appendix 3
communications audit 19
community relations 4, 30, 38, 54, 102–3, 106
company newspapers 235–9
company results 41, 107
complaints 23, 35, 89
  about advertisements 265–6
computer graphics 79, 226
computerised newsrooms 154, 180, 185, 194, 208
Confederation of British Industry 23, 271, 280
confidence 37–38, 94, 99–100, 167, 245
confidentiality 245, 247–48
conflicting interests 246
consumer panel 23, 99
consumer relations 4–5
contact reports 74
content analysis 87–88
continuations 193
contract printers 51, 158
Control of Misleading Advertisements Regulations
  1988 266
controlled circulation 56
Co-op 88–9, 182, 195, 197, 232
Copyright Act 1956 224
  Copyright, Designs and Patents Act 1988 224
copywriting 197–198
Cornhill Insurance 23, 25, 104, 138, 139
Coronation Street 58, 106
corporate catering 139
corporate identity 22, 30, 41–2, 64, 108, 138, 274
  style book 108
corporate image 21, 22, 30, 41–2, 91, 99, 101, 106, 107–
  8, 136, 138
Corporate Television Communications 228, 232
corporate video 68, 188–9, 227–29, 235, 268
cost effectiveness 17–18, 19, 28, 39
Council of Ministers 268
Countrywide Communications London Ltd 195–6, 232
CPC (Corn Products) 37
Cranfield School of Management 15, 146, 147, 257
credibility 7, 11, 13, 15, 165
credit for achievement 30, 38, 92, 99, 101–2
cricket, test match 23, 25, 138, 139
Crime Watch 13
crisis management 5, 33, 92–3, 148
Croft Port 141–2
Croydon Airport 225
CSS International Holdings 134
cultural sponsorships 136

Cuprinol 32
Currys 33
customer interest, maintaining 13–14, 97–98

Daihatsu 37
Daily Express 265
Daily Mail 51
Daily Mail Ideal Home Exhibition 129
Daily Mirror 51, 52, 56, 236
Daily Record 52
Daily Telegraph 52, 54
Dalgety Spillers Foods Ltd 33, 266
darts sponsorship 137
dates 192
Datsun 40, 88
DDI, India 231, 254
dealer audit research 23, 98
dealer magazine 4, 32
dealer relations 4, 29, 36, 91, 98, 167
definitions
    advertising 11
    investor relations 247
    propaganda 15
    public relations 9–11, 17, 20
    publicity 166
delisting, brands 36
Denmark 132
Department of Trade and Industry 40, 155, 204, 252,
    254, 255–6, Appendix 5
    environment claims 267
    joint ventures 125
    new products from Britain service 254–5
desk research 23
desktop publishing 238–9
Development Business 264
Dewe Rogerson Ltd 239
Dickens, Charles 235
Digital 228
direct mail 20, 37, 62, 100
Direct Mail Preference Service 37
direct response marketing 62
directories 53, 57–58, 101–2
discussion groups 25
Distillers 33, 99
diversity 37, 98–99
Dixons 33
dolphins 195–6, 232
Drambuie Liquer Co 232
drop capitals 187, 188
Dublin Institute of Technology 259–60

Eagle Star 265
Earls Court 125
EBC Germany 230
EC directives 39, 266
    advertising 266
    packaging 266–7
    television requirements 230
Economist, The 8, 105, 190, 249, 280
Ecowater Systems 182
Edelman, Daniel J. 239, 265
edit suite 231

editorial space universe 88
Editors 20, 50, 54, 114, 158, 160, Appendix 3
educational literature, print 61
educational sponsorships 136
EIBIS International 40, 105, 160–1, 212, 252, 255,
    Appendix 5
embargoes 191–2, 193, 195, 197
emotive language 182
emphasis 190
empty nest, nester 264, 270
end(s) 186–7, 190, 196, 199, 206, 295
engineering consent 9–10
English Heritage 100
'envelope, the' 243
envelopes 193
environment 248–9, 266–7
Environmental Claims in Advertising 267
essay writing 157
Esso 135
Euro Disney 232
European Commission 268
European Parliament 39, 268
Evaluating Media Coverage 88
evaluation of results 18, 21, 278–9
Ever Ready Derby 104, 138, 139
Eversheds Ltd 61
exclusive feature article 209–19
    cost of 212
    negotiating publication 211–12
Exel Logistics 172
Exhibition Industry Federation 125
Exhibition Industry Report 125
exhibitions 29, 125–32
    in developing countries 131–2
    official opening 126, 127
    press office 41, 126, 128, 157
    press officers 30, 40–1, 82, 106, 126–7, 129–30
    press preview 126–27
    press room hints 130–1
    private 132
    public 60
    support for exhibitions 129–30
    support for exhibitors 81–3, 125–129
Exhibitions Bulletin 125, Appendix 3
expedition sponsorship 137
expenses 66, 70, 71
export manager 29
export public relations 30, 39–40, 104–5, 250–6
extended family 269

facts 176, 182, 184, 190
facts book 74
familiarising of name 138
family revolution 269–0
Farnborough Air Show 128, 256
favourable 2, 3, 8, 11, 15, 22, 41, 42, 84, 166, 172
feature article 165, 209–19
    advantages of 217
    and advertisements 213
    by outside contributors 210
    by public relations source 210–11
    by staff writers 209–10
    cost of 218–19

feature article *cont'd.*
  how to write 214
  negotiating publication 211–12
  permission 214
  plots for 214–15
  presentation 217
  researching 215–16
  seven-point model 215–17
  Two-Ten service 212
  why they may fail 214
fees 19, 21, 66, 67, 71, 83, 186
  ad hoc 73
  annual 73
  arbitrary 72
  hourly rate 73
  limitations of 149–50
  methods of assessing 72–3
  other than from clients 245
  retainer plus charges 72
  time bank 73
fertility rate 264
Fiat 107
Fife-Clark, Sir Tom 15
fifth estate 7
films 225
financial interests 245, 246, 247
financial relations 4, 28, 44, 93–4, 101
Financial Times, The 8, 52, 90, 92, 105, 174, 190, 191, 220
  appointment stories 174
  overseas editions 53, 252
Findus 13
fire-fighting exercise 3
flags 64
flexography 51, 158
flotation, share 93, 94, 140
flower shows 135
football 134, 135, 139, 140
Football League 134, 139
for immediate release 188, 189, 197
Ford Europe 228
  Communications Network 228
Ford News 236, 237
Foreign and Commonwealth Office 256
foreign language print 253, 256
Fours Ps 147, 166, 167
France, French 13, 56, 99, 143, 269
free advertising 15, 31, 66, 85, 230
free draws, illegal 265
free newspapers 50, 53, 54
freedom of the press 50
freelance writers 210
freelances 151
Freight Transport Association 177–79, 204–5
Friday night drop 152
Friends of the Earth 279
front organisation 244
FTSE 100 280
full points, stops 184, 191

Gallina, Emil 230
Gambon, Michael 143
General Election 1992 50
Germany 6, 49, 52, 56, 87, 231

Ghana 89, 104, 199
Girobank 32, 200
Goebbels, Paul Josef 15
Gold Paper No.6 15
Gold Paper No.7 9
Golden Wonder Ringos 266
golf sponsorships 137
good neighbour policy 38, 102–3, 281
Goodbye to the Low Profile 152
goodwill 10, 31, 38, 61, 104, 280
Goodyear airships 64
Gracie, William McAuley 274
Granada TV 106, 139, 143
Grand National 138
Great Ormond Street Children's Hospital 139
green products 266–7
Greenpeace 232
grey revolution, the 264–5
Guardian, The 8, 92, 174
Guinness 33, 61, 99, 142
Guinness Book of Advertising 137
Guinness Book of Records 137
Gulf states 52, 104
Gulf War 139, 230
gun lobby 268
Gwyther, Matthew 264

Hales Trophy 232
half-tone screens 221
halo-effect 31, 99
handout 6, 172
Hanson, Lord 7, 104
hard news 155, 173
Harris 24
hats 40
headlines 11, 187, 206, 238
Hearst, William 7
Heineken Export Lager 266
Heinz 33, 106
Help the Aged 231
Hickin, Dr Norman 274
Hill and Knowlton 230, 254, 265
Hints to Exporters 252
Hollis Press and Public Relations Annual 19, 58, 100, 102, 135, 160, 205, 207, 252, Appendix 3
Hollis Sponsorship and Donations 135, 205–6, Appendix 3
Honda 40, 133, 139
Hong Kong 218
  Trade Association 232
  TV 233
hospitality 75–6, 83, 104, 109, 139
hostility 3, 12, 18, 19, 21, 23, 40, 90, 105–6
hot-air balloons 64, 138–9
hot metal 51, 55
hourly rate 19, 73
house colour 22, 42, 64
  style 64
house journal, external 235, 238, 253
  language versions 238
  Singer magazine 238
  Travelers Insurance magazine 238
house journal, internal 34, 57, 62, 100, 107, 159, 168, 212, 235–9

advertisements 236, 237
  budgeting 78–1
  cover charge 237
  eight considerations 79–80
  frequency 237
  planning issues 237–8
  printing 239
  production 238–9
  readership 237
  title 237
House Magazine, The 239
housewife 270–1
human resources management 168

ICI 7, 37
ignorance 3, 12, 13–14, 18, 19, 21, 23
image 21, 34
  change of 29, 30, 88–90
  corporate 21, 22, 30, 41–2, 91, 98, 101, 106, 107–09, 136, 138
  current 19, 22
  favourable 2, 11, 41, 42
  mirror 19, 22
  multiple 22
  optimum 22
  parental 36, 99
  perceived 22
  product 22
  seven kinds of 21–2
  studies 23–4, 91, 99
  tracking 88
Impact Calendars 61
Incorporated Society of British Advertisers 267
indention 196–98, 206, 207
Independent, The 8, 50, 51, 53, 174, 271
Independent Broadcasting Authority 140, 142
independent local radio 39, 111
Independent on Sunday 264
Independent Radio News 111
Independent Saturday Magazine, The 8, 54
Independent Television Association 141
  copy clearance 267
Independent Television Commission 38, 51, 142, 230, 267
  complaints about commercials 266
  Sponsorship Code 51, 142
Independent Television News 59, 111, 230, 231
India, Indian 49, 231, 252, 254
Indonesia 131, 251, 255
induction material 28, 168
in-house department 11, 65, 67, 83, 146–48, 173
  advantages of 148
  costs of 67–70
  disadvantages of 148–9
  personnel 67–68
inside information, insider trading 245–6, 247–48
Institute of Public Relations 10, 11, 14, 44, 72, 84, 151, 166, 173, 218, 258, 259, Appendix 4
  Code of Professional Conduct 85, 153, 166, 242–7
  Handbook 229, Appendix 3
  Register of Members' interests 39, 244
  Sword of Excellence awards 18, 283
instructions 23

intellectual property 224
Interchange Group 236
interest and value 7, 173, 220
International Association of Business Communicators 229, 262, Appendix 4
International Distillers & Vintners 142
International Freighting Monthly 172
International Herald Tribune 53
International Public Relations Association 9, 15, 248–9, 262, Appendix 4
  Code for Communication on Environment and Developments 248–9
  Code of Athens 9, 248
interval sample 26
interviewer 25–6
Intruders, The 275
investment analysts 4, 27
investor relations 242, 247–48
invitations 109–10, 114–16, 121
italics 188–9, 190
ITT 91–2, 98, 99
ITV 53, 54, 140, 141, 142, 230
  Chart Show 142
  World Cup football series 140
  Rugby World Cup 140–1

Japan, Japanese 12, 13, 104, 136, 138, 232, 255, 265
jargon 250–1
Jeffreys, Janie 252
Jenkins, Peter 50
job numbers 21, 74
job titles 164–5
journalists 51, 136, 152, 153, 154, 155, 161–3, 174, 175, 186, 207, 208, 243, 281
journey cycle 36
JQ Films 232

Kanawa, Dame Kiri Te 141
Karting 139
Kelloggs Golden Oatmeal Crisp 266
Kenco London to Brighton Veteran Car Run 231
Kent County Council 197
Kinnock, Neil 50
knocking advertisements 266
Kotler, Philip 10, 13, 31, 147, 166, 167
Kronenbourg 142, 143

Laming, Mike 264
languages 50
laser clayshooting 139
LBC 60
Lean Cuisine 13
Lee, Ivy Ledbetter 7, 173
Legal and General 142–3
Legoland 132
Letherby and Christopher 139
letterpress 51, 54, 55, 158, 221
library shots 59
life-styles 13, 26, 131, 264–5
Lilly, Eli 136
Lincoln, Abraham 281
listings, deregulation of 51, 54

listings magazines 51, 54, 174
livery 22, 42, 64
Lloyds Bank Clothes Show Live Exhibition 139
   Fashion Awards 139
   Fashion Challenge 139
   Young Musician of the Year 139
lobby correspondents 39, 192
lobbying 103–4, 268
local authorities 37, 39, 45, 69, 146, 147, 278
logo 22, 42, 99, 140, 142, 189, 283
London Chamber of Commerce and Industry 218, 219,
   257–58, Appendix 4
London Marathon 137, 138, 139
London Philharmonic Orchestra 136
Lowell Offering 235
Lucas 37, 42

magazines
   Chamber of Commerce 53, 57
   children's 56
   house journals 34, 57
   listings 56
   local 57
   professional 56
   specialised 56
   technical 56
   trade 56
   weekend 54
   women's 56, 158
Magid Associates, Frank N. 232–3
Maigret, Chief Inspector 142, 143
mailing list 48, 50, 86, 129, 157, 159–60, 173, 174, 199
Malawi 89
Malay, Malaysia 49, 104, 131, 251
Malaysia Airline 237
management–employee relations 4, 28, 85, 95–6, 158
Management Today 280
manhours, labour, time 19, 20–1, 28
Manx Pied Piper 279
margins 193
market education 13, 23, 27, 29, 31, 36, 90–1
Market Research Society 24
marketing 10, 11, 13, 31, 147, 153, 165–6
   antipathy with public relations 165
   director, manager 28, 167
   mix 167
Marketing Business 134, Appendix 3
marketing research 10, 19, 21, 23–4, 90, 100–1
Marks and Spencer 92, 136
Marlboro 133
Mars 33
   London Marathon 139
Mary Rose exhibition 132
mass market 26, 58, 134
maximising profits 36, 167
Maxwell, Robert 7
Mawell-Lefroy, Professor 272
Mazda 40
McDonalds 264
McDougall's Cookery Book 35, 137
McKern, Leo 142
media
   content analysis 87

coverage 15, 19, 21, 31, 90, 106, 134, 137, 138, 139,
   275
effect of 87
evaluation of 85–7
for a fee 21
measurement of 87–88
picture record 87
quality 86
rating chart 86
ratio of publications 86
relations 42, 153, 154
television 230–1, 232, 275
tone 86–7
value of 85
volume of 85, 90
Media Dimensions 142
media, existing commercial 20, 50, 51–60
   private created 20, 50, 60–4
   relations 30, 42, 108
Media Measurement 88
media, overseas 252, 254, 255
Members of Parliament 39, 62, 103, 104, 239, 268, 277
Mercedes-Benz 40, 200–3
Merrill Lynch 228
Mexican Statement, The 10–11, 18
MicroPhone 11 239
Midland Bank 136, 183, 207
Miles, Louella 134
mime 226
misleading information 244
Mobil 152
mobile cinema 50
monitored scripts 21, 23, 85–6
moral rights 224
MORI 24
Morse, Inspector 142
motor racing 133, 135
multinationals 37, 135
mutual understanding 10
Myanmar 89

Napier University, Edinburgh 260–1
national brand 36
National catch a cockroach month 278–9
National Exhibition Centre 125
National Health Service 90, 104, 264
national newspapers 52–3
National Opinion Polls 24
National Power 140
National Readership Survey 26, 50, 85
National Trust 38, 100
Nationwide 89
Neighbourhood Watch 13
networked consultancies 254, 265
New Horizons (BP) 267
news agencies 186
News Analysis Institute 87
News At Ten 53, 111, 158
news reader 229, 232
news release heading 187–88

news releases 11, 50, 51, 85, 108, 153, 154, 157, 159, 165, 172–79, 180–3, 184–94, 214, 216, 273
  analysis of 195–208
  how to write 172–79
  journalistic writing 157
  layout of 178
  length of 186–7
  marketing of 157–58, 173
  opening paragraph 172, 176, 180–3, 185
  presentation of 184–94, 217
  seven-point formula 175–7, 179, 180
  six kinds of 175
  timing of 158, 160
  typing of 187–88
news sense 155–6
newsletter 234
newspapers
  civic 54
  free 50, 53, 54
  national 53
  regional 53, 54
NHS (Amendment) Act 278, 283
Nielsen, A.C. 31
Nigeria 23
Nissan 40, 88
Northern Rock Building Society 265
Norwich Union 238
Nuclear Electric 228
nuclear family 269
numerals 190–1

objectives 3, 10, 15, 18, 20, 21, 28–43, 84
  achieving the 34 objectives 88–108
  34 possible 29–42
Observer, The 54
Ocean Transport 99
off the record 161
Office of Fair Trading 266
offset-litho 221
O'Gorman Fund for Children, Paul 139
Olympia 125
Olympus cameras 134
One Foot in The Grave 264
open days 30, 38, 41, 106
Open University 32, 205
opening paragraph 172, 176, 180–3, 185, 203, 204, 206, 216
  examples of 181
  for feature article 215, 217
opinion leaders 12, 20, 30, 40, 44, 85, 105–6
opinion poll 21, 24, 26, 89, 90, 99, 103
opportunities to see 86
Option One 230
Oracle teletext 140
over-50s 264–5
overseas, media 252, 254, 255
  news agencies 252
  press conferences/receptions 254
  press correspondents 253
  press mailing services 253
  public relations consultancies 253–4
overseas public relations 250–6
Overseas Trade 252, Appendix 3

own label 36
Oxford English Dictionary 20

P & O 30, 232
Pacific Rim 232, 233, 269, 273
packaging 30, 37, 167
  EC directives 266–7
PageMaker 238
PAL television system 226, 231
Panasonic 135
paragraphs 187–88
  closing 215, 216
  opening 172, 176, 180–3, 185, 203, 204, 206
  short 197, 199, 200, 208, 215
participatory sponsorships 139
Partridge Films 232
Pasco Associates, Alan 134
Peaudouce 231
pensioners 30, 41, 106–7
Pepe jeanswear 142
Pepsodent 40
perimeter boards 133
Persil Concentrated 266
personnel management 168
  manager 28, 168, 234
Peugeot 88, 239
Phillips, David 88
phone-in polls 25
photography 52–3, 193, 220–4
  black and white 223
  captioning 223–4
  colour 223
  copyright 224
  faults to avoid 222
  hints 223
  quality of pictures 221
  telling a story 220
  use of public relations pictures 221–2
  working with the photographer 220–1
photogravure 56, 158, 221
  PIMS 59, 69, 114, 160, Appendix 3, Appendix 5
Players Special 133
plot for news release 176, 177
  for feature article 214–15
police, the 13
policy, change of 29, 30–1, 89
political polls 24, 26
political relations 39, 62, 103
pollution 38, 100, 266
population, (research) 25
post production 79, 226
postal surveys 25, 89
  posters 61
  PowerGen 140, 142
PR, a 7
PR agency 6–7, 147
  exercise 8
PR Planner 20, 50, 158, 160, Appendix 3
  Europe 253, Appendix 3
PR Week 6, 7, 56, 151, 207, 218, 280, Appendix 3
praise, self 157, 172, 173, 206
predator 33
prejudice 3, 12–13, 18, 19, 21, 23, 90, 138

presentation 184–194
  elements of 185–194
  three purposes of 184
press agentry 7, 156
Press Association 54, 160, 173–4
press conference 109
  planning 111–118
press cuttings 15, 21, 23, 70, 84, 102, 105, 159, 161, 173, 189, 194, 275
press facility visit 76–79, 111
  briefing 122
  budgeting 76–7
  catering, accommodation 119–20
  invitations 121–2
  news story facilities 122
  party numbers 119
  planning 118–2
  timing 122–3
  transport 120–1
press kits 41, 116, 122, 131, 157
press office 158–60
press officer 11, 152–63, 173, 174, 184, 209
  qualities of 155, 156–58
press reception 75–6, 109–10
  budgeting 76
  catering 116–17
  date 112
  gifts 117
  identifying guests 116
  invitation 109–11, 114–16
  managing event 117–18
  planning 111–118
  press kits 116
  timetable 109–10
  venue 112–13
press relations 42, 108, 152–63
  costs of 70
  dos and don'ts 161–3
  evaluation of 15
press release 172
pressure groups 99, 268
price 167
price sensitive announcements 248
Prince's tuna 197
priorities 42–3
privatisation 32, 33, 37, 93, 94, 140
probability sample 26
product recall 5, 9, 28, 32–3, 35, 92–3
  manager 28
  pre-testing 31, 90
  publicity 31
profit sharing 28
progress reports 74
pronouns 181
propaganda 11, 15, 164
properties 59
public office holder 244
Public Relations 239, Appendix 3
public relations
  as part of other duties 164–69
  cost effective 17–18
  counsellors 6, 150–1

exercise 3
  purpose of 8–9, 14
  strategy 27
  transfer process 11–14, 84
public relations consultancy 6–7, 19, 65, 66, 70–5, 146–7, 157, 173, 186
  advantages of 149
  commissions 66–7
  costs of 70–1
  disadvantages of 149–50
  estimates for proposals 74–5
  fees 19, 21, 66, 71, 148
  presentations 72
  skeleton budget 5
  types of 150–1
Public Relations Consultants Association 6, 10, 72, 151, 242, 247–48, Appendix 4
  Charter 248
  Independent Professional Consultants Group 151
  Investor Relations Code of Practice 243, 247–48
  Investor Relations Register 247
  public relations practitioner, attributes of 14, 17
publicity 147, 156, 164, 165
publicity manager 167–68
publics 8, 9, 10, 18, 20, 21, 44–48, 102
  eight basic 44
puffery 165, 172, 182, 187, 189, 197, 199, 206
punctuation 191

qualifications 257–63
quango 29–30, 38, 103
Quantel Paintbox 79, 226
Quark Express 238, 239
questionnaire 96
questions, research 24
quota sample 25, 26
quotation marks 190
quotations 175, 183, 189, 197, 200, 201, 203, 216

Racal 239
radio 59–60, 111
  advantages of 60
  Two-Ten services 60, 160
Radio Authority 39, 52, 142
  Code of Practice 267
  Sponsorship Code 51, 142
Radio Rentals 229
Radio Times 51, 54
random location 26
  number 25
  sample 25–6
  walk 26
rate card 15
rationalisation 30, 31, 89
RBL (Research International) 141
readership 26, 50, 85
recognition, agency 6, 7
recommendations 280
recycling 267
regional press 53–4, 158
re-location 29, 35, 97
Renault 266

Rentokil Ltd   v, 30, 32, 88, 271–83
  case study   271–83
  Environmental Services   283
  film, video unit   275
  Library   136, 276
  media coverage   275
  public company   279–80
  public relations specification   274–5
Rentokil Review   237, 282
Rentokil Roundabout   273
reputation   31, 33, 246, 280, 281
results, assessing   84–108
  advertisement value   15, 85
  three ways   84–5
Retail Motor Industry Federation   182, 187, 190, 192
retailer   31, 33, 90, 91
retainers   19, 72–3
Reuters   192, 231, 254
road shows   32
Rockwell News   239
Rolls-Royce   94
Romeike and Curtice   105
Rothman-Honda   133
Rover   88
Rowland Company, The   280
Royal Mail International Business Travel Guide   252,
  Appendix 3
Royal National Lifeboat Institution   38
Royal Protocol   123–4
Royal Warrant   272, 283
Rumpole of the Bailey   141, 142
Russia   12–13, 89

Saab Scania   232
Sainsbury, J.S.   30, 139, 267
St Ivel Gold   117
St Mark and St John College, Plymouth   261
Sakurauchi, Yoshiom   12
sales conferences   36
  manager   29
  promotion   36, 167
  reports   23
sample, sampling   25–6
satellite news service   253
satellite television   50, 105, 134, 231
  business video   68, 188–9, 227–29, 235, 254
  media tours   231
  news gathering   231
Save the Children   15, 89
Schmertz, Herb   152, 162
Scottish Television   50
Sea Cat   232
Sea Containers   232
Secombe, Harry   136
selling in, selling out   36
semantic differential   96, 99
service industries   269
Servis UK Ltd   93
ServiScene   276, 282
Shah, Eddie   51
Shandwick   254, 265
share issues   4, 20, 29, 33, 93–4, 168
share lists   37

Sharp   135
Shell   135
  Film Unit   225
shift studies   24
show jumping   138, 139
Simenon, Georges   143
Sinclair C5   13
Singapore   104, 132, 218, 255
Singer sewing machines   40
Single European Market   40, 251, 253, 265
single parent family   270
single stroke keying   51, 154
Six-Point Public Relations Model   9, 10, 18–21, 27, 151
  constraints imposed by   18–19
Sky News   231, 232
slide presentations   36, 110
snooker sponsorships   137
soap operas   139
social grades   26–7, 52, 141, 142, 143
  and the UK nationals   52
Society of Food Hygiene Technology   277
Society of Public Relations Agencies   6
socio-economic groups   26–7
software   238–9
SOLAADS   176, 177
Sony   13
  Music   140–1
  sponsorship of ITV Rugby World Cup   140–1
Sony/Umatic videos   79, 226, 236
Sophus Berendsen   272
sound, dubbed   79, 226
  voice over   226
special correspondents   210
Spillers   33
Spitting Image   13
spoken word   63, 64
  bad habits   63
  behaviour when speaking   63–4
sponsored awards   136
  books, 135, 136–7
sponsored programmes on TV and radio   139–2
  costs of   140, 142
  credits   140, 142, 143
  research   140, 141
sponsorship   23, 25, 30, 38, 39, 85, 99, 104, 107, 133–43
  advertising objectives   133–4
  broadcasting codes   51
  choices   135
  kinds of   136–7
  marketing objectives   134
  objectives   135
  participatory   139
  public relations advantages   138
  public relations spin-offs   138
  purpose and suitability   133–4
  reasons for   133
  spin-offs   138, 140
  sports   137
staff recruitment   29, 34–5, 94–5
  stability   34, 95–6
  training   34
Sterling Pharmaceuticals   37

still photographer 226
Stirling University 257, 261–2
Stock Exchange 33, 94, 242, 247, 279
stock market 29, 33, 93–4, 282
stringers 186
Stritch, Elaine 136
subbing 198, 203, 208, 212
subheadings 187
subject 176, 177, 178, 180, 206
Sumitomo Corporation 12
Sun, The 52, 53, 56, 90, 138, 235
Sunday Express 56
Sunday Times 50, 54
Sunday Trading 265, 270
super-calendered paper 235
superlatives 157, 173, 176
supermarket 36, 265, 267, 270
symbols 190–1
syndicated articles 212

tabloids 8, 50
  house journals 234–5
take-over bids 4, 33
tangibility 2–5, 10, 19, 28, 84, 88, 102
Tate and Lyle 99
Taylor Woodrow Group 198–199
'taxi' money 243
telephone surveys 25
television 58–9, 111
  archival material 59
  coverage 134, 137, 139
  decreasing advertising value 134
  interviews 63
  programmes 59, 111
  properties 59
  sponsorship coverage 133
  Top 20 58
Televisual 228, Appendix 3
tennis sponsorship 137
terrorists 31, 33
Tesco 30
test marketing 31
Thailand 89
Thames Barrier exhibition 132
Thaw, John 142
Thompson, Clive 271, 273
Thomson, Lord 50
Thomson Holidays 13
time-bank 21, 73
time-sheet 19, 21, 66
Times, The 52, 174
tobacco companies 133
tone 23, 86
Toshiba 40, 167
Toshiba's Year of Invention Awards 136
Toyota 37, 40
TSB 265
Trade Descriptions Act 92
trade press 32, 36, 209
  terms 36
trailing spouse syndrome 35
training, shop staff 32, 36, 167
trans-continentals 37

translations 161, 238, 250–1, 255, 256
Traverse-Healy, Tim 15
truth 246
TV Globo, Brazil 231, 254
TV newscasters 111
TV Quick 56
TV Times 51, 54, 140
Two-Ten Communications 40, 60, 160, 192, 253,
  Appendix 5
  computerised satellite service 253
  feature article system 212
  radio services 60, 111
typography 22, 42, 64

UK Press Gazette 50, Appendix 3
underlining 190
understanding 2, 8, 10, 11, 12, 38, 61, 90, 100, 138,
  238, 244
undertakers 265
uniformity 42
Unilever 280
Unipart 228
unique 197–198, 206
unity 42
Universal Declaration of Human Rights 9
universe 25
unleaded petrol 269
USA 6, 7, 8–9, 32, 49, 104, 139, 168, 228, 229, 230, 239,
  265, 268
USA Today 53
US Food and Drug Administration 230

VAG 266
value of coverage 85
Van der Maiden, Professor 15
VAT 268
Vauxhall 266
venues for press events 12–13, 119
Veteran Car Run 231
VHS 79, 226, 236
video, business, corporate 68, 188–9, 227, 269
video-cassette recorder 225, 264
videoconferencing 228, 231
video house magazine 34, 226, 227, 236, 273
  news release 51, 59, 105, 111, 229–3, 254, 269
Video Press Release Ltd 229, 230
videotapes 34, 35, 36, 41, 107, 110, 136, 138, 225–38
  budgeting 78–9
  distribution 226
  documentary 225–6, 227
  formats 79, 226
  production 225–226
  purpose 225
  reviews of 30, 40, 106
  sponsored 136
  still photographs 226
  types of 226
vineyards, English 13
Visage Productions 228
Visnews 51, 59, 85, 105, 228, 229, 254
vocabulary 176, 182, 214
  limited 251

volume of coverage 85, 90
voluntary bodies 12, 29, 37, 38, 46, 100–1, 146, 153

wall newspaper 236
Wall Street Journal, The 53
weather bulletins, forecasts 140, 142–3
Weasel, the 8
web-offset-litho 51, 54, 55, 158, 221, 236
Wellcome 280
Wells, Bob 239
West Herts College 257, 258–9
West tuna, John 197
Westphal, Bob 272
Whale and Dolphin Conservation Society 182
Whitbread Round-the-World Yacht Race 135
White, Dr. Jon 15
Willings Press Guide 160, 253, Appendix 3
Wilson, Des 268

window, interview 231
Wings of Gold 236
Wish You Were Here 142
woodworm 32, 272
woolly bears picnic 278
WTN Productions 229, 230, 231

Yamaha organs 138
  motor-cycles 138
Yardley 134
yearbooks 53, 57–58, 100, 102
Yellow Pages 57
York, Duchess of 231
Yuppie 264

Zambia 89
Zimbabwe 89